Dictionary of
CONFUSING
WORDS AND
MEANINGS

Dictionary of
CONFUSING WORDS AND MEANINGS

ADRIAN ROOM

Guild Publishing
London

First published in 1985
by Routledge

11 New Fetter Lane, London EC4P 4EE

Reprinted 1986
This edition published 1988 by Guild Publishing
by arrangement with Routledge

Phototypeset in Linotron Baskerville 9 on 10 pt
by Input Typesetting Ltd, London
and printed in Great Britain
by T. J. Press (Padstow) Ltd, Padstow, Cornwall

INTRODUCTION

This Dictionary is a revised and enlarged blend, in a single volume, of two earlier books: *Room's Dictionary of Confusibles* (first published in 1979) and *Room's Dictionary of Distinguishables* (1981). The aim of those books was to try and sort out a selection of words that are annoyingly similar in sound or meaning, with the former called 'confusibles' and the latter 'distinguishables'. 'Confusibles', thus, are words that not only have a similar sound and spelling, and a common or at any rate apparently common link of meaning, but are even often mutually related linguistically. Examples are pairs such as 'banister' and 'baluster', 'luxurious' and 'luxuriant', 'dominating' and 'domineering'. 'Distinguishables' are words that may be unlike each other in sound or spelling, but are closely related in meaning, such as 'boat' and 'ship', 'referee' and 'umpire', 'town' and 'city'. Many 'distinguishables' are in fact nouns.

English is plagued with words of both kinds, and the wrong use of one in place of another is something that can not only bother us but even disturb and embarrass, or at least frustrate. Someone says, 'He's a real bon viveur', for example, and while mentally sorting out the exact meaning of this we also wonder 'Shouldn't that be "bon vivant"?' Or we may find ourselves saying, 'We've been allocated three tickets', and then wondering whether we should have said 'allotted'. And how about the excited child who runs home and exclaims 'I brought that book!' 'Brought' or 'bought'? Perhaps even both? Such doubts arise in writing, too, and with the many quirky English spellings also to bother about, it is hardly surprising that several 'lookalike' and apparent 'meanalike' words cause problems there as well. And this is to say nothing of the misprints one all too often comes across in the media (can they in fact *all* be misprints?), to add to the general verbal confusion. (In its Court & Social column of 10 January 1985, *The Times* mentioned that the Queen Mother was Colonel-in-Chief of the 'Royal Anglican Regiment'. No doubt, wrote a correspondent subsequently, in a letter to the Editor, the regiment's regimental march was 'Onward Christian Soldiers'.)

Many such pairs of words are more or less coincidental 'false friends', where there is no actual linguistic link, such as 'loot' and 'booty', 'Pom' and 'Peke', 'gad' and 'gallivant', 'mould' and 'mildew'. It is simply the chance similarity of sound and sense that causes the difficulty.

Looking more closely at such pairs (or larger groups), it is possible, however, to pin down some particular areas where confusion may occur. It may be helpful to identify these, and reveal them for what they are, so that we know what we are up against when we next venture into their hypnotic territory!

The first area is that of 'hard' words generally, ones that form part of our passive vocabulary rather than being in the familiar wordstock on which we actively draw daily to say or write what we wish to communicate. Among such pairs may be ones such as 'abrogate' and 'abdicate', 'assiduous' and 'sedulous', 'faculties' and 'facilities'. These need careful distinguishing if our meaning is to be clear, or if we are to understand exactly what a speaker or writer intends.

The second, more specialised area, but rather a large one, comprises words in technical fields with which we may not be very familiar. Such a field may be in science, for example, or in sport, politics, education, or any other sphere where we do not really feel at home. Many of us have our own field in which we are specialists of a kind, but we cannot be specialists in all the other fields as well, and when we encounter words from those unfamiliar areas, in the media, for example, there can be difficulties. If we are not a scientist, we may thus have problems with such pairs as 'apogee' and 'perigee', 'albumen' and 'albumin', 'polythene' and 'polystyrene', even 'genus' and 'species', and 'comet' and 'meteor' (and which of those, if either, is a 'shooting star'?) Or take medicine, even of the most homely or 'aches and pains' kind. What is the difference between 'measles' and 'German measles' (or 'rubeola' and 'rubella')? If you twist your ankle on a kerbstone, have you 'strained' it or 'sprained' it? Perhaps you have 'wrenched' it, or simply 'ricked' it? It may help to know which is correct, if only to tell the doctor! And if the doctor himself says that you may have fractured your 'fibula', where is this in relation to your 'tibia'? Other specialised fields have similar frustrations.

The third area, perhaps, consists of those words which you can confidently identify in meaning, but whose different endings cause doubts. We have already mentioned 'luxurious' and 'luxuriant'. Quite clearly, both are related to 'luxury', but to give what particular shade of meaning or usage? Is a soft warm bed a 'luxurious' one or a 'luxuriant' one? Can one lie in summer on 'luxuriant' grass or 'luxurious' grass? If you half mow the lawn, have you 'partly' mown it or 'partially'? There are several closely linked words of this type. Similar hesitations can be caused by words whose second half or ending is identical, yet whose first parts are quite different. Such words may even be opposites, so it is even more important to get the right one! Examples are 'windward' and 'leeward', 'subject' and 'object' (a 'subject' of interest or an 'object' of interest?), and even 'overtone' and 'undertone'.

Certain suffixes can cause difficulties in some of the 'specialist' categories mentioned, especially in science, so that only a real expert can tell you what the difference is between 'chlorine', 'chloride', 'chlorate' and 'chlorite'. Some of these suffixes were purposely devised by scientists for their own esoteric purposes (so that '-ite', for example, denotes the name of the salt of an acid whose own name ends in '-ous', with 'nitr*ite*' therefore being a salt of 'nitr*ous*' acid.) This may be beautifully logical and consistent, but hardly helps the poor non-scientist who may come across such a word on a container or preparation of some kind, and wonder exactly what he is dealing with.

A special area of difficulty can be caused by the quite large numbers of foreign words that have been adopted by English, some in their native spelling and complete with their native accents. Examples here might be 'au fait' and 'au courant', 'baroque' and 'rococo', and even menu French 'mousse' and 'soufflé'. Many individual foreign words and phrases cause problems to the insular English, and our usual reaction is to ignore the precise meaning and go instead for a face-saving schoolboy-type pun. So the Chancellor of the Exchequer (or someone in the news) is 'hors de combat', is he? That will teach the old warhorse! Or not all the wedding guests have arrived yet, *tant pis*. Never mind, auntie will be here when she has finished powdering her nose.

A final type of confusing word is a much more homely one, and much more natural than the rather 'rarefied' scientific and other specialised words already mentioned. This is the sort of word that has a sound matching its meaning, or at least suggesting it, and surprisingly often one finds that there can be a whole group of similar words that all share the same shade of meaning. A word like 'slope', for example, is very like 'slip', and in some contexts it may be difficult to decide whether one wants to say 'slope off' or 'slip off' to mean 'leave quietly and unobtrusively'. The need to produce the right word may be all the more urgent, in fact, since words and phrases like this are mostly used in speech rather than in writing, where there is more time to stop and consider. Both these particular words, with their initial letter-group 'sl-', belong to quite an extensive family of words that all suggest a 'down-gliding' movement. Others in the group are slack, sleek, sleep, sleeve, slender, slide, slither, slobber, slop, slow, slumber and slump. Did the slinky snake slide, slither or simply slip through the open door? Do Eskimos travel with sleighs, sleds or sledges? These words (see **sleigh** in the Dictionary) are part of this group, too.

The whole phenomenon is technically known as 'phonaesthesia' (literally 'sound-feeling' or 'sound-sensitivity') and this term is used by linguists to apply to words that share a common sound and sense, especially a basic one of this type. The late Professor Simeon Potter defined phonaesthesia as 'sound-meaning associations which would seem to be not merely echoic or onomatopoeic but rather linguistically innate and universal'. Not surprisingly, many such words are genuine 'confusibles' for our purpose, and for others the reader is recommended to refer in the Dictionary to **babble, clang, encumber, scamp** and **solid.**

Exploring and categorising such groups can be a fascinating pastime, and also a useful one, and the reader may like to consider other letter-groups besides 'sl-' for similar sense patterns, and similar 'confusibles', therefore. Many words that being with 'st-', for example, often denote a fixed or rigid state, such as stable, stand, static, stay, steady, step, sterile, stick, still, stone, stop, stout and 'state' itself. Should we therefore 'take a stand' (or 'make a stand') or 'adopt a stance', perhaps? If something does not move, is it 'static' or 'stationary'? Or take the opening letters 'fl-', which begin many words denoting a light, delicate movement, such as flake, flap, flick, flicker, flirt, flitter, float, flounce and flurry. In this group, if you wish to escape, should you 'fly' or 'flee'? Do the little birds flit, flitter or flutter from tree to tree? Did you 'flick' that cloth or 'flap' it? Again, there could be a difference! Finally, although it is tempting to go on and hunt for more, let us consider some confusingly similar sounds and senses from another such group. Did the dog 'drivel' or 'drool' as you prepared its meal? Perhaps it 'dribbled'? Was it the drops of rain or the dripping rain that drenched you? Are those dull-coloured dresses 'dreary' or 'drab'? Have your spirits 'drooped' or 'dropped' altogether after all these alternatives?

Whether it is 'confusibles' or 'distinguishables' that are in question, this Dictionary, like its predecessors, endeavours to sort them out and clarify them. The actual arrangement of the Dictionary is straightforward. In the headings of the entries, the words are usually given in the order 'familiar before unfamiliar' or 'common before less common'. In some cases, a pair of words may have a traditional order, and this is usually kept to, such as 'port' and 'starboard', 'hawks' and 'doves', 'hardware' and 'software'. Words that are not the first in a heading are cross-indexed separately in their correct alphabetical place.

The definition in brackets after the headwords is the 'common factor' or 'sense link' that frequently springs to mind, even when it is not quite the right one. A 'privilege' and a 'prerogative' are really quite distinct in their meaning, therefore, but the general sense of both words, together with their similar appearance, can justify the definition given for them of 'special right or advantage'. In a few cases, words that are sometimes believed to have different meanings, but actually mean one and the same thing, are included in their own entry. An example can be found for the words 'gorse', 'furze' and 'broom', which are all names of a single plant, the shrub botanically known as *Ulex europaeus*. Again, it does not follow that *all* meanings of a word will be given in an entry. It is only the confusing 'overlap' that is concerned with here. Readers who wish for more detailed information on the various senses of a word, or would like more examples of usage than are given here, should consult a good, up-to-date dictionary, such as the latest edition of the *Concise Oxford* or *Chambers Twentieth Century Dictionary*. Both Collins and Longman have published good English dictionaries, too, and the latter (*Longman Dictionary of the English Language*) has a number of special comments (so-called 'essays') dealing with the very kind of word, similar in sound or sense to another, that forms the basis of this present Dictionary.

The *Dictionary of Confusing Words and Meanings,* as already mentioned, is not only a revision of the two earlier dictionaries but an expansion of them, so that although a very few entries have now been omitted (mainly ones dealing with obsolete usages), fifty new ones have been added, making a grand total of around 3000 words to be individually treated in pairs or larger groups. Many of the new words now included came from my own material. Several, however, were suggested by correspondents good enough to propose them after the publication of the former books. I would here particularly like to thank Keith Thomas, of Canberra, Australia, who wrote more than once with interesting suggestions for inclusion, Walter Perdeck, of Groningen, Holland, who sent a similar list, and Mrs Margery Green of Chalfont St Giles, who kindly transcribed and despatched an agreeable selection of actual 'clangers' in words and meanings that she had collected over the years from the media, notably radio and television and the local press. I owe the new entry 'oh/o' to an anonymous correspondent who sent me a postcard on which, apart from my name and address, these were the sole words. If he or she should chance to read this, my thanks for the contribution and also the briefest communication I can remember ever receiving.

As can probably be imagined, the collating and combining of the entries of the two previous dictionaries to make this new one was a sizeable 'paste and scissors' task, as well as an editorial one, and for timely and willing assistance in the physical preparation of the new material I would like to acknowledge the help of Louise Hamer, who completed the assignment in under a week, thus enabling me to meet my own deadline.

Finally, any comments that readers may feel like sending on their own pet 'confusions', whether included in the Dictionary or not, will always be welcome. We who speak English, or are learning the language, are after all the masters, and we must make these annoying differences our servants, not our stumbling-blocks!

Petersfield, Hampshire   Adrian Room

What is the difference between a warder and a jeweller? One watches cells and the other sells watches.

Age-old schoolchildren's **riddle,** which is a **conundrum** containing a double **pun.** (See **pun** itself for the difference between the three of these, and even **warden** for the difference between him and a **warder.**)

A

abaft/abeam (not ahead – of a ship at sea)
Draw an imaginary line through the centre
of a ship at right angles to it. Anything
behind this line will be 'abaft' – as distinct
from 'astern', when it will be to the rear of
the stern. Anything actually on this
imaginary line, to left or right – port or
starboard – will be 'abeam'.

abbey see (1) **cathedral**, (2) **monastery**

abdicate/abrogate/arrogate/derogate
(cancel or alter a person's status)
To 'abdicate' is to renounce formally, as
most commonly by a monarch of the throne.
The verb can also apply to other kinds of
authority or standing, so that one can 'abdicate' one's power, office, duties or rights.
To 'abrogate' a law is to cancel it or annul
it. To 'arrogate' something is to seize or
claim it without right, as when a person
'arrogates' certain privileges to himself. To
'derogate' is to lessen or detract from in
some way: to 'derogate' a person's authority, for example, is to undermine it, and
to 'derogate' someone's rights is to restrict
them. The 'ar-' prefix in 'arrogate' is a form
of 'ad-', that is, 'to', with the '-rogate' root
of three of the verbs meaning 'ask'.

abdomen see **stomach**

abeam see **abaft**

ability see **capability**

ablaut see **umlaut**

abolition/dissolution/prorogation
(ending or annulling of something)
The terms are used for the ending of something that has been legally or politically
sanctioned or established. 'Abolition' means
ending for good, and is used in particular
of slavery and capital punishment – both of
which were suddenly found to be shameful
and entirely undesirable. 'Dissolution' is

used more of the breaking up or dispersal
of something, especially parliament for a
new session, or historically the suppression
('Dissolution') of the monasteries by Henry
VIII in the 1530s. 'Prorogation' is the
discontinuing of the meetings of parliament
without a 'dissolution', that is, the official
ending of one session, when parliament
'stands prorogued', until the day of meeting
of a new session. The 'prorogation' of parliament usually extends from late July or early
August to October or November, when
another session will begin.

abrogate see **abdicate**

abrupt/brusque/brisk (peremptory)
'Abrupt' has the basic sense of 'sudden',
and referring to someone's manner can
suggest rudeness, and imply a discourteous
interruption. An 'abrupt' manner can, of
course, actually be a sign of shyness, but it
tends to be more the hall-mark of extroverts
than of introverts. 'Brusque' suggests a
businesslike manner, not necessarily a
discourteous one. Here, too, brusqueness
can indicate the introvert, especially if it
takes the form of a kind of gruffness. If
'brush-off' suggests 'brusque' so much the
better: the word ultimately goes back to the
Latin *bruscus* (broom). 'Brisk' is the most
extrovert of the three, with no suggestion of
shyness. The word implies a lively efficiency
and frequently connotes an almost hale and
hearty state, as when one walks at a 'brisk'
pace in a 'brisk' wind.

absolution see **acquittal**

abstruse see **obscure**

abuse/misuse (as verb: use improperly; as
noun: improper use)
To 'abuse' something is to use it wrongly
or badly, as when 'abusing' a privilege or
one's authority. To 'abuse' a person is to
malign him. To 'misuse' something, on the
other hand, is simply to use it for a purpose
for which it was not intended, as one's knife
for putting cheese into one's mouth. All too
often a rarish word gets 'misused' – but
hardly ever 'abused'.

Abwehr see **Bundeswehr**

abyss see **crevice**

accent see **dialect**

acciaccatura see **appoggiatura**

accident/incident (mishap, casualty or disaster, sometimes with loss of life)
An 'accident' is a general word for a disaster or mishap of some kind, such as a road 'accident' or a train 'accident'. Common 'accidents' that make news locally or nationally are fires, crashes and explosions. An 'incident' can be any of these, but the word is normally used by those who deal with it professionally, such as a rescue service (for example police or firemen) or reporters. An 'incident' at sea might thus mean a collision of ships or a fire or explosion on a ship. 'Incidents' are usually seen as single occurrences in the professional life of the people involved, such as military personnel or hospital staffs. An 'incident' can also, however, be a diplomatic encounter of nationalities at a border, with or without casualties, and an 'incident' outside a pub may be not much more than a minor public disturbance, a drunken brawl or threat of violence. These are not 'accidents'. The media sometimes seem to find it difficult to decide which word to use when reporting a disaster or tragedy. *The Times*, for example, when reporting (in its issue for 12 January 1985) an event headlined 'Three killed in Pershing accident', begins by talking of an 'accident' but ends by referring to it as an 'incident'. Even the professionals sometimes hesitate. A senior London fireman, interviewed on television about an explosion in

a block of flats, began a sentence 'This accident . . .' but then corrected himself to 'This incident . . .', almost as if the former word were not quite 'professional' enough.

accidental see **incidental**

accord/account (independently, in the phrases 'of one's own accord', 'on one's own account')
The two phrases are sometimes confused both in meaning and formation ('on' for 'of', and vice versa). To do something 'on one's own account' is to do it with some kind of initiative, whether by oneself or for oneself. Something done 'of one's own accord', however, is done voluntarily, without prompting. Here, too, a measure of initiative is suggested.

accordion/concertina (portable musical instrument with reeds and bellows)
The 'accordion' first appeared in Vienna in the 1820s. The early models had buttons at both ends – unlike the modern 'piano accordion', which has a piano-style keyboard for the right hand – and were so-called 'single action', meaning that the instrument's reeds, arranged in pairs, gave one note on the press or push and another on the draw or pull. Later models, and always the 'piano accordion', have 'double

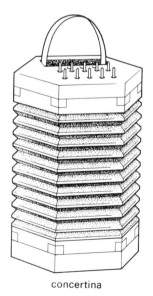

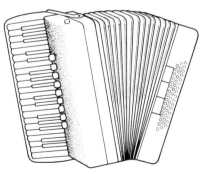

piano accordion

concertina

action', meaning that both reeds in a pair are tuned to the same note so that both the press and the draw of the bellows will give an identical note. The 'concertina' appeared a few years after the 'accordion' in London, with its characteristic hexagonal bellows and buttons, never a keyboard, at both ends. 'Concertinas' are almost always 'double action', with the reeds producing the same note when the bellows are either compressed or expanded. There is, however, a type of German 'concertina', known in its more sophisticated form as an 'Anglo-German concertina' (just an 'Anglo' to professionals), which is 'single action', like the early 'accordions'. On both English and German 'concertinas' alternate notes of the scale are produced by the right hand and the left, but in the so called duet-system 'concertina' a complex chromatic scale is provided for each hand. Although largely superseded by the 'accordion' in the twentieth century, the 'concertina' must not be under-rated: Tchaikovsky has four of them in the score of his second orchestral suite, opus 53.

account/bill/invoice/statement

(document stating debit, credit or balance) An 'account', in commercial terms, is a record of money or goods or services received and expended, as typically an 'account' settled with a firm monthly by a private customer. A 'bill' – as if we didn't know – is a note of charges for goods delivered or services rendered, payable either on receipt or entered in an 'account'. An 'invoice' is a list of goods sent or services performed, with prices and charges. Firms usually indicate if an 'invoice' also serves as a 'bill'. A special type of 'bill' is a 'bill of exchange'. This involves the payment of money and is an official order in writing, signed by the person giving it, to pay a particular sum to a specified person or to the bearer – that is, to the person who presents it. A well known form of 'bill of exchange' is a cheque. A 'statement' is a formal record of a customer's or client's liabilities and assets, or of an amount due to a tradesman or firm. A bank 'statement' – in full, 'statement of account' – records transactions made through a bank, by cheque and otherwise, over a given period,

the balance, or amount one has in the bank ('when overdrawn marked OD'), being noted on the occasion of each transaction.

account (in phrase 'on one's own account') see **accord**

acerbic see **acid** (sharp, stinging)

ache/pain (sensation of bodily discomfort) An 'ache' can be dull or sharp, and is usually fairly persistent, as a 'headache', 'toothache' or 'backache'. A 'pain' is usually sharp rather than dull, but is sudden and normally of short duration, as a 'pain' in one's leg from cramp or in one's ankle from a sprain. 'Pain', too, may be mental or emotional, as the 'pain' of parting, but 'ache' – apart from 'heartache' – is usually a physical thing. English spelling is capricious, heaven knows, but why can't 'ache' be spelt 'ake'? The answer is that it once was, at least the verb was, while the noun, spelt as now, was actually pronounced 'aitch'. This went on till about 1700, when the noun, keeping its spelling, came to be pronounced the same way as the verb 'ake'. (Compare the similar pair of 'make' and 'match' – where, however, the noun is still pronounced with a 'tch'.)

achievement/exploit/feat (special accomplishment) An 'achievement' often implies a number of setbacks and difficulties, all of which had to be dealt with and overcome, resulting finally in success. An 'exploit' connotes bravery of some kind, or an act performed with ingenuity or even cunning. The word comes to English from the Latin, via French, meaning 'something unfolded', almost so that one sees it as a flowering or blooming, which can be looked back on and admired. A 'feat' implies the carrying out of something difficult, usually a single act of some kind, as a 'feat' of showmanship or of strength. It's a word not frequently used in English, no doubt because of the rather ludicrous image conveyed by such a phrase as 'Walk in space – astronaut's great feat'. In the original Latin it means, rather prosaically, 'something done'.

acid/acrid/acerbic (sharp, stinging)

Apart from its use as a chemical term, 'acid' basically denotes a sharpness or sourness of taste, as of a lemon or an 'acid' drop. Applied to a person it implies a sharp temper or kind of caustic hostility, as seen in an 'acid' remark or an 'acid' tongue. In addition to sharpness, 'acrid' suggests a stinging or smarting quality; an 'acrid' remark is a biting one, and stronger than an 'acid' one. In its literal sense, 'acrid' is often used for smoke and fumes that sting the eyes and nose. 'Acerbic' is less often used as an adjective than 'acid' or 'acrid', but as a noun ('acerbity') is quite often used of words spoken bitterly and usually snappily, as when one is stung into making some kind of retort. The literal sense of 'acerbic' is 'sour-tasting'.

acid/alkali (corrosive chemical substance)
Chemically, the two are opposites, as shown by litmus paper, which is turned red by an 'acid' and blue by an 'alkali'. Since they are chemically opposites, the one therefore neutralises the other, which is why a primitive way of reducing the irritation of an insect bite ('acid') is to put washing soda on it ('alkali'). In a complementary way, too, an 'acid' reacts chemically with an 'alkali' to form a salt. The first known 'acid' was vinegar. Chemically (again), the definition of an 'acid' is a substance which in solution in an ionising solvent (usually water) gives rise to hydrogen ions. An 'alkali' is a base – today the more common word in chemistry – that is soluble in water, when it forms a caustic or corrosive solution, as caustic soda (sodium hydroxide) or ammonia. The word, like a surprising number of words starting 'al-' (alcohol, algebra, alcove) is Arabic, and means 'the calcined ashes': 'alkalis' were formerly obtained from wood and bone ashes.

acquittal/exoneration/absolution (freeing from blame)
An 'acquittal' is a release from a particular accusation. The word has a legal ring to it, and in law it actually means a setting free not only from the guilt of an offence but also from the suspicion of an offence. (Someone who has been officially acquitted of a criminal offence may plead *autrefois acquit* or 'formerly acquitted' if subsequently charged

with an offence that is legally the same.) An 'exoneration' is a clearing from the blame of an offence – even when the person concerned has actually admitted to the act. The word is of Latin origin, meaning 'disburdened'. An 'absolution' has something of a religious overtone: the formal act of a priest pronouncing the forgiveness of sins to those who are penitent and confess them. Of the three words here, however, 'absolution' is the most general in meaning.

acrid see **acid** (sharp, stinging)

Act/Bill (type of parliamentary law)
An 'Act', in Parliament, is properly a 'Bill' that has been passed by both the House of Commons and the House of Lords and assented to by the Queen. A 'Bill' is a draft 'Act' of Parliament which can be presented to either House, either as a Public 'Bill' (the majority), which involves measures relating to public policy, or as a Private 'Bill', which relates to matters of individual, corporate or local interest. (The latter is not the same as a Private Member's 'Bill', which is a Public 'Bill' introduced by a private member, that is, an MP who is not a minister.) A 'Bill' is passed by three readings in the House in which it was presented, and is then sent to the other House. When it has passed through these stages and received the Queen's formal assent, it becomes an 'Act' – in legal vocabulary, a statute. However, under the provisions of the Parliament 'Acts' 1911 and 1949, a 'Bill' passed by the House of Commons may receive the royal assent and become an 'Act' without the agreement of the Lords.

act (thing done) see **action**

action/act (thing done)
An 'action' applies in particular to the doing of something, whereas an 'act' refers to the thing done. One can thus take avoiding 'action' – the thing one does is to avoid – as the result of a deliberate 'act' – one that is intentional and thus has a definite consequence. An 'act', too, is usually of short duration, while an 'action' may take some time and indeed consist of several individual 'acts'. This temporal difference is illustrated by such legal terms as 'Act of God' and 'civil action'.

activate/actuate (set working)
'Activate' has the basic sense 'make active' and as such is used mainly in scientific expressions, as to 'activate' sewage (aerate it) and 'activate' carbon (make it more active). 'Actuate' is a more general word whether used in a literal sense of things – to 'actuate' a switch is to operate it – or in a figurative sense of people, where it is usually passive, as when one is 'actuated' by selfish motives. It is in fact close in meaning to 'motivated'.

actuate see **activate**

acuity/acumen (sharpness of mind)
'Acuity' – related to 'acute' with its sense of sharpness – is used of any human faculty and applied to any of the five senses as well as the mind. 'Acumen', however – sometimes wrongly accented on the first syllable instead of the second – is applied to mental sharpness only, suggesting a penetrating mind or a discerning one. It is therefore a virtual synonym for 'perspicacity' – itself a confusible (see **perceptive**).

acumen see **acuity**

acute see **chronic**

addenda see **supplement** (at end of book)

adder see **viper**

addled see **muddled**

adjacent/adjoining (close to, next to)
If one thing is 'adjacent' to another, it borders it or is next to it, without necessarily touching, as a field that is 'adjacent' to the road and 'adjacent' angles in geometry. An 'adjoining' object, however, has a common point with some other object, as an 'adjoining' room or yard, which leads off or into some other part of the premises.

adjoining see **adjacent**

adjure/conjure (entreat)
Both these verbs – each accented on the second syllable – have the general sense of making an earnest request. To 'adjure',

however, as implied in its origin from Latin *adjurare* (swear), suggests that the person entreated is put under some kind of oath, whereas to 'conjure', with its origin in Latin *conjurare* (swear together), is properly better applied to more than one person. The verbs are very bookish, though, and can be easily avoided by means of such alternatives as 'implore', 'urge' or 'beg'.

admission/admittance (right to enter)
The difference is between physically entering a place – as in the familiar notice 'No admittance except on business' – and the granting of the right to join a particular group of people, as the 'admission' of a guest to one's club, a patient to hospital, or an immigrant into a foreign country. *Partridge* points out that when these two factors are combined, as when one goes to the cinema or enters a sporting contest, 'admission' is used, often referring to the price demanded – 'Admission £2.50'.

admission (acknowledgment of guilt)
see **confession**

admittance see **admission** (right to enter)

ado see **to-do**

adventuresome see **adventurous**

adventurous/adventuresome/venturesome/venturous (bold)
An 'adventurous' person is one who seeks adventure, with the implication that a risk is being taken or that courage is needed. Such a person may well have an 'adventurous' spirit, and enjoy trips that for one reason or another are 'adventurous'. An 'adventuresome' youth, however, takes more of a risk than a purely 'adventurous' one – his involvements may well be foolhardy ones. Rasher still is a 'venturesome' youth, who constantly takes risks and whose exploits are usually hazardous. The word is frequently used to describe a mood or inclination. 'Venturous' is close to 'venturesome' in meaning but describes more the nature of the enterprise than the attitude that prompted it. If a prisoner, one would make a 'venturous' bid for freedom rather than a 'venturesome' one.

11

adverse to see **averse to**

advice note/delivery note (document indicating that goods are on their way)
An 'advice note' is sent by the supplier to the customer before the invoice (see **account**). It is sometimes sent in advance of the goods, or alternatively together with them. A 'delivery note' is similar, but it always accompanies the goods and is often in duplicate, the recipient signing one copy and returning the other. The signed copy is then taken by the deliverer back to the vendor as evidence that the goods have been delivered.

aeon see **era**

aerodrome/airport/airfield (place where aeroplanes take off, land, and are housed and serviced)
An 'aerodrome' is a general word for an 'airfield' that is usually a smallish, civil and private one. An 'airport' is a large 'aerodrome', especially one for public passengers, and often of international status, with several large buildings. 'Airport' is very much a twentieth-century word, arising on an analogy with a sea **port**. An 'airfield' is much more than just a field, of course. The word particularly applies to service (RAF) air bases. The term gained popularity after the Second World War. Churchill, in his *The Second World War,* wrote, 'For "aerodrome" either "airfield" or "airport" [should be used]', adding, 'the expression "airdrome" should not be used by us'. So far, it has not been.

aerospace see **airspace**

aesthetic/ascetic (refined – of taste)
The basic meaning of 'aesthetic' is appreciating what is beautiful. If one has a well developed 'aesthetic' sense one is, by implication, more artistic than practical. But in their different ways both an athlete and an artisan will have an 'aesthetic' sense if they are aware of the beauty of what they create, in spite of the fact that the artisan, at least, is involved in a practical craft. Someone whose outlook is 'ascetic' is also aware of the finer things of life, but in his case his aims are usually harshly idealistic, with the implication that abstention is the best means of achieving the end. The word has religious connotations – it is therefore not

surprising to find its origin in the Greek *asketes* (monk).

affect/effect (exert influence on)
To 'affect' something is to have an 'effect' on it. Smoking thus 'affects' your health. If something 'affects' you it concerns you. The possible harm caused by smoking thus 'affects' all of us. To 'effect' something – the verb cannot apply to people – is to bring it about. Heavy smoking may well 'effect' a deterioration in your health, therefore. The difference lies in the prefixes: 'affect' has *ad–* (towards); 'effect' has *ex–* (out). The first of these denotes a cause; the second . . . an 'effect'.

afflicted see **inflicted**

African elephant/Indian elephant (species of elephant)
These are two vintage distinguishables, eminently suitable for quizzes and general

note ears

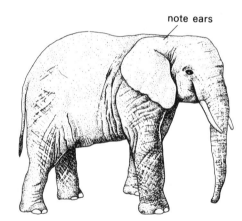

African elephant

Indian elephant

knowledge contests. 'The African elephant is distinguished from the Asian elephant by its larger ears and flatter forehead', says *Everyman's Encyclopaedia*. Probably the ears are the obvious feature: the 'African elephant's' ears come right down over its shoulders, while the ears of the 'Indian elephant' are strikingly small by comparison. The 'African elephant' is also in fact rather a darker grey, and inclined to be fiercer. It is also rarer than its Asiatic cousin. A further, delicate distinction is that the 'African elephant' has two sensitive 'finger-tips' at the end of its trunk, whereas the 'Indian elephant' has only one.

aggravate/exacerbate/exasperate
(irritate)
To 'aggravate' something is to make it worse, as by scratching a mosquito bite. To 'aggravate' a person is to annoy him – a use of the word that some people deplore. To 'exacerbate' a thing – the word is related to 'acerbic' (see **acid**) – is to increase its bitterness or harshness, especially a disease or someone's bad mood. To 'exasperate' someone is to irritate him in the extreme, usually to a degree of frustration. The root of the word is Latin *asper* (rough).

agnostic see **atheist**

airfield see **aerodrome**

airport see **aerodrome**

airspace/aerospace (space in which aircraft fly)
The two terms are confusingly similar. 'Airspace' is the territorial air – the equivalent of territorial waters – that lies above a country and that is within its jurisdiction. One thus has 'violation of "airspace"' when an aircraft of one country flies through the air over another country who will not permit such an incursion for political or strategic reasons. 'Aerospace' is the umbrella term for the region of flight of aircraft *and* spacecraft, that is, flight in the atmosphere and outer space. More commonly the word is used of the technology of such aviation. The expression is American in origin, although Britain uses it in this sense and indeed had a Minister for 'Aerospace' in the Conservative government of 1970–4.

albumen/albumin (substance found in the white of an egg)
Both words derive from Latin *albus* (white). 'Albumen' actually *is* the white of an egg – as a general scientific term – or else the nutritive matter, called the endosperm, round the embryo of a seed. 'Albumin', a narrower chemical term, is the name of a class of proteins soluble in water. Some biochemists, however, equate 'albumin' with 'albumen', and dictionary definitions of both words vary considerably.

albumin see **albumen**

ale/bitter/mild/stout/lager (type of beer)
The word 'ale' is now a historic one for beer except as used commercially or as a trade name, such as India Pale Ale ('IPA'), a pale or light beer originally brewed for export to India. 'Mild' and 'bitter' have names accurately reflecting their respective tastes: 'mild' beer is not strongly flavoured with hops, 'bitter' is. ('Mild and bitter' is a mixture of the two, which rather seems to negate the point of the flavouring.) 'Stout' is a strong, dark beer with roasted malt or barley, while 'lager' is 'continental beer', a light kind of beer which properly is kept in cold store (German *Lager*, 'store') for some months to mature and then drunk chilled. All beers have long been a staple drink in England, with 'stout' something of a connoisseur's beverage (Guinness is a well-known brand of it), and 'lager' increasing in popularity from the 1970s.

alkali see **acid** (corrosive chemical substance)

allegiance see **loyalty**

allegory see **analogy**

Allhallows see **All Saints' Day**

allies/Axis (united forces in Second World War)
Both words denote an alliance of countries. The 'allies' were the armed forces of the allies of Britain, in particular the Americans, French and Russians. These fought against the 'Axis', the name used for the alliance of Germany, Italy and Japan and

originating historically from the Rome-Berlin Axis of 1936. The idea was that the 'axis' was the line joining Rome and Berlin – and later extended to Tokyo – with the alliance being the pivot on which the countries revolved. But there was also a London-Washington 'axis', and subsequently a Moscow-Peking one.

alligator see **crocodile**

allocate/allot (appoint as one's due or share)
To 'allocate' something is to set it aside for a specific purpose. One can thus be 'allocated' a place to park one's car, or a room in a hotel or hostel. To 'allot' something is to give it, but with an implied restriction, and the understanding that one is sharing something. If you are 'allotted' five minutes to make your speech, you must thus share the overall time with everyone else. There's no choice; that will – quite literally – be your lot.

allot see **allocate**

All Saints' Day/All Souls' Day/All-hallows/Hallowe'en (late autumn festival of religious origin)
'Hallow' means 'holy', so that 'Allhallows' is another name for 'All Saints' Day' on 1 November, when the Anglican and Roman Catholic churches commemorate all the saints, thus including all those who have no day of their own at any other time in the year. The day after this is 'All Souls' Day', dedicated by the church to the memory of the faithful departed. These are strictly religious festivals. 'Hallowe'en', originally 'All-hallow-even', is thus the eve of, or day before, 'All Saints' Day', 31 October, which in the old Celtic calendar was the last night of the year. The pagan ceremonies of the day were not very successfully transformed by the church into the eve of a major religious festival. They survive quite healthily in the form of 'Hallowe'en' parties and other traditional customs smacking romantically of witchcraft and general **black magic**.

All Souls' Day see **All Saints' Day**

allure see **lure**

alternately/alternatively (relating to one of two)
'Alternately' means one after the other, in time or space; 'alternatively' means one *instead* of the other. It's as simple as that.

alternating current/direct current (type of electric current)
'Alternating current' (AC) is the one most commonly found in the home and in commercial use. The voltage 'alternates', that is, the flow reaches a maximum in one direction then decreases and reverses until it reaches a maximum in the opposite direction. This cycle is repeated continuously. 'Direct current' (DC) has a flow that does not change direction. This is the current produced in batteries and fuel cells. It lost out commercially to AC in the 1880s because it cannot be transmitted over long distances at a high voltage and then transformed economically at a low voltage. DC made something of a comeback in the 1960s and is sometimes used today in conjunction with predominantly AC systems. (In 'underground' or 'hippie' jargon 'AC/DC' means 'bisexual', the reference being to an electric appliance that can operate on both types.)

alternatively see **alternately**

alto see **treble**

amah see **ayah**

amatory see **amorous**

amber/umber/ochre (shade of yellow or brown)
'Amber', deriving ultimately from an Arabic word meaning 'ambergris', is the colour of the fossil resin, pale yellow, or of the resin itself, which is yellowish brown. Conventionally it is the colour of the 'caution' traffic light and urine. 'Umber' is a type of earth, perhaps originally from Umbria, in Italy, that produces a reddish brown pigment, known also as burnt 'umber'. 'Ochre' is also an earth – a metallic oxide of iron ranging in colour from pale yellow to orange and red and, like 'umber', used as a pigment.

amend/emend (change, alter)
To 'amend' something is to improve it. A bill 'amended' in Parliament is thus altered for the better. The very common verb 'mend' is in fact derived from it, with the improving sense still clear in such an expression as 'mending' one's ways. To 'emend' something, on the other hand, is to correct it, remove the errors from it. The word is most often used with reference to a text of some kind that has been corrected. The noun of 'amend' is 'amendment'; of 'emend' it is 'emendation'.

amiable/amicable (friendly)
'Amiable' is used of a person or his nature or facial expression, so that an 'amiable' workmate might well have an 'amiable' smile to indicate his 'amiable' disposition. 'Amicable' refers to something done with goodwill, in particular an agreement or combined undertaking such as an exchange of views. It is always pleasant when differences can be settled in an 'amicable' way, which can happen when one of the sides is, for once, in an 'amiable' mood.

amicable see **amiable**

ammunition/munitions (offensive weapons)
'Ammunition' comprises virtually all missiles and means of attack fired from weapons of all kinds and includes weapons that are their own means of attack such as bombs, mines and chemical agents. The 'am-' is not a prefix, as the word derives from French *la munition,* which was originally taken as *l'amunition.* 'Munitions' widens the offensive to embrace both 'ammunition' and weapons of all kinds. A 'munitions' factory may thus produce not only shells but the guns that fire them.

amok see **berserk**

amontillado/Montilla/manzanilla/ marsala (type of sherry or sherry-type wine)
Only two of these are true sherries. 'Montilla' is a dry, sherry-type wine made in the region around Montilla, in southern Spain, and 'marsala' is a light-coloured wine resembling sherry shipped from the Sicilian port of Marsala. 'Amontillado', however, so called from its likeness to a 'montilla', is a real sherry, a medium dry one, its dry equivalent being called 'fino' and the sweet variety 'oloroso'. 'Manzanilla' is a very dry pale sherry, with its name not deriving from a place but from the Spanish word for 'camomile' (see **calamine**). The sherry itself comes from the vineyards at the mouth of the Guadalquivir in southern Spain – properly from the town of Sanlucar, eight miles west of Seville, near which, intriguingly, there is in fact the small village of Manzanilla.

amoral see **immoral**

amorous/amatory (loving)
An 'amorous' poem could, if the writer chose, be an erotic or even lewd one. An 'amatory' poem, however, is simply one written by a lover. Similarly an 'amorous' look could mean business, but an 'amatory' look is just one given by someone in love. Put another way, 'amorous' may imply the physical aspect of love; 'amatory' pertains to love in the abstract.

amplifier see **loudspeaker**

amps see **volts**

amulet see **charm**

anaesthetic/analgesic (as noun: deadener of pain or bodily sensation)
The prime purpose of an 'anaesthetic' is to deaden sensation locally or generally, the latter resulting in unconsciousness. An 'analgesic' may also deaden sensation, but its basic aim is to relieve or remove pain by blocking the transmission of nerve impulses. A mild 'analgesic' is aspirin, a strong one is morphine. Both words have the Greek prefix *an–* denoting absence of, respectively, feeling and pain.

analgesic see **anaesthetic**

analogy/allegory (artistic device whereby one thing is compared to another, unlike it)
The essential feature of an 'analogy' is that although two things may partially resemble each other, or be alike, they are basically of

quite a different nature. Compare death to sleep and you have an 'analogy'. You also have a metaphor if you say death *is* sleep, and it's an extended metaphor that is the basis of an 'allegory', which is a story told in symbolic terms. Examples of an 'allegory' are, in literature, *Pilgrim's Progress*, and, in art, Holman Hunt's *The Scapegoat*.

Anderson shelter/Morrison shelter (type of air-raid shelter in Second World War)
The 'Anderson shelter', named after Sir John Anderson, British Home Secretary at the outbreak of the war, was a smallish prefabricated shelter, usually half buried in the back garden. The 'Morrison shelter' was essentially an indoor construction, made of steel and shaped like a table. It was designed to give protection if the house collapsed, and was named after Herbert Morrison, British Secretary of State for Home Affairs from 1940 to the end of the war.

anger/fury/rage/indignation (strong sense of annoyance)
These are specialised types of temper. 'Anger' often involves a strong feeling of revenge for a wrongdoing, and may be suppressed or suddenly expressed. 'Fury' is great 'rage' – which itself is violent 'anger'. This leaves 'indignation', which usually implies a moral or 'proper' 'anger', especially when directed against something unworthy or outrageous. See also **fury** itself.

angle/tangent (point where one line meets another or leaves it)
An 'angle' is a space between two meeting (straight) lines. A 'tangent' is a line that meets a curved one at a point and has the same direction at this point, so touches it. Both words are used figuratively, as the 'angle' or viewpoint from which something is considered, or a speaker or writer who goes off at a 'tangent' – suddenly diverges from the matter in hand. (In this latter phrase, the line is seen as leaving the curve, not meeting it.)

animal/mammal (living creature, usually warm-blooded)
All 'mammals' except man are 'animals', but not all 'animals' are 'mammals', although popularly the two words are equated. Strictly speaking, 'mammals' are all 'animals', including man, that nourish their young with milk from their *mammary* glands, i.e. from the breast of the female, and that usually have their skin more or less covered with hair. (Whales are an exception here, because of the hydrodynamics needed for their mostly submarine existence.) 'Mammals', too, are usually four-footed and warm-blooded. On the other hand, 'animals' in a loose sense can include just about any living creature, even reptiles and fish, so that the word is contrasted with 'plant' rather than 'mammal'. Popularly, however, 'animals' equate with 'mammals' as defined here, and the word embraces those creatures with which man is most familiar in homes, fields and zoos.

announce/pronounce/proclaim (declare publicly)
'Announce' is the general word – to say what is going to happen. One thus 'announces' one's plans for the future or the time of the proposed next meeting. To 'pronounce' something is to declare it solemnly or authoritatively, frequently in public. The key point in the Anglican marriage service is when the priest 'pronounces' that the man and woman 'be Man and Wife together'. To 'proclaim' something is to 'announce' it – but widely, so that it is generally known, as the results of an election. Something 'proclaimed', such as a holiday, may result from a decision of some kind.

annual/perennial (occurring every year)
If something is 'annual' it happens every year, once a year. We are all familiar with 'annual' visits to the dentist, tax returns and Christmas parties. The literal meaning of 'perennial', from Latin *per* (through) and *annus* (year) is 'lasting right through the year', i.e. continuous. The word is often used, though, to mean 'recurrent', as a 'perennial' problem. The noun 'perennial', meaning the plant, is technically regarded as one that lasts more than two years, as distinct from the 'annual', which lasts one year, and the 'biennial' (see **biannual**).

anorak/parka (warm weatherproof jacket with a hood)

The 'anorak' originated in the Arctic as a Greenland Eskimo word for the skin or cloth hooded jacket worn in the icy polar regions. It is now the word for a similar jacket, often a blue or green quilted one, used for everyday wear as an outdoor coat. A 'parka' is similar, but tends to be used for specific purposes such as mountaineering. It, too, is an Eskimo word in origin, but from much further east, from the Aleutian Islands, off the south-west coast of Alaska. The garment is in fact more of a thick smock, slipping over the head, than the 'anorak', which usually has a front fastening, as a zip. Genuine Eskimo 'parkas' are much longer, too, reaching to the thighs or even knees. Many so-called 'parkas' today, however, are simply glorified 'anoraks', although they usually have a fur-lined or fur-fringed hood and thus resemble the Eskimo original, which is fully lined with caribou, seal or other fur. (Eskimo women wear 'parkas' that have an extra hood in which a small child can be wrapped.)

antagonist/protagonist (leader of a cause or campaign)

A 'protagonist' is, properly, the leading character in a novel or play. Possibly under the influence of the better known 'antagonist' it has come to acquire the popular meaning of one who champions or supports a cause. But an 'antagonist' is really someone opposed to someone else, an opponent. Confusion over 'protagonist', too, has occurred through Greek *protos* (first) being misunderstood as the prefix 'pro-' (for).

Antarctic see **Arctic**

antiquarian/antiquary (one dealing in old or historical objects)

Basically, an 'antiquarian' is a person who is interested in old objects and an expert on them. An 'antiquary' – the accent is on the first syllable – is by contrast someone who tends to concentrate more on old objects that are curiosities rather than, say, the findings of an archaeological expedition. This is not to say that an 'antiquary' is not an expert; he can in fact be a real professional or specialist, even if his occupation seems more of a hobby than a full-time occupation. The two words can overlap, though, since they have a common link with antiquities and antiques. As an adjective, 'antiquarian' can apply to antiquities or to 'antiquary', hence, referring to the latter, an 'antiquarian' bookshop.

antiquary see **antiquarian**

antiseptic/aseptic (preventing disease)

It's a matter of prefixes: an 'antiseptic' agent is directed against (Latin *anti*) sepsis, whereas something that is 'aseptic' is free (Greek *a-*) from the germs of disease. One thus applies 'antiseptic' ointment to a wound and then covers it with an 'aseptic' dressing.

antiseptic (sterilising agent) see **disinfectant**

anxiety see **apprehension**

aphorism see **maxim**

apogee/perigee (extreme point)

The two are opposites. The 'apogee' of one's career is the highest point of it, its climax. The terms are from astronomy, the 'apogee' being the point in the orbit of a heavenly body when it is farthest from the earth, and the 'perigee' – not used much figuratively – when it is nearest to it. A possible false association with 'peroration' may be a factor in the confusion that sometimes occurs. The '-gee' is 'earth', as in 'geology'.

apostle/disciple (follower of Christ)

'Apostle' is the word used in the Gospels, and in subsequent writings, to refer specifically to the twelve chief 'disciples' chosen by Christ: Peter, Andrew, James, John, Philip, Bartholomew, Thomas, Matthew, James the Less, Thaddaeus, Simon and Judas Iscariot. (After the suicide of Judas, Matthias was voted in to replace him.) Traditionally, too, Paul and Barnabas are regarded as 'apostles', since they, together with the twelve 'disciples', fulfilled the technical requirement for bearing the title: they had 'seen the Lord'. The word actually derives from the Greek for 'one sent', 'ambassador'. The term 'disciple' is synonymous with 'apostle' in many ways – all of the above were both 'disciples' and 'apostles' – but the word is used less specifically to apply to any follower of Christ, whether he had actually seen Him or not. The word means simply 'learner', 'pupil'.

apothecary see **chemist**

appendix see **supplement** (at end of book)

appoggiatura/acciaccatura (type of musical grace-note)
Two admittedly rather specialised words, but which are pure music to look at, to say ('ap-poj-yat-*oo*-ra', 'atch-yac-cat-*oo*-ra' – Italian style), and of course to hear played professionally. An 'appoggiatura' is a grace-note that normally takes half the time value as the note on which it leans (Italian *appoggiare*, 'to lean'), although it steals the emphasis of this main note, which follows gently like the resolution of a discord, as it often is. An 'acciaccatura' is a grace-note that in theory is timeless, and so squeezed in as quickly as possible before the main note is played – or even played at the same time as the main note, then immediately released. (The origin here is Italian *acciaccare*, 'to crush'; the note is sometimes called a 'crushnote', which is not anything like as evocative.)

appoggiatura

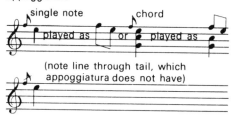

acciaccatura

apprehension/anxiety (feeling of concern)
'Apprehension' usually involves a greater or lesser degree of fear or uneasiness, with at the same time an implicit hope that what may come will not after all turn out for the worst, as a feeling of 'apprehension' when opening a reply to one's letter to the tax inspector. (With 'neat' fear one almost always expects the worst, but 'apprehension' may mean that one will get away with it.) 'Anxiety' suggests a rather lengthy state of 'apprehension', possible at not such a keen level. The word is actually related to 'anger'.

apricot see **peach**

apron/pinafore (garment worn in front of the body to protect the clothes)
The 'apron' is essentially the garment of the housewife and mother – to whose 'apron'-strings spoilt children or hen-pecked husband can be tied. The word is like 'adder', that is, it should be 'a napron' rather an 'an apron'. (It derives from Old French *naperon*, meaning 'small table-cloth'. For more about 'adder', the word and the beast, see **viper**.) A 'pinafore' or 'pinny' is similar, but is usually worn by a young child – of either sex – to protect its clothes, as when eating or messily playing. More decoratively, it can be worn as a fashionable garment by girls or women over a dress. Compare, in this respect, a 'pinafore' dress, which is one without a collar and sleeves worn over a blouse or jumper. 'Pinafores' were originally 'pinned afore', i.e. pinned on to the front of the dress.

aqueduct/viaduct (type of bridge, often with a series of arches)

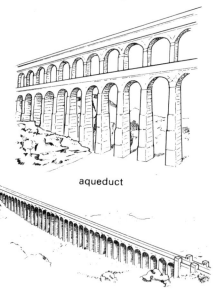

aqueduct

viaduct

An 'aqueduct' is for water only. The word particularly applies to Roman bridges of this type, some of which still exist and are still used for carrying water, as the fine one at Segovia, Spain. A 'viaduct' is designed to carry a road or railway over a ravine or valley. Holborn 'Viaduct' in London, about a quarter of a mile long, was completed in 1879 over the valley of the 'Hole Bourne', or part of the River Fleet, to connect Holborn Circus with Newgate Street.

arbiter/arbitrator (judge)

An 'arbiter' is a person who has the power to judge, or who thinks he has. 'I'll be arbiter of that, thank you', says someone who feels his authority or standing is being challenged. An 'arbitrator' is someone called upon to settle some kind of dispute, with the implication that he will examine the background of the point at issue. The word has a legal or political ring about it. Both an 'arbiter' and an 'arbitrator' arbitrate, with 'arbitration' being the official word to describe what an 'arbitrator' does. An 'arbiter' can get away with making an arbitrary decision; an 'arbitrator' certainly cannot.

arbitrator see arbiter

arbour/bower (shady or private retreat)

An 'arbour' has its sides and roof formed mainly by trees or climbing plants, as a type of natural summer-house. The word actually comes from Old French *erbe*, 'herb' (as modern French *herbe*, 'grass'), but the initial 'e-' became 'a-' by association with Latin *arbor*, 'tree'. A 'bower' is simply a place with closed-in foliage, whether natural, as an 'arbour', or man-made, as a summer-house. It would be agreeable if the word were related to 'bough' or 'flower', but it actually derives from a Germanic word meaning 'dwelling-place'. The street and section of New York known as The Bowery gets its name not from 'bower' but from the Dutch word for 'farm', *bouwerie*, to which the street originally led. (The farm was owned by the Governor, Peter Stuyvesant.)

arcane see arch

arch/arcane (secretive)

'Arch' is usually used to mean 'knowing', 'sly', with the implication that a secret is being withheld. The *SOED* says the word is usually used of women and children, but there is no need for this qualification since anyone can give an 'arch' smile or an 'arch' look. The word is nothing to do with arching one's eyebrows; its origin is the prefix 'arch-' used as an independent adjective by association with such cunning characters as arch-knaves and archrogues. 'Arcane', deriving from Latin *arca* (chest) – which also gave Noah his Ark – means 'secret' in the sense of 'obscure' or 'mysterious'. From the 1960s it became something of a vogue word, and itself rather 'arcane'.

archdeacon see dean

Arctic/Antarctic (polar region)

Which is which? The 'Arctic' is the region round the North Pole, which lies under the constellation of the Great Bear – Greek *arktos* (bear) – while the 'Antarctic' is 'anti' it, round the South Pole. The occasional confusion between the two may be caused by the fact that although Britain and the USA are geographically close to the 'Arctic', it is the feats of British and American explorers in the 'Antarctic' that remain prominent in the mind, boosted by the history books and films such as *Scott of the Antarctic*.

arise see rise

aristocrat see autocrat

armoury/arsenal (weapon store)

An 'armoury' is a store for weapons and other military equipment but not in general, for ammunition. By contrast, an 'arsenal' is a repository of weapons and military equipment of all kinds, as well as ammunition. It is also the word for a building of this kind where troops are trained, such as Woolwich Arsenal (now transferred to Sandhurst), London, which was also the training ground of the soccer team Woolwich Arsenal (now transferred to Highbury). A less common meaning of 'arsenal' is that of the building where military equipment of all kinds is manufactured. The word goes back via the Italian *arsenale* (dock) to the Arabic *darsina'a* (workshop), whose initial 'd' disappeared somewhere along the line.

19

arouse see **rouse**

arpeggio see **solfeggio**

arrogance see **vanity**

arrogate see **abdicate**

arsenal see **armoury**

Art Deco see **Art Nouveau**

artery see **vein**

artful see **arty**

arthritis see **rheumatism**

artist/artiste (artistic performer)
An 'artist' need not be just someone who practises one of the fine arts, such as a painter or sculptor; in a more general sense it is someone who shows skill or cleverness, that is, art, in what he does, as an angler or orator. The word 'artiste' was introduced into English from the French in the nineteenth century as a consequence of the limited sense of 'artist'. Today it is used mainly of actors and singers, of either sex, but can be readily extended to include such creative experts as stylists and chefs, especially to suggest a professional excellence. It retains its near-French pronunciation of 'arteest'.

artiste see **artist**

Art Nouveau/Art Deco (style of art in fashion in the early twentieth century)
'Art Nouveau' (new art) came first. It flourished between about 1890 and 1910 throughout Europe and the USA and was characterised by the use of long, flowing lines and curves. Germany called it the *Jugendstil* (youth style) and Italy the *stile Liberty*, after the London drapery firm started by Arthur Liberty in 1875. 'Art Deco', with name derived from the 1925 exhibition in Paris of the 'Arts décoratifs et industriels modernes', is the term that came to be used in the 1960s for the style that developed in the 1920s and became prominent in the 1930s. It had the aim of adapting the application of the 'Art Nouveau' style to the design of mass-produced furniture, posters, plastic ornaments and the like. A revived interest in the style and its objects developed in the 1970s.

arty/crafty/artful/arty-crafty (skilfully artistic)
An 'arty' person is not so much skilfully artistic as ostentatiously so, wearing 'arty' clothes or sporting an 'arty' tie. 'Crafty' originally meant skilful but is now used to mean sly, cunning – indeed, even 'devious'. 'Artful', too, means cunning, but with a certain ingenuity. Dickens's 'Artful Dodger' picked pockets with a nice combination of slyness and artistry. 'Arty-crafty', now a rather dated word, denotes a kind of earnest but trivial artistic interest. Its origin lies in the Arts and Crafts Exhibition Society, founded in London in 1888. Devotees of the arts and crafts movement were regarded by some with the same degree of suspicion or disparagement as displayed today in some quarters for champions of hydroponics, macrobiotics and numerology.

arty-crafty see **arty**

ascetic see **aesthetic**

Asdic see **radar**

aseptic see **antiseptic**

ashes see **cinders**

asphalt see **tar**

asphyxiate see **smother**

ass see **donkey**

assail see **assault**

assassin see **murderer**

assault/assail (attack)
To 'assault' someone usually implies physical violence, often criminal in nature. This is reflected in the legal term 'assault and battery' where 'assault' is an 'attempt or offer to beat another' and 'battery' the

actual beating. To 'assault' a person's sense of decency is to shock or scandalise him. To 'assail' a person is usually figurative, meaning to attack him violently with abuse, pleas, arguments and the like. You can 'assail' the lawn, however, if the grass is overlong, by making a determined attack on it with a mower, just as you yourself can be 'assailed' by doubts – bombarded by them. See also **attack**.

assault (act of force) see **attack**

assay see **essay**

assent/consent (as verb: agree)
The difference is really that between active and passive. If you 'assent' to someone's view or suggestion, you need little persuading. The word is almost a synonym of 'accede' or 'acquiesce'. To 'consent' to something, however, is to give it your positive agreement, often having weighed up the matter before making a decision. A father may readily 'assent' to his daughter's marriage, or reluctantly 'consent' to it.

assert/asseverate (state as being true)
Both verbs have the sense of declaring something, with 'asseverate' implying a formal or solemn declaration. 'Asseverate' suggests 'severe', and correctly so, as the two words are related.

asseverate see **assert**

assiduous/sedulous (conscientious, determined)
To be 'assiduous' in one's work or a particular task is to be steadfast in one's application. In spite of the fact that the word derives from the Latin *assiduus* (sitting down to) it could well apply to an athlete training for a contest. If the persistence is there, so is the assiduousness – or assiduity. 'Sedulous' means very much the same, but implies that attention is paid to detail. A proof-reader should 'sedulously' study the text for misprints, for example. The noun is 'sedulity' or 'sedulousness'.

assignation see **assignment**

assignment/assignation (set task)

An 'assignment' is a task or piece of work that has been specially allotted to a particular person or group of people. The term is used in American education to denote a pupil's or student's task, as an 'assignment' of ten arithmetic problems or an essay on the Boston Tea Party. 'Assignation' is more the actual act of assigning, and in America has the additional connotation of the arranging of an illicit meeting between lovers.

assume see **presume**

assure/ensure/insure (make sure or certain)
In the commercial sense, 'assure' strictly speaking applies to the arrangement of insurance against something that is certain to happen as, in particular, death (life 'assurance'), so that one can 'insure' against other occurrences that may or may not happen, such as floods or accidents. 'Assure' in this specifically defined sense still exists in the names of some insurance companies, as that of the London Assurance, one of Britain's oldest. In a different sense, both 'assure' and 'ensure' are close in meaning: 'make safe or sure', 'guarantee'. The distinction can be seen in a phrase such as 'success is assured', meaning simply that it is certain. 'Success is ensured' means that particular steps or actions have been taken to guarantee it. In American usage 'ensure', in the commercial sense, is sometimes used as a variant of 'insure'.

astonished/astounded/dumbfounded (amazed, greatly surprised)
'Astonished' suggests a reaction to something unexpected or remarkable or inexplicable, as an actor's superb – or abysmal – performance or one's first chemistry experiment at school. One would be 'astounded' if the surprise made one unable to think or act, as when one is lost for words at a friend's generosity. The word is more forceful than 'astonished'. 'Dumbfounded', as it suggests, implies a striking dumb with amazement. A forthright female 'no' to a popped question must have caused many a would-be husband to be 'dumbfounded'.

astounded see **astonished**

astrology see **astronomy**

astronaut/cosmonaut (spaceman)
Both perform essentially the same task: the difference is in nationality – an 'astronaut' tends to be American and a 'cosmonaut' Russian. The Russians themselves make a similar distinction – a Soviet spaceman is a *kosmonavt*. Both derive from Greek: respectively 'star sailor' and 'space sailor'.

astronomy/astrology (study of the stars)
'Astronomy' is the word for the scientific study of the stars in particular and celestial bodies generally. 'Astrology', which has been enjoying something of a cult revival in western society from the 1970s, is the science or art – considered by many to be no science or art at all – of judging the occult influence of the stars and planets on the lives of humans. In ancient times 'astrology' embraced what is now called 'astronomy', and was divided into natural 'astrology', which consisted in calculating the movements of the heavens, and judicial 'astrology', which studied, as 'astrology' does today, the supposed influence of the stars on human life and destiny. It is perhaps rather surprising that 'astronomy', not 'astrology', has come to be the word used for the scientific study: there are far more '-ologies' in science than '-onomies'. The 'astro-' element in each, of course, means 'star'.

atheist/agnostic (one not inclined to believe in God)
Everyone knows what an 'atheist' is: his Greek privative prefix *a–* (without) marks him as someone who denies the existence of God or of divine beings. An 'agnostic', with the same prefix, is not, as often held, someone who doesn't know whether there is a God or not, but someone who believes it is impossible to know or prove anything about the existence of God. An 'agnostic', therefore, says that the existence of God cannot be proved – or disproved. The word was invented by T. H. Huxley in his *Science and Christian Tradition*, published in 1870, from the Greek *agnostos* (unknowable), as the opposite of 'gnostic'. See also **deist**.

atmosphere/stratosphere/ionosphere/ troposphere/tropopause (layer of gas surrounding the earth)
The 'atmosphere' is properly the envelope of gas, in the shape of a sphere, that surrounds the earth. It comprises, going outwards, the 'troposphere', which extends from sea level up to about seven miles, the 'stratosphere' – seven to fifty miles in altitude – and the 'ionosphere' – the upper region of the 'atmosphere' extending from around fifty miles in a succession of ionised layers – the first called the Heaviside layer – to a distance of several hundred miles. Between the 'troposphere' and the 'stratosphere' is the 'tropopause', a boundary layer. Most aircraft fly somewhere in the 'stratosphere', while clouds and 'weather' are in the 'troposphere'.

atomic bomb/hydrogen bomb (type of thermonuclear bomb)
The 'atomic bomb', or atom bomb, has a force that comes from nuclear fission, e.g. uranium (235) or plutonium, which when combined form an assembly which starts an uncontrolled chain reaction. Its first – and most inglorious – military use was when dropped on Hiroshima after the Second World War (6 August 1945). The 'hydrogen bomb' derives its power from fusion. It is a fission, or atomic, bomb surrounded by a layer of hydrogenous material. The temperature resulting from the explosion of the fission bomb causes the fusion of the hydrogen nuclei to form helium nuclei. It is many more times more powerful than the 'atomic bomb', and as yet has never (D.G.) been used in warfare. It has, however, been tested by the major powers.

atomic number/atomic weight (unit of measurement of a chemical element)
The 'atomic number' is the number of protons in the nucleus of an atom of a given element, for example for oxygen it is 8, for hydrogen 1, for gold 79, for radium 88. The 'atomic weight' is the average weight of the atoms of a given specimen of an element measured in atomic mass units, one of which approximately equals 1.7×10^{-24} grammes. For oxygen the atomic weight is thus 15.9994, for hydrogen 1.0079, and for uranium, the heaviest naturally occurring

element, 238.029. Today the preferred term for 'atomic weight' is 'relative atomic mass', as since 1961 the carbon-12 atom has been the usual basis of calculations, not the oxygen-16 atom.

atomic weight see **atomic number**

attack/assault (act of force, armed or unarmed)
An 'attack' is a generally forceful act directed against somebody or something, whether physical or verbal (which in a sense could be even more damaging). An 'assault' is an 'attack' that is specifically hostile, whether literally or figuratively. Legally an 'assault' is 'an attempt or offer to beat another, without touching him' – which means that '"assault" and battery' involves the actual 'beating'. See also **assault** as a verb.

attendance centre see **remand home**

attest see **testify**

attic/loft/garret (small room at the top of a house)
An 'attic' is usually up in the roof of a house, where it is a small room with a skylight. Where it exists, it is often used as a boxroom or 'junk room', unless enterprisingly converted into an extra bedroom or study or 'pad'. (An 'attic' under a mansard roof is itself called a mansard – a mansard roof being one that has two slopes, the lower steeper than the upper.) A 'loft' can be an alternative word for an 'attic' – in America it may mean an upper room in general, or even a whole storey – but normally is the word for the space or area approached by a trap-door that lies directly under the roof and often containing the main water tank and various other plumbing or heating arrangements. It, too, can frequently be converted into a proper room, and at the least insulated to preserve the heat in the rooms below it. A 'garret' is a less common word for a rather mean or wretched 'attic', traditionally or romantically sometimes regarded as a place for impoverished painters and poets. Thomas Chatterton, the young 'Gothic' Poet of the eighteenth century, indeed led such a life – and tragi-

cally poisoned himself in a Holborn 'garret' when still only seventeen.

attorney see **lawyer**

au courant see **au fait**

auction bridge see **contract bridge**

audience see **audition**

audition/audience (important interview)
An 'audition' is a trial arranged for a would-be performer by an impresario or agent. An 'audience' is an interview granted by a monarch or other high personage to an individual. Both words are literally a 'hearing', as 'audible' and the more common sort of 'audience' that listens to a performance.

au fait/au courant (informed)
If you are 'au fait' with something you have a practical knowledge of it, you know how it works or is arranged. The French phrase *mettre au fait* means to give someone information about something, acquaint him with it. To be 'au courant', on the other hand, means to be up to date with news or recent developments, literally 'in the course' of things.

auger see **awl**

augury/auspice (omen)
Originally 'augury' was the practice of an augur, the Roman official who interpreted omens. It now simply refers to any sign or indication, as an 'augury' of success – or equally of failure. An 'auspice', by contrast, is a good omen, one that occurs in favourable circumstances, or circumstances seen as boding well for the future. The divining of such omens was carried out by the watching of birds, the classical birdwatcher being called an *auspex*. In the plural, the word means patronage, of course, as when work is done under the 'auspices' of some organisation or sponsor. The adjective can be a confusible: see **auspicious**.

aura/aurora (unnatural emanation)
The word 'aura' has passed from a medical term – the sensation like a cold current of

air experienced before an attack of epilepsy or hysteria – to the subtle emanation said by spiritualists to surround a person like an atmosphere. From this latter sense it has come to be used of the special air or character of a person, such as an 'aura' of wisdom or simplicity. 'Aurora' originally meant the dawn (it is the Roman name of the goddess of the dawn), then later something suggesting the dawn. Today the word is used for the phenomenon known as the aurora borealis or northern lights, the luminous display seen in or near the region of the North Pole. 'Aura' may occasionally be half-associated (wrongly) with 'aroma', since this, too, is a type of emanation with a figurative as well as a literal meaning.

aurora see **aura**

auspice see **augury**

auspicious/propitious (favourable)
'Auspicious' indicates that the time or moment is right for success in the future. It has an overtone, too, of importance, so than an 'auspicious' occasion or an 'auspicious' moment is one that not just points to a good future but is memorable in itself. 'Propitious' – which sometimes acquires a false association with 'prosperous' – indicates favourable conditions not so much in the future as at the moment. One can thus talk of 'propitious' weather, or of meeting in 'propitious' circumstances.

authoritarian see **authoritative**

authoritative/authoritarian (having authority)
An 'authoritative' manner implies that the person in question has authority – speaks or acts as one who knows, or is in a position to know. An 'authoritarian' manner suggests that subjection to authority is favoured – usually that of the person possessing such a manner.

autocrat/plutocrat/bureaucrat/aristocrat (kind of ruler or person in authority)
An 'autocrat' is an absolute ruler, such as a monarch who holds and exercises powers of government by an inherent right, with no restrictions. A 'plutocrat' is a member of the wealthy ruling class (if there is one). A 'bureaucrat' is one of the officials who rule, especially a remote civil servant or minister, and one who operates by a fixed routine rather than by a rational or considered policy. An 'aristocrat' is a member of the nobility or of the upper classes, especially someone who is distinguished by his genteel manners or general 'superiority' in habits, dress, speech and the like. The four 'crats' (the element is Greek for 'power', 'rule') have names that denote their distinguishing characteristics, respectively 'on one's own', 'wealth', 'office', and 'best'.

autogyro see **helicopter**

automatic see **pistol**

avenge/revenge (inflict pain or harm in return for pain or harm)
The two words were once interchangeable. Today 'avenge', a more objective and impersonal verb, suggests a legitimate vindication, as of a wrong or an offence against oneself. A murder might be 'avenged', but not 'revenged'. With 'revenge' the pain or harm inflicted might in fact be imaginary or non-existent. A worker who wants to 'revenge' himself on the way his boss treats him may have an axe to grind rather than the wish to right a manifest wrong. The noun of 'avenge' is 'vengeance'; of 'revenge' it is . . . 'revenge'.

averse to/adverse to (opposed to)
To be 'averse to' something is to be disinclined towards it. If you are 'not averse to' an alcoholic nightcap, you are really saying you are in favour of it. To be 'adverse to' a thing – the word is used more of things than of people, as conditions 'adverse to' one's interests – is to be opposed or unfavourable towards it. The difference is in the prefixes, with 'averse' having a reduced 'ab-' (away) and 'adverse' having 'ad-' (towards).

avid/rabid (greedy)
'Avid' implies a general greediness: an 'avid' interest is a keen one, a person 'avid' for success desperately desires it. 'Rabid' suggests a furious intensity, so that a 'rabid' hunger is almost a morbid one. The words

derive respectively from Latin *avidus* (eager) and *rabidus* (raving), with the second related to 'rabies'. 'Rabid' is sometimes half-confused with 'ravage': see **ravishing**.

avoid/evade/elude (escape from, keep out of the way of)
To 'avoid' a thing or a person is to steer clear of him, shun him. To 'evade' someone or something is to escape him/it by cunning or trickery, as when one 'evades' the taxman or a question. To 'elude', as when one 'eludes' one's creditors or 'eludes' pursuit, is to escape not just by cunning but by real artifice. A word that 'eludes' you has, for the moment, fallen into oblivion. For another confusible of 'elude', see **escape**.

awake see **wake**

awaken see **wake**

award see **reward**

awl/bradawl/auger (instrument for boring holes)
An 'awl' is used for piercing small holes, mainly in leather or wood. A 'bradawl' is an awl used for boring holes in wood specifically for brads – small nails with small heads. An 'auger' is a carpenter's tool larger than a gimlet with a spiral groove, also for boring holes in wood. It's a word that like 'apple' and 'apron' originally had an initial 'n' ('a nauger'). (Its spelling must be distinguished from 'augur' – see **augury**.)

axiom see **maxim**

Axis see **allies**

ayah/amah (nurse or maid in the East)
An 'ayah' is an Indian nurse or lady's maid. Although in fact a Hindi word it derives from the Portuguese *aia*, the feminine of *aio* (tutor). An 'amah' is similar – though possibly more amahs are wetnurses – and also from the Portuguese (*ama*, nurse), but the word is used mainly by Europeans in the Far East, not in India.

B

BA see **BOAC**

babble/rabble/gabble/rabbit/burble/blather (talk rapidly or incoherently)
The degree of rapidity, incoherence, or general wordiness can perhaps be best expressed by associations: for 'babble' – 'baby', for 'rabble' – 'rapid', for 'gabble' – 'gab' (gift of the), for 'rabbit' – 'ramble', for 'burble' – 'bubble', for 'blather' – 'baloney' (which has its own confusible, **blarney**). All can be followed by 'on'; 'rabbit' virtually always is.

babel see **bedlam**

baboon see **gorilla**

BAC see **BOAC**

bacilli see **bacteria**

back/rear (location of something behind something else)
'Back' has the implied opposite 'front', and often indicates a position both behind something and outside it, as a small garden at the 'back' of a house (and a tiny lawn at the front). 'Rear' usually refers to the final or end section of something, as the 'rear' of a train or a 'rearguard' bringing up the 'rear' of an armed force (as the opposite of the vanguard).

bacteria/bacilli (disease-producing organisms)
'Bacilli' *are* 'bacteria', in fact – only 'bacilli' produce spores and 'bacteria' do not. They are the simplest group of non-green vegetable organisms and are involved in fermentation and putrefaction as well as the production of disease. They are rod-shaped (Greek *bakterion* and Latin *bacillus* both mean 'little stick') as distinct from *cocci* which are spherical and *spirilla* which are

spiral, among others. The singular of 'bacteria' is 'bacterium'; of 'bacilli' it is 'bacillus'.

badinage see **banter**

BAe see **BOAC**

balcony/gallery/circle/dress circle
(section of the auditorium of a theatre situated above the stalls, that is, above floor level)
Going upwards, the 'circle' is a curved section of seats on the first or a higher floor, which may be divided into two such sections, the lower being called the 'dress circle' (in which evening dress was once *de rigueur*) and the higher the 'upper circle'. Above the 'circle' comes the 'balcony', which is also effectively – and may even be called – the 'upper circle'. In a cinema the 'balcony' is a fairly general word for any seats upstairs. Highest of all is the 'gallery', traditionally the cheapest and most vociferous section of the audience. However, the highest tier may be called the 'balcony', not the 'gallery', especially in a smaller theatre, and in the USA the 'balcony' turns out to be what in a British theatre would be the 'dress circle'. Cinemas, too, may settle for a 'circle' of some kind instead of a 'balcony'. The terms are thus entertainingly imprecise and variable.

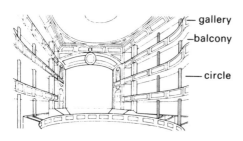

balcony/verandah (platform in front of a house on which one can walk or sit)
A 'balcony' is almost always a suspended platform with railings or a parapet outside an upper floor window. A 'verandah' (or veranda) is an open portico or gallery at the front of a house or along the side with a roof supported on pillars. The word is of Hindi origin: the structure is a special feature of houses in India.

baleful/baneful (evil)
Strictly speaking, 'baleful' means 'full of bale', an old-fashioned word for evil. The most common sense of the word today, though, is 'lugubrious' or 'dismal', as a 'baleful' look or expression, sometimes seen on the faces of bored monkeys in zoos and elderly judges in courtrooms. 'Baneful' – literally 'full of bane' – is even stronger, since 'bane' is an old word for murder or death. It now means 'destructive' or 'poisonous'. One might thus talk of the 'baneful' effect of tobacco or a 'baneful' habit. The modern sense of 'bane', as in 'He/She is the bane of my life', is considerably toned down from the original.

ballad/ballade (kind of narrative poem or song)
There is a technical difference between these two very similar terms, and this is in the verse form. A 'ballad' has stanzas or verses of four lines, of alternating four-feet and three-feet length, and with only the second and fourth lines rhyming. The first stanza of Charles Causley's literary (and modern) 'ballad' 'Mother, Get Up, Unbar the Door' illustrates this:

> Mother, get up, unbar the door,
> Throw wide the window-pane,
> I see a man stand all covered in sand
> Outside in Vicarage Lane.

A 'ballade', by distinction, usually has three stanzas of eight lines, with the same three or four rhymes throughout, and ending with an *envoi* of four lines, the whole rhyme scheme thus being ABABBCBC BCBC. Furthermore, the last line of the first stanza serves as a refrain repeated in the last line of each stanza and of the *envoi*. Thus a somewhat complex form! The 'ballade' was revived with a certain degree of success in modern times by G. K. Chesterton and others. To illustrate the rhyme-scheme, here is a stanza from his *A Ballade of an Anti-Puritan*:

> They spoke of progress spiring round,
> Of Light and Mrs. Humphry Ward

It is not true to say I frowned,
  Or ran about the room and roared;
I might have simply sat and snored
  I rose politely in the club
And said, 'I feel a little bored;
  Will some one take me to a pub?'

ballade see **ballad**

balmy see **barmy**

baloney see **blarney**

baluster see **banister**

ban/bar (prohibition or restriction)
A 'ban' is a formal or authoritative prohibition, or one made by public opinion. A
'bar' is a kind of temporary 'ban', as an
obstruction or objection. Of course, both a
'ban' and a 'bar' can be lifted, but one
almost expects a 'bar' to be. Legally, a 'bar'
is an objection which nullifies an action or
claim, or a stoppage of an alleged right or
action.

baneful see **baleful**

banister/baluster (one of a series of pillars
supporting a rail)
The main difference is that 'banisters' – the
word in the plural can refer to the pillars or
the rail itself – are usually indoors, running
down a stairway, and that 'balusters' are
normally outside and are the stone pillars
supporting a parapet across a bridge, say,
or along the edge of a terrace. A whole row
of 'balusters' complete with rails forms a
balustrade. Both 'banister' and 'baluster'
ultimately derive from the Greek *balaustion*
(pomegranate flower). The reference is to
the ornamental shape of many pillars.

banjo see **guitar**

bank card see **credit card**

bankruptcy see **insolvency**

banquet see **feast**

banter/badinage (teasing talk)
'Banter' is good-humoured chaffing, often
on a particular topic. Stag nights and
wedding receptions are frequently noted for
the 'banter' directed at the groom. 'Badinage', as its French origin suggests (from
badiner, to jest, joke), is more stylish, and on
the whole also lighter and more delicate.
The origin of the word 'banter' is not
known.

bar/barrier (obstruction, obstacle)
When used figuratively, 'bar' suggests an
acceptable or reasonable obstacle or
condition, as a 'bar' to promotion after a
certain age. A 'barrier' has the connotation
of something stronger, more of an impediment, but nevertheless an obstacle that can
be overcome with an effort or patience.

bar (prohibition) see **ban**

barbarian see **barbarous**

barbaric see **barbarous**

barbarous/barbaric/barbarian (savage,
uncivilised)
The Greek word *barbaros*, possibly related to
babble and also the Latin derivative
barbarus, was used to designate a foreigner or
stranger, someone who 'babbled' in another
tongue. The word resulted in the name of
the Barbary Coast in north west Africa and
earlier, the people known as Berbers who
lived there. Such 'barbarians' were, to the
Greeks and Romans, uncivilised folk, and
this is the general sense of the word today.
'He is a real barbarian', means that he is
uncouth, ill-mannered, discourteous or
whatever. 'Barbarous' means 'like the
barbarians' – cruel and inhuman, so that
one can talk of 'barbarous' customs, laws or
treatment. 'Barbaric' is a milder word, often
meaning little more than 'in bad taste' or, of
something impressive, 'crude'. Thus yelling
football fans can, to some ears, make a
'barbaric' noise, and baroque architecture,
to some eyes, has a 'barbaric' splendour.

baritone see **tenor**

barmy/balmy/palmy (crazy, carefree)
Both 'barmy' and 'balmy' mean 'silly' or
'crazy'. Dictionaries disagree as to which
spelling came first or indeed as to the origin
of the words. Barm is actually the froth on

fermenting malt liquor, but it is hard to see how this means 'crazy'. 'Balmy', however, could literally mean 'like balm', that is (punningly) 'soft'. Yet another explanation is that 'barmy' has its origin in the former Barming Asylum, near Maidstone, Kent: someone destined or fit for the establishment was said to be 'barmy'. So the confusion lies more in the spelling and the origin than the meaning. 'Palmy', however, means prosperous and flourishing, and no irresponsibility is implied in the phrase 'the palmy days of youth'. The reference is a literal one, to palm trees, and 'bearing the palm'. ('Do you allow dates?' a distinguished visitor asked the headmistress of a girls' school while waiting to present the prizes. 'Oh yes,' replied the good lady, 'so long as they don't eat too many.')

baron/baronet (one of lowest ranks of the nobility)
A 'baron' in Britain holds a title that is either hereditary or, as laid down by the Life Peerages Act of 1958, for life only. 'Barons' are known as 'Lord X', where X is either a surname, often the title-holder's own, or the name of a place historically linked with his family. A 'baronet' is a member of the lowest hereditary British order, and ranks below a 'baron'. The wives of both – in the case of a 'baron', the baroness, therefore – are called 'Lady X', the X being the same as their husband's name. 'Barons' exist or existed also on the European continent, although the title in both France and Germany is given only by courtesy. The word originally meant simply 'man': compare modern Spanish *varón*, meaning 'male', 'man'. For some more elevated noble ranks see **duke** and **marquis** and also, for a more general view of the nobility, **lord**.

baronet see **baron**

baroque/rococo (florid style in architecture and painting)
'Baroque', derived from the Portuguese *barroco* (irregular) via the French, is a style that was developed in sixteenth-century Italy. Its hall-marks were lack of symmetry, bold and convoluted forms, and exaggerated pictorial and ornamental effects. It can be seen today in the churches of Roman Catholic countries such as Spain and Austria and as echoed in the paintings of such artists as Rubens, Caravaggio and Murillo. 'Rococo', said to be derived from French *rocaille* (shellwork, rockwork), was the final stage of the 'baroque' period, in roughly the first half of the eighteenth century. Different materials were used, such as stucco, wood, metal, and tapestries, the key feature of the style being the use of ornamentation in the form of shellwork, scrolls and the like.

barque/barquentine/brigantine/brig
(type of sailing ship)
A 'barque' has three or more masts, all of them square-rigged (with sails set at right angles) except the aftermost, which is fore-and-aft. A 'barquentine' also has three or more masts, but the foremast is square-rigged and all the others fore-and-aft. A 'brigantine' has two masts, with the foremast square-rigged and the mainmast having a fore-and-aft mainsail and square topsails. The 'brig' is also two-masted, but both masts are square-rigged. All very shipshape.

barquentine see **barque**

barrel-organ/hurdy-gurdy (musical instrument played by turning its handle)
The two names have a popular and a specific meaning. The 'barrel-organ', to the man in the street (literally), is, or was, the street piano played in the time-honoured way by an Italian with a pet monkey. (It largely disappeared after 1922 when Mussolini came to power and recalled all Italians engaged in street music.) This same instrument was also known as a 'hurdy-gurdy', which is also, however, the name of quite a different instrument: a sort of violin with a rosined wheel acting as a circular bow. This sounded two drone strings by being turned with the right hand, while the left hand played piano-type keys. Meanwhile the 'barrel-organ' proper was an instrument with a pin-studded cylinder (or barrel) turned by a handle, and a mechanism for opening pipes or striking metal tongues. As such it was not a street instrument but one originally used in churches in the late eighteenth and early nineteenth centuries. The

'barrel-organ' of the street piano kind has a barrel, it is true, but was certainly not an organ in the accepted sense of the word.

barrier see **bar**

barrister see **lawyer**

base/basis (foundation)
'Base' is normally used literally, with a number of technical and scientific meanings, although 'to base' can mean 'to put on a basis'. 'Basis', by contrast, is usually a figurative word meaning 'determining principle'. The plural of 'base' is 'bases' and of 'basis' – 'bases' (pronounced 'baseez').

basin see **bowl**

basis see **base**

basketball see **netball**

bastard/dastard (cruel or brutal person)
Literally, of course, a 'bastard' is an illegitimate child, hence (formerly) one to be despised, and hence (in common use today) a term of abuse, especially for a violent or cruel person. Oddly, 'dastard' has come to have the same application – a term of abuse for a person who commits a brutal act, especially when the victim is not given a chance. Originally the word meant 'coward' – specifically a mean or sneaking one.

bathos see **pathos**

battalion see **corps**

battle see **war**

bay/gulf/bight/inlet/cove (bow-like expanse of water)
A 'bay', the most common word, does not necessarily have to be landlocked, i.e. approached by a strait (see **sound**). It can have quite a shallow curve, as the 'Bay' of Biscay. 'Gulf' implies a deeper recess, however, with a narrower width of entrance. Most 'gulfs' are fairly large or important in some way, as the 'Gulf' of Mexico which gave its name to the 'Gulf' Stream. A 'bight' is a less common word for a curve or recess of the coast or a river bank. German 'Bight',

a sea area for shipping forecast purposes, is the stretch of sea off the north-west coast of Germany. An 'inlet' is much smaller: a small arm of the sea, almost a creek. A 'cove', which tends to have pleasant seaside or smuggling associations, is a small 'bay' or recess in the shoreline of the sea, a lake, or a river, especially a sheltered one. One might expect it to be related to 'cave' or 'cover', but it actually comes from an Old English word *cofa* meaning 'chamber'.

bay window/bow window (projecting window)
A 'bay window' is often curved, but can also be rectangular or polygonal. A 'bow window' is curved only. 'Bow windows' have something of a historical or stylish ring to them. Mr Micawber went to bed planning to add 'bow windows' to the house 'in case anything turned up'.

bazaar see **fête**

BEA see **BOAC**

beach see **shore**

bear/bull (type of share on the stock exchange which can be profitable)
The terms really apply to the speculators: a 'bear' reckons that conditions are unfavourable, so he sells his shares hoping to buy them in later (assuming they go on falling) and make a profit. A 'bull' does the opposite: buys hoping to sell later at a profit, on a rising market. An old proverb talked of 'selling the skin before you have the bear'. The story behind 'bull' is obscure, although both the animal and the shareholder are headstrong.

beast/brute (wild animal; savage person)
'Beast' suggests a large animal such as a lion ('King of Beasts'), tiger or elephant, and a coarse (in any sense), cruel or filthy person. 'Brute' is used less often of animals. Of a person it suggests stupidity, lack of intelligence, or want of reasoning. The words are frequently accompanied by adjectives reflecting these attributes, such as 'dirty beast', 'drunken brute', 'wicked beast', 'callous brute'.

bedlam/babel (noise and confusion)
The words can be traced back to, respectively, the biblical towns of Bethlehem and

29

Babylon, with 'bedlam' directly originating from the Bethlehem (or Bethlem) Royal Hospital in south east London – a lunatic asylum that in 1930 was transferred to new premises at Shirley, near Croydon, Surrey. As a common noun it implies noise and disorder as well as confusion. 'Babel' has its immediate derivation in the Tower of Babel (with 'Babel' the Hebrew name of Babylon) in Genesis 11, where the confounding of language took place. It suggests an uproar or hubbub, or incoherent speech as at a rowdy meeting. The resemblance of 'babel' to **babble** is fortuitous.

beefcake see **cheesecake**

beginning/start (initial stage or part of something)
'Beginning' is a general word, as the 'beginning' of the month (the first few days of it) or the 'beginning' of a programme (the opening moments of it). 'Start' implies the distinct, perhaps sudden, first phase or opening action of something, as the 'start' of a race (the important moment when the participants suddenly begin to move) or the 'start' of a new career (the first part of a milestone in one's life). 'Start' is one of the few common words beginning with 'st-' that does *not* have something to do with standing still – as these last two words and others such as 'state', 'stick', 'stop' and 'stubborn'.

begrudge/grudge (give or grant unwillingly)
To 'begrudge' someone something is to be envious of their possession of it. To 'grudge' a thing to a person, however, is to give it or grant it to him reluctantly. One friend can 'grudge' you a loan of £20, and another can then 'begrudge' you this loan since he could have done with it himself.

bellicose see **belligerent**

belligerent/bellicose (militant, warlike)
'Belligerent', used literally or – frequently – figuratively, means 'warlike', 'pertaining to war', as a 'belligerent' tone of voice or a 'belligerent' code of conduct. 'Bellicose' implies seeking to wage war or actually doing so, so that of people it often means something close to 'pugnacious', as a 'bellicose' old man.

belly see (1) **billow**, (2) **stomach**

belt/zone (region with special characteristics)
A 'belt' is a strip or band of land or territory, as a green 'belt' that encircles a city to prevent sprawling development, or a commuter 'belt' or dormitory 'belt' further out from a city, where those who work in the city live and from which they travel daily. The word is a fairly informal one, and the actual idea of 'strip' may be rather vague. It is quite vague in 'zone', which is the formal word for a region of any shape – although often circular. Examples might be a danger 'zone', a smokeless 'zone', the British 'zone' in Berlin, or the so-called Torrid 'Zone', between the Tropics of Cancer and Capricorn. However, 'zone' actually derives from the Greek word for 'belt' or 'girdle', so the 'strip' concept is basically there. 'Zone', incidentally, is not related to 'zodiac', even though the latter is a 'heavenly belt'.

Benedicite see **Benedictus**

Benedictus/Benedicite (canticle in Book of Common Prayer)
Both words are from the Latin *benedicere* (to bless), with 'Benedictus' the past participle (blessed) and 'Benedicite' the imperative (bless!). They are the first words of Latin texts. The 'Benedictus' occurs twice in the Anglican liturgy: the first time as a canticle in the service of Morning Prayer (as an alternative to the *Jubilate*), the second in the new alternative Order of Communion, into which it was introduced from the Roman Mass. The first 'Benedictus' begins the sentence translated 'Blessed be the Lord God of Israel'; the second has the English version 'Blessed is He that cometh in the name of the Lord' (found in the Book of Common Prayer only, Psalm 118, v.26, l.1 where the second word is 'be', not 'is'). The 'Benedicite', whose opening words in English are 'O All ye Works of the Lord, bless ye the Lord', is a canticle preceding the 'Benedictus' in the order of Morning Prayer, and is an alternative to the *Te Deum*. It is an extract from the apocryphal Book of Daniel, where it was purported to be sung by the 'Three Holy Children' in Nebuchadnezzar's burning fiery furnace.

beneficent see **benevolent**

benevolent/beneficent (well disposed)
Strictly, 'benevolent' is *wishing* to do good for others, or being generally amiably disposed, while 'beneficent' is *doing* good for others by conferring gifts on them. An ideal Father Christmas is presumably as 'benevolent' as he is 'beneficent'.

berserk/amok (frenziedly out of control)
The words are sometimes confused, although people 'go berserk' but 'run amok'. To go 'berserk' is to become suddenly violent and destructive, as reputedly were the berserkers or berserks, the giant warriors in Scandinavian legend who were filled with wild frenzy in battle. To run 'amok' – not related to 'muck' – is to become violently murderous or homicidal, as Malays are claimed to. (The word is of Malay origin.) The word has a quite acceptable alternative spelling 'amuck'.

biannual/biennial (twice a year – or once every two years)
'Biannual' means 'happening twice a year'; 'biennial' means 'happening every other year'. As a noun, 'biennial' is used of plants that live for two years. These confusibles can be easily avoided by using 'half-yearly' and 'two-yearly'. The Latin prefix *bi–* (two) is even more ambiguous in 'bi-monthly', which can mean either 'twice a month' or 'every two months'. Here, too, Anglo-Saxon alternatives are preferable – 'twice-monthly', 'two-monthly'.

bias see **prejudice**

biathlon see **marathon**

bicentenary/bicentennial (200th anniversary)
A 'bicentenary' is a 200th anniversary, with the word as an adjective meaning 'pertaining to a 200th anniversary'. A 'bicentennial' is preferred American usage with the same meaning: the word became familiar to Britons in this spelling in 1976 with the celebration of the 200th anniversary of the US Declaration of Independence. As an adjective, 'bicentennial' means 'lasting 200 years' or 'recurring every 200 years'. See also **centenary**.

bicentennial see **bicentenary**

biennial see **biannual**

bight see **bay**

bile/gall/spleen (bitter liquid secreted in the body or organ secreting this)
Both 'bile' and 'gall' are terms used for the liquid which is bitter and yellowish and secreted in fact by the liver. One of the main functions of 'bile' is to aid digestion, but it was formerly known as 'choler' and regarded as one of the four so-called humours (the others being blood, phlegm and melancholy). Figuratively it has the sense of 'peevishness'. The connection with 'gall' – itself having the figurative sense 'bitterness of spirit' or 'rancour' – is that 'bile' proceeds from the liver into the 'gall' bladder, where it is concentrated and from which it is discharged after meals. 'Spleen', like 'bile', also means 'peevishness' – as when one 'vents one's spleen' on someone, although it is not a liquid but an organ near the heart end of the stomach in which the blood undergoes certain corpuscular changes. It was formerly thought to be the seat of courage, melancholy, ill humour and the like.

bill see **account**

Bill see **Act**

billiards/snooker/pool (game of 'poking balls about a smooth table to score by sending them into small pockets', J. B. Pick, *The Phoenix Dictionary of Games,* Phoenix House, 1954)
'Billiards' is the game with three balls: a red, a white, and a spot-white (white ball with a spot on), with each player aiming to strike his own ball (white or spot-white) to hit the red and his opponent's and, preferably, pocket the red in so doing. 'Snooker' has all the coloured balls: fifteen red (scoring one each), one each of yellow (scoring two), green (three), brown (four), blue (five), pink (six) and black (seven) and one white ball, the latter used as a cue ball by the players in turn. A player is 'snookered' – a term that has come to be used figuratively in the sense 'stymied' (the golfing equivalent), 'frustrated' – when a

31

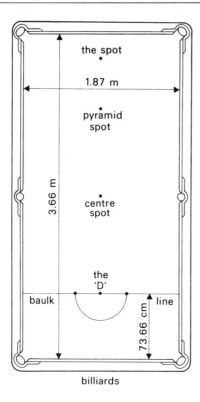

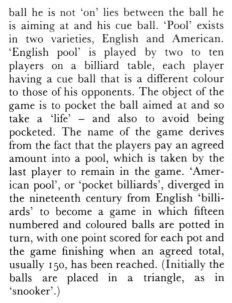

billiards

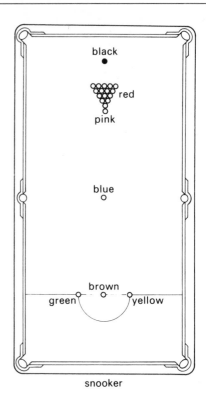

snooker

ball he is not 'on' lies between the ball he is aiming at and his cue ball. 'Pool' exists in two varieties, English and American. 'English pool' is played by two to ten players on a billiard table, each player having a cue ball that is a different colour to those of his opponents. The object of the game is to pocket the ball aimed at and so take a 'life' – and also to avoid being pocketed. The name of the game derives from the fact that the players pay an agreed amount into a pool, which is taken by the last player to remain in the game. 'American pool', or 'pocket billiards', diverged in the nineteenth century from English 'billiards' to become a game in which fifteen numbered and coloured balls are potted in turn, with one point scored for each pot and the game finishing when an agreed total, usually 150, has been reached. (Initially the balls are placed in a triangle, as in 'snooker'.)

billion see **million**

billow/belly (swell out)
The words are related in origin, with 'billow' used mainly of the swelling of large waves at sea or the surging of a mass of smoke or fog. 'Belly' – also related to 'bellows' – is used mainly of something that stays swelled out, such as sails on a ship. Curtains in the wind, however, usually 'billow'.

billow/breaker/roller (wave at sea)
A 'billow' is a great, surging wave – and poetically the sea itself. The word is not related to 'bellow' or 'pillow' but is of Scandinavian origin. A 'breaker' is an ocean wave with a breaking crest – this is the wave used for surfing. A 'roller' is a long, swelling wave that 'rolls' in towards the coast.

bison see **buffalo**

bitter see **ale**

bitters see **vermouth**

bitumen see **tar**

black humour/sick humour (type of 'warped' humour)
'Black humour' aims to present tragedy or bitter reality in comic terms. It often treats sad or macabre subjects (death, divorce, serious illness, murder) in this way. Classic examples of black comedies in the twentieth century are Edward Albee's *Who's Afraid of Virginia Woolf?* (1962, film version 1966), dealing with the intense 'love-hate' relationships of a middle-aged, alcoholic couple, with few holds barred, and the plays of Joe Orton such as *Entertaining Mr Sloane* (1964) and *Loot* (1966) which involve, among other things, a funeral, murder, blackmail and homosexual eroticism. 'Sick humour' also deals in the macabre and in human misfortunes, but at a less intense level and with more of a pathological 'twist'. It is most common in the form of the 'sick joke', the most original of which can usually be savoured in the 'raconteurs' corner of a pub on a Friday or Saturday night. Cynics – or sober realists – see both phenomena as symbolic of the ever-increasing moral disorientation and decadence of western society in the twentieth century.

black magic/white magic (type of supernatural power)
'Black magic' is evil magic, evoking devils. It involves the use – or abuse – of supernatural powers for selfish ends, as in sorcery, necromancy (making predictions by communicating with the dead) and the raising of the dead generally. 'White magic' is good magic, evoking angels, and involves the selfless use of supernatural powers to promote the good of others. (There is also natural magic, which evokes no personal spirit.) So, at any rate, say the experts on these things. But 'black magic' is the kind most down-to-earth mortals will have heard of and been attracted to, if only because of brand-name associations.

Blackshirts/Brownshirts (members of militant organisation)
The 'Blackshirts' were the Italian Fascists. Neo-Fascists and other offshoots of this organisation also frequently wear a black shirt as part of their uniform. In Britain the 'Blackshirts' of Oswald Mosley's British Union of Fascists were notorious in the 1930s. The 'Brownshirts' were Hitler's Stormtroopers, otherwise the SA. The term is sometimes used loosely of any Nazis.

blanch see **blench**

blancmange see **jelly**

blare see **blast**

blarney/baloney/boloney (nonsense)
'Blarney' is used to mean flattering or cajoling talk. 'Let's have none of your blarney, now!' If that sounds Irish, it's because the gift of talk of this kind, especially wheedling flattery, is said to be given to whoever kisses the Blarney Stone, in the village of the same name near Cork in southern Ireland. 'Baloney', and its alternative spelling 'boloney', means at the most 'nonsense', 'rubbish', and at the least, 'waffle'. The word is said to be linked with the 'polony', or Bologna sausage, from the eponymous town in Italy. This is conjectural, however, and may well itself be 'baloney'.

blast/blare/bray (raucous noise)
A 'blast' is essentially loud and piercing, as of trumpets, whistles, horns or sirens. A 'blare' is more loud and raucous, as of a radio playing at maximum volume, a loudspeaker, or brass instrument played *cuivré*. A 'bray' is first and foremost the harsh and breathy cry of a donkey, but can also be used of trumpets, especially when the sound is discordant, or of a loud, human, asinine laugh. The three words are frequently used as verbs.

blast-off see **lift-off**

blatant/flagrant (undisguisedly offensive)
'Blatant', delightfully defined by *Chambers* as 'calumniously clamorous: egregiously vulgar', can be used of things and persons. Of things it has the sense 'shamelessly obvious', as a 'blatant' lie or error. Of a person, it implies a lack of concern over his bad behaviour by the offender, as is shown by a 'blatant' liar or plagiarist. 'Flagrant', glossed by Johnson in his *Dictionary* as

'flaming into notice', has a similar sense to 'blatant' but is a stronger word. 'Flagrant' disregard for rules suggests that one not only flouts them, but does so with relish. *Partridge* quotes Anthony Eden, in a speech made in 1936, as using the wrong word of the pair when he spoke of a 'blatant breach of good faith'.

blather see **babble**

blaze/blazon (vividly exhibit)
There are three meanings to 'blaze': to burn brightly, as of a fire; to proclaim, as with a trumpet; to mark trees by chipping off the bark, as when indicating a trail. The third of these meanings in fact derives from the 'blaze', or white mark, on a horse's head, which in turn has its origin in the first sense. To 'blazon', from an Old French word *blason* (shield), of unknown origin and not related to any form of 'blaze', is to show something or display it conspicuously or publicly, as, literally, heraldic arms on a shield. It is difficult to believe, though, that one of the two words does not influence the meaning of the other.

blazon see **blaze**

blench/blanch (turn pale or white)
'Blench' is the more general word, meaning to make, or go, pale or white. But when used with such words as 'fear' – 'She blenched with fear' – it also acquires the other sense of 'blench': to shrink or quail. 'Blanch' is confined more to a literal use, as of 'blanching' almonds by peeling them. Here the influence is of 'bleach', so that the two in some senses are virtually synonymous: linen can be either 'blanched' or 'bleached' on the grass.

blink see **wink**

blizzard see **snowstorm**

bloater see **herring**

bloom/blossom (come into flower)
The difference is a delicate one: to 'bloom' is to be in the *first* stage of full flower, as literally or, when used of a person, to be in a state of health and vigour and beauty (or

handsomeness). One thus talks of the 'bloom' of youth: youth itself may last several years, but it is the first full attainment of it that is the 'bloom'. To 'blossom' is to flower, but at the same time to give promise of fruit to come. One can thus say of someone that he is 'blossoming' into a talented writer, or that she is 'blossoming' into a gifted actress.

blossom see **bloom**

bludgeon see **cudgel**

Blue Book see **White Paper**

blush/flush (of person: redden with embarrassment or other emotion)
One usually 'blushes' from embarrassment, shame, modesty or shyness. One 'flushes' from something stronger, from any sharp, sudden emotion, in fact, such as pride, anger, joy or great shame. Often, however, the cause of a 'flush' is a good one such as success or victory. The word seems to derive from a combination of 'flash' and 'gush' under the influence of 'blush'. Occasionally, too, there is confusion between 'first flush', the initial elation of victory, etc. and 'at (the) first blush', meaning 'at (the) first glance'.

blusterous see **boisterous**

blustery see **boisterous**

BOAC/BEA/BAC/BA/BAe (aircraft or airway company)
'BOAC', the British Overseas Airways Corporation, was founded in 1939. In 1972 it merged (formally in 1974) with 'BEA', British European Airways, founded in 1946, to form 'BA', British Airways. 'BAC', the British Aircraft Corporation, was set up in 1960, as a merger of the aircraft and guided weapons interests of the Bristol Aeroplane Company (20 per cent), English Electric (40 per cent) and Vickers (40 per cent). It has produced many important names in the aerospace industry, including the Viscount, Vanguard, VC10, One-Eleven and, best known of all, the Concorde, which is now flown jointly by 'BA' and Air France. 'BAe' is British Aerospace, a formerly nationalised

corporation, which was formed in 1976 and acquired the assets of 'BAC' as well as those of Hawker Siddeley and Scottish Aviation. It was privatised in 1981, however, when half of its shareholding was sold by the government to private investors (with the other half sold in 1985). It is the largest airframe manufacturer in Britain.

boa constrictor see **python**

boar see **pig**

boat/ship (vessel used for travelling on water)
'A "boat" is small, a "ship" is large' is as far as most people are prepared to distinguish. In general true, of course – although one can be more precise. As distinct from a 'boat', a 'ship' is a relatively large sea- or ocean-going vessel, usually over 500 tons in weight. Of sailing vessels, a 'ship' has three or more masts with square rigging. There are two notable exceptions to the 'small-large' distinction. Submarines are officially 'boats' (compare the term 'U-boat' as applied to German submarines in the First World War, itself derived from the German *Unterseeboot*). The other exception relates to the ore-carrying vessels, ore 'boats', that ply on the Great Lakes of the USA. When it comes to methods of propulsion, 'boats' can be propelled by any of the four methods: oars, paddles, sail or power (as steam or engine). 'Ships', on the other hand, are propelled virtually exclusively by sail or power only. 'Boat' is, however, often used loosely to apply to any vessel, especially to a passenger one, as in 'What sort of cabin did you have on the "boat"?' In spite of a certain overlap between different types of 'boat' and 'ship', usage is more or less standardised for many vessels. Thus one has a fishing 'boat', rowing 'boat', motor 'boat', ferry 'boat', paddle 'boat', 'lifeboat', 'houseboat', 'speedboat', 'gunboat', motor torpedo 'boat' (or MTB), 'showboat' and, as a once popular type of aircraft, flying 'boat'. An early form of mail 'boat' was a packet 'boat' – which in fact gave the French word (*paquebot*) that today means 'passenger liner'! Most 'ships' are more specialised in their function, so that one has a 'warship', 'battleship', hospital 'ship', 'lightship', slave 'ship', container 'ship' and, by transference, 'airship' and 'spaceship'. The overlap occurs for sailing 'boats' or 'ships', 'steamboats' or 'ships', passenger 'boats' or 'ships' and, historically, the 'Q-boat' or 'ship', otherwise the mystery 'ship' – a 'warship' disguised as a tramp steamer in the First World War with the aim of decoying German submarines.

boater see **panama**

boating see **sailing**

bog see **marsh**

boiled/broiled (cooked)
'Boiled' means cooked in water (normally), as eggs, vegetables, potatoes and some kinds of meat such as beef, mutton and lamb. 'Broiled' means 'cooked by direct heat', as in an oven or under a grill, of fish or poultry. A 'broiler' is a young chicken ready for 'broiling'. The word is related to French *brûlé* (burned).

boisterous/blustery/blusterous (rough and buffeting)
'Boisterous' is usually applied to violent natural forces such as the wind or the sea. Of behaviour it suggests roughness and rowdiness, as of noisy boys – which two words evoke the adjective – while of a mood it hints· at a rough playfulness. 'Blustery' and 'blusterous' suggest more a temporary roughness, and they lack the playfulness that 'boisterous' can imply. A 'blustery' wind is rather a threatening one, and a 'blusterous' mood is a boastful or bragging one.

bollard see **bulwark**

boloney see **blarney**

bon vivant/bon viveur (one who enjoys wining and dining)
'Bon vivant' is the older term, from the French meaning literally 'good liver' (i.e. one who lives well). It is close to the sense of **gourmand**, with overtones of one who wines and dines unwisely, and rather too well. 'Bon viveur' which is also French for

'good liver' – although the French itself is spurious, and a concocted phrase – has a sense similar to 'bon vivant' but with an air of respectability, of a 'man about town'. The term, too, is applied not merely to one who is an expert on food and drink but who is knowledgeable on such gentlemanly pursuits as touring and travel. Fanny Cradock and her husband adopted the joint nom de plume 'Bon Viveur' for their reports of hotel and restaurant meals around Britain in the *Daily Telegraph*.

bon viveur see **bon vivant**

boogie-woogie see **swing**

boot/shoe (item of outer footwear)
In general, a 'boot' comes above the ankle – well above it for most Americans – and a 'shoe' stops below it. 'Shoe', moreover, is a general word for any variety of footwear, indoor or outdoor, that does not cover the ankle, as slippers, sandals, plimsolls, clogs and brogues. Most 'boots' have a fairly specialised use, either professionally or functionally, as army 'boots', football 'boots' and wellington 'boots', or for fashion wear, as 'snakeboots' and desert 'boots'.

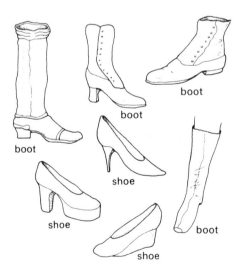

boot

boot

boot

shoe

shoe

shoe

boot

booty see **loot**

bop see **swing**

bordeaux see **burgundy**

border/boundary/frontier (line or boundary marking the limit of a territory)
A 'border' is close in meaning to a 'boundary', except that it often includes territory on either side of a 'boundary', as the 'Border', geographically if loosely so called, between England and Scotland, Northern Ireland and the Irish Republic, and, in America, between the USA and Mexico – hence, in the latter case, 'south of the "border"'. From this it follows that a 'boundary' is a line, real or imaginary, that marks the limit of a territory, the furthest extent reached by a geographical or administrative area, such as a county 'boundary' or a stream that forms the 'boundary' between two parishes. A 'frontier' is similar, but usually implies that the territory beyond the 'border' is different in some way, in terms of geography, politics, language or culture. Perhaps the most familiar is the 'frontier' that is the boundary of a country, with its customs officers, checkpoints and, usually, 'frontier' guards. In the USA, the 'frontier' is that part of the country which forms the 'border' of a settled or inhabited region, so that beyond it lies something of a wilderness or, seen differently, a virgin land. Davy Crockett became internationally known – perhaps more thanks to Disney than to history – as 'king of the wild "frontier"'. He was active on the 'frontier' in western Tennessee in the early nineteenth century.

borstal see **remand home**

bough see **branch**

boundary see **border**

bourbon see **burgundy**

bower see **arbour**

bowl/basin (round dish for liquids or solids)
A 'bowl' is a deep 'basin', especially one for food, as a breakfast 'bowl' or fruit 'bowl', or for liquid, as a wine-'bowl' or, less palatably, washing-up 'bowl'. It is thus both wide and deep, like the grave envisaged by

the girl whose true love had abandoned her for the pleasures of a tavern in the town. A 'basin', by comparison, is more wide than it is deep, as a hand-'basin'. Sometimes the difference is small, as between a sugar 'basin' and sugar 'bowl', which are virtually interchangeable. The words also have a geographical sense, when a 'bowl', more an American term, is a 'bowl'-shaped region, as the Western Dust 'Bowl', and a 'basin' a land-locked harbour or the area drained by a river and its tributaries, as the Thames 'basin'.

bowling see **bowls**

bowls/skittles/ninepins/bowling (game in which a heavy ball is rolled down a course to strike a target)
'Bowls' (in the USA 'bowling') is the game in which biased or weighted balls ('bowls') are rolled over a smooth green to bring them as near as possible to the jack, a small white ball, to to knock an opponent's bowl out of the way as a tactical manoeuvre. 'Skittles' is a game popular at fairs and fêtes (where it may go under such a name as '"bowling" for a pig'), in which nine wooden pins at the end of an alley are to be bowled down with a wooden (unweighted) ball. 'Ninepins', therefore, is an alternative (mainly British) name for this game, and a version of this went to America some time ago, whence it mysteriously returned as 'tenpins', otherwise tenpin 'bowling' or just 'bowling' – the automated game in which hard rubber balls are bowled down lanes to strike machine-operated pins. But how did nine come back as ten? The explanation is simple: 'ninepins' was declared illegal under American law; a tenth pin was therefore added; tenpins by any count is not 'ninepins'; tenpin 'bowling' evades the law! Tenpin 'bowling' caught on in Britain in a big way in the 1960s, when many alleys or 'bowls' were constructed on former theatre or cinema sites. 'Bowling', it will be noticed, is a general name for all four sports (as well as the term for the special delivery of the ball by a bowler in the game of cricket).

bow window see **bay window**

boxer see **bulldog**

bracken see **ferns**

bradawl see **awl**

Brahma see **Buddha**

brain see **mind**

brains see **mind**

brains trust/brain trust (group of experts vouchsafing an opinion)
A 'brains trust' is a group of experts or 'brains' who give impromptu answers to questions – not necessarily giving any information, but quite often simply engaged in discussion. The phrase became familiar from the wartime radio *Brains Trust* – a panel of Sir Julian Huxley, Professor C. E. M. Joad and Commander Campbell, under the chairmanship of Donald McCullough – who answered questions put to them by the public. The term was borrowed from the American 'brain trust' of the 1930s, which was a group of experts called in to advise Roosevelt in his first administration. This corresponded to what became known in Britain as the 'think tank', the nickname for the Central Policy Review Staff initiated in Edward Heath's government (1970-4) but subsequently disbanded (in 1983). (The term 'think tank' is also of American origin.)

brain trust see **brains trust**

brambles/briers (collection of thorny or prickly plants or bushes)
'Brambles' are specifically blackberry bushes. (The word is related to 'broom'.) 'Briers' (or briars) normally means the thorny branches of the wild rose from which also **hips** come.

branch/bough (limb of a tree)
A 'branch' can be any limb of a tree; a 'bough' is one of the main ones, which in turn may have its own 'branches'.

brandish see **flourish**

brandy/cognac (type of spirit)
'Brandy' is a spirit distilled from wine or, sometimes, fermented fruit juice (as apple 'brandy', plum 'brandy' or cherry

'brandy'). The word is properly 'brandy-wine', from Dutch *brandewijn,* 'burnt (i.e. distilled) wine'. 'Cognac' is French 'brandy', usually regarded as the finest of all 'brandies'. Properly it is distilled from the wine of the region around Cognac, a town in western France.

brass/bronze (metal alloy)
'Brass' is a yellow alloy of copper and zinc; 'bronze' is a brown-coloured alloy chiefly of copper and tin, and known from very early times. The instruments of 'brass' mentioned in the Bible, however, were in all probability made of 'bronze', since it is not known what the exact composition of the metal was.

bravado see **bravery**

bravery/bravado/bravura (show of courage)
'Bravery' is courage or valour in general. 'Bravado', from Spanish *bravada,* is a specific act of bravery or daring designed to impress or intimidate – or to conceal timidity. 'Bravura', an Italian word (spirit), is mainly associated with music, in which it denotes a passage, usually a difficult one, played or sung with skill and gusto. More generally it is a display of daring, or simply a brilliant performance or attempt at one.

bravura see **bravery**

bray see **blast**

breaker see **billow** (wave at sea)

Bren gun/Sten gun (type of machine-gun)
The 'Bren gun' came first. It was manufactured at Brno, Czechoslovakia in 1937 and its construction was perfected at a small-arms factory at Enfield, Middlesex. Thus 'Bren' is an acronym of the first two letters of each place. The 'Sten gun' first saw the light of day in 1942. Unlike the 'Bren', it was a light sub-machine-gun firing 9mm cartridges. It, too, was produced at Enfield, but its first two letters are those of the initials of the inventors, Major S. Sheppard and Mr T. Turpin, a Civil Servant. (Although according to one authority, the '-en' is borrowed from 'England')

bridle see **rein** (part of horse's harness)

briers see **brambles**

brig see **barque**

brigade see **corps**

brigantine see **barque**

brim see **rim**

Bri-Nylon see **nylon**

brisk see **abrupt**

Britain see **England**

British Isles see **England**

brochure/pamphlet (type of booklet or leaflet)
A 'brochure' is normally a commercial publication, for example of a travel agency or a motor dealer. A 'pamphlet' is either a small, unbound discourse on some subject, especially a political or religious one, as a tract or a manifesto, or, loosely, any leaflet, even a single sheet. The word suggests an exotic or erratic spelling of 'leaflet', but it actually comes from *Pamphilet,* which was the popular name of a twelfth-century comic love poem in Latin entitled *Pamphilus, seu de Amore* ('Pamphilus [that is, "love-all"] or about Love'). *Brochure* is French for 'stitching'.

broiled see **boiled**

broker see **stockbroker**

bronze see **brass**

broom see **gorse**

Brownshirts see **Blackshirts**

brush see **bush**

brusque see **abrupt**

brute see **beast**

bucentaur see **Minotaur**

Buddha/Brahma (Indian god)
'Buddha' ('The Enlightened One') is the title given by Buddhists to the founder of their faith, who flourished in the fifth century BC. Buddha's real name was actually Sayyamuni, and he is the latest of a series of Buddhas who will continue, it is thought, indefinitely. 'Brahma' ('Creator') is the supreme god of Hinduism. Later Hinduism has a trinity in which 'Brahma' is the personal Creator, Vishnu the Preserver, and Siva the Destroyer. Buddhism arose as a reaction to Brahmanism and in particular to its caste system: Buddhists believe that all people are equal.

buffalo/bison (ox-like animal)
There are three kinds of 'buffalo': *Bubalis bubalis* of Asia, originally from India, valued as a draught animal, *Syncerus caffer*, or Cape 'buffalo', of South Africa, and *Bison bison*, of North America, and thus the American 'buffalo' – or 'bison' (or wild ox). This is the one that turned William Frederick Cody into 'Buffalo' Bill, the champion 'buffalo' killer of the Plains of Kansas. His total haul was 4,280 in eight months, or around eighteen a day, which must have meant at least one unfortunate 'buffalo' before breakfast as a starter. Seen objectively, the Indian 'buffalo' is a heavy animal with coarse black hair and long, curving horns; the Cape 'buffalo' is less heavy and has horns that are very broad at the base, where they almost meet; the American 'buffalo' (the 'bison') has a humped body and small horns.

buffer/bumper (device for deadening the impact or reducing the force of a blow to a vehicle)
'Buffers' usually come in pairs, especially on railway vehicles or at the end of a track. A 'bumper', in contrast, is found on cars and other road vehicles, where it is designed to reduce damage in a collision. In the USA, railway 'buffers' are 'bumpers', while 'bumpers' on a car are fenders – a word that can also, however, mean the wings or mudguards of a car or other vehicle.

buffet see **café**

bugle see **cornet**

builder/mason (constructor of houses and buildings)
A 'builder' usually means a master craftsman, especially one contracted to build houses. A 'mason' is a craftsman who works in stone. He does not build buildings, but bits of buildings, i.e. masonry or stonework. It would be logical if the word came from 'mansion' or French *maison*, 'house', but in fact it rather unexpectedly derives from Latin *maccare*, 'to beat', and may, perhaps, be related to 'mattock'.

bull see (1) **bear**, (2) **ox**

bulldog/boxer/bull-terrier (dog with a bull-like or pugnacious face)
Actually, 'bulldogs' are not so called because they look like bulls but because they were bred for baiting bulls. The breed has come to typify tenacity, determination and courage, characteristics seen also in Winston Churchill, who was popularly likened to the animal. The original 'boxer' was a dog called Flocki shown in Munich in 1895, the offspring of a bullfighting terrier bitch and a 'bulldog' called Tom. Today the breed is taller and more slender than the 'bulldog', but like it a good guard and an affectionate companion. (Why 'boxer'? Does it look like one? The name may come from the dog's manner of 'boxing' with its forepaws when it begins to fight.) A 'boxer' was thus a crossbreed, and so is a 'bull-terrier', which is a cross between a 'bulldog' and a terrier, and famous as the original 'Bill Sykes tyke' of pits and rat haunts. It is characteristically an all-white dog, and of a somewhat brutalised appearance. There are also so called 'coloured' 'bull-terriers' – ones with brindle or black predominant.

bullock see **ox**

bull-terrier see **bulldog**

bulwark/bollard (solidly built structure on a ship)
The 'bulwark' – not connected with bulls but, apparently, 'bole' (of a tree) and 'work' – is the solid part of the ship's side that extends above the deck. A 'bollard', possibly also deriving from 'bole', is a vertical post on which hawsers are made fast, both on a

ship and on the quayside. 'Bulwark', but not 'bollard', can be used figuratively to indicate a protecting force or agent: 'He's been a real bulwark in my trials and tribulations.'

bumper see **buffer**

bun/roll/scone (small bread or cake)
A 'bun' is usually soft, round, and sweet, and often contains currants. A number of varieties exist, as an iced 'bun', with icing on top, Bath 'bun', spiced, with currants inside and iced, Chelsea 'bun', rolled with currants, and the like. A 'roll' can be round or long – as the bridge 'roll', which is smallish and soft – and is customarily served with the soup or starters at lunch or dinner, when it is eaten with or without butter and, in polite society, torn asunder with the fingers rather than neatly cut with a knife. The 'scone', which has Scottish associations, if only through the Stone of Scone – which is not a type of rock-cake or edible at all, but a coronation stone from Scone, near Perth – is a cake of barley-meal or oatmeal or wheatflour, with or without currants, traditionally baked on a griddle and eaten with a little butter and, although somewhat gilding the lily, sometimes a little jam. Scots tend to say the word to rhyme with 'con', although south of the border it often rhymes with 'cone', a pronunciation still regarded in some circles as 'non-U'.

Bundesrat see **Bundeswehr**

Bundestag see **Bundeswehr**

Bundeswehr/Bundesrat/Bundestag/ Reichswehr/Reichstag/Reichsrat/ Abwehr (German state department)
Those titles which incorporate the word 'Bund' (German for 'Federation', i.e. of West Germany) are all post-war, and the 'Reich' equivalents (literally 'realm', 'empire') all existed between 1919 and 1945. The 'Bundeswehr' is the West German Army, while the 'Bundesrat' and 'Bundestag' are, respectively, the upper and lower houses of the West German parliament. Those words incorporating 'Reich' apply to the earlier equivalents, with the 'Reichstag' also being the building where the house met

in Berlin. (It was destroyed by fire in 1933.) The 'Abwehr' ('Resistance') was the German counter-intelligence section in the Second World War. The second elements of the names derive from *Wehr* (defence), *tagen* (to meet, sit in conference) and *Rat* (council).

burberry see **raincoat**

burble see **babble**

burden see **load**

bureaucrat see **autocrat**

burglary see **theft**

burgundy/bordeaux/bourbon (type of wine or spirit)
There are many varieties of 'burgundy', both red and white. It is a full, dry wine produced in the Burgundy region of France. 'Bordeaux' wines, from the region of the same name in the south of France, include red wines such as Médoc and St Emilion, and white wines such as the sweet Sauternes and dry varieties of Graves. 'Bourbon', as no American will need to be told, is not a wine but a type of whisky distilled in the USA and popular with both goodies and baddies in novels and movies – and in real life. It was originally produced in Bourbon county, Kentucky: it's a nice quirk that the county name was imported from France.

burlesque see **parody**

burrow see **den**

bush/shrub/scrub/brush (single low, woody plant, or a stretch of such plants)
'Bush' is both the familiar small tree (botanically a small cluster of 'shrubs' growing as a single plant) and a stretch of wild, uncultivated land in Australia or Africa with – or even without – such 'bushes'. A 'shrub' is usually regarded as larger than a 'bush' but smaller than a tree, a collection of them forming a 'shrubbery'. 'Scrub', not used often in the plural, is a collective term for 'shrubs' or low trees, especially as in the Australian 'bush'. 'Brush' or 'brushwood' more or less equals 'scrub', that is, it is

densely growing 'bushes' and 'shrubs'. (The word is probably related to 'brush' in the sense of 'implement with bristles for sweeping'.) This quadruple set of confusibles can prove rather thorny.

business see **occupation**

bust see **sculpture**

bustle/hustle/hassle (as verb: hasten, harass)
To 'bustle' is to hurry with a great show of energy. The word is probably influenced by 'busy' and 'bundle'. To 'hustle', in turn no doubt influenced by 'hurry' and 'bustle' and perhaps 'jostle', is to force (someone) hurriedly or roughly, as when someone is 'hustled' into a car or through a door. The verb 'hassle' is of American origin and suggests 'harass', which it basically means. All three verbs are used as nouns.

butter/margarine (yellow, creamy foodstuff used in cooking and as a spread)
Advertisers do their best to assure us that there is only a minimal difference between 'margarine' and 'butter' ('Fancy calling Stroke margarine!'). Some 'margarines' do in fact contain a small percentage of real 'butter', although 'margarine' is legally not 'butter' at all, but a 'butter' substitute. The chief difference between the two is not in their appearance or even use, but in their content: 'butter' is made from the fat of an animal's milk, usually a cow's, when this milk, or its cream, is churned. 'Margarine' is made from edible vegetable oils and animal fats in cultured skimmed milk. Furthermore, while 'margarine' may contain preservatives, it is illegal for any preservatives to be used in 'butter'. Can there really be anything in common between 'marge' and the attractive girl's name Margaret? The answer is yes: they both basically mean 'pearl'. It was originally wrongly thought that all oils and fats, including the ones used to make 'margarine', contained so called 'margaric acid', which is pearl-white in colour. In many ways, and especially nutritionally, since by law it is now compulsorily fortified with vitamins A and D, 'margarine' today is a very worthy substitute for 'butter', and

so called 'soft' 'margarine', which is cholesterol-free, has found favour in many households. (Whether the 'g' in the word is pronounced 'soft', as in 'tangerine', or 'hard', as in 'marguerite', is a matter of taste, as the substance itself is.)

buttercup/celandine (plant with yellow flowers found in fields and woods)
The 'buttercup' is a member of the genus *Ranunculus*, which also includes anemones and marsh marigolds. It has five green sepals (which form the calyx, or envelope of the flower) and five fullish yellow petals. The 'celandine' is properly a member of the poppy family, although the lesser 'celandine' is a member of the 'buttercup' family. It has three sepals and usually eight petals and is often found near water, which the 'buttercup' does not necessarily prefer. The petals of the lesser 'celandine', too, are noticeably slimmer than those of the 'buttercup'.

butterfly/moth (flying insect with large showy wings)
The difference is this: 'butterflies' are usually day-flying creatures and brightly coloured with knobbed or club-shaped antennae ('feelers'), and hold their wings vertically when at rest. 'Moths' are normally nocturnal and dull-coloured, with spindle-shaped, threadlike or comblike antennae, and hold their wings (with one or two exceptions) flat when at rest. On closer examination, moreover, most 'moths' will be found to have a connecting hook for fastening their wings together, which 'butterflies' do not have.

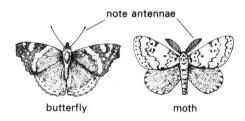

note antennae

butterfly   moth

by heart/by rote (from memory)
Something learned 'by heart' has been consciously or unconsciously committed to memory and can be recited at recall, as a

poem, the procedure for operating a machine and the like. A thing learned 'by rote' has been learned mechanically, parrot-fashion, with no real thought for the meaning. The origin of the latter is not too clear – it does not seem to be connected with Latin *rota* (wheel).

by-pass/ring road (road avoiding a town or its centre)
A 'by-pass' is a main road that 'passes by' a town or other congested area and provides an alternative route for through traffic. A 'by-pass' that goes right round a town (with the appropriate turn-offs to a motorway or other main route) is called a 'ring road'.

by rote see **by heart**

C

cabaret see **musical**

cabinet-maker see **carpenter**

cachou see **cashew**

café/buffet/cafeteria (public place for meals, snacks and refreshments)
The origin of the 'café' is in the coffee-houses of France (French *café* meaning 'coffee', and a word familiar as part of the name of a well-known instant variety). With such a fine gastronomic pedigree – French is the language of gourmets *par excellence* – it is perhaps surprising that the word has descended to mean little more than just an inexpensive snack-bar, a 'caff', in fact. There are some restaurants of note, however, that preserve the classy tone of the word, as the long established 'Café' Royal in London. A 'buffet' – the word is also

French in origin, formerly meaning 'stool', but now 'sideboard' – is also found at both ends of the social scale, as a 'buffet' supper, where guests serve themselves from groaning tables or even sideboards, or a station 'buffet', which is really a kind of cosmopolitan, but typically British, 'café'. (A 'buffet' car on a train serves snacks, as distinct from a dining car, which is a rail-running restaurant.) A 'cafeteria', in essence, is a 'café' where customers serve themselves by fetching their food and drink from a counter and carrying it to a table. The word is rather loosely used, though, and some 'cafeterias' offer excellent waitress service and no self-service at all. The word is American-Spanish for 'coffee-shop'.

cafeteria see **café**

calamine/camomile/calomel (medical or medicinal preparation)
'Calamine' is a soothing liquid for the skin, especially to offset the effects of sunburn, rash, etc. It contains zinc oxide and is in origin related to the Latin word *Cadmia* (Cadmian earth) which gives cadmium. 'Camomile' is a medicinal preparation from the strong scented foliage and flowers of the herb of the same name. The herb itself derives its name from the Greek *chamaimelon* (earth apple). 'Calomel' is a tasteless solid – actually mercurous oxide – used in purgative medicines. Its origin is said to be in the Greek words *kalos* (beautiful) and *melas* (black), which seems odd since the substance itself is white.

calf/heifer (young cow)
A 'calf' is the word for the young of a cow, male or female, in its first year. A 'heifer' is a young cow in general, or in particular one that has not had more than one 'calf'. For young horse words see **colt**.

callow see **shallow**

calomel see **calamine**

camomile see **calamine**

camouflage see **disguise**

Campari see **Cinzano**

candelabra see **chandelier**

cannabis/marijuana (hallucinogenic drug prepared from hemp)
According to the World Health Organisation, 'cannabis' does not encompass resin alone – which would be hashish (*Cannabis indica*) – but is a general term for the flowering or fruiting tops of the hemp plant, its leaves, and sometimes its stems and seeds, used as a drug by being smoked, drunk (in an infusion) or eaten. 'Marijuana' is the name of a specific type of 'cannabis' plant – *Cannabis sativa*, sometimes called American 'cannabis' – that unlike 'real' 'cannabis', which comes mainly from India or North Africa, is grown in the western hemisphere. 'Marijuana' is usually smoked and is relatively mild compared to 'real' 'cannabis' as used in other countries. Most American 'marijuana' is grown in Mexico. Although hallucinogenic, both drugs are technically regarded as non-addictive or non-habit-forming, i.e. as 'soft' drugs, not hard drugs.

cannon see **gun** (both entries)

canon see **dean**

canopy/panoply (protective covering)
The Greeks had a special word for a bed with mosquito curtains – *konopeion* (in turn from *konops*, 'mosquito'). This is the origin of 'canopy', which is now any suspended or supported overhead covering for anything or anyone from a bed to a bishop. A 'panoply', from a Greek word meaning literally 'all arms', is technically a complete suit of armour but can also be used, in a more stylish or poetic sense, for a complete covering of anything, especially if it is protective or impressive, such as the 'panoply' of a Red Indian chief or the weaponry and electronic gadgetry of a modern fighter aircraft.

cantata see **oratorio**

canter see **trot**

canyon see **ravine**

cap see **hat**

capability/capacity/ability (quality of being able to do or act)
'Capability' is basically the quality of being 'capable' in any way, as physically, intellectually or emotionally. 'Capacity' suggests power, often of the mind, as when someone has the 'capacity' for hard work. 'Ability' usually implies the possession of a particular attribute that enables one to do a particular thing. One person thus might have the 'ability' to run very fast (he will do this when he has to), another the 'ability' to overcome her blushing (she will do so when the occasion demands it). All three words, however, overlap somewhat in their meanings.

capacity see **capability**

capital punishment see **corporal punishment**

capsule see **probe**

Capuchin/Carmelite/Carthusian/Cistercian (member of a religious order)
All four are Roman Catholic orders. The 'Capuchins' are Franciscan friars who wear a long cowl, their name deriving from the Italian *cappuccio* (hood). The 'Carmelites' are monks or nuns who now exist in several orders. Their original order, however, was founded on Mount Carmel in Palestine in the twelfth century. The 'Carthusians' are monks whose order was founded in 1086 near the town of Grenoble in the French Alps, with their first monastery called La Grande Chartreuse – a name that in its turn has given us 'chartreuse', the liqueur made by the monks there, and 'Charterhouse'. (Charterhouse public school was founded, together with a hospital, on the site of a 'charterhouse' or 'Carthusian' monastery in London. The school transferred to Godalming in Surrey in 1872 and took its name with it.) The 'Cistercian' order of monks and nuns was founded in the south of France near Cîteaux in 1098.

car see **coach**

carabineers see **carabinieri**

carabinieri/car(a)bineers/Carbonari (special armed force)

The Italian Army Corps who serve as the police are called the 'carabinieri'. They are armed with rifles ('carbines'). 'Carbineers' or 'carabineers' were armed soldiers. In England the name was preserved in the regiment known as the 3rd Carabiniers, now incorporated in the Royal Scots Dragoon Guards. The 'Carbonari' (literally 'charcoal-burners') were a nineteenth century secret political society active in southern Italy and also France and Spain whose aim was to bring about a republican government. They are said to have evolved from medieval charcoal-burners, and went to the extent of calling their meeting-place a 'hut', the outside area the 'forest' and their opponents the 'wolves'.

carbineers see **carabinieri**

Carbonari see **carabinieri**

carbon dioxide see **carbon monoxide**

carbon monoxide/carbon dioxide
(poisonous gas)
'Carbon monoxide' (CO) is a gas formed when carbon burns with an insufficient supply of air, hence its latent presence in car exhaust fumes. 'Carbon dioxide' (CO_2) or 'dry ice' is the gas in fizzy drinks and fire extinguishers and is basically what we breathe out, having breathed in mainly oxygen. Its danger as a poisonous gas lies in its presence as 'choke damp' in mines.

carborundum/corundum (hard abrasive substance)
'Carborundum' – properly a trade name formed from 'carbon' and 'corundum' – comes in powder or blocks and is used for such purposes as grinding tools and refractory lining in furnaces. 'Corundum', a word which ultimately goes back to the Sanskrit for 'ruby', is a mineral aluminium oxide used both as a precious gem and for the manufacture of bearings in such fine machinery as watches and motors. Mixed with iron oxides and spinel (another hard mineral) it becomes emery.

carcajou see **cockatoo**

carcass see **corpse**

cardinal see (1) **crimson**, (2) **ordinal**

careen see **career**

career/careen (move rapidly)
To 'career' – the word is related to 'car' – is to run or move at speed, so that a vehicle can 'career' round a corner or down a hill. In the USA the word is often used synonymously for 'careen', which properly is to turn a ship onto its side for cleaning or caulking. The derivation here is Latin *carina* (keel): when a ship is on her side the keel will be exposed. See also the related confusible **heel over**.

caretaker/curator/janitor/custodian
(official appointed to look after premises)
A 'caretaker' either takes charge ('caretakes') in an owner's absence or, more commonly, is the person who looks after a public building such as a school or office block. The latter sense is a British one, corresponding to the American 'janitor'. A 'curator' is the keeper or 'custodian' of a museum, where a 'custodian' is one who has the custody of special records, documents or particular historical objects. A 'custodian' is also, however, one who guards or is specially responsible for people who are 'in care' in some way, as prisoners or a ward, although in the latter case the term is normally in fact 'guardian'.

cargo see **freight**

caribou see **cockatoo**

caricature see **cartoon**

Carmelite see **Capuchin**

carmine see **crimson**

carnation/pink (garden plant with sweet-smelling white or pink flower)
A 'carnation' is a cultivated clove 'pink', that is, the clove-scented 'pink' botanically known as *Dianthus caryophyllus*. (The Sweet William, or bunch 'pink', belongs to this family.) The 'pink', therefore, is a general name for the plant of the genus *Dianthus* that has not only white or pink flowers, but

crimson or variegated ones. How did the 'carnation' get its name? Originally, perhaps, it was 'coronation', although one theory claims it derives from Latin *carnatio,* 'flesh-colour' (compare 'carnal' or 'carnage'). The reference is not to real flesh, but to the rather more lurid colour of flesh in paintings. See also **crimson**.

carnation (shade of red) see **crimson**

carnelian see **crimson**

carp see **cavil**

carpenter/joiner/turner/cabinet-maker (specialist in woodwork)
A 'carpenter' is a craftsman in wood or woodwork, especially of a rough, solid kind, as in a house or boat. A 'joiner' makes furniture, house fittings, and other woodwork that is lighter than that of a 'carpenter'. (He joins, basically with glue, rather than builds.) A 'turner' is a craftsman who works with a lathe, and a 'cabinet-maker' is not just someone who makes cabinets but who is a skilled joiner. The first three words (not 'cabinet-maker', which is a seventeenth-century word) denote ancient crafts, which is why they also occur as surnames (although the surname Turner denotes someone who may have worked in materials other than wood, such as metal or bone).

carpus see **tarsus**

carriage see **coach**

Carthusian see **Capuchin**

cartoon/caricature (amusing or grotesque drawing)
Originally and properly, a 'cartoon' was a full-size drawing on stout paper as a design for a painting, tapestry, mosaic, or the like (see, for example – literally, if possible – the Leonardo da Vinci 'cartoon' of the *Virgin and Child* in the National Gallery, London). The word then came to mean a full-page illustration, especially a satirical one on politics, in a newspaper or magazine (see some of these in early numbers of *Punch*). Eventually it came to be used of any amusing or witty drawing, with or without

a caption, a sequence of which is a 'strip cartoon', telling a story or recounting an incident or episode. Another spin-off is the 'animated cartoon', or just 'cartoon', as perfected, for example, by Walt Disney in the cinema. A 'caricature' is a grotesque representation of a person – less often, a thing – exaggerating his characteristic traits. This may well be in the form of a 'cartoon', of course. 'Caricature' can also apply to any representation like this, as a written account or a mime. The word is not related to 'character' but comes from Italian *caricare,* literally 'to load' (compare English 'charge'). 'Caricatures' are, after all, 'loaded' portraits. 'Cartoon' is also Italian in origin, meaning 'large card' (compare English 'carton').

cashew/cachou/jujube (small lozenge or sweetmeat)
'Cashew' is the nut, from the tree growing in tropical America. 'Cachou' is the pill or pastille for sweetening the breath, especially after smoking. Confusion is increased since it used to contain, among other condiments, 'cashew' nut. Trees of the botanical genus *Ziziphus* gave their name to the 'jujube', which properly refers to the fruit, resembling a small plum, of these trees. By extension it came to mean a small, sweet lozenge. Winston Churchill used to suck them, and drop them, when sitting in the Commons.

cashmere/kerseymere/cassimere (type of woollen cloth)
'Cashmere' is a fine, downy wool from Kashmir goats and often popular for making shawls. It is also a wool fabric of twill weave, in imitation of the real thing. 'Kerseymere', by contrast, is a coarse woollen cloth, a ribbed twill. Its name is a variant of 'cassimere', which became altered by association with Kersey, a village in Suffolk, formerly a wool-making centre. 'Cassimere', which in turn is a variant of 'cashmere', is a plain or twilled woollen cloth usually used for men's clothes. All three words are thus quite closely interwoven.

cassimere see **cashmere**

castigate see **chastise**

cat see **reach**

cataclasm see **catastrophe**

cataclysm see **catastrophe**

**catacomb/hecatomb/catafalque/
cenotaph** (place for preserving dead
bodies or for commemorating the dead)
Historically, 'catacomb', or in its Latin form
catacumbae, was the name of the cemetery of
St Sebastian on the Appian Way, with the
word itself of unknown origin. The term
came to be applied to an underground
cemetery, especially one with tunnels and
recesses for the coffins and tombs such as
those around Rome or in Paris. A 'hecatomb' is nothing to do, except indirectly,
with 'tomb'; it is a great mass killing or
slaughter – originally the public sacrifice
of a hundred oxen, from the Greek *hekaton*
(hundred) and *bous* (ox). A 'catafalque' is
an elevated structure on which a dead body
lies in state or is carried. The word is related
to 'scaffold'. A 'catafalque' is usually in the
form of a tomb or a 'cenotaph', literally
'empty tomb', like the memorial to the dead
of both World Wars in Whitehall, London.

catafalque see **catacomb**

catalogue see **list**

catastrophe/cataclysm/cataclasm
(disaster or violent upheaval)
'Catastrophe' is the general term, from the
Greek word meaning 'overturning'. A 'cataclysm', literally a 'washing down', is usually
reserved for a social or political upheaval,
although the term is also used by geogra-
phers to refer to a physical action which
produces a change in the earth's surface
and causes flooding. A 'cataclasm', literally
'breaking down', is a disruption of the
normal order of things. Here too the word
has a scientific use: in geology it refers to a
breaking down process of rocks.

catchphrase see **cliché**

cathedral/abbey/minster (large or
important church)

A 'cathedral' – in full, 'cathedral church' –
is the principal church of a diocese, where
the bishop has his throne or seat (Greek
kathedra, 'chair') and in whose city he lives,
in either a palace or a more modest residence. An 'abbey' is the term either for a
religious community (see **monastery**) or for
an important church as, notably,
Westminster 'Abbey', which was once
attached to a religious house. (Officially,
Westminster 'Abbey' is neither a 'cathedral'
nor an 'abbey', but a collegiate church. It
was built on the site of a monastery called
the 'west "minster"' – that is, a 'minster'
that was west of the city of London. It must
not be confused with Westminster
'Cathedral', which is the principal Roman
Catholic church in England.) A 'minster',
then, is the title of certain large or important
churches that were originally associated
with a monastery. A noted example is York
'Minster' – actually a 'cathedral' and
famous for its grandeur and fine medieval
stained glass – which was built on the site
of a monastery.

cave/cavern (hole under the ground or in
the side of a hill or cliff)
A 'cavern' is a very large 'cave', often
regarded as containing something worth
having – or avoiding – as a vast underground chamber where treasure is stored
or danger lies hidden. A 'cave', the more
common word, is a more mundane thing,
where primitive man lived or some bears
still do live, although Aladdin's 'cave',
where he found his magic lamp, is rather
more out of this world.

cavern see **cave**

cavil/carp (find fault with in an irritating
manner)
To 'cavil' is to raise irritating, often trivial,
objections. To 'carp' means almost the
same, but in addition suggests that the
objections are unreasonable. 'He's always
carping at the way she dresses.' It has a
suggestion of persistent nagging – perhaps
because of a suggestion of 'harp'. There's
some basis for this, as Latin *carpere* (to
pluck) lies behind both 'carp' and 'harp'.
'Cavil' derives from Latin *cavillari* (to make
captious objections) and is related to
'calumny'.

celandine see **buttercup**

cellar see **vault**

Celtic/Gaelic (native language of Scotland or Ireland)
Properly, 'Celtic' is a whole group of Indo-European languages, including Irish, Scottish (or 'Gaelic'), Welsh, Breton, Manx and, until it died out, Cornish. All these tongues are spoken by the descendants of the Celts, a west European race that included the Gauls and the Ancient Britons. 'Gaelic' is commonly used to denote the language spoken by the Scottish branch of the Celtic family. Linguists also use it, however, to apply to the language of the Scottish *and* Irish and Manx Celts, as well as the language of ancient Ireland. With other terms such as 'Goidelic' and 'Brythonic' the plethora of words relating to the languages of the British Isles borders on the babelic.

cement see **concrete**

cenotaph see **catacomb**

censor/censure (as verb: to condemn, ban)
To 'censor' something is to act as a censor by cutting, toning down, editing, blue-pencilling or whatever. To 'censure' a thing or a person is to criticise it or him severely. One thus 'censures' a person's behaviour or one's current unfavourite fashion or art form. The adjective of 'censor' is 'censorial' and of 'censure', 'censorious'. The respective nouns are 'censorship' and 'censure'.

censure see **censor**

centaur see **Minotaur**

centenary/centennial (hundredth anniversary)
A 'centenary' is a hundredth anniversary, with the adjective the same as the noun. The American equivalent term is 'centennial', although the identical adjective is also used in British English to mean 'lasting or occurring every hundred years'. Colorado is nicknamed the 'Centennial State' as it was admitted as a state in the 'centennial' year

of the existence of the USA (1876). For similar distinctions see **bicentenary**.

centennial see **centenary**

centipede/millipede (insect with hundreds of legs)
The 'centipede' does not have a hundred legs, but anything from 14 to 177 *pairs*. There are around 2,800 species, and they belong to the even less aptly named class *Chilopoda* (thousand legs). 'Millipedes' belong to the class *Diplopoda* (double legs). There are about 8,000 species and they have not a thousand legs as their name suggests, but up to 400, i.e. 200 pairs.

centre see **middle**

cerebellum see **cerebrum**

cerebrum/cerebellum (part of the brain)
Both are anatomical terms. The 'cerebrum' is the front and upper part of the brain, with the 'cerebellum' lying behind it and below it. The second word is a diminutive of the first, which is the Latin for 'brain', in turn giving the English word 'cerebral'.

ceremonial/ceremonious (pertaining to, or showing, ceremony)
'Ceremonial' serves as an adjective for both 'ceremony' and 'ceremonial', so that ceremonial' dress is the formal dress worn for either. 'Ceremonious' means 'full of ceremony' in the showy or fussy sense, as a 'ceremonious' occasion (a grand one) or a 'ceremonious' gesture of the hand (a rather snooty one).

ceremonious see **ceremonial**

cerise see **violet**

certificate see **degree** (academic qualification)

cesarevitch see **czarevitch**

chain store/multiple store (shop that is one of several similar owned by one company)
A 'chain store' may specialise in one main item of goods, as one of the many shoe shops

that belong to a particular company, or sell a range of goods. A 'multiple store' will always sell a range of goods (a 'multiple' choice), such as Woolworths or the Co-op.

chairman see **president**

chancel see **choir** (area in church)

chandelier/candelabra (branched support for several lights)
Most 'chandeliers' hang from the ceiling. Originally they all held candles, hence the word's origin in French *chandelle*. A 'candelabra', strictly 'candelabrum', is really an ornamental branched candlestick, from the Latin word for 'candle'. It doubles up as a 'chandelier', however, in actual usage, although the French word seems more popular.

channel see **sound** (narrow stretch of water)

chantry see **choir** (area in church)

chapel see **church**

chaperone/cicerone/chatelaine (female in authority)
A 'chaperone' is a 'mature' woman who accompanies, escorts or otherwise monitors a younger woman in public. The original 'chaperone' wore a 'chape' or cape. A 'cicerone' is not necessarily a woman. The term is used of a guide who explains the curiosities or antiquities of a place, such as a museum or historical site. Cicero was one of the world's record speakers, many guides emulate him; hence the title. A 'chatelaine' could not be male: she was the lady of the castle, and is now the mistress of a household, especially an elegant or fashionable one. All three words are rather mannered, but by no means obsolete.

charger/courser (war horse)
The aim of a 'charger' was not to charge in battle but to carry (from this now secondary meaning of 'charge'). A 'courser' was also a 'charger' but since the seventeenth century the word has come to be used of a race horse rather than a war horse, one that 'courses'.

charm/talisman/amulet/mascot (object believed to bring good luck)
A 'charm', in general, is anything worn to avert evil or bring luck or otherwise aid its owner. A 'talisman' is similar – it is supposed to have the power to work wonders – but specifically is an inscribed stone or ring said to ensure safety or bring good fortune. An 'amulet' is a 'charm' worn to ward off evil, but not necessarily to bring good luck. A 'mascot' is a person, animal or thing supposed to bring luck to an individual or group of some kind, as a regimental 'mascot' (traditionally, and rather bafflingly, a goat) or a team 'mascot' (a small boy footballer who wears the team strip and features in team photographs). Many people, from schoolchildren taking exams to racing drivers in contest on the track, have a 'lucky "mascot"' such as a cuddly toy or other whimsy that they take with them to bring them success and frustrate the knavish tricks of their rivals.

chart see **map**

chary see **wary**

chasm see **crevice**

chasten see **chastise**

chastise/chasten/castigate (punish)
'Chastise' is a variant of 'chasten' with the basic meaning 'inflict corporal punishment'. 'Chasten', which is related to 'chaste' and 'castigate', means 'inflict suffering on, in order to improve morally'. Its past participle is in common use as an adjective, as a 'chastened' look. 'Castigate' has a meaning close to 'chasten', except that the punishment inflicted is often verbal and the aim is not to improve but to correct. It has a secondary meaning, 'severely criticise'. All three words are close in meaning, with perhaps 'chastise' and 'castigate' the closest, and all are ultimately derived from Latin *castus* (pure).

chatelaine see **chaperone**

check/mate/checkmate (final or near final position in chess)
'Check' is the call to inform your opponent that his king is exposed to a direct attack.

'Mate' and 'checkmate' mean the same, although 'mate' is the term normally used in chess, with 'checkmate' often having a figurative meaning. This is the call you make to announce that your opponent's king is in an inextricable 'check', so that the game is over – you have won. The ordinary verb 'to check' meaning 'to stop' derives from this, but 'checkmate' does not mean that you have 'checked your mate' or something: it is a distorted rendering of the Persian *shah mat*, 'the king is dead'.

checkmate see **check**

cheesecake/beefcake (picture or pose of the human form designed to emphasise its attractiveness)
Unlike the genesis of Adam and Eve, 'cheesecake' came first, ex the USA. The word's earliest recording is in 1934, and it soon came to be used of pin-ups and pictures of attractive women in general, especially ones that emphasised their sex appeal. The idea is that 'cheesecake' is rich and sweet and tasty – compare 'crumpet' in its popular sense. 'Beefcake' appeared after the war as a not-too-serious rival, when photos of husky film stars with fine physiques became popular. 'Cheesecake' can also indicate the quality of the subject portrayed – the 'luscious legs look' – while 'beefcake' may also imply, as *Chambers* puts it, 'brawn as distinct from brain'. 'Beefcake' as a comestible is unknown.

cheesecloth see **muslin**

cheetah see **leopard**

chef see **cook**

chemist/apothecary/pharmacist (dealer in medicinal drugs)
A British 'chemist' is an American 'druggist', just as a British chemist's shop is a drug-store across the Atlantic. The American term is more realistic, in fact, since a 'chemist' is also the term for one skilled in chemistry, which a 'chemist' (as found in the High Street) is very likely not. An 'apothecary' is a now obsolete term for a 'chemist' (or druggist). However, in Britain the Society of 'Apothecaries' still exists as a body authorised to license students to prac-

tise medicine by passing its special examination. Perhaps the British 'chemist' should be renamed a 'pharmacist', who is not only skilled in pharmacy (the preparation and dispensing of drugs) but a pharmaceutical 'chemist' – that is, the 'chemist' we usually mean, with the shop that sells drugs.

cheque card see **credit card**

cherish see **nurse**

cherubic see **chubby**

Chianti see **Cinzano**

chick see **chicken**

chicken/chick/hen/fowl (bird bred for its meat and eggs)
Do you keep 'chickens' or 'hens'? Are all 'chickens' 'hens', or all 'hens' 'chickens'? We must sort out the flesh from the fowl. A 'chicken' is the normal word for the domestic bird (*Gallus gallus*) of either sex that is still quite young and that is regarded as potential meat. Hence the use of the word in food descriptions and menus (roast 'chicken', 'chicken' Kiev, 'chicken' 'n' chips, and the like). A 'chick' is a baby 'chicken', especially one that has just been hatched (and that appears, attractively round, fluffy and yellow, in Easter cards and spring advertising displays). A 'hen' can of course be the female of any bird, with the male being a 'cock', but with regard to poultry, it is a female 'fowl' that is usually older than a 'chicken' (say, over a year old) and that is kept for its eggs, not its meat. (One thus talks of 'hens'' eggs not 'chickens'' eggs.) A 'fowl', in full 'domestic fowl', is a more comprehensive word that includes not just 'chickens' and 'hens' (and their attendant cockerel) but other birds similarly kept, such as geese, ducks and turkeys. These are bred almost exclusively for their meat, however, although ducks' eggs can prove something of a delicacy. In Old English, 'fowl' was the general word for 'bird' until the latter superseded it.

chicken pox/smallpox (contagious disease with red spots)
'Chicken pox' is a fairly mild disease commonly contracted by young children

and often occurring in epidemics. 'Smallpox' is a much more unpleasant thing: an acute virus disease with fever and pustules that usually leave permanent scars. The 'pox' denotes the 'pocks' they produce. The link between 'chicken pox' and the farmyard bird is a false one (although the name can, misleadingly, be sometimes used, especially in the USA, for fowl pest). 'Chicken' here means 'child', a usage not now common – but compare Macduff's 'all my pretty chickens' in *Macbeth*. 'Smallpox' is not 'small' in the general sense – just the reverse – but so named to distinguish it from the 'great pox', syphilis (also called 'the pox').

child/infant/minor (legal term for a young person)
The meaning of 'child' varies according to different statutes. In Part 1 of the Children Act, 1958, for example 'child' means a young person under eighteen, while in the Education Act, 1944, it means a person not above compulsory school age (at present sixteen). In general, though, a 'child' is a young person under the age of fourteen, i.e. one who has not reached the so-called 'age of discretion' at which he is judged fit to manage his own affairs. An 'infant' was a person under the age of twenty-one, which was regarded as 'full age', when all persons were considered competent to do everything the law required them to do. The Family Law Reform Act, 1969, however, reduced the age of majority from twenty-one to eighteen, and at the same time provided that any person not of full age may be described as a 'minor' instead of an 'infant'. 'Minor', then, is the now common term for a young person under the age of eighteen.

chilli see **pickles**

chime see **peal**

china/pottery/porcelain (type of earthenware)
'China' was a term used originally to distinguish 'porcelain' from China from European 'pottery'. Subsequently the word came to apply to both without distinction. 'Pottery' is literally anything made out of clay by a potter on a wheel – especially, of

course, a pot – but the word is properly used for all ware that is opaque, whereas 'porcelain', now regarded as the 'true' 'china' Worcester, Wedgwood, and the like, is translucent. Both 'pottery' and 'porcelain' are further divided by experts into, respectively earthenware (fired at a temperature below 1200 degrees C) and stoneware (above 1200 degrees C) for 'pottery', and hard-paste and soft-paste 'porcelain' – where the 'hard' and 'soft' refer not to the degree of 'hardness' and 'softness' of the clay but to the degree of firing necessary in the kiln. Hard-paste porcelain, too, contains kaolin – a fine white clay originally from the Chinese mountain of Kaolin (its name meaning 'high hill'). 'Porcelain' is one of the most unusual words in the English language, since it ultimately derives from Italian *porcellana*, 'little sow' (i.e. small female pig) via French *porcelaine* 'cowrie shell', 'porcelain'. The association is a bizarre one: a cowrie shell is translucent, and at the same time resembles a sow's vulva. One wonders precisely whose fantasy created such original comparisons.

Ch'ing see **Ming**

chive/endive (salad plant)
The 'chive' is related to the leek and onion and has long slender leaves used as seasoning. The leaves of the 'endive', a species of chicory, are finely divided and curled and, when blanched, used for salad.

chlorate see **chlorine**

chloride see **chlorine**

chlorine/chloride/chlorite/chlorate
(poisonous gas or related compound)
'Chlorine', so named by Sir Humphrey Davy from its colour – the Greek for 'green' is *chloros* – is a greenish-yellow poisonous gas (Cl) that is irritating to breathe. With the other word it's a matter of suffixes: a 'chloride' is a chemical compound of two substances, one of which is 'chlorine'; 'chlorite' is a salt of chlor*ous* acid; 'chlorate' is a salt of chlor*ic* acid.

chlorite see **chlorine**

choir/chancel/chantry (area surrounding the altar in a church)
The 'choir' in a church extends from the crossing (the intersection of the nave and the transepts) to the east or altar end; in a cathedral it is the area between the nave and the main altar. In both it houses the choir in their choirstalls. The 'chancel', which is not related to 'chant', is the space round the altar, usually enclosed, for the clergy. Its origin is in latin *cancelli* (bars, lattice) which originally enclosed it. 'Chantry' is, however, related to 'chant'. It is a small chapel or altar in a church or cathedral endowed for priests to sing masses, usually for the soul of the endower.

choir/chorus (group or band of singers)
A 'choir' is a fixed or regular group of singers, as a church 'choir', school 'choir', the Bach 'Choir', and so on, which may or may not have soloists. A 'chorus' is a special group of singers who usually gather to perform a particular piece, as an opera or oratorio, in which there will, by contrast, be soloists or principal singers. However, the words are sometimes used more or less interchangeably, and *The Oxford Companion to Music*, rather unexpectedly, does not distinguish between them.

chop/cutlet (slice or cut of meat)
A 'chop' is normally a slice of meat that includes a rib-bone and is cut from the loin. A 'cutlet' is usually cut from the neck, when it will be a neck-'chop', or from a part that contains *no* bone. The word is doubly misleading in origin, since it comes not from 'cut' but from French *côtelette*, which in turn comes from Latin *costa* meaning 'rib' – which, today at any rate, it does not contain.

chord see **cord**

chortle see **chuckle**

chorus see **choir** (group of singers)

chrome/chromium (shiny metallic substance)
'Chrome' is, in fact, 'chromium', of which it is the French form. The word is used especially to apply to the various coloured pigments such as 'chrome' yellow or 'chrome' oxide which are compounds of the shiny metallic element 'chromium'. Both words derive from Greek *chroma* (colour).

chromium see **chrome**

chronic/acute (type of disease or illness)
The former word is often wrongly used instead of the latter, largely because 'chronic' has become a colloquial word for 'bad', 'serious' in its own right (as a 'chronic' noise or a 'chronic' remark). Properly, however, a 'chronic' illness is a protracted or longlasting one, such as 'chronic' asthma or 'chronic' malnutrition. (The word ultimately comes from Greek *chronos*, 'time'.) An 'acute' illness is the opposite: one that is 'short and sharp', such as 'acute' toothache or 'acute' influenza.

chrysalis/cocoon (case protecting an insect pupa)
A 'chrysalis' is either the case or the whole pupa, especially, of course, of a butterfly or moth. The rather learned word derives from the Greek for 'gold', the colour of certain 'chrysalises' (or chrysalides, or – rather too correctly – chrysales). A 'cocoon' is usually silky, and especially applies to the case of a silkworm, from which, in fact, the silk actually comes (which is why the wretched pupating creature is plunged into hot water, so that its carefully wound case can be as carefully unwound). However, even a 'cocoon' is strictly speaking a 'chrysalis', since it is a pupa.

chubby/cherubic/seraphic (baby-faced or sweet-expressioned)
'Chubby' is really 'round and plump', though when applied to cheeks can suggest an endearing, baby-like nature or appearance. 'Cherubic', of course, is 'cherub-like'. Cherubs were often portrayed in art as beautiful, winged children with 'chubby' innocent faces. 'Seraphic' is, similarly, 'seraph-like'. Whereas cherubs form the second order of angels, seraphs belong to the highest order. They, too, are represented in art as pretty children – more often simply as a child's head with wings. 'Seraphic' suggests more 'blissful' than 'chubby', especially when applied to a smile.

51

chuckle/chortle (as verb: laugh softly with satisfaction)
'Chuckle' implies a laughing to oneself, with quiet amusement or modest satisfaction. 'Chortle' is Lewis Carroll's famous 'chuckle' and 'snort' combined, from *Through the Look-ing-Glass*. In the poem *Jabberwocky*, Carroll says of the warrior whose 'beamish boy' had killed the Jabberwock that 'He chortled in his joy'.

chum see **crony**

church/chapel (place of worship, for some a regular one)
In Britain, at any rate, 'church', meaning both the building and the body of Chris-tians, has an 'establishment' connotation. But then the Church of England, which is the one meant, is indeed quite literally the established church of the land, so the conno-tation need not be a derogatory one. But if 'church' does mean 'them', then 'chapel', which normally means a Nonconformist building or body, must be 'us', so what about those for whom 'church'-going is 'us'? The split (or distinction) will probably be of little significance to members of either – for them religious worship is what really matters – yet the division is there, if only when it comes to an intermarriage. 'His people are "church", but hers are "chapel"!' There are, however, Anglican 'chapels', such as the separate place of worship, with its own altar, in a large 'church' or cathedral – where the 'chapel' dedicated to the Virgin Mary is called the 'Lady Chapel' – or the building or room that is the place of worship in a school or institution, and non-Anglican 'churches', as, obviously, Roman Catholic ones. A division can often be found in virtually any section of society – if that is what you are looking for.

churchwarden see **sidesman**

cicerone see **chaperone**

cider/scrumpy/perry (sparkling alcoholic drink made from fruit)
'Cider' is made from fermented apple juice. 'Scrumpy' is a rough brew of 'cider' famous in the West Country, where cider-apples are widely grown. 'Perry', a more or less exclus-ively British drink, is made from the juice of pears. 'Cider' is produced in a number of different varieties, drier and sweeter, and not all are necessarily sparkling. In the USA, moreover, 'cider' usually means *un*fer-mented apple juice, i.e. non-alcoholic.

cinders/ashes/clinker (residue of a fire)
'Cinders' are usually reasonably 'solid' or substantial, and may contain matter that is still combustible. 'Ashes' are essentially powdery (and usually grey), and cannot be further subjected to combustion. 'Clinker' – not so called because it 'clinks' but deriving from a Dutch word – is a fused, solid mass of incombustible matter remaining after the burning of coal (unlike 'cinders', which are generally smaller, and can be the remnants of coal, wood, or any combustible matter). A further distinction between 'cinders' and 'ashes' is that 'cinders' may be either hot or cold, while 'ashes' are nearly always thought of as cold or 'dead'.

Cinemascope see **Cinerama**

Cinerama/Cinemascope (system of projecting a cinema film onto a wide screen)
Both terms are really proprietary names. 'Cinerama' – from 'cinema' and 'panorama' – was all the rage when it first appeared in 1951. The film was projected on to a wide, curved screen by three projectors simul-taneously with stereo sound. Two years later came 'Cinemascope' (or 'Cinema-Scope') – from 'cinema' with the suffix '-scope'. This was an improvement in that although the basic system was the same, the film was projected by one projector. The first film shown in 'CinemaScope' was the American *The Robe* (1953). Subsequent single-lens 'Cinerama' was virtually indis-tinguishable from 'Cinemascope'.

cinnabar see **cinnamon**

cinnamon/cinnabar (red-coloured substance)
'Cinnamon' is the aromatic bark of a type of laurel tree in the East Indies. When the bark is dried the resultant substance can be

used as a spice or in medicine. It is yellowish or reddish brown in colour. 'Cinnabar' is mercuric sulphide, a mineral used as a red pigment. Its name ultimately goes back to the Arabic *zinjarf* (red lead).

Cinzano/Chianti/Campari (type of Italian wine or aperitif)
'Cinzano' is Italian vermouth, obtainable as red, rosé or white, sweet or dry. 'Chianti' is a dry red – less often white – wine, sold in distinctive straw-covered bottles. The name is also used indiscriminately of certain rather inferior Italian wines. 'Campari' is an aperitif consisting of bitters and usually drunk with soda. 'Cinzano' and 'Campari' are named after their manufacturers, 'Chianti' is properly from the Chianti Mountains in Tuscany.

cipher see **code**

circle see **balcony** (section of the auditorium of a theatre)

Cistercian see **Capuchin**

cite see **quote**

citizen/denizen (inhabitant, resident)
A 'citizen' is the (usually native) inhabitant of a city or country. The word 'denizen' derives from Old French *deinz* (within) by assimilation in the fifteenth century with 'citizen', and refers to the inhabitant or resident of any place, but normally one who was originally an alien and has been adopted. The word can apply also to animals and plants that have migrated, as well as to words borrowed from a foreign language.

citron see **citrus**

citrus/citron (sour yellow fruit)
The 'citrus' is a tree or shrub of the genus *Citrus* whose fruit includes the lemon, lime, orange, grapefruit and 'citron' itself. The 'citron' resembles a lemon but is larger and has a thicker rind.

cittern see **zither**

city see **town**

civic see **civil**

civil/civic/civilian (pertaining to a civilian or a citizen)
'Civil' is a general word that normally implies 'citizen', either as the native inhabitant of a state, as in such terms as 'civil' law or 'civil' affairs, or as a member of a military, ecclesiastical or political society. One thus has, respectively, a 'civil' award (not a military one), a 'civil' marriage (not a religious one) and the 'Civil' Service (as distinct from the military services). 'Civil' may also apply to the citizen as an individual, and define his 'civil' duty or 'civil' rights. 'Civic' has the basic sense 'pertaining to a city', as a 'civic' centre or a 'civic' function, although here it can extend to refer to a citizen seen as the inhabitant of a city, for example, in 'civic' pride or 'civics', the school subject which is training in citizenship. 'Civilian' usually means simply 'non-military', as in the 'civilian' population. Of an airline, however, one has, in this sense, 'civil' rather than 'civilian', so there are 'civil' passenger aircraft, and the body organising the National Air Traffic Services in Britain is entitled the 'Civil' Aviation Authority.

civilian see **civil**

clang/clank/clink/clonk/clunk (sharp sound made by one hard object striking another)
These onomatopoeic words can be usefully distinguished to apply to different objects. An iron gate slamming and a heavy bell struck 'clang'. Heavy chains rattling 'clank' – so does a suit of armour. Spoons placed on saucers and one wine glass brought into contact with another 'clink'. A plate or dish falling upside down on the floor 'clonks' – a slangish word but a valid one. A milk bottle set down on a doorstep and a car door slammed to 'clunk'.

clank see **clang**

class/form (set of pupils in a school)
'Class' is a general word used in both primary and secondary state schools, although 'class' is normally reserved for primary or junior schools and 'form' often

53

used in secondary, especially grammar schools, as the fifth 'form' or sixth 'form' (the most senior). In independent schools 'form' is generally preferred to 'class' at any level, although there are always exceptions. The difference is thus one of usage.

classic/classical (relating to class or the classics)
'Classic' is the attribute of something that is of the highest 'class' and serves as a standard or establishes one, as a 'classic' case or a 'classic' example. A 'classic' novel is one that has come to be regarded as one of the best, and so is now famous. 'Classical' applies to the 'classics', usually Roman or Greek, or to 'classicism'. There is thus a difference between a 'classic' play, which is one that serves as a standard (as the 'classic' novel just mentioned), and a 'classical' play, which is, say, a Greek or French one. Both words can overlap to mean 'refined', so that one can talk of 'classic' or 'classical' purity. 'Classical' music, however, is regarded as being opposed to romantic or light or popular, i.e. it is respectively pre-1800 (roughly), serious or traditional.

classical see **classic**

clavichord see **harpsichord**

claw/talon (pointed nail on the foot of an animal or bird)
A 'claw' is a general term, so that cats, dogs, lions, starlings and eagles, to name a few, have 'claws', and so by extension (literally) do lobsters, crayfish and the like. A 'talon' is the 'claw' of a bird of prey, as a vulture or hawk. It should really mean little more than 'heel', or at most 'hind "claw" of a bird', as it does in French and a number of other languages. The meaning '"claw" of a bird of prey' is peculiar to English.

cleanliness see **cleanness**

cleanness/cleanliness (state of being clean)
'Cleanness' refers to a temporary or permanent state of being clean. 'Cleanliness' implies being kept in a clean state and is often used figuratively, as 'cleanliness' of thought or heart.

clearway see **motorway**

clench/clinch (make fast, secure)
'Clench', an earlier word than 'clinch', means, 'grasp or close firmly', as one's fist, teeth or jaw. 'Clinch' has a wider use. Literally it means to drive a nail in or grasp one's opponent tightly in boxing or wrestling. Figuratively it means to settle decisively, as an argument or deal.

clerihew see **limerick**

cliché/catchphrase/hack phrase (popular saying or quotation)
A 'cliché' is a stereotyped expression, especially a hackneyed one that careful speakers and writers normally try to avoid. (The word has its French origin in the term for the literal stereotype used by printers to produce identical copies of something: the word is said to derive from the sound made by the matrix as it falls on to cooling metal). Examples of 'clichés' are: 'to all intents and purposes', 'at this moment in time', 'lock, stock and barrel' (which has now long lost its former originality), 'here today and gone tomorrow', 'you could have knocked me down with a feather', and so on. A 'catchphrase' is really what it says: a phrase that has caught on, and quite often originating from or associated with a particular group, such as servicemen, pub drinkers, entertainers (many 'catchphrases' reach their public through radio and television), sportsmen, and the like. Most 'catchphrases' are in fact whole sentences, and like 'clichés' are constantly in the process of becoming more and more dated, until they die out altogether to be replaced by new ones. In fact, 'catchphrases' can become 'clichés', although 'clichés' only very rarely become 'catchphrases'. Examples of 'catchphrases' are: 'I'll have your guts for garters' (which might have meant what it said originally), 'There's a lot of it about', 'Win some, lose some', 'Play it again, Sam', 'One drink and I'm anybody's', 'That makes two of us', and so on. A 'hack phrase' is simply an overworked or hackneyed phrase of any kind, perhaps more often a 'cliché' than a 'catchphrase'. It is usually remarkably trite and even meaningless, such as 'mark my words' and 'know what I

mean' and even 'you know'. Readers who wish to investigate the phenomena more closely should consult the works of Eric Partridge, who compiled dictionaries of both 'clichés' and 'catchphrases'.

clinch see **clench**

clink see **clang**

clinker see **cinders**

clocks back see **clocks on**

clocks on/clocks back (adjustment of clocks by one hour to mark start or end of summer time)
When does which happen? You put 'clocks on' or forward by one hour in the spring, with the immediate result that you lose an hour's sleep and the more lasting consequence of having lighter evenings and, for a while, darker mornings. You put 'clocks back' by one hour in the autumn, thus gaining an extra hour in bed for once, temporarily lighter early mornings, and a dreary succession of dark evenings. If in doubt when to do which, try the American mnemonic: 'Spring forward, fall back' ('fall', of course, being autumn).

clonk see **clang**

clue/cue (sign, indication)
A 'clue' guides one in the direction of the solving of a problem or a mystery – but does not necessarily lead to the final solution. One might thus see a 'clue' to a friend's strange behaviour in his recent row with his boss. A 'cue' gives a hint or a suggestion. As such, it is not so positive as a 'clue'. So, put another way, your friend's encounter with the management might be a 'cue' to his strange behaviour.

clunk see **clang**

coach/carriage/car (passenger vehicle as unit of a railway train)
'Carriage' is the general and popular word, as a 'first class "carriage"' or a 'crowded "carriage"'. 'Coach' is a more official word, and normally the one used by railway authorities, as in announcements about 'the

front three "coaches"'. A 'car' is a specific type of 'carriage', as a dining or restaurant 'car', buffet 'car', or sleeping 'car'. In the USA, 'car' is used in a wider sense to mean 'carriage', a 'railroad "car"'.

coarse/crude/rude (rough, vulgar, offensive)
Basically, 'coarse' has the implication of lack of refinement, inferiority, as of 'coarse' language or manners. 'Crude' – literally 'unrefined' as in 'crude' oil or sugar – suggests that there is a distinct absence of polish or tact, so that a 'crude' joke is, to some, not only unfunny but offensive. 'Rude', apart from its meaning of 'robust' or 'sturdy', as in 'rude' health, implies a definite offensiveness or lack of politeness, partly because of roughness, partly through want of courtesy. A 'rude' reply is one that is consciously offensive; a 'crude' one may be unintentionally so, simply because the person knows no better.

coast see **shore**

coat/jacket (outer garment usually with sleeves and buttoning or fastening down the front)
A 'coat' is a general word for a top garment usually designed for outdoor wear, as an 'overcoat', 'raincoat' or car 'coat'. Many 'coats', however, have specific uses indoors, as a 'housecoat', morning 'coat' or 'waist-coat'. The latter is not even (usually) a top garment, and a 'petticoat' is certainly not – although it once was the word for an outer skirt. All 'jackets' are 'coats', which is why the two words are often used interchangeably, but unlike 'coats' they are normally short, whether for outdoor or indoor wear, as a donkey 'jacket', lumber 'jacket' and shooting 'jacket' (outdoor), or dinner 'jacket', sports 'jacket' or bed-'jacket' (indoor).

cockatiel see **cockatoo**

cockatoo/cockatiel/marabou/caribou/ kinkajou/carcajou/sapajou (exotic bird or animal)
The 'cockatoo' is a crested parrot, a native of the East Indies and Australia. The 'cockatiel' is also an Australian parrot, and

crested, but is smaller. It is common as a cagebird. The 'marabou' is a large stork, a native of Africa. Its soft downy feathers under its wing and tail have found favour with some women as an adornment for their hat. The 'caribou' is a species of North American reindeer. The 'kinkajou' is a small, brown, furry animal related to the racoon that lives in trees in Central and South America. The 'carcajou' is the American glutton, and the 'sapajou' is the capuchin monkey, a native of South America.

cockle/mussel (edible shellfish)
'Cockles' are smaller and rounder – or more exactly more heart-shaped. They vary in colour from brown to red or yellow and are usually found under a layer of sand. 'Mussels' are twice as long as 'cockles' and are found sticking to rocks, and to one another, in large colonies. They are dark blue or dark greenish-brown in colour. Both are regarded as tasty delicacies, but to define the difference between them in this respect one would have to ask an expert, such as the Irish girl Molly Malone, who 'wheeled her wheelbarrow thrqugh streets broad and narrow, Crying, "Cockles" and "mussels"! alive, alive, oh!' (But perhaps she merely sold them and never sampled her own wares?)

Cockney see **Londoner**

cocoon see **chrysalis**

cocotte see **coquette**

cod/halibut (fish yielding oil from its liver)
The 'cod' is a standard-shaped, i.e. cylindrical, fish important for food. 'Cod' liver oil is a useful source of vitamins A and D. The 'halibut' is a large flatfish, with its eyes and colouring on one side only. Its liver oil yields mainly vitamin A.

coddle/cosset (pamper)
One usually 'coddles' invalids or children by pandering to their whims and generally overindulging them. To 'cosset' someone is to treat him as a pet, lavish attention on him. 'Cosset' is a dialect word for a pet lamb.

code/cipher (secret symbols or language for messages)
A 'code' is essentially a system of signals, using letters, figures, word groups or symbols, while a 'cipher' is a form of secret or disguised writing, or the key to it. In cryptology, a 'code' system is a specialised form of substitution in which whole words, long phrases, and even sentences are replaced by arbitrary equivalents, such as other words, groups of letters or figures, or combination of these. A 'code' book or 'permutation table' would be used for encoding or decoding messages. A 'cipher' system involves a variety of devices such as transposition of letters, the use of grilles, and substitution (as figures for letters). A very simple 'cipher' system would be so-called monoalphabetic substitution, where one letter of the alphabet stands for another

Cipher

L	E	X	I	N
G	T	O	A	B
C	D	F	H	K
M	P	Q	R	S
U	V	W	Y	Z

1. Message: **AM FOLLOWING ON NEXT TRAIN**

2. Plain-text: **AM FO LX LO WI NG ON NE XT TR AI NX**

3. Cipher: **GR QF EI XG YX LB BX LX EO AP HA LI**

Cryptogram

4. **GRQFE IXGYX LBBXL XEOAP HALI**

Code

One-part code

A B A B A – A
A B A C E – Abandon-ing-s
A B A D I – Abandoned
A B A F O – Abate-ing-s
A B A G U – Abated
A B A H Y – Abeyance
A B E B E – Abide-ing-s
A B E C I – Abide
. . . . . – ....
Z Y Z Y Z – Zone-s

Two-part code

Encoding

K A B O L – A
S T O L G – Abandon-ing-s
E X I F O – Abandoned
Z U M R A – Abated
A B A B A – Abeyance
R O A B Y – Abide-ing-s
. . . . . – ....
B I K U R – Zone-s

Decoding

A B A B A – Abeyance
A B A C E – Procedure
A B A D I – To purchase
A B A F O – Commenced
A B A G U – Do not think
A B A H Y – Recorded
. . . . . – ....
Z Y Z Y Z – According to

(as B for A, C for B, and so on). Ships' signalling flags are a form of 'code', with the Blue Peter, for example, meaning 'Am about to sail', and Nelson's famous message 'England expects . . .' expressed in a series of flags. (He intended the second word of the message to be 'confides', but this was not in the signal book and would have had to be represented by seven flags. He therefore changed it to 'expects' for which a single flag existed.)

codger/curmudgeon (eccentric or crusty old person)
A 'codger' – possibly the word is related to 'cadger' – is usually an old, rather odd person. The term can be quite an affectionate one. 'He's a nice old codger' (cp. the gentlemen who deal with the *Daily Mirror*'s equivalent of 'Letters to the Editor'). A 'curmudgeon' is definitely not an affectionate term. It implies meanness or stinginess. Its actual origin is unknown, although Dr Johnson in his *Dictionary* quoted an anonymous correspondent of his who ascribed it to the French *coeur méchant* (spiteful heart)!

cogent see **coherent**

cognac see **brandy**

coherent/cohesive/cogent (binding, meaningful)
'Coherent' literally means 'sticking together' and thus 'consistent' or 'logical', as in a 'coherent' report or policy. 'Cohesive', with the same basic meaning, emphasises the binding or uniting force. The word is chiefly used of physical objects, such as a 'cohesive' mass of some material, but one can talk of the 'cohesive' force of, say, a party or league of some kind. 'Cogent' means 'convincing', as when a speaker makes a number of 'cogent' points.

cohesive see **coherent**

coif see **quiff**

cole see **coleslaw**

coleslaw/slaw/kale/cole/kohlrabi (kind of cabbage)
'Coleslaw', from two Dutch words, means literally 'cabbage salad' and is a salad of sliced white cabbage. 'Slaw' is sliced or chopped cabbage eaten usually cold, i.e. uncooked, or less often, hot i.e. cooked. 'Kale' is a kind of cabbage with wrinkled leaves, although the name is also used for borecole or broccoli. 'Cole' is a general name for different kinds of cabbage, in particular rape. 'Kohlrabi', a word that is a blend of German *Kohl* (cabbage) and Italian *cauli rape* (cabbage turnips), is a variety of 'kale' with a stem swelling into a bulblike formation.

coliseum/Colosseum (large theatre)
A 'coliseum', now more familiar as the name of a number of theatres, cinemas, dance halls and the like, is properly any place for meetings or public entertainment. It is the generic variant of the 'Colosseum', the great amphitheatre in Rome built by Vespasian. Both words are, unsurprisingly, related to 'colossal'.

collaborate see **co-operate**

collate see **collect**

collect/collate/collocate (bring together, set in order)
To 'collect' is basically to 'bring or gather

together', as a crowd, stamps, or water in a ditch. The actual order of gathering is often unimportant. To 'collate' is to compare things – usually texts, articles, written or printed entries and the like – in order to see if they agree or disagree. One might thus 'collate' one's entries for a competition, or one's notes for a lecture. There is a suggestion of 'collecting' as well. To 'collocate' is to arrange in proper order. A linguistic expert might thus 'collocate' the languages of West Africa. The term often suggests a place, as when a commanding officer 'collocates' his battle forces for action at a particular point.

college of advanced technology see **technical college**

college of education see **teacher training college**

collocate see **collect**

collude/connive/conspire (act or plot together)
'Colluding' implies a secret understanding, especially when something illegal or dishonest is involved. Agreeably, the word originates from the Latin verb meaning 'play with'. A similar sort of game is 'conniving', which suggests supporting something wrong, which one secretly approves, by deliberately avoiding showing any disapproval – by being, in other words, a secret accessory, or by turning a blind eye. This last sense is closest to the Latin original, meaning 'shut the eyes with'. 'Conspiring' – this time literally 'breathing together' – simply suggests agreeing to do something unlawful or illegal, especially secretly. This is the strongest, most active word, with 'connive' the weakest, least active.

colony/dominion/protectorate/ dependency (country or state dependent to some degree on another)
'Colony' these days does not normally mean 'country occupied by and ruled by another', but in the United Kingdom is usually taken to mean 'British Crown colony', officially defined as 'a territory belonging by settlement, conquest or annexation to the British

Crown'. This means fully or partially self-governing 'colonies' such as Belize, Bermuda and Hong Kong where a British Governor is appointed. A 'dominion' was the former title (before 1939) of the self-governing territories of the British Commonwealth, as Canada, Australia and the (then) Union of South Africa. The term was abandoned in 1947 when these became members of the Commonwealth. A 'protectorate', too, is a term that now no longer exists. Strictly speaking, it applies to a weak state protected by a stronger one, or technically, 'a territory not formally annexed, but in respect of which ... Her Majesty has power and jurisdiction'. The last of the British 'protectorates' were the Solomon Islands, which were granted their independence in 1978. A 'dependency', in British parlance – more correctly a Crown 'Dependency' – is a term applied to the Isle of Man and the Channel Islands. These are not strictly speaking part of the United Kingdom, but have their own legislative assemblies and systems of local administration, and their own courts. At the same time they have a special relationship with the United Kingdom because of their geographical proximity to it and their long connection with the British Crown. They are thus not fully 'dependent' from the point of view of government, but 'dependent' more on good will – and the tourist trade.

Colosseum see **coliseum**

colt/foal/filly (young horse)
A 'colt' is a young male horse, usually from when it is taken from its dam to four or five years old. A 'foal' is a young horse generally, or even a young donkey. A 'filly' is a young female horse, with the same specification as for a 'colt'. (Rather unexpectedly, the word is not related to French *fille* but is of Germanic origin). For young cow words see **calf**.

column see **pillar**

Comecon see **Comintern**

comedy/farce/slapstick (stage play of a light, amusing character)
'Comedy', the opposite of tragedy, can be

satirical, but usually represents everyday life and has a happy ending. 'Farce' can be properly distinguished from 'comedy' by its tendency to derive amusement through the ingenious manipulations of a series of intricate situations in which stereotyped or 'stock' human characters are involved. The plot is often an amatory one (a 'bedroom farce'), with the main subjects in and out of wedlock – and bed. Some 'farces' have become famous, as the so-called Aldwych 'Farces' in the 1920s and 1930s, mostly by Ben Travers, and the Whitehall 'Farces' of the 1950s and 1960s, managed by Brian Rix. Many present-day domestic 'comedies' on television are 'farces' of a lesser rather than greater degree of originality. A special type of 'farce' is 'slapstick', which usually involves good, low, knockabout fun, with much physical action (custard pies, pratfalls, silly walks and the like) and general rumbustiousness. 'Farce' and 'slapstick' are words that have interesting origins. 'Farce' comes from Latin *farcire*, 'to stuff' (compare, at a much more sophisticated level, the *haute cuisine* term *farci*). The idea was that such 'comedies' were 'stuffed' into interludes or intervals as 'fill-ins'. A 'slapstick' was a special type of stick, consisting of two flat pieces of wood hinged together, which when slapped on someone's backside produced a resounding 'crack' but inflicted minimal physical discomfort.

comet/meteor/meteorite (bright, moving object in the sky)
A 'comet' is quite often confused with a 'meteor', but in fact is nothing like it. It is a hazy, star-like patch in the sky with a lengthy tail pointing away from the sun, round which it slowly moves in a near oval orbit. The brightest 'comet', and one of the best known, is Halley's, which reappears every 75 years. Its last appearance was in 1986. A 'meteor' is the 'shooting star' or fireball. 'Meteors' generally move in streams round the sun, although they are often observed singly. They are caused by particles called 'meteoroids' entering the atmosphere at high speed and becoming luminous by compression of the air. 'Meteors' usually burn up before they reach the earth's surface, but if they are not completely consumed, the surviving frag-

ment of rock or metal is called a 'meteorite'. Most 'meteorites' are quite small, but large ones have caused spectacular craters in Arizona, for example, and in Siberia. 'Comet' comes from the Greek word for 'hairy', a reference to its tail, while 'meteor' derives from Greek 'lofty', 'high in the air' – whence also, of course, 'meteorology' as the term for the scientific study of the weather.

comfy/cosy (snug and homely)
'Comfy' is a pet abbreviation for 'comfortable', talking of some familiar or homely object, as a 'comfy' chair or a pair of 'comfy' slippers. 'Cosy' – spelled 'cozy' in the USA – really means 'snugly comfortable', as a 'cosy' chair or a 'cosy' corner. Figuratively it means 'intimate', as when one has a 'cosy' little chat, although it can acquire a disparaging sense in such a phrase as a 'cosy' job, which is a cushy one, or a 'cosy' profit, which is an easy and large one.

comic/comical (causing amusement)
The essential difference is that 'comic' describes something that is supposed to be funny, and 'comical' – usually – something that is not. So one has on the one hand a 'comic' play, actor, novel or song, but a 'comical' sight, manner, face or gait. As a noun, 'comic' can mean a low-grade comedian.

comical see **comic**

Cominform see **Comintern**

Comintern/Cominform/Comecon
(Communist organisation)
The 'Comintern' was the Third Communist International, founded in 1919 and dissolved in 1943. It united various Communist countries and advocated violent or revolutionary measures. The 'Cominform' was an organisation existing from 1947 to 1956 established by the Communist parties of nine European countries including the USSR, France and Italy, for mutual advice and coordinated activity. 'Comecon', the acronym of '*C*ouncil for *M*utual *Econ*omic Aid', is a confederation of nine Communist countries, including the USSR, Mongolia and Cuba, to coordinate their

economic development. Founded in 1949, it is a kind of Eastern bloc Common Market.

command see **order**

commandant see **commander**

commander/commodore/commandant (high military rank)
A 'commander' is, in general, the chief commissioned officer, irrespective of rank, of a military unit, otherwise the 'C.O.'. When it comes to the three services, officers of equivalent rank, in descending order, are:
Navy commodore, commander, lieutenant commander
Army lieutenant general, lieutenant colonel, major
Air Force air commodore, wing commander, squadron leader
The WRNS equivalent of 'commodore' is 'commandant'. Moreover, apart from the naval rank, a 'commodore' is the senior captain of a line of merchant vessels and also the title of the president or head of a yacht club. Generally speaking a 'commandant' is the commanding officer of a particular place or body of troops, as of the Royal Army Medical College or an army barracks.

commissar see **commissioner**

commissary see **commissioner**

commission see **committee**

commissionaire see **commissioner**

commissioner/commissionaire/ commissary/commissar (public official)
A 'commissioner' is in principle someone appointed by a commission to carry out specified work. From this come such official titles as Parliamentary 'Commissioner', Health Service 'Commissioner', 'Commissioner' of Police, and so on. A 'commissionaire' is either, more familiarly, the uniformed doorkeeper at a hotel or club, or a member of the Corps of 'Commissionaires', which employs ex-servicemen, policemen, firemen and merchant navy seamen. A 'commissary' is the (military) officer of a commissariat, which supplies provisions,

transport and the like. It is also the title of someone given special power by a superior, or otherwise a deputy, such as the representative of a bishop in his absence. A 'commissar' was the title of the head of a government department, a 'commissariat', in the USSR before there were ministries and ministers, i.e. 1917-46. (His full title was 'People's Commissar'.)

commissioner for oaths see **solicitor**

committee/commission (body set up to carry out a special function)
A 'committee' is usually formed by and out of a larger body to carry out, investigate, report, research, debate or the like a special matter that probably concerns the whole of the larger body, as an executive 'committee' or a complaints 'committee'. A special type of 'committee' is a working party, which is specially set up to investigate a particular problem or question. A 'commission' is not necessarily appointed by a larger body but is set up to perform special duties and almost always report on its findings. Often it is a 'once and for all' body: when it has completed its mission it is disbanded. A 'committee', on the other hand, although its members may change, runs for a lengthy period, especially a standing 'committee', which may even be a permanent one.

commodore see **commander**

commonplace/platitude/truism (unoriginal or trite or obvious statement)
A 'commonplace' is a statement made so often that it is far from original, in other words an everyday saying, as the pathetic 'These things are sent to try us'. It was originally a notable saying, in fact, and entered in a 'commonplace book'. A 'platitude' is a dull or trite statement made solemnly as if fresh or profound but actually rather boring and stale, as many hackneyed sayings and catch phrases. A 'truism' is similar, in popular usage: an obvious truth, as the hackneyed statement 'You only die once'. Properly, though, it is a much more interesting thing: a proposition that states nothing that is not already implied in one of its terms. An example might be, 'I don't

like to go to bed too late', which really means 'I don't like to go to bed later than I like to go', since 'too late' means 'later than I like', 'too late for me'. However, 'commonplaces' and 'platitudes' and 'truisms' turn up regularly in our daily conversation.

communism see **socialism**

commute/compound (mitigate a punishment or sentence)
To 'commute' a punishment is to change it for one less severe, as when an offender has his sentence 'commuted' to five years' imprisonment. To 'compound' a crime – which on the face of it would seem to make it worse – is to agree, for financial consideration, not to prosecute or punish. For this word in another role see **compound**.

compact see **contract**

company see (1) **corps**, (2) **firm**

competition/contest (act of rivalry in which one aims to win)
A 'competition' almost always suggests an undertaking – usually a sporting one – in which one has an active 'opposition' and hence strives to do one's best. A 'contest' can be an individual attempt to gain an objective or to hold on to what one has gained, although by implication there will be an opposing force of some kind. A 'contest', too, suggests more of an effort or struggle than a 'competition', more of a trial of strength, or even of countering the claim or position of another.

compile see **compose**

complacent/complaisant/compliant
(pleasant or agreeable)
If one is self-satisfied, pleased with oneself, one may be said to be 'complacent', especially if secretly delighting in one's advantages. To be 'complaisant' is to be obliging with the aim of pleasing, but to be 'compliant' is to yield to another's wishes, whether to please or not.

complaisant see **complacent**

complement see **supplement** (additional part)

complex see **complicated**

compliant see **complacent**

complicated/complex (difficult)
'Complicated' means 'difficult' because of several factors or points that must be taken into account, as a 'complicated' argument or a 'complicated' task. 'Complex' means 'difficult' because of an involved combination of factors, as a 'complex' problem or a 'complex' way of life.

compose/compile/concoct (arrange, constitute)
To 'compose' something is to put it or arrange it in order to make a single finished product, often something written. One thus 'composes' a poem, a piece of music or a letter. To 'compile' something is to put (usually written or literary) materials in order so as to form a complete book or unit of some kind. In this way one can 'compile' an index, a register or a dictionary. Whether one 'composes' or 'compiles' a crossword is a matter of precision: to 'compose' it implies imaginative or intellectual originality; to 'compile' it suggests setting the individual components – clues and words – in order. To 'concoct' a thing is to 'compose' it hastily, in fact to 'cook it up', as the origin of the word in Latin *concoctus* (cooked together) suggests.

compose (be made up of – or make up) see **consist of**

compound/confound/confuse
(complicate)
To 'compound' is to 'combine', as when a leader 'compounds' his followers – builds up a band of them. To 'confound' is to mingle in such a way that the individual components cannot readily be distinguished, or to throw in disorder or confusion. To 'confuse' is to combine without order or to fail to distinguish. In fact one often 'confuses' two things but 'confounds' more than two. Incidentally, it won't do to 'confuse' 'compound' with

'confound'. For 'compound' in another sense, see **commute**.

compound (mitigate a punishment or sentence) see **commute**

comprehensive school/secondary modern school/grammar school
(type of secondary school)
'Comprehensive schools', which in England and Wales comprise some 90 per cent of state secondary schools, are those that take pupils, usually at age eleven, without reference to their ability or aptitude – without any kind of entrance test or exam, in other words – and provide a wide, supposedly 'comprehensive' range of secondary education for all or most of the children in a given district. (In Scotland secondary education is almost entirely comprehensive or non-selective.) 'Secondary modern schools' provide mainly a general education with a practical bias, while 'grammar schools' concentrate on a specifically academic course. Both of these allocate places after an aptitude test – the former 'eleven plus' – and until 1980 were being phased out. As a result of the gradual abolition of those 'grammar schools' that are direct grant schools, however, most schools of this type have now become fully independent, i.e. have joined the private sector of education and charge fees to all pupils. A number of 'grammar schools' are thus familiar as 'public' schools (which in typically convoluted British parlance means just the opposite).

comprise (of) see **consist of**

comptroller see **controller**

compulsive/impulsive/impetuous
(instinctive, spontaneous)
How does a 'compulsive' gesture differ from an 'impulsive' one? 'Compulsive', a word borrowed from psychology, is normally used in the sense 'strongly irrational'; thus someone who has a 'compulsive' desire for food cannot refrain from eating. By contrast, 'impulsive' suggests spontaneity, something done without thought for the consequences, as an 'impulsive' movement or an 'impulsive' act of generosity. 'Impetuous' implies

an eagerness that borders on the rash, so that an 'impetuous' act of generosity might well make a large hole in one's pocket.

computer programmer/systems analyst
(person working with computers)
A 'computer programmer' writes the set of instructions or program to the specifications of the 'systems analyst', who thus analyses the program in computing terms and writes the specifications for the programs that follow. Put another way, and as something of an over-simplification, the 'analyst' plans what the computer must do, and the 'programmer' instructs the computer to do it. Many 'programmers', of course, are also 'analysts', but not all 'analysts' are 'programmers'. Both are sometimes called 'liveware' (see **hardware**).

conceit see **vanity**

concert/recital (performance of a musical work)
'Concert' is a general word derived from Italian *concerto* meaning performing together, as a symphony 'concert'. A 'recital' is a more intimate thing, a programme given by one player or singer, or perhaps by two, as in a violin and piano 'recital'; it is always more personal and on a smaller scale than a 'concert'.

concertina see **accordion**

conciliate see **reconcile**

concoct see **compose**

concrete/cement (hard stonelike material)
Surprisingly often one hears people talking about a 'cement' path when they mean a 'concrete' one. 'Concrete' is made by mixing 'cement' – which is its binding agent – sand, broken pieces of stone and the like with water. This amalgam then hardens and you have an artificial stonelike surface. 'Cement' itself is made by burning a mixture of clay and limestone and is used in powder form.

condemn/contemn (disapprove of)
To 'condemn' something is to declare it to be bad or undesirable. To 'contemn' – a

much rarer word, mainly only in legal use – means to treat with contempt, to scorn or despise. Since the noun and adjective 'contempt' and 'contemptible' are in reasonably common use, it's perhaps surprising that the verb is so rarely found.

conduit/culvert (water duct or course)
The basic difference between the two is that a 'conduit' carries water over a reasonable distance ('conducts it'), whereas a 'culvert' takes water across under something such as a road or railway. Both are normally underground, with a 'conduit' usually being a longish pipe or tube and a 'culvert' a fairly wide drain or sewer leading a shortish distance. The origin of 'culvert' is uncertain: there may perhaps be a link with the French *couvert* (covered).

confession/admission (acknowledgment of guilt or offence)
The two are very close, but a distinction can be made. A 'confession' is usually of something 'bad', as a fault, crime, debt, dread or guilty secret. An 'admission' is also this, but has a suggestion of 'allowing', and can imply a personal, unprompted resolve to tell the truth, especially of a lesser evil. 'I admit that it was all my fault', one might say. But an interrogator, especially one investigating a serious crime, says 'Confess!'

confine/contain (limit, restrict)
To 'confine' something is to keep it within its recognised or acceptable limits, as when an invalid is 'confined' to his room or one 'confines' oneself to a few words. To 'contain' something is to check it to prevent it from breaking its normal bounds, such as 'containing' one's temper, the enemy, or an outbreak of disease. The implication is that something 'contained' would, if not checked, rapidly spread or increase.

confound see **compound**

confuse see **compound**

conga see **tango**

congregation/convention/convocation (meeting, assembly)
All three can be used, in rather special senses, of the assembly of an ecclesiastical, academic or political body. As titles, one has 'Congregation' for the senate of Cambridge University, and the body of resident MAs at Oxford University, as well as for the permanent committee of the Roman (Catholic) College of Cardinals; 'Convention' for the period of English history when Parliament assembled without a summons from the sovereign, such as the one that restored Charles II to the throne in 1660; 'Convocation' for the ecclesiastical assemblies of the provinces of Canterbury and York in the Church of England that meet two or three times a year to discuss church laws, and also for the legislative assembly of Oxford University.

conjugal/connubial (pertaining to marriage)
There is a sizeable overlap in the use of the terms but on the whole it's a matter of rights and rites. 'Conjugal' means 'pertaining to the state of marriage', that is, to a married couple, as in 'conjugal' rights or 'conjugal' bliss. 'Connubial' relates to the marriage ceremony, so that one has 'connubial' vows and 'connubial' rites. The words, Latin in origin, mean respectively 'joined together' and 'married together'.

conjure see **adjure**

conjuror/magician (one skilled in the art of magic)
A 'conjuror' (also spelt 'conjurer') is a person who practises sleight of hand, not necessarily so that the quickness of the hand deceives the eye, but with manual dexterity. A 'magician' is more of an all-rounder. The word is not only a general one for a 'magic-maker' but also has mystic or even religious connotations, since it derives from the magi or ancient Persian priestly astrologers, of whom three, the Magi, or Three Wise Men, came from the East to Bethlehem to bring offerings to the infant Jesus. For more about magic see **black magic**.

connive see **collude**

connote see **denote**

connubial see **conjugal**

consent see **assent**

consequent/subsequent (following)
'Consequent' means 'following as a result or effect', so that one might have a 'consequent' meeting to discuss proposals made at an earlier one. 'Subsequent' means 'following' in any way, so that a 'subsequent' meeting is simply one that happens to take place after an earlier one, or in fact after anything at all that had occurred earlier.

conserve/preserve (keep carefully)
To 'conserve' something is to keep it safe and sound, guard it against loss or damage – hence the 'conservation' of rural areas, old buildings and the like. To 'preserve' something is to keep it for a long time in a good condition, or keep it as it is now, so that one 'preserves' fruit, the peace and one's health. Illogically, if one 'preserves' fruit one can end up either with a 'preserve' or a 'conserve'; the latter suggests that sugar and other additives assist in the retention of the product's natural properties.

consistently/persistently (constantly)
To do something 'consistently' is to do it repeatedly but always in the same manner, as when someone works 'consistently'. If something is done 'persistently' it implies that the repetition is deliberate or calculated, as a correspondent who 'persistently' ignores your requests for a reply to your letter, or a child who 'persistently' late for school.

consist in see **consist of**

**consist of/consist in/comprise
(of)/constitute/compose** (be made up of – or make up)
A rather tricky collection. 'Consist of' is used of one thing being made up of one or more parts, components, materials, etc. Thus concrete 'consists' of cement, sand and stones mixed with water. 'Consist in' is usually followed by a verb, and means, more or less, 'be defined as': cheerfulness 'consists in' not letting things get you down. 'Comprise' can mean both 'consist of' – a house may 'comprise' three bedrooms, sitting room, dining room, kitchen and bathroom – and also 'make up', as the pages that 'comprise' this book. In other words 'comprise' can relate from singular to plural or plural to singular, if the one comprehends the other. 'Comprise of' is also found, possibly because of the common use of 'of' with the past participle, as a course 'comprised of' ten lectures (which is the same as 'consisting of'). To 'constitute' is to make up: health and wealth can 'constitute' happiness. 'Compose' means much the same as 'constitute' but implies a degree of unity, often of dissimilar elements, as the varied ingredients that 'compose' a Christmas pudding.

conspire see **collude**

constantly see **continually**

constellation/nebula/galaxy (mass of stars)
A 'constellation' is the area of sky round a group of stars having an imaginary outline, when seen from the Earth, that gives them their name, as Ursa Major, otherwise the Great Bear, or seen through other eyes Charles's Wain (or even, seen more irreverently, the Bent Saucepan). Astronomers now recognise eighty-eight constellations that more or less cover the sky. A 'nebula' and a 'galaxy' need to be rather more carefully distinguished. A 'nebula' is a bright area in the heavens due either to a 'galaxy' or to a large cloud of distant stars. Today, increasingly, the term tends to be used for visible condensations in interstellar space, while all extra-galactic systems are 'galaxies', which admittedly is something of a paradox. In common use, however, a 'galaxy' is one of two things: either (as the 'Galaxy') another name for the Milky Way (Greek *galaktos* means 'milk'), or one of the many independent systems of stars, gas, dust and so on that exist in space, especially the one (again, the 'Galaxy') that contains the earth. The confusion between the two is partly due to the fact that 'galaxies' were first described as 'nebulae', since they were only hazy or nebulous objects in telescopes. Later, but not much more helpfully, they were known as 'island universes' or 'extra-galactic "nebulae"'. Apart from our own

'galaxy', only two are visible to the naked eye. These are the Magellanic Clouds in the southern sky, which look like two detached portions of the Milky Way. (They are named after the explorer Magellan, who circumnavigated the world.)

constitute see **consist of**

consulate see **embassy**

consultant/specialist (doctor experienced in a particular field of medicine or surgery)
A 'consultant' is so called because he is consulted not by his patients but by his colleagues in the hospital where he works, since he has specialised knowledge. A 'specialist' is a doctor, usually in a hospital, who devotes his attention to a particular class of diseases, for example an orthopaedic 'specialist'. A 'specialist' may thus be a 'consultant', which in hospital appointments is regarded as a senior rank of medical officer.

contagious see **infectious**

contain see **confine**

contemn see **condemn**

contempt/disdain (strong disapproval)
'Contempt' is disapproval combined with disgust or mockery, especially of something regarded as 'beneath one'. 'Disdain' is similar, but has more of an overtone of moral correctness and of a standing attitude towards something. The word is related to 'deign', that is, something one does not deign to consider. See also **scorn**.

contemptibly/contemptuously (with contempt)
If a person has behaved or acted 'contemptibly' he is usually held in contempt. A person who has behaved 'contemptuously' however, has himself expressed contempt for someone or something else. The same distinction goes for 'contemptible' and 'contemptuous'. See also **contempt**.

contemptuously see **contemptibly**

contest see **competition**

continually/continuously/constantly (repeatedly)
All three suggest a succession of occurrences. 'Continually' suggests that the recurrences are very close together, with small breaks or even none at all. Someone who is 'continually' cleaning his car thus does it very frequently, seemingly always. 'Continuously' suggests a succession that really is unbroken. If it rained 'continuously' last night it never stopped raining. 'Constantly' suggests that the action was repeated in the same manner, probably producing the same results each time. A person's proneness to colds, for example, might make him 'constantly' absent from work.

continuously see **continually**

contract/compact (agreement)
A 'contract' is a formal agreement, usually written and signed, as in marriage, or an engagement to perform, make regular payments and the like. A 'compact' is any mutual agreement, not necessariiy a formal one. It is close to 'covenant', as a 'compact' made between two colleagues to help each other out or engage in mutually beneficial activities, legal or illegal. Formally, it almost has the sense of 'treaty', as in a peace – or aggression – 'compact'.

contract bridge/auction bridge/whist (card game for four players)
'Contract bridge' is a development of 'auction bridge' that originated in France as *plafond* ('ceiling') before the First World War. The 'contract', basically, is an undertaking to make a stated number of tricks. The main difference is that in 'contract bridge' the side that wins the bid can earn only the actual number of tricks bid towards the game, all additional points being credited above the score line. In 'auction bridge' ('auction' from the bidding) all the tricks won, whether bid or not, score towards the game. 'Whist' is perhaps the doyen of full-pack partnership games: the object is to score tricks, a trick being gained by the partners who play the highest card of a suit, or the highest trump card. Each trick over six counts one point, with part-

ners scoring five points for a game and two games for a rubber. 'Whist' was the forerunner of bridge, which was superseded by 'auction bridge' in 1911 with this in turn giving way to 'contract bridge' in 1928. 'Whist' is still flourishing (in 'drives') in town venues and village halls up and down the country.

contralto see **treble**

contrary/converse (opposite)
A 'contrary' opinion is one that is either opposed to another or different from it. A 'converse' opinion, on the other hand, is always opposed to another.

controller/comptroller (public officer who controls or manages a department)
'Controller' is the more common word, used in several titles for the head of a government or public office, where it often approximates to 'director' or 'chairman', such as the 'Controller' of Her Majesty's Stationery Office, the 'Controller' of the Navy (a high-ranking admiral), or, in the BBC, the 'controllers' who are the heads of the various television and radio networks (BBC1 and 2 and Radio 1, 2, 3 and 4). However, the first two examples here correspond in sense to a 'Comptroller' since they are the financial executives of the bodies mentioned, and this 'financial' aspect is always present behind 'comptroller' (which arose simply as a variant spelling of 'controller' under the influence of French *compte*, 'account'). Examples of 'comptroller' as a title are thus the 'Comptroller'-General of the Patent Office and (separately) of the National Debt Office, the 'Comptroller' and Auditor General who heads the National Audit Office (formerly the Exchequer and Audit Department), and the 'Comptroller' of the Royal Mint. The title is commonly found, too, in the royal household, which has not only a 'Comptroller' of the Household itself (i.e. of the Queen's Household), but of the Lord Chamberlain's Office and of the households of other members of the royal family, where the holder of the title may also be a 'Private Secretary' or 'Equerry' (or even all three).

contumacy/contumely (offensive behaviour)

Both words are accented on the first syllable; both express an objectionable attitude. 'Contumacy' is rebelliousness or wilful disobedience; 'contumely' is blatant contempt expressed in words or actions. The first word derives from Latin *contumax* (stubborn); the second from Latin *contumelia* (swelling together), with the former possibly derived from the latter.

contumely see **contumacy**

conundrum see **pun**

convalescent home see **nursing home**

convention see **congregation**

converse see **contrary**

convocation see **congregation**

cook/chef (one who prepares food professionally)
Both 'cook' and 'chef' can be used as titles (forms of address), although presumably not so many people today are in a position to say 'I'll have a word with "cook"'. (The designation was originally always masculine, in fact.) The French word 'chef' – implying 'head' 'cook', so that there are other 'cooks' working under him – was first used in English to mean the head 'cook' in the kitchen of a large household. The broad difference today, of course, is that anyone can be a 'cook', even if just for a *mauvais quart d'heure*, but a 'chef' is always a full-time professional.

cooker see **oven**

co-operate/collaborate (work together)
To 'co-operate' is to unite in work, to act jointly. The verb is often used of someone reluctant to be helpful, as when prisoners do not 'co-operate' with the authorities. To 'collaborate' is similar in meaning, but implies that the working together is for a specific purpose. Here the joint effort is much more likely to be for a sinister end, as of traitors who 'collaborate' with the enemy. There is an overlap, however, and some speakers and writers use the words indifferently.

coppice see **wood**

copse see **wood**

coquette/cocotte (flirt)
A 'coquette' is a woman who seeks to gain the attention or admiration of a man out of vanity or for show. A 'cocotte' does likewise, but as a means to a different end – she is a prostitute, originally a Parisian one. Both words are related in some way to French *coq* (cockerel), of which they are a feminine form. Both *cocotte* and *poule* in modern French are words for 'hen' – and 'tart'.

cord/chord (string – or string-like object)
Both spellings are used for 'vocal cords/chords', yet 'cord' is the basic word for 'type of thick string'. The confusion is largely caused by a musical 'chord', in the sense 'notes played together' or 'string of an instrument'. This latter meaning is now found only in such set phrases as 'touch the right chord' or 'strike a chord' (recall), or in poetry – although Adelaide Ann Procter's 'Lost Chord' ('Seated one day at the organ, . . .') was 'one chord of music, like the sound of a great Amen', i.e. not a single string. The geometrical type – a straight line joining any two points on a curve – is 'chord'.

corn/grain/wheat (staple agricultural crop)
'Corn' is the tricky word, since its meaning and usage varies geographically: in England it generally means 'wheat', in Scotland and Ireland 'oats', and in North America 'maize'. Moreover, it can mean the same as 'grain', i.e. the actual edible fruit or seed of a cereal, as well as a collective word for a whole crop before or after harvesting, as a 'field of "corn"' – which might mean 'wheat' *or* oats *or* maize, or any food-grass. 'Wheat' is a specific cereal plant: the one with the four-sided head used for making flour for bread and regarded as highly nutritious. So all 'wheat' is 'corn', and all 'corn' is 'grain', and most 'grain' is 'wheat'. No wonder all flesh is as grass.

cornet/bugle (instrument of the trumpet family)
The 'cornet' is halfway in size between a

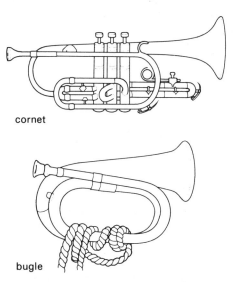

cornet

bugle

trumpet and a 'bugle', with the same open (unstopped) notes and compass as a trumpet, and the same method of operation – valves opened and closed by pistons. It is associated chiefly with brass bands and solitary players on street corners. The 'bugle', very much a military instrument, is roughly the same length as a trumpet but has a wider bore. It differs from both the 'cornet' and the trumpet in that it has no valves, and so can basically produce not much more than five open notes, in ascending order: middle C, G, C, E, G. These are enough, in fact, to play Reveille. 'Come to the cookhouse door, boys', and a number of other military orders. Its name comes from Latin *buculus*, 'young ox', from whose horns the instrument was originally made.

coronary see **stroke**

coronet see **crown**

corporal punishment/capital punishment (penalty inflicted physically)
The two are emotive subjects, and in the heat of the moment may be confused. 'Corporal punishment' is that of the human body, traditionally by flogging, beating, slapping or smacking. Any child who has been subjected to it will know that there are mental undertones and overtones to the

process as well as physical. 'Capital punishment' is execution – by any means, although the implication is by beheading, from Latin *caput, capitis* (head). 'Corporal', too, has its origin in the Latin – *corpus, corporis* (body).

corporation see **firm**

corps/division/brigade/battalion/ company/regiment/troop/squadron/ platoon/section/squad (military formation)
The 'corps' is the largest unit of an army, usually comprising two or more 'divisions' and additional support arms. The next largest unit is thus the 'division'. This is a major formation containing the necessary arms to sustain combat. Smaller than a 'division', and usually commanded by a brigadier, is a 'brigade', which will also have its support arms and services. One of three units (usually) in a 'brigade' is a 'battalion', which in turn is comprised of two or more subordinate units, normally 'companies' or 'regiments'. A 'company' will be commanded by a major or captain and a 'regiment', usually, by a colonel. Of these two latter units, therefore, the 'regiment' is the 'higher ranking'. It is also the chief permanent recruiting and training unit of the army and for tactical control it is itself organised into 'companies', 'battalions' or 'squadrons', much as a 'brigade' is. For some time a 'regiment' was roughly equated with a 'battalion', however (not a 'brigade'), and the two terms were used interchangeably. In most modern armies, though, the 'regiment' is the higher unit. (In 1957 the US Army in fact eliminated its infantry 'battalions' and 'regiments', replacing them with 'battle groups'. A further reorganisation, begun in 1961, called for the restoration of infantry 'battalions' as self-sufficient units of 800 to 900 officers and men, each 'battalion' being divided into four 'companies'). A 'troop', meanwhile, is a subdivision of a cavalry 'regiment' of about 'company' size, usually commanded by a captain. A 'squadron' is the principal division of a cavalry 'regiment' or armoured formation and is of sufficient size to contain two or more 'troops'. A 'platoon' is the subdivision of a 'company' and is normally under the command of a lieutenant and

divided into three 'sections'. Finally, a 'section' is divided into two or more 'squads', the army's smallest units, each of which has typically a dozen men. The exact function, size and ranking of each unit varies from country to country and period to period, so that it is impossible to give precise figures for the number of men in any one unit or to say what the exact composition of a formation will be. Such factors vary with changing tactical and strategic requirements. Moreover, increasing disbandments, amalgamations and arms reductions further complicate the picture. Thus the grading given here is mainly one of size, from biggest to smallest.

corpse/carcass (dead body)
A 'corpse' is the dead body of a human; a 'carcass' the dead body of an animal. For once, therefore, a neat and straightforward distinction. The word 'carcass' suggests 'case' – in fact it is sometimes spelt with a final 'e' instead of double 's' – but its origin is something of a mystery. *Webster* suggests possibly Persian *tirkash*, 'arrow-bearing', which is ingenious. (But might not the initial 'car-' have something to do with 'flesh', as in 'carrion'?)

corridor see **passage**

corrode see **erode**

cortège see **suite**

corundum see **carborundum**

corvette/vedette (fast naval vessel)
Originally, a 'corvette' was a three-masted sailing ship, ultimately derived from Latin *corbita* (ship of burden). In the modern sense it is a lightly armed fast vessel used for escorting convoys and midway in size between a destroyer and a gunboat. A 'vedette', from Italian *vedere* (to see), is a small naval launch, unarmed, used for reconnaissance work.

cosmonaut see **astronaut**

cosset see **coddle**

costumier/couturier (designer, maker or seller of clothes)

A 'costumier' makes or sells costumes, and also hires them to actors. A 'couturier' – from French *couture* (sewing) – designs and makes women's clothes. His – and also hers – is the art of the 'haute couture', the world of fashion.

cosy see **comfy**

couch/sofa/settee/divan (upholstered seat for two to four persons)
A 'couch' has a back and sometimes arm rests. A special sort of 'couch' is the one found in doctors' surgeries and psychiatrists' consulting rooms, which has a raisable head end – and on which one lies, not sits. A 'sofa' usually has comfortable, padded 'arms' or ends and a comfortable back. (The word is not related to 'soft' but comes from the Arabic, in which it is the term for a part of the floor raised so as to make a seat.) In the USA a large 'sofa' is often known as a davenport, especially when it can be converted into a bed. The name is said to be that of the original maker. A 'settee' is virtually the same as a 'sofa', although it may not have ends. It's a 'non-U' word, says Professor Ross, in *Don't Say It*, as is 'couch'. (Presumably he sanctions 'sofa'.) A 'divan' normally has no back or arms. Properly, it is the word for a long, low seat against a wall, as in the Middle East. These days it often doubles up as a spare or 'guest' bed or 'put-you-up', when it is called a 'divan-bed'. 'The thing itself', says the Professor, 'used to be non-U but is perhaps no longer so' (judgment made in 1973). The word is directly related to the French for 'customs', *douane,* and ultimately derives from Persian *dīwān,* 'court', 'bench'.

councillor/counsellor (professional adviser)
A 'councillor' is essentially the member of a council, as a 'town councillor'. A 'counsellor' – one who counsels – is the common term in the USA to mean, among other things, a lawyer, especially one attending a trial, or a student's tutor. The word exists in some titles in Britain, however, notably as 'Counsellor of State' and, at a local and more homely level, 'marriage guidance counsellor'.

counsellor see **councillor**

count see **duke**

course see **field** (area of play)

courser see **charger**

court see **field** (area of play)

courtesy see **politeness**

couturier see **costumier**

cove see **bay**

covert see **den**

cradle/crib (baby's bed or cot)
A 'cradle' is a bed mounted on rockers to send baby to sleep (in theory). A 'crib' is properly a receptacle for animal feed with bars, hence a small bed with latticed or barred sides. A combination of both meanings of 'crib' gives a third use of the word for a model of the manger-scene at Bethlehem as found in churches at Christmas-time.

crafty see **arty**

crass see **gross**

craving see **longing**

crawfish see **crayfish**

crayfish/crawfish (edible crustacean)
The 'crayfish' closely resembles the lobster, but is much smaller. The 'crawfish' actually is a lobster. The name denotes, especially, the spiny or rock lobster or *langouste.* 'Crawfish' is also, confusingly, the preferred American spelling of 'crayfish'. Both words have become firmly confused with 'fish' – which they are not. The origin lies in Old French *crevis* or *crevice;* the name of the creature in modern French is *écrevisse.*

credible/creditable/credulous (believable)
'Credible' means both 'believable', as a 'credible' story, and 'trustworthy', as a 'credible' backer or supporter. 'Creditable'

means 'deserving credit', as a 'creditable' performance, or a 'creditable' result in an examination. 'Credulous' refers to someone who is over-ready to believe or gullible, or to a person's attitude or appearance, as a 'credulous' child, who will believe anything he is told.

creditable see **credible**

credit card/cheque card/bank card
(special card authorising the obtaining of goods or cash)
A 'credit card', issued chiefly through banks but also by commercial organisations, is mainly used for the settlement of an account or services, as in a shop, hotel, restaurant or garage. Familiar types of 'credit card' are the Access, VISA (incorporating Barclay-card) and American Express ones. A 'cheque card', or 'bank card' (or banker's card), is a 'payment guarantee' card issued by a bank to enable the holder to cash a cheque up to £50 at any bank or to support payment by cheque. A Barclaycard, for customers of Barclays Bank only, acts not only as a 'credit card' but also as a 'cheque card', as now do many others both within and outside the VISA system. Holders of 'credit cards' are issued with a monthly account which, if not settled fully within a specified period (usually 25 days from the date of the statement), attracts interest.

credulous see **credible**

cretin see **idiot**

crevasse see **crevice**

crevice/crevasse/abyss/chasm (rent or split, usually deep)
The only one that is not deep is 'crevice', which is a small crack that forms an opening, usually in something solid, as hard ground, rock or ice. A 'crevasse' is a deep cleft, usually in ice. An 'abyss' is a bottom-less, or seemingly bottomless, gulf, from the Greek word meaning 'without bottom'. A 'chasm' can be literal, when it is a deep or wide cleft or gorge, or figurative, when it denotes an abstract rending force, as the 'chasm' of death.

crew cut/Eton crop (hair style in which hair is cut very short)
A 'crew cut', of which skinheads affect(ed) an exaggerated version, is a style in which a man's or boy's hair is cut short all over. The term apparently originates, as do many colourful phrases in the English language, from the USA, where at one time the boat crews at Harvard and Yale universities went in for close-cropped hair. An 'Eton crop' is, though, of ultra-British origin. It is – or was, since it was mostly in vogue before the Second World War – a style in which a woman's hair was cut short all over and sleeked, like that of the pre-war, but rarely post-war, Eton boy.

crib see **cradle**

cricket see **grasshopper**

crime/offence (wrongdoing, lawbreaking)
In general usage, a 'crime' is a more serious thing than an 'offence'. Legally, a 'crime' is either an act which is forbidden by law, or the omission to perform an act which is commanded by law, and as such is often contrasted with a civil injury, which is the violation of another's right. 'Crime', too, is a violation of man-made laws, whereas an 'offence' can be against a divine law, as an 'offence' against morality.

Crimplene see **poplin**

**crimson/carnation/carmine/
incarnadine/cardinal/carnelian**
(shade of red)
It is remarkable that so many similar words should denote more or less the same colour. 'Crimson', is a deep, purplish red, as one sees in a 'crimson' complexion. 'Carnation' is a light red, almost pink – the colour of the flower, in fact. Its origin is the Latin *carnatio* (fleshiness), the reference being to the colour of flesh in paintings. 'Carmine' is virtually the same as 'crimson'; basically it is the pigment obtained from cochineal. The rolling Shakespearean 'incarnadine' has a primary suggestion of flesh colour, but a secondary sense of blood colour – the latter due to association with the words of the horrified Macbeth. 'Cardinal' is deep, rich red, the colour of a cardinal's robes.

'Carnelian', yet another word influenced by the flesh (Latin *caro, carnis*), is strictly speaking a red or reddish variety of chalcedony. A variant form of the word is 'cornelian': neither spelling should be confused with 'c(a)erulian' which is sky-blue.

crisis see **emergency**

crocodile/alligator (large fearsome reptile living in rivers)
The 'crocodile' lives in the rivers of tropical Africa (especially the Nile), Australia and America. The 'alligator' is less cosmopolitan. It exists in only two species: the first inhabits the Mississippi and other large rivers of America, the second is found in China, in the Yangtse Kiang. Geographical disposition apart, there is a physical distinction between the creatures. The 'alligator' has a broad head, a depressed, blunt muzzle, and unequal teeth, whereas the 'crocodile' has a narrower head, a rounder, sharper nose, and equal teeth. Though one may feel disinclined to examine them too closely, it is the teeth, in fact, that provide the ultimate difference: the 'alligator' has two teeth – one on each side of the lower jaw four back from the front – that are elongated and fit into sockets in the upper jaw when its mouth is closed; with the 'crocodile' these two teeth project outside its snout. Those experienced in these things

note protruding 4th tooth   crocodile

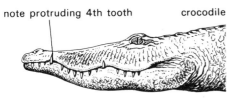

crocodile   alligator

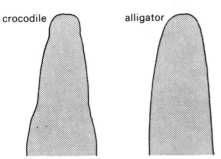

additionally claim that 'crocodiles' are livelier than 'alligators' and so more likely to attack a supposedly hostile human. But the dental distinction is the foolproof one.

cromlech/dolmen/menhir (type of large ancient standing stone)
A 'cromlech', from the Welsh *crom* (bent) and *llech* (stone) is a circle of single, standing stones, such as the one at Avebury. Unhelpfully, the word is also sometimes used to mean 'dolmen'. This is an ancient tomb or burial chamber looking rather like a rough and ready table with three or more upright stones and a horizontal flat stone on top. 'Dolmens' exist especially in Wales, Cornwall and Ireland as well as in Brittany. The name seems to be an invented one, from Breton *tol* (table) and *men* (stone), although some authorities derive it from Cornish *doll* (hole) and *men* (stone). There is no doubt that 'menhir' is simply Breton *men hir* (long stone). This is a single stone whether on its own or, as at Avebury, Stonehenge and the famous *alignements* at Carnac in Brittany, with others.

crony/chum (close friend or 'mate')
A 'crony' is normally a close friend of long standing, especially one associated by workplace, hobby and the like. The word apparently derives from Greek *chronos*, 'time', with reference to this long fidelity. A 'chum' is a now rather dated name in the 'close friend' sense, although the word is quite often used to address an acquaintance or even a complete stranger, the latter often in a rather hostile sense, such as 'Look, chum, I know what I'm doing'. In the sense 'close friend' it has probably been superseded by 'mate' or some other word (such as 'buddy', 'oppo' or whatever, depending on the background). 'Chum' now has a rather 'upper class' ring to it, also, which is explained by the fact that it arose as a slang word at Oxford. Its equivalent at Cambridge was thus, not surprisingly, 'crony' (hence, perhaps, the classical connection of the word).

cross-ply tyres see **radial tyres**

crotch/crutch (fork of the human body)
'Crotch' is used of the fork itself as a

location, of the genital organs situated there, or of this area of a pair of trousers, pants and the like. 'Crutch' is a popular anatomical term for the same area, with the usage not extended to other meanings. A particularly unpleasant below-the-belt blow is a kick in the 'crotch'.

crow/rook/raven (large black bird)
The 'crow' is smaller – about 20 inches long – and less heavily billed than the 'raven'. It feeds chiefly on the ground, where it walks around rather sedately. The 'rook' belongs to the same family as the 'crow' (*Corvidae*) and is roughly the same size. It can be distinguished from it, however, by its gregarious nature – it lives with its many companions in rookeries – and the white skin at the base of its bill and its 'trousers'. The 'raven', also in this family, is the largest of the three – up to 26 inches long. As a scavenger, it is often found where the others are not, for example on beaches, in the mountains, or in a town. Its colouring is more blue-black than pure black, like the 'crow', and its voice is deeper. It is from their voice or call, in fact, that all three birds get their name: compare words such as 'caw', 'croak' and 'creak', also imitative. (Not so easy to see this origin in the 'raven', but it always was a devious bird.)

crown/coronet/tiara (head covering worn as sign of royalty, nobility, or elegance)
The 'crown' is the more or less sumptuous bejewelled head-covering worn by a monarch, as a king, queen, emperor or tsar. A 'coronet', as its diminutive ending suggests, is a small 'crown', especially one worn by a peer or peeress. A 'tiara' does not necessarily denote rank, but may be worn, as a type of ornamental 'coronet', above the forehead, on formal occasions such as dances or banquets or receptions. In this sense it is an exclusively feminine adornment. The pope, however, always wears a 'tiara' on certain important occasions: it is a form of triple 'crown', one surmounting the other, of traditional beehive shape and gemmed with three diadems.

crude see **coarse**

crumpet/muffin (type of tea-cake eaten hot with butter)

Both are toasted and eaten with butter, with the American 'muffin' being the equivalent of an English 'crumpet'. English 'crumpets' are in general smaller, thicker, and denser than 'muffins' and are almost always eaten as tea-cakes in winter, whereas 'muffins' were also eaten for breakfast and were not so seasonal in their appearance. (A hundred years ago both were equally popular for tea-parties, which came to be known as 'muffin'-worries and 'crumpet'-scrambles accordingly – that is, a special variety of bun-fight.) 'Muffin' now has something of a romantic ring to it, while 'crumpet' has taken on a new meaning to denote 'sexually attractive woman' or, loosely, 'sex' in general. How this happened – why 'crumpet'? – is not too clear, but there is obviously an association, mainly figurative, with the attributes of the cake when ready to be consumed (as 'hot', 'juicy', 'luscious'). Compare the use of other comestibles in a similar way, as **cheesecake**.

crumple/rumple (crush or press into irregular form or folds)
'Crumple' is used of the crushing of any kind of cloth or clothes, such as shirts, sheets, coats and curtains. 'Rumple' implies that the crushing or pressing is into smaller folds – a 'rumpled' sheet is thus merely a disarranged one – and is extended to mean 'ruffle' or 'tousle' applied to hair or an animal's coat.

crush/pash (infatuation, or the object of it)
A 'crush' is usually regarded as a feminine affair, the infatuation of a schoolgirl for her teacher (male or female) or, less often, of a woman for a man. 'Pash' can apply to both sexes – of both, for both – but its main application is among schoolchildren with the target object either a teacher or a fellow pupil of the opposite or the same sex. In origin 'crush' suggests a passionate compulsion, and 'pash' a compulsive passion.

crustacean see **mollusc**

crutch see **crotch**

crypt see **vault**

crystalline see **pristine**

CSE see **GCE**

cucking-stool see **ducking-stool**

cudgel/bludgeon (short heavy stick used as a weapon)
A 'cudgel' is any stick used as a weapon; a 'bludgeon' – suggesting 'blunt', although the origin of the word is unknown – is more of a club, with one end heavier than the other. Both instruments provide the verbs that mean 'hit' (with the respective weapon). In addition one can 'cudgel' one's brains – rack them, and take up the 'cudgels' – join the defence on behalf of someone or something.

cue see **clue**

culvert see **conduit**

cupola see **dome**

curate see **vicar**

curator see **caretaker**

curling see **hurling**

curmudgeon see **codger**

currant see **raisin**

current account/deposit account (type of bank account)
A 'current account' is the standard 'pay in and withdraw' account, using cheques, standing orders and the like, for which the bank may charge. A 'deposit account' is one that earns interest – formerly 2 per cent below Minimum Lending Rate until this was abolished in 1981 – and in theory not able to be drawn on without notice. Depositors have a pass book recording their balance. A bank customer may well have both types of account, although if his 'current account' goes 'into the red' the bank will not set this right by transferring from his 'deposit account' unless it is so instructed.

curriculum/syllabus (plan or course of study)
A 'curriculum' provides information with regard to the courses available at a particular educational establishment, and gives, basically, all the subjects offered, together with a brief plan of the way the various courses run or are programmed (or timetabled). A 'syllabus' is an outline or summary of a particular course, or a list of what will be covered or what books will be required, especially with an examination in mind. The basic difference between the two is thus the 'run' of the 'curriculum' (the word actually derives from Latin *currere*, 'to run') and the 'content' of the 'syllabus'.

custodian see **caretaker**

cutlet see **chop**

cuttlefish see **octopus**

cyclone see **whirlwind**

cyclotron/synchrotron/ synchrocyclotron (nuclear accelerator)
The 'cyclotron' is the basic device. It imparts very high speeds to electrified particles by means of successive electric impulses. A 'synchrotron' is a 'cyclotron' in which the strength of the magnetic field is increased as the particles gain energy. By contrast a 'synchrocyclotron' is a 'cyclotron' in which the frequency of the electric field is *de*creased as the particles gain energy. The '-tron' suffix derives from 'electron'.

cynical/sceptical (distrustful)
'Cynical' means 'disbelieving' with a suggestion of disapproval. One can thus have a 'cynical' outlook or make a 'cynical' remark. 'Sceptical' is not so strong as 'cynical'; it implies a doubt, and usually a mild one, as might be expressed in a 'sceptical' look, or by a 'sceptical' smile. Both Cynics and Sceptics were members of schools of Greek philosophy. The Cynics strove to develop the ethical teachings of Socrates (especially that virtue is the only good); the Sceptics held that real knowledge of things is impossible.

cynosure see **sinecure**

czarevitch/cesarevitch/czarina/

czarevna (member of the Russian imperial family)

Spellings of the titles vary, with 'ts-' often preferred to 'cz-' and '-wich' an alternative ending to '-vitch'. All, of course, are related to the czar (or tsar). The 'czarevitch' was originally the son of a czar; later the title became that of the czar's eldest son. The 'cesarevitch' was the title of the eldest son as heir to the throne. From it derives the 'Cesarewitch', the Newmarket race which in 1839 was instituted by the 21-year-old eldest son of Nicholas I, who was to become Alexander II. The 'czarina' – in Russian actually *tsaritsa* – was the wife of the czar, i.e. the Empress of Russia. The 'czarevna' was the daughter of the tsar. All words, as 'czar' itself, are related to 'Caesar' and 'Kaiser'.

czarevna see **czarevitch**

czarina see **czarevitch**

D

Dacron see **nylon**

daffodil/narcissus (pale yellow spring flower)

There are many forms and hybrids of 'daffodil' and 'narcissus', but the 'true' or wild 'daffodil', with its long 'trumpet', is the species of 'narcissus' classified as *Narcissus pseudonarcissus*. This means that 'narcissus' is also a name of many applications, but it more narrowly applies to the species *Narcissus poeticus*, which is heavily scented with white petals, a small orange-rimmed corona and a short 'trumpet'. The name, as well as the flower, is poetic because of its association with the mythological Greek youth who fell in love with his own reflection in the water, subsequently pined away (or threw himself in), and was changed into the flower. Yet the name of the flower does not derive from the yearning young Greek but comes, it seems, from the plant's numbing properties – 'narcissus' the narcotic, in fact. Another member of the 'narcissus' family is the jonquil, of which there are various kinds, but all having clusters of flowers and short, broad coronas.

dais see **rostrum**

dally see **delay**

damask/dimity (fabric with distinctive design)

'Damask', originally produced in Damascus, is a reversible fabric of linen, silk, cotton or wool with woven patterns, most usually seen in the dining room as a tablecloth. 'Dimity' – from the Greek *dimitos* (of double thread) – is a thin cotton fabric, white, dyed or printed, and woven with a stripe or check of some kind of heavier yarn. It appears mainly in bedrooms as a bedspread, although it's also used for hangings and occasionally for clothes. Its stripes are sometimes raised and may be complemented by fancy figures.

damp/moisture/humidity (slight wetness)

'Damp' usually suggests an undesirable and possibly superficial wetness, especially one that can be treated or removed, as rising 'damp'. 'Moisture' implies a natural or acceptable wetness, as the 'moisture' of the soil or the lips. 'Humidity' is a term for a measure of the amount of 'moisture' in the air.

dandruff/scurf (small flakes of dead skin in the hair of the head)

There is very little difference between the words. If any, it is that 'scurf' is the word for the actual scales or small shreds of dead skin (which are in fact being cast off all the time), and 'dandruff', the medical term for which is seborrhoeic dermatitis, is the condition of having 'scurf' on the scalp. ('Scurf' must not be confused with 'scurvy', a much more serious disease caused by a deficiency of vitamin C formerly attacking sailors who lived without any fresh vegetables.)

dappled/piebald/skewbald (mottled, of a horse or pony)

A 'dappled' horse is a spotted one, such as a 'dappled' grey which is mainly grey with darker grey mottling or a 'dappled' bay which is bay (reddish brown) with darker mottling. A 'piebald' horse is white with black patches: the term derives from 'pie' (magpie) with 'bald' in the sense of 'marked with white'. 'Skewbald' horses are a mixture of white and some other colour, usually brown. The word seems to be modelled on 'piebald' but the 'skew' is hard to explain. Perhaps it has its origin in the Old French *escu* (shield) in reference to the 'quartered' appearance.

daring/derring-do (courage)

'Daring' is 'adventurous courage', 'boldness' as in a 'daring' escape or rescue. 'Derring-do' is something of a phony hybrid. It came about through a misunderstanding on the part of Spenser, who took the phrase 'derryng do' in a fifteenth century poem to be a noun – it in fact is 'daring to do'. It still serves as a pseudoarchaic epithet of 'daring' with the sense 'romantically heroic'. For another Spenserian slip, see **Sabbath**.

dash see **rush**

dastard see **bastard**

day nursery see **nursery school**

dazed/dazzled (bewildered by brightness)

Both words have a sense extended to include anything that stuns or overwhelms. Basically, 'dazed' implies a bewilderment, as when one is 'dazed' on hearing dramatic news, whereas 'dazzled' suggests a brilliance of some kind, literal, as of a flashlight, or figurative, as of a woman's radiant beauty.

dazzled see **dazed**

deadly/deathly (like death, or causing it)

Both words have both meanings, although 'deathly' is almost always figurative. One can thus talk of 'deadly' poison or a 'deadly' enemy, but a 'deathly' pallor or a 'deathly' hush.

dean/archdeacon/canon (clerical dignitary)

A 'dean' controls the services in a cathedral, and with the chapter – 'canons' of the cathedral – supervises its fabric and property. The title also applies to the head of Westminster Abbey (not properly a cathedral) and certain other churches, such as St George's Chapel, Windsor. In the Roman Catholic Church, 'dean' is the title of the head of the Sacred College of Cardinals, in Rome. In the Church of England, a 'rural dean' is the head of a group of parishes in a particular diocese. The term is not exclusively ecclesiastical, though, since in many universities and colleges the 'dean' is the title of a fellow who has special disciplinary and advisory responsibilities. (At Oxford and Cambridge he is specifically responsible for undergraduate discipline.) It can also be the title of the head of a university faculty or department. In origin, the word comes from Latin *decem,* 'ten': the *decanus* was the chief of a group of ten. An 'archdeacon' – literally, 'chief of the deacons' – ranks next below a bishop in the ecclesiastical hierarchy and has administrative authority delegated to him by a particular bishop. He generally supervises the discipline of the clergy under him and administers church property. He holds a territorial title, for example, 'Archdeacon of Lindsey'. A 'canon' is a member of the clergy belonging to a cathedral or collegiate church. 'Residentiary' 'canons' comprise the chapter of the cathedral. As such, they are members of a permanent salaried staff responsible, under the 'dean', for the maintenance of the services, upkeep of the fabric and the like. 'Nonresidentiary' 'canons' are unsalaried but may have certain privileges and responsibilities: the title can sometimes be awarded as a kind of honorary promotion for dedicated service.

deathly see **deadly**

debate/deliberate (discuss, consider)

The meanings of the words overlap up to a point, although 'deliberate' has the overtone of 'weigh up', which in fact it literally means. Both actions can be carried out by one person on his own, in spite of the implication of a joint discussion or consideration.

decathlon see **marathon**

deceitful see **deceptive**

decent/decorous (seemly, proper)
'Decent' suggests that good taste or standards or appearance are involved, as a 'decent' family or a 'decent' respect for law and order. With 'decorous' the emphasis is more on outward appearance or behaviour, as can be seen in someone's 'decorous' manner or heard in his 'decorous' speech. The shades of propriety merge, however, so that the related 'decorum' can mean both 'decency' and 'decorousness'.

deceptive/deceitful (deceiving)
It's a matter of intention: something or someone 'deceptive' may not intentionally be so; a 'deceitful' person, however, is one who deliberately deceives.

decidedly/decisively (definitely, markedly)
Confusion can lead to 'decisively' being used instead of 'decidedly' as when a team is wrongly said to have won a 'decisively' easy victory. 'Decidedly' means 'undeniably', as when someone is 'decidedly' forthright or outspoken; 'decisively' means 'showing decision', so that a matter is dealt with 'decisively' – or conclusively.

decisively see **decidedly**

decorous see **decent**

decree see **degree** (official edict)

dedication see **devotion**

deductive/inductive (relating to process of reasoning)
'Deductive' reasoning is that in which a general statement is applied to a particular one, such as saying 'All cows are animals; this is a cow; therefore it is an animal.' This is formally known as syllogism. 'Inductive' is the opposite: a general principle is made as a result of the study of individual cases. It may, though, not lead to a one hundred per cent truth, since all individual cases would have to be studied. An example of

'inductive' reasoning is 'All calendars I have seen show twelve months in the year: I can therefore expect all calendars I see in the future to show twelve months in the year.'

deep-freeze see **refrigerator**

deer see **stag**

defective/deficient (faulty, having a shortcoming)
Something that is 'defective' may be just imperfect, as 'defective' eyesight or a book which turns out to be a 'defective' copy. Something 'deficient' is always faulty, however, since it lacks its full quota of attributes. Thus a 'deficient' supply is one that falls short, and a person who has a 'deficient' memory has one which is unable to recall properly.

deficient see **defective**

deflation see **inflation**

degree/certificate/diploma (formal academic qualification or the document that attests this)
A 'degree' is a university qualification awarded on successful completion of a three-year course or longer. As such it is usually in the form of a 'pass' or **honours degree**, with different classes in some universities, and is officially a first 'degree', otherwise a BA. A subsequent 'degree' would be an MA – a so-called higher and further degree – although a specialised qualification obtained subsequently might be a 'diploma'. Such specialisation is a distinguishing feature of a 'diploma', although today many former 'diplomas' are now termed 'degrees', with 'diploma' reserved for a less academic qualification – or one generally regarded as less academic. Also, a 'diploma' is the equivalent of a 'degree' as awarded by a non-university institution, for example a technical college. A 'certificate' is often, of course, simply a formal record of a person's birth, marriage, death, medical condition and the like, although it can apply to the attainment of proficiency in the academic sense, as **GCE** and CSE. In this sense it is close to 'diploma'. If both a 'certificate' and a

'diploma' are awarded in a particular field of study, then the 'diploma' is usually higher and awarded at the end of a longer course. Compare, in this respect, the Ordinary National 'Certificate' (ONC) at higher education level, awarded after two years part-time, and the Ordinary National 'Diploma' (OND) gained at the end of a full-time or sandwich course that involves wider and deeper study than the ONC.

degree/decree (official edict or statute)
Apart from the many senses of 'degree' as a unit of measurement, as well as other technical uses (e.g. in music and genealogy), the word is best known for the academic award that is made by a university or college to a student on the successful completion of a course of study. With luck, he or she will be awarded an **honours degree** (which see, as well as **degree** itself (above) for more detailed background.) A 'decree' is not really an award, but an official ruling or law made by someone in authority, for example in a divorce court. Those who sometimes confuse the two may like to remember that 'degree' is related to 'grade' (both with 'g'), while 'decree' is related to 'decern' (both with 'c').

deist/theist (person who believes in God)
A 'deist' is a person who acknowledges the existence of God, but who holds that religion is based on human reason rather than divine revelation. A 'theist', by contrast, is someone whose belief in God is based on both reason *and* revelation, i.e. in a God who rules the universe as well as having created it. Originally, a 'deist' was the opposite of an 'atheist' (who denies the existence of God), and was synonymous with 'theist' until about the end of the seventeenth century. After this, the present distinction came to be made. See also **atheist** itself.

delay/dally/dilly-dally/dither/shilly-shally (be slow or indecisive)
The basic word is 'delay' – 'be slow or tardy'. 'Dally' implies a loitering or lack of determination, as when a profligate 'dallies' away his youth. 'Dilly-dally' and 'shilly-shally' are similar – the latter deriving from the semi-jocular query 'Shill I? Shall I?',

although 'dilly-dally' suggests that hesitation leads to time being wasted, while 'shilly-shally' implies that indecision itself causes a waste of time. 'Dither' puts the emphasis on the hesitation, which is often accompanied by some kind of confusion or agitation.

delegate/relegate (consign, refer, classify)
To 'delegate' a task to a person is simply to give it to him. To 'relegate' something is often to place it in a lower position, as a football team in the League divisions, or an unwanted circular in the waste paper basket. 'Relegate' can, however, simply mean 'refer', as of a matter to a committee for discussion, or 'classify', as of a newly discovered scientific species to a particular family.

deliberate see **debate**

delicious see **delightful**

delightful/delicious/delectable (very pleasing, very pleasant)
'Delightful' means 'highly pleasing' in any way, as a 'delightful' meal, a 'delightful' holiday, a 'delightful' piece of music or a 'delightful' new neighbour. 'Delicious' means more or less the same, but with particular reference to the senses of taste and smell, so that it is good to eat a 'delicious' apple with its 'delicious' smell. The word can also mean 'very amusing', as a 'delicious' story or a 'delicious' remark made by an innocent child. 'Delectable' really combines the two, so that one can enjoy a 'delectable' view or a 'delectable' **steak and kidney pie** (which see). However, the word also seems to be popularly associated with 'delicate' and 'selectable', so that when applied to people has a more 'personal' connotation: 'Sarah Smith, the delectable actress' is thus more immediately appealing and attractive than 'Sarah Smith, the delightful actress', where the word applies more to her art than to her personal charm.

delivery note see **advice note**

delusion/illusion (mental deception)
There is a nice difference between these

classic confusibles. A 'delusion' is deception caused by something actually being other than it seems, as when a person is under the 'delusion' his food is being poisoned. 'Delusions' thus often refer to something sinister or harmful. An 'illusion' is deception caused by something *appearing* to be other than it really is, so that what is visualised may not exist at all. Thus a mirage is an 'illusion', not a 'delusion'. 'Illusions' are not necessarily unpleasant; they can often be pleasant, or at least harmless. There are, however, certain instances when either word can be used equally meaningfully, as 'If you think you're clever you're under an illusion (a delusion).'

Democrat see **Republican**

demonstrate/remonstrate (show, point out)
Both words have as their root the Latin *monstrare* (show). To 'demonstrate' something is to show it clearly, normally for some specific purpose, as when a suspect 'demonstrates' his innocence – proves it by pointing to particular facts or circumstances. To 'remonstrate' is to protest against something by pleading as if 'demonstrating'. The same suspect might 'remonstrate' with his accusers by protesting his innocence; only if he can clearly 'demonstrate' it, however, will he not be regarded as guilty.

den/lair/covert/burrow (home of a wild animal)
A 'den' is the word for the home of any wild beast, especially one that is a cave, as for a lion or tiger. A 'lair' is not so much a dwelling place as a lying place, that is, a place where a wild animal can rest. A 'covert', too, is not a home in the full sense of the word, but a place of shelter, and in particular a thicket where game animals can hide, or where they happen to be hidden anyway. A 'burrow' is a hole excavated for living in by an animal such as a fox or a rabbit. Some 'burrows' have special names depending on the animal inhabiting it: a badger's 'burrow', for example, is a set (or sett).

denims see **jeans**

denizen see **citizen**

denominator see **numerator**

denote/connote (mean, signify)
'Denote' has the direct meaning 'indicate': a high temperature usually 'denotes' fever, therefore, and thick, black clouds often 'denote' an approaching storm. 'Connote' means 'denote secondarily' i.e. signify something additional to the primary meaning. Thus 'home' 'denotes' living accommodation but it 'connotes' comfort and security.

department/faculty/school (section of a university)
A 'department' deals with a particular field of study, as for example, a 'Department' of English. As such, it usually forms part of a 'faculty', so that the 'Department' of Chemistry, for example, might form part of the 'Faculty' of Science. It follows that a 'faculty' is engaged in the study of a major field of learning such as theology, the arts, law, music, medicine, science, engineering or agriculture. Birmingham University, for example, has five 'faculties': Arts, Science and Engineering, Medicine and Dentistry, Law, and Commerce and Social Sciences. In the USA both words are extended to mean the staff of the respective sections. In some universities several related 'departments' are grouped together as a 'school'. At Leeds University, for example, the 'School' of Chemistry consists of the 'Departments' of Inorganic Chemistry, Organic Chemistry, and Physical Chemistry. This use of the word 'school' originated in the Middle Ages at Oxford, where subjects were arranged in 'schools', not 'faculties' – a practice that continues there even today.

department/ministry (major division of the government)
In the British government, all 'ministries' are 'departments', but not all 'departments' are 'ministries'. 'Ministry', in fact, is a title that has arisen in the twentieth century for certain government 'departments', and is headed, as are most 'departments' themselves, by a minister. Examples are the present 'Ministry' of Defence, and 'Ministry' of Agriculture, Fisheries and Food, and the former 'Ministry' of Food.

Examples of current British 'departments' are the 'Department' of Education and Science, 'Department' of Health and Social Security, and 'Department' of the Environment. Some divisions of the government, although headed by a minister, are called neither a 'ministry' nor a 'department', for example, the Home Office and the Foreign and Commonwealth Office. Many ministers, too, are formally called 'Secretary of State', such as the two who head the divisions just mentioned, the Home Secretary and the Foreign Secretary. Sometimes, as well, there is a special title for the minister, as the Chancellor of the Exchequer who is the head of the Treasury (again, not called a 'department' or 'ministry'), and who is thus the equivalent of the finance minister in other countries. Finally, some 'departments' are not headed by a minister at all, but by a permanent official. This is the case in 'departments' where questions of policy do not arise, such as the Central Office of Information, the Inland Revenue, and the Customs and Excise, which are all run by officials from the Treasury. In Britain, all heads of a 'department' are responsible to Parliament. In the United States, however, heads of 'departments' (all called 'Secretary' except in the 'Department' of Justice, headed by the Attorney General) are responsible to the President, not to Congress.

dependency see **colony**

deplore/deprecate/depreciate (feel reproach or disapproval for)
To 'deplore' a thing is to regret it, usually deeply. To 'deprecate' something is to express strong disapproval of it. If I therefore 'deplore' your behaviour I am upset by it; if I 'deprecate' it I say that I disapprove of it and probably give my reasons. To 'depreciate' has the basic sense 'lower in value', but can also mean 'disparage'. If a speaker makes several good, valid points, why 'depreciate' them simply because you don't agree? See also, out of interest, **self-deprecation**.

deposit account see **current account**

depository/repository (place where things are left or kept)

A 'depository' is a place such as a storehouse or depot (the word is a French cousin) where furniture and the like are kept safely. A 'repository' is on the whole smaller, such as a room, cupboard or chest where things are put for safe keeping or stored – or a place where something is discovered, as a back garden that turns out to be a 'repository' of tin cans and buried bones. Its use is extended to mean 'warehouse' or any place where things are sold, and also to designate the special place where a dead body is deposited.

deprecate see **deplore**

depreciate see **deplore**

depredation see **deprivation**

depressed area/distressed area/development area (area of economic depression or unemployment)
All three terms are government jargon. A 'depressed area' was one in which there was economic depression and unemployment, and a 'distressed area' one in which unemployment was marked. The terms are pre-war ones and the subsequent terms for such areas became, respectively, a 'development area' and a 'special development area'. Both these were officially known as 'assisted areas' in which incentives were offered by the government to encourage industrial development and the movement of office and other service employment.) In 1984, however, a revision of the terms was made, so that a 'development area' was the prime one to receive regional aid, and an 'intermediate area' became the one to receive only selective assistance.

deprivation/depredation (loss)
'Deprivation' is the act of being deprived of something, so that one loses it: war often entails many 'deprivations'. 'Depredations' – the word is normally used in the plural – means 'destruction and robbery', as the 'depredations' that can be caused by birds on fruit bushes or locusts on crops. The word is related to 'prey'. War can also, of course, bring its 'depredations' as well as its 'deprivations'.

depth see **height**

derogate see **abdicate**

derring-do see **daring**

déshabillé see **dishabille**

design see **plan**

designed/destined/predestined
(planned, ordained)
'Designed' means 'intended', even if the desired aim is not actually achieved, as a train 'designed' to travel at over 100 m.p.h. 'Destined' implies that the result is achieved, whether it was desired or not – almost 'foreordained', in fact. Yuri Gagarin was thus 'destined' – and also 'designed' – to be the first man in space. 'Predestined' emphasises the preceding stage of something that (frequently) fails to achieve the desired aim, as an attempt to climb Everest which was 'predestined' to failure: looking back, you can see that it was never likely to have succeeded.

despot see **dictator**

destined see **designed**

destiny see **fate**

detention centre see **remand home**

developed countries see **developing countries**

developing countries/underdeveloped countries/developed countries (class of country determined according to its economic status)
The 'developing countries' – a term now generally favoured instead of 'underdeveloped countries' – are those that have a relatively low *per capita* income compared with the 'developed countries' of North America and western Europe. In most 'developing countries' the majority of the population are engaged in agriculture, with other distinctive features being low rates of literacy, the observance of traditional customs, and the absence of a middle class. Most 'developing countries' are in Asia, Africa, Latin America, and Oceania, and many of them are former colonies. A collective term for them, especially from the viewpoint of countries not politically aligned with communist or western (capitalist) countries, is the 'Third World'.

development area see **depressed area**

deviate see **digress**

devoted/devout (dedicated)
'Devoted' implies a positive show of loyalty, as with a 'devoted' husband, friend or admirer. 'Devout' expresses more of an attitude, one of sincerity and earnestness, as is shown by the 'devout' supporter of a campaign. The word has a religious connotation, which gives it a suggestion of reverence or even fanaticism.

devotion/dedication (loyalty to someone or something)
'Devotion' implies a personal attachment, often an earnest or caring one, and a loyalty in which one is not only involved but wishes to be involved. 'Dedication' has more an implication of duty and perseverance, of a personal committal that may be from choice or from altruistic or external motives. 'Devotion', too, often connotes enthusiasm, while 'dedication' suggests a rather lofty single-mindedness. Perhaps the different shades of meaning can be seen best reflected in the basic senses of the words: 'devotion' is related to 'vow', 'dedication' to 'declare'.

devout see **devoted**

dialect/accent (form of speech differing from the standard)
Broadly, a 'dialect' has different *words* from the standard form of the language, while an 'accent' has a different *pronunciation*. The distinguishing features of a 'dialect' are thus its different grammatical structure and different vocabulary, as found, for example, in the Cornish 'dialect' or the Kentucky 'dialect'. A 'dialect' will, however, almost certainly be spoken with a particular 'accent', especially by a native of the place – although it is perfectly possible to speak standard or 'received' English with a regional 'accent' such as a Yorkshire one.

dialogue/duologue (conversation between two or more persons)
A misleading and rather devious couple, whose exact sense is indicated by the prefixes. A 'dialogue' – the prefix does not mean 'two' but, literally, 'through', 'by means of' – is a conversation between two *or more* persons. A 'duologue', where the prefix does mean 'two', is between two persons only, as in a play. The word was formed by analogy with 'monologue'.

diameter see **radius**

dictator/despot (absolute ruler)
A 'dictator' is a ruler who has absolute control in a government, either without hereditary right or without the free consent of the people. Hitler, Mussolini and Franco are traditionally regarded as 'dictators'. The term 'despot' extends a little wider to denote any absolute ruler, especially one who is a noted tyrant or oppressor. Both words are near-synonyms for autocrat.

diesel oil see **petrol**

difference/distinction (perceivable dissimilarity or disparity)
The 'difference' between two things is the complete or partial lack of identity between them, usually as perceived by one of the senses – they look different, sound different, etc. The 'distinction' between one thing and another is the dissimilarity between them perceived as the result of analysis and/or discrimination, as this dictionary attempts to do. One can in fact have a '"distinction" without a "difference"', which is a way of talking about a discrimination that is artificial or false.

diffident see **indifferent**

digress/diverge/deviate (turn aside)
One 'digresses' mainly when speaking, by wandering from the main topic. Two roads will 'diverge' if they run off at an increasingly widening angle from a common point. To 'deviate' is to turn, literally or figuratively, from a particular path or course, often only slightly or temporarily.

dilemma see **predicament**

dilly-dally see **delay**

dimity see **damask**

dinner see **lunch**

diploma see **degree** (academic qualification)

diplomacy see **tact**

dipsomaniac see **hypochondriac**

direct current see **alternating current**

direction see **order**

director see (1) **president**, (2) **producer**

discerning/discriminating (choosing and distinguishing carefully)
'Discerning' tastes are ones that take minor features into account as well as the major, obvious ones. The word thus implies depth or acuteness of judgment. 'Discriminating' implies a similar attention to detail, but has the additional connotation of a rejection as well as a selection.

disciple see **apostle**

discomfit see **discomfort**

discomfort/discomfit (make uneasy)
To 'discomfort' a person is to disturb his comfort or happiness in some way, as bad news can do. To 'discomfit' is to confuse or disconcert: an airport strike can 'discomfit' your holiday plans considerably. The word is bookish, though, and need not often 'discomfit' you.

discovery see **invention**

discrepancy/disparity (difference)
A 'discrepancy' implies that the difference should not in fact exist, as when one finds a 'discrepancy' in one's bank statement: the figures are not as they should be and not as they usually are. A 'disparity' emphasises the inequality of the difference: one expects the two things to be more alike. People are always ready to point to the 'disparity' in years when a forty-year-old marries someone half this age.

discriminating see **discerning**

disdain see **contempt**

disease see **illness**

disguise/camouflage (concealment of identity)
'Disguise', a fairly general word, usually implies changed dress or at the least a false beard or a wig and dark glasses. 'Camouflage' is a more specialised thing: the disguise of military vehicles, weapons and the like (including weapon-carrying aircraft and ships) by means of smoke screens, patchy paintwork, artificial greenery or foliage, and so on. The design of such 'camouflage' is selected in such a way that the camouflaged object blends with its background and thus is difficult to detect. Animal 'camouflage' works in much the same way, so that the wings of a moth, say, will merge with the bark of the tree on which it is resting, making it less conspicuous to possible predators. It is a popular misconception, incidentally, that the chameleon changes its colour as a form of 'camouflage' to match its background: its colour changes are the result of environmental factors such as light and temperature or of 'emotions' such as victory or defeat in battle with another chameleon. 'Camouflage' is a French word in origin meaning, simply, 'disguise'.

dishabille/déshabillé (state of undress)
Both words are from the French. 'Dishabille', usually pronounced 'disabeel', is the state of being undressed, partly dressed, or dressed carelessly or negligently. 'Déshabillé', also written without accents, is 'days-a-bee-ay' and is usually reserved for a specifically coy state of undress. Strictly speaking, one is *in* 'dishabille' but *en* 'déshabillé'. The second term, however, has lost much of its stylishness now that the phenomenon itself has become so commonplace.

disinfectant/antiseptic (medically cleansing or sterilising agent)
A 'disinfectant' is a chemical agent that destroys bacteria, whether for personal or household use. An 'antiseptic' is an agent that counteracts sepsis by 'preventing' the growth of bacteria. Some agents, of course, are both, which presumably is the ideal combination.

disinflation see **inflation**

disinterested/uninterested (not interested)
The two are not synonyms, and can make a useful distinction. 'Disinterested' means 'impartial', as a 'disinterested' report or account. 'Uninterested' implies boredom through lack of interest. Some AGMs cause members to lapse into an 'uninterested' state. The noun of 'disinterested' is 'disinterest' or, if marked, 'disinterestedness'. Of 'uninterested' the noun is usually 'uninterest', or less often 'uninterestedness'.

disparity see **discrepancy**

dispel see **disperse**

disperse/dispel/dissipate (scatter, drive away)
'Disperse', meaning 'cause to go in different directions', usually applied to an organised body that can be tangibly split up, as a crowd or clouds. Of something intangible, or barely tangible, such as fog or smoke, both 'disperse' and 'dispel' are virtually interchangeable. 'Dissipate' has the additional sense of 'reduce to smaller parts', as of money or resources. When it comes to the nouns, 'dispersal' refers to the act of dispersing, 'dispersion' to the state of having been dispersed.

dissembling/dissimulating/simulating (pretending)
A 'dissembling' nature is one whose real quality is concealed. 'Dissimulating' and 'simulating' are opposites: 'dissimulating' meaning 'pretending not to have what you really do have' (or not to be what you really are); 'simulating' means 'pretending to have (or be) what you do not have (or are not)'. The last two are most often used as active verbs, while 'dissembling' is frequently used as an adjective.

dissentient see **dissenting**

dissenting/dissident/dissentient
(disagreeing)
'Dissenting' means 'feeling or thinking differently'; 'dissident' suggests a strong or active disagreement, as of a 'dissident' voice or vote; 'dissentient' lays the emphasis on one's own views by comparison with those of the majority – at the time of the Reformation in England the Protestants were both 'dissident' and 'dissentient'.

dissident see **dissenting**

dissimulating see **dissembling**

dissipate see **disperse**

dissipated see **dissolute**

dissolute/dissipated (self-indulgent, morally lax)
'Dissolute' describes more the state – one of almost permanent dissipation. One could thus lead a 'dissolute' life, with 'dissolute' friends. With 'dissipated' the emphasis is on the action itself: a person's 'dissipated' appearance has a positive cause. The word is often used as a stronger variant of 'dissolute'. It has also, of course, the emotively neutral meaning 'scattered' (see **disperse**).

dissolution see **abolition**

distemper see **whitewash**

distinct/distinctive (marked)
'Distinct' means 'clear', 'easily noticed', as of a 'distinct' improvement in the economy or a 'distinct' nip in the air. The word frequently implies a comparison. 'Distinctive' means 'serving to distinguish' or 'characteristic', so that someone who speaks with a 'distinctive' authority is expected to do so, since such authority is one of his characteristics.

distinction see **difference**

distinctive see **distinct**

distracted see **distraught**

distrait see **distraught**

distraught/distressed/distracted/distrait
(mentally or physically disturbed)
A person who is 'distraught' usually behaves irrationally under the pressure of a deep emotion such as fear or grief. A 'distressed' person is one seen to suffer as the result of a strong emotion or some kind of pain. With 'distracted' the disturbance is nearly always a mental one, and there is not necessarily any implication of physical suffering. The word can, in fact, mean little more than 'diverted'. 'Distrait', from the French, means 'absent-minded' – not so much 'distracted' as 'abstracted'.

distressed see **distraught**

distressed area see **depressed area**

distrust/mistrust (not trust)
The weaker word is 'mistrust', as in similar pairs of words with these prefixes such as 'disbelief/misbelief'. It means 'not trust' to any degree, even a slight one: if you 'mistrust' my motives, you have doubts about them. 'Distrust', on the other hand, means 'regard (one hundred per cent) with suspicion': if you 'distrust' my judgment you have no faith in it. Put another way, 'mistrust' is a more negative word; 'distrust' a positive one.

disturb/perturb (unsettle, agitate)
'Disturb' tends to apply to a physical or mental unsettling – a sudden hammering on the door at night would probably 'disturb' you both physically and mentally. 'Perturb' applies mainly to a mental state: one can be 'perturbed' by bad news or a vivid account of something unpleasant.

dither see **delay**

divan see **couch**

diverge see **digress**

divers see **diverse**

diverse/divers (various)
'Diverse' has the meaning 'of different or various kinds', such as 'diverse' opinions, painting materials or habits. 'Divers' is simply a quaint or poetic word meaning

'several', as in 'divers' complaints. It used to mean 'diverse', however, hence the 'divers manners' referred to by St Paul at the beginning of his Epistle to the Hebrews.

divine/dowse (search for water or metal hidden underground)
'Divine' is a more general word, meaning basically 'make known'. To 'divine' water is to discover it by means of a 'divining' rod of some kind. To 'dowse' – in spite of its appearance no relation to 'douse' – is more to search for water in this way. Thus 'divining' implies a finding; 'dowsing' merely a searching.

division see **corps**

dizziness/giddiness/vertigo (sensation of whirling or revolving)
'Dizziness' is usually experienced in the head, resulting in a dazed state (the words are similar, but not actually related) and tottering steps or an unsteady stance. 'Giddiness' emphasises the rapid whirling motion experienced when looking down from a height, for example, with a sudden sensation of unsteadiness or even nausea. 'Vertigo' is the medical term for either of these, or even both together, whether the cause is physical or psychological. All three are equally unpleasant.

doctor/surgeon/physician (medically qualified practitioner)
A 'doctor', formally a 'physician', usually means a general practitioner (GP), that is, a 'doctor' advises and prescribes medicines and treatments for all kinds of diseases and conditions, as opposed to a **consultant** or specialist. In the USA, the term 'doctor' can also be applied to a dentist or a veterinary surgeon. A 'surgeon', who has also received a full medical training, practises surgery, usually of one speciality or another. He is addressed in Britain as Mr (not 'doctor'). In the Navy and the Army all medical officers are called 'surgeons'. A 'physician' is the technical and old-fashioned name for a 'doctor' and in fact means a teacher. For a list of local 'doctors' in the Yellow Pages telephone directory you must search under 'physicians and surgeons' since there is no classification under 'doctor'.

doddering/doting (senile)
Literally, 'doddering' is descriptive of one who dodders or trembles, shakes, and otherwise shows the enfeebled physical powers of extreme old age. A 'doddering' old man is really no more than an aged one, therefore, although the word is often used with the overtone of 'senile'. 'Doting' really does mean 'senile', with the lack of emotional stability that the word implies. The reference is to a feeble old man's pathetic affection – he 'dotes' on the past or a world in which he is no longer young.

doe see **stag**

dolmen see **cromlech**

dolphin/porpoise (small member of the whale family)
The 'porpoise' is usually smaller than the 'dolphin' and is chubbier in shape, with a blunt snout rather than a beak-like one. Both creatures are intelligent, the 'dolphin' to the extent that it is sometimes said to have a learning ability second only to that of man, performing complex tricks for public entertainment in dolphinariums.

dolphin

porpoise

dome/cupola (rounded roof on a church or other building)
A 'dome' is a rounded vault with a base

that is circular, elliptical or polygonal. A 'cupola' is a small 'dome' that either forms the roof or simply adorns it. For a fine example of a 'dome', see St Paul's, London, or St Peter's, Rome. For some typical 'cupolas', see the bulbous roofs of virtually any Greek or Russian Orthodox church – and also the Royal Pavilion at Brighton.

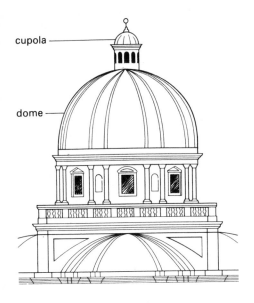

cupola

dome

dominating/domineering (controlling, governing)
'Dominating' can apply to an authority that is reasonable or unreasonable: a 'dominating' position may be simply a commanding one; a 'dominating' manner is usually a bossy one. 'Domineering' suggests a tyrannising or overbearing position, so that a 'domineering' manner is an unpleasantly haughty one.

domineering see **dominating**

dominion see **colony**

don/fellow (senior member of a university or college)
A 'don' is a rather vague word to mean any senior member of a college, especially one at Oxford or Cambridge, whether a college head, a 'fellow' or a tutor. It can be used rather disparagingly to denote a stuffy or bombastic academic, as Hilaire Belloc's 'Remote and ineffectual Don'. Rather surprisingly for an 'establishment' word, the term originates in the Spanish title (meaning something like 'lord'), as in Don Quixote or Don Juan. A 'fellow' is the term for an incorporated (i.e. 'regular') senior member of a college. It can also be used of a graduate receiving a stipend for a period of research and, in some universities, of a member of the governing body. A 'fellow', too, is the title of the senior member of a learned society, as a 'Fellow' of the Royal Society. It is rather an unusual word in having both a formal, academic meaning (senior member) and an informal, familiar one (bloke, chap, 'fella'). Its origin is unexpected, also: a 'fellow' was once a 'fee-layer', one who laid down money in a joint undertaking.

donkey/ass/mule (animal like a small horse renowned for its stubbornness or stupidity)
A 'donkey' is an 'ass', and an 'ass' is a 'donkey': they are one and the same beast. Originally 'donkey' was regarded as a slang word, even as late as the early nineteenth century; originally, too, it rhymed with 'monkey'. Today it is the more common name for the animal, which differs from a horse not merely in just being smaller but in having a tuft of hair at the end of its tail, no warts on its hind legs, and especially, the presence of stripes, although not in the domestic 'donkey'. A 'mule' is properly the offspring of a he-'ass' and a mare, or, popularly, of a she-'ass' and a stallion (which properly is a hinny). The 'hybrid' sense of 'mule' is also seen in the related word 'mulatto', which is the word for the child of a white-skinned person and a black. 'Donkeys' are proverbially stupid or stubborn, but not always actually so. Through biblical associations they are also regarded as patient and humble creatures. In the USA 'donkey' is preferred to 'ass' since the latter word also means 'buttocks' and even 'sexual intercourse' ('piece of ass').

doom see **fate**

doting see **doddering**

doubtful/dubious (unwilling to believe, open to question)

'Doubtful' suggests that more evidence is needed for something to be believed, as when one is 'doubtful' about a person's ability, or a book is of 'doubtful' content. 'Dubious' implies greater uncertainty than 'doubtful', so that 'dubious' hopes of winning are very small and a book of 'dubious' content has little merit and is not regarded as worth the buying or reading. 'Dubious' company is company that is morally suspect; 'doubtful' company *may* be morally suspect.

dove see **pigeon**

doves see **hawks**

downstage see **upstage**

dowse see **divine**

doze/drowse/snooze (be briefly or lightly asleep)

To 'doze' is to sleep lightly or fitfully, especially when feeling tired but not wishing to fall asleep properly. To 'drowse' is to half-succumb to weariness and to be close to falling fast asleep. To 'snooze' is to have a pleasant daytime nap or short sleep, such as when relaxing in the garden on a warm summer's day, or even in one's office after a good lunch. A 'snooze' can also be the short relapsing into sleep that can occur on waking in the morning, especially when the desire to get up is not strong. Hence the 'snooze' button on many bedside radios and alarms: press it, and it will wake you after a particular number of minutes, allowing you to 'drowse off' again, or simply to 'doze'.

drab/dreary (dull, tedious, colourless)

'Drab' is a more negative word, suggesting lack of colour or cheerfulness. Oddly, it derives from the French *drap* (cloth), meaning material that is undyed and therefore cheerless. 'Dreary' is a positive word suggesting sadness, active tedium and – possibly by association with 'weary' – tiredness and fatigue. Thus a 'drab' voice is an expressionless one, while a 'dreary' voice is a boring, depressing one.

Dracula see **Frankenstein**

dragoman see **dragon**

dragon/dragoon/dragoman/gorgon (fearsomely powerful person)

Applied figuratively, a 'dragon' is a fierce or violent or domineering person, often one in authority. A 'dragoon' is properly a cavalryman or a mounted infantryman with a musket (the word derives from French *dragon* – the term for the hammer of a firearm). The noun is not in common use, although the verb – 'to force by rigorous and oppressive measures' – is quite common. Some 'dragons' do indeed 'dragoon'. A 'dragoman' is really in the wrong box – he is a professional interpreter in the Middle East, more to be revered than feared. All three words, however, fall under the additional influence of 'Draconian' meaning 'harsh', 'very severe', as were the laws of the Athenian statesman Draco in the seventh century BC. A 'dragon' is usually female; a 'gorgon' always is. The Gorgons, from the Greek *gorgos* (terrible), were the three mythological sisters whose glance turned their beholder to stone. The word still comes in handy to describe a repulsive-looking woman.

dragoon see **dragon**

dram see **gram**

dramatist/playwright (writer of plays)

A 'dramatist' writes mostly dramas (in effect, a play of any kind, not necessarily a serious one) or dramatic poetry. A 'playwright' also writes plays ('wright' meaning 'maker', not 'writer'), but often combines his play-writing with another activity, as 'actor and playwright' or 'novelist and playwright', or perhaps regards himself, or is regarded, as less of a professional or 'dedicated' writer of plays than a serious-minded, full-time 'dramatist'. Perhaps the difference is similar to that between 'lyricist' and 'song-writer': it's really a question of how one views the activity and the person who does it.

draught horse/dray horse (strong horse used for pulling loads)

A 'draught horse' is – increasingly was – one that works on a farm drawing loads, pulling ploughs and the like. A 'dray horse' is a strong carthorse or other powerful horse that is used for pulling a 'dray' – a low cart without fixed sides as that used by breweries.

dray horse see **draught horse**

dreary see **drab**

dress/frock/gown (main garment worn by a woman or girl)
'Dress' is the general word for the garment that in essence combines bodice and skirt. It is also, of course, an even more general word for the clothing of both sexes, especially when the clothes are formal, as 'morning dress'. 'Frock' is virtually the same as 'dress', but a more restricted word, and used in particular of girls' 'dresses', as a party 'frock' or a pretty 'frock'. Narrowly, the word means the long 'gown' worn by a monk, or priest formerly – hence 'unfrocked', of a priest who has been officially deprived or relieved of his status in the church. 'Gown' is used in specialised instances (as in the last sentence) for the long, loose, flowing garment worn as part of an official costume or 'dress', as a judge's 'gown', surgeon's 'gown', or a university student's 'gown'. More commonly, though, it is the word for a 'dress' that is elegant or fashionable, especially a long one.

dress circle see **balcony** (section of the auditorium of a theatre)

dresser see **sideboard**

driving licence/vehicle licence/road fund licence (type of licence needed for a vehicle to travel on a public road)
A 'driving licence' is the one that must be held by the driver of a vehicle. It is normally either a 'full' licence, held until he is 70 years old, or 'provisional', valid for one year while he is learning to drive (that is, before he has passed his driving test). This is the licence that is 'endorsed' for traffic offences. A 'vehicle licence' and 'road fund licence' are one and the same thing – a licence that must be bought periodically, usually annu-

ally or quarterly, permitting a vehicle to be on the road. The holding of this licence is indicated by the licence disc that is usually displayed in the bottom left-hand corner of the windscreen.

drove see **flock**

drowse see **doze**

dryad/naiad (nymph)
'Dryads' were thought to live in trees: the word has no connection with 'dry' – as distinct, say, from a water nymph – but comes from Greek *drys* (tree). 'Naiads' were indeed water nymphs, said to live in streams and springs. Their name is related to the Greek verb *naein* (to flow). For more mythological maidens see **nymph** itself.

dubious see **doubtful**

ducking-stool/cucking-stool (former type of punishment chair)
A 'ducking-stool', as its name implies, was a seat like a chair (usually on the end of a plank) in which an offender was ducked in a local pond or river by way of punishment. A 'cucking-stool' could also be used for this, but was likewise a seat to which offenders such as dishonest traders were simply tied so that they could be pelted with unpleasant missiles, jeered at, and otherwise subjected to abuse, rather in the manner of a person in the **stocks** (which see). Since an offender could be in the chair for some time, however, the seat was a 'close-stool' or basic form of commode. Hence the origin of the name, which means literally 'defecating chair'. (Its medieval Latin name was *cathedra stercoris*, 'chair of excrement'.)

duke/earl/viscount/count (rank of the nobility)
A 'duke', the highest of the four, can be either a royal 'duke', who is a prince, or ruler of a duchy (there are at present only five royal 'dukes' in Britain: of Edinburgh, York, Cornwall, Gloucester and Kent, three of these princes), or the title of a nobleman of the next highest rank after a prince, and next above a marquess. (There were twenty-six dukes in Britain in 1987, from Abercorn to Westminster.) An 'earl' holds the next

rank below a marquess. His wife is called a countess (for 'counts', read on). A 'viscount' ranks below an 'earl' (or a 'count') and next above a baron. The title is also held by the son or younger brother of an 'earl' or 'count'. 'Counts' as such no longer exist in Britain, although they do in France, as *Comte,* or Germany, as *Graf,* or Italy, as *Conto.* In fact after the Norman Conquest, 'earls' were called 'counts' for a while, and it is just one of the quirks of British history and the English language that although we still have counties and countesses, there are no 'counts' to oversee either.

dumbfounded see **astonished**

duologue see **dialogue**

dusk/twilight (time between daylight and darkness)
'Dusk' is a darker stage of 'twilight', when things cannot be clearly discerned. Loosely, 'twilight' is the period between sunset and darkness – or, less often, between night and sunrise. Astronomically, it begins when the Sun's centre is 18 degrees below the horizon, which is the angle at which no light from the Sun can reach an observer. Civil 'twilight' begins when the Sun's centre is 6 degrees below the horizon. This is usually half an hour to an hour after sunset, and determines lighting-up time (which for sake of convenience is from half an hour after sunset to half an hour before sunrise). The word means 'half light', or more exactly 'between light', since it comes between day and night (or night and day).

duty see **tax**

dwarf see (1) **goblin**, (2) **midget**

dynamite/gelignite/TNT (type of high explosive)

'Dynamite' is the oldest of the three. It was invented and named in 1866 by Alfred Nobel – founder of the Nobel Prizes – as a powerful ('dynamic') high explosive of nitroglycerine mixed with some absorbent substance such as kieselguhr (a type of sand). 'Gelignite' is a gelatin type of 'dynamite', with less nitroglycerine but with an

oxidant such as potassium nitrate. Its chief use is for blasting. 'TNT', or *trinitrotoluene* – otherwise $CH_3C_6H_2(NO_2)_3$ – arrived in the twentieth century and has a use that can be military or general. Its chief advantage over its two rivals is that, although exploded by detonators, it is unaffected by ordinary friction or shock.

E

earl see **duke**

earth see **world**

eatable/edible (fit or able to be eaten)
'Eatable' applies to something that is palatable. More often than not, its opposite is used, so that 'uneatable' is used of food that is unpleasant or difficult to eat for some reason, as an oversalted stew or an underdone potato – 'quite uneatable'. 'Edible' means 'suitable for eating', such as an 'edible' fungus or plant. If something is 'inedible' it cannot be eaten however well it is prepared.

eccentric/erratic (deviating from the normal)
An 'eccentric' person deviates markedly from the normal; what he does is noticeably unusual. An 'erratic' person behaves in an irregular, inconsistent or unpredictable manner; you are not sure what he is going to do next. To this degree, an 'erratic' person can be said to be 'eccentric', since most people are normally consistent and reasonably predictable.

Ecclesiastes/Ecclesiasticus (book of the Bible)
'Ecclesiastes' is a book of the Old Testament, perhaps written about 250 BC. Its name, via Late Latin, comes from the Greek word meaning 'member of the assembly'.

Its Hebrew title, occurring in the Bible only in this book, is *Koheleth*, 'the preacher', apparently with reference to the 'herald' who summoned an assembly. Although the book is ascribed to Solomon, this is simply a literary device, and its true author is unknown. It is noted for its pessimism and even agnosticism, and in effect represents an unresolved conflict between faith in God and the vanity of human life. (One of its most famous quotations is 'Vanity of vanities; all is vanity'). 'Ecclesiasticus' is a book of the Apocrypha, where it is the longest book in the Bible. Its Latin title means 'church book', whereas in Greek it is called 'The Wisdom of Jesus, Son of Sirach' (or simply 'Wisdom of Sirach'). Its original name in Hebrew is said to have translated as 'Proverbs'. It consists of a whole range of practical morals and exhortations, and is the source of many famous quotations, such as 'Let us now praise famous men' and 'Their name liveth for evermore', as well as the heartfelt 'Of making of many books there is no end'. It was probably written, by the scribe Jesus ben Sirach, in about 180 BC.

Ecclesiasticus see **Ecclesiastes**

éclat/élan (spirit)
Two French words meaning respectively 'flash' and 'dash'. 'Éclat' implies a brilliance of some kind, of success, reputation, performance or display. An orator of great 'éclat' thus speaks skilfully and with polish – and is no doubt famous for his eloquence. 'Élan' indicates ardour or zeal rather than accomplishment: someone who plays the part of Henry V with 'élan' does so with spirit but would have to play it with 'éclat' to give a really professional performance.

eclectic see **esoteric**

economic/economical (relating to the economy)
The words overlap, with one frequently used as the other. But to differentiate: 'economic' pertains to the economy, as an 'economic' crisis, to economics, as in the science of 'economic' geography, or to economy in the sense 'thrift', as in an 'economic' rent. 'Economical' is confined to this last sense,

and means 'thrifty', as an 'economical' detergent (you need use only a little).

economical see **economic**

edible see **eatable**

edification see **education**

education/edification (instruction, enlightenment)
'For your edification . . .' someone begins ominously. Is he aiming to teach us a home truth or two? In origin, 'edification' is not related to 'education' but to 'edify', from Latin *aedificare* (to build). 'Edification' is the 'building up', therefore, of one's morality, and has the aim of increasing one's knowledge of right and wrong as well as improving one's mind. 'Education' is in its strictest sense the imparting of knowledge pure and simple.

effect see **affect**

effective/effectual/efficacious/efficient (producing results)
'Effective' means 'producing an effect', so that one can give an 'effective' speech or take 'effective' steps to solve something. 'Effectual' means 'producing a particular effect' – one that was possibly not intended, as when warm week-end weather leads to an 'effectual' mass exodus of city dwellers to the country. 'Efficacious' means 'capable of producing an effect' – but usually a medical one, and with the implication that the result is conditional on the application of the means, as an 'efficacious' medicine (it will work only if you take it). 'Efficient', of things or people, means 'effortlessly effective', as of a plan or an organiser. 'Efficacious' has a choice of nouns: 'efficaciousness', 'efficacity' or 'efficacy' – but the last can also double as the noun for 'effective'.

effectual see **effective**

effeminate/effete (unmanly, feeble)
'Effeminate' means 'womanish' of a man, hence 'unmanly', as of an 'effeminate' gesture, walk or voice. 'Effete' means 'worn out', hence 'weak', 'useless'. Oddly, the word applies properly to women, since it

derives from Latin *effetus* (exhausted by bearing children). The word is thus related to 'foetus'.

effete see **effeminate**

efficacious see **effective**

efficient see **effective**

e.g./i.e. (abbreviation indicating that more precise information follows)
Both abbreviations are of Latin phrases, namely *exempli gratia* (for sake of an example) and *id est* (that is). 'E.g.' indicates that one or more specific examples follow what has been mentioned in general terms. Thus many crustaceans, 'e.g.' crabs, lobsters and shrimps, are edible. ('E.g.' introduces examples of what a crustacean is.) 'I.e.', on the other hand, gives an explanation of what has been mentioned, so that many crustaceans, 'i.e.' those sea creatures that have legs and a hard shell, are edible. ('I.e.' introduces an explanation of what a crustacean is.) The two abbreviations are often confused, especially in official notices. One hospital appointments card, for example, asks patients to 'notify the appointments clerk of any change in their personal particulars (i.e. change of address)'.

egoist/egotist (self-centred person)
The difference, in essence, is that an 'egoist', although self-centred, is not necessarily deliberately so; an 'egotist' is.

egotist see **egoist**

élan see **éclat**

elated see **elevated**

elder/older (older or senior)
'Elder' means 'older' only in family relationships, as an 'elder' brother or sister. Of two specified people, it means 'senior', as the 'elder' of two partners. 'Older' means 'older' in all other senses.

elect/élite (chosen group)
The 'elect' comprise any persons chosen for something – not necessarily the best. The 'élite', from the French *élire* (to elect) are, by contrast, the best, the most choice – usually of some group or set that is already of high or recognised quality, such as the 'élite' of the aristocracy or of the entertainment world.

elemental see **elementary**

elementary/elemental (basic, fundamental)
Literally, 'elementary' means 'pertaining to elements', so in some cases has a meaning close to 'primary'. Commonly, however, it means 'basic', 'simple', as in an 'elementary' fact, or argument for or against something. 'Elemental' means 'pertaining to the elements' – either chemical elements or, often, the forces of nature or of some spirit, as in the 'elemental' beauty of the polar regions or the 'elemental' grandeur of a symphony or portrait.

elevated/elated/exalted (raised up, set high)
'Elevated' has both a literal and figurative usage, so that an 'elevated' position can be a high one or a senior one. 'Elated' means 'proudly jubilant' – 'feeling high', in a way. 'Exalted' means 'nobly elevated', as an 'exalted' rank or 'exalted' style of writing.

elf see **goblin**

élite see **elect**

elope see **escape**

elude see **avoid**

embassy/consulate/legation/high commission (official residence of the diplomatic representative in a foreign country)
An 'embassy' is the residence of the ambassador, a diplomatic agent of the highest rank. The 'consulate' is the resident of the consul, who though not officially a diplomat is a diplomatic agent carrying out particular administrative duties, such as issuing visas, renewing passports and the like, as well as – and chiefly – fostering the commercial interests of his country and aiding its citizens in a foreign city. Many

countries thus have both an 'embassy' and a 'consulate', often in quite different buildings. A 'legation' is the residence of the legate, now an obsolete term for an ambassador, and in practice that of a diplomatic minister such as a chargé d'affaires (an ambassador's deputy) or an envoy (who ranks above a chargé d'affaires but below an ambassador). A 'high commission' is the residence of the High Commissioner, which is the title of the head of an 'embassy' from one Commonwealth country to another. 'Residence' here, of course, means not just dwelling place but central office.

emend see **amend**

emerald/jade (green stone, or its colour)
'Emerald' is a precious stone, bright green in colour and a variety of beryl. 'Jade' is a hard green stone (or a blue or white one), used as an ornament or for implements, and varying from bluish green to yellowish green in colour.

emergency/crisis (serious situation)
Both words are beloved by headline writers: '"Emergency" union meeting', 'Oil tanker "emergency"', '"Crisis" discussions', 'England face "crisis"' (they might lose the next test match at cricket). Distinguishing, however: an 'emergency' is a serious situation that has arisen and which has to be dealt with urgently, as a plane making an 'emergency' landing; a 'crisis' is not just a grave situation but properly the turning point in one, on which everything depends, as a financial 'crisis', personal or nationwide. 'Emergency' is misused slightly more often than 'crisis', perhaps, when it means 'sudden serious situation'. (Possibly, too, the word itself suggests 'urgent', which reinforces this misuse.)

emigrant see **immigrant**

émigré see **immigrant**

Emmy/Grammy/Tony (American performing arts award)
An 'Emmy' – said to be an alteration of 'Immy', a jargon term for an image orthicon tube – is a statuette awarded by the American Academy of Television Arts and Sciences to an outstanding television programme or performer, the Oscar of television, therefore. A 'Grammy', from 'gramophone', is a gold-plated record awarded by the National Academy of Recording Arts and Sciences for achievement in gramophone recording. A 'Tony', named after the American actress Antoinette Perry, is the Broadway equivalent of an Oscar, i.e. an award for the theatre. See also **platinum**.

emotional/emotive (pertaining to the emotions)
'Emotional' means 'affected by or appealing to the emotions', as an 'emotional' greeting or an 'emotional' girl. 'Emotive' means 'tending to affect the emotions', 'not impassive'. Abortion is thus an 'emotive' issue.

emotive see **emotional**

empathy see **sympathy**

empirical/pragmatic (relating to practicalities rather than theories)
These rather impressive-looking words sometimes feature in the utterances of politicians and economists, so it is just as well to know what they mean. 'Empirical' (nothing to do with 'empire' or 'imperial') refers to something that derives from experiment and observation rather than theory, such as medical treatment. In philosophy, the reference is similarly to experience rather than to logic from first principles. The origin of the word is in Greek *empeirikos*, 'practised'. 'Pragmatic' refers to behaviour or procedure that is dictated more by practical consequences than by theory, so that the important thing is what is immediately suitable or convenient, without heed for moral or intellectual considerations. Greek *pragma*, from which the word derives, means 'deed', 'act'. So the two words look respectively at the practical lessons of the past and the practical outcome of the immediate future, with a minimum of moralising or reasoning. Many of our day-to-day judgments are both 'empirical' and 'pragmatic' without our realising it.

encumbent see **incumbent**

encumber/lumber (burden)

The words are close in meaning, although 'encumber' has more the sense of 'hamper', and 'lumber' that of 'saddle'. A passage thus 'encumbered' with furniture is one that it is difficult to get through, an obstructed one; a passage 'lumbered' with furniture is one that has an undue quantity of bulky furniture in it. The origins of the words reflect this distinction: 'encumber' derives from French *encombrer* (to block up), while 'lumber' seems to be from the other 'lumber' – to move clumsily, as to 'lumber along' – with a strong association with 'lumber', the now obsolete word for a pawnbroker's shop. 'Cumbersome' probably derives from 'encumber'. (For two confusible colleagues, see **incumbent**). The element '-umb-' or '-ump-' suggests clumsiness or bulkiness in a number of words – besides these particular two there are: 'clump', 'lump', 'bump', 'bumble', 'rumble', 'fumble', 'dump', 'tumble', 'stump', 'plump', 'mumps', 'hump', 'slump', 'stumble', among others. The Clumber spaniel, however, is not a noticeably heavy or awkward dog, although it is the largest of the English sporting spaniels. It was developed at Clumber Park, Nottinghamshire, towards the end of the eighteenth century.

endemic see **epidemic**

endive see **chive**

enemy/opponent/foe (person or persons hostile to one, an adversary)
An 'enemy' is a hostile opposition, personal or general, domestic or military, literal or metaphorical. An 'opponent' is not necessarily hostile, but simply someone who is acceptably matched against you, as in a sport or a debate. A 'foe' is a rather rarefied 'enemy', especially a fearful or spiritual one. The word seems to imply, too, a consequent danger, as a deadly 'foe'. The word is related to 'feud', not 'fear', however.

England/Britain/Great Britain/British Isles/United Kingdom (native land of the English or British)
The various names present special difficulties to non-English-speaking people, in whose languages 'England', for example,

tends to mean the whole of the 'British Isles', including Ireland. In spite of nebulous areas, it is possible, however, to make certain reasonably clear distinctions. 'England' is the southern and chief country of the island of 'Great Britain', as distinguished from Scotland to the north and Wales to the west. 'Britain' is a fairly informal name, and possibly a more emotive one, for either 'Great Britain' or, more commonly, the whole of the 'United Kingdom'. 'Great Britain', thus, comprises 'England', Scotland and Wales. It is 'Great' not so much for its age or authority but as opposed to 'Little' Britain, better known as Brittany, so named from the flight to this land of Celts from (historic) 'Britain' when the Angles and Saxons invaded their native country in the fifth and sixth centuries. The 'British Isles' is the name for the islands that comprise 'Great Britain' and Ireland (both Northern Ireland and the Irish Republic), including small islands such as the Orkney and Shetland Isles to the north and the Scilly Isles to the south-west. The Isle of Man and the Channel Islands, however, although not normally regarded as belonging to 'Great Britain' are often included in the 'British Isles'. The 'United Kingdom' is the most official of all the names, and its full version, the 'United Kingdom' of 'Great Britain' and Northern Ireland, is administratively self-explanatory.

engraving/etching (drawing or picture made by cutting into stone or metal)
An 'engraving' is done by cutting words, a pattern or a drawing in metal, stone, wood, glass, or other incisable substance. An 'etching' is a form of 'engraving' in which the cutting is done not with a cutting tool but with acids or corrosives, and moreover on metal only. The metal plate to be etched is first coated with a thin layer of gums, waxes and resins (the'"etching"-ground') through which the drawing or pattern is scratched. The plate is then placed in an acid bath and the acid bites or 'eats' (which is the origin of the word 'etch') into the lines traced. The actual etching has to be executed in mirror form, back to front, so that the positive print it produces is the right way round on paper. The 'etching'

originated from the custom of etching designs on armour: those responsible for doing this, either enterprisingly or lazily, found it easier to etch this way instead of cutting.

enormity see **enormousness**

enormousness/enormity (wickedness)
'Enormousness' is the noun of 'enormous', usually literally, so that you can talk of the 'enormousness' of a castle, of someone's appetite, or of the ocean. Less commonly, however, 'enormousness' can mean 'great wickedness', as the 'enormousness' of someone's offence. 'Enormity' is frequently used to mean 'enormousness', but really refers to the quality of being *too* large, so that whatever it is is outrageous, monstrous or shocking, or especially wicked. You can thus speak about the 'enormity' of a crime, a lie, a deception or a person's behaviour. However, 'enormous' has long been used to mean 'shocking', and the two nouns have been equated since the seventeenth century. Even the poet Donne wrote (in 1631) about 'the enormousness of our rebellious sin', using the now less common sense of the word.

enquiry/inquiry (request or demand for information)
Pedants claim there is a distinction. For the record, then: 'enquiry' is simply 'asking', as an 'enquiry' about one's health or where to book a seat on a train. 'Inquiry' is more of an investigation, so that police carry out 'inquiries' into a case. Most dictionaries, however, make no distinction between the two.

ensure see **assure**

enthralled see **thrilled**

en-tout-cas see **passe-partout**

enviable see **envious**

envious/enviable (expressing envy, or worthy of it)
'Envious' expresses envy, as an 'envious' expression, desire or look. 'Enviable' is 'causing envy', as an 'enviable' position, salary or charm.

envy/jealousy (feeling of resentment caused by someone else having something that one does not have oneself)
'Envy', one of the seven deadly sins, does not necessarily imply a feeling of ill will, but often simply a longing for something that someone else has, even if it is theirs by right. 'Jealousy' is a much more personal thing, a feeling that the other person's right to what he has is not as great as one's own, with a consequent sense of rivalry, as a tussle of love or a contest for promotion at work; you have the prior claim, you know you have!

épée see **foil**

epic/epos (long 'heroic' poem)
An 'epic', in the strict literary sense, is a long narrative poem, on a grand scale, about the deeds of warriors and heroes. An 'epic' can be primary (oral) or secondary (literary). Examples of a primary 'epic' are Homer's *Iliad* and *Odyssey* and the anonymous *Beowulf*, while secondary 'epics' include such works as Virgil's *Aeneid* and Milton's *Paradise Lost*. (Primary 'epics' may, much later, appear in a written version; basically, however, they are composed orally and recited. Secondary 'epics' appear only in written form.) An 'epos' is an early 'epic' poem of the primary kind, as the Homeric works above mentioned. Both words originate in Greek *epos* (word, song). 'Epic' has since come to be applied on a wider scale to a heroic-type novel or film such as Tolstoy's *War and Peace* (novel and film) and the grandiose cinematic creations of Cecil B. de Mille who as the clerihew records:

> Was feeling ill
> Because he couldn't put Moses
> In the Wars of the Roses.

epidemic/endemic/pandemic (wide spread disease)
An 'epidemic' is a disease that affects many people at the same time, such as a flu 'epidemic' or the former typhoid 'epidemics' that used to plague European countries. An 'endemic' (the word is more often used as an adjective) is a disease that is not brought in from outside but is native to the people or region concerned, affecting only the local

population. A 'pandemic' is an extensive 'epidemic' that ranges widely, such as the Black Death did. The three words derive from three Greek words that mean literally, respectively, 'among the people', 'in the people' and 'all the people'.

epigram/epitaph/epigraph (short saying or inscription)
An 'epigram' is a witty or pointed saying or a short satirical poem. An 'epitaph', from the Greek for 'funeral oration', is a commemorative 'epigraph' such as those seen on tombs. An 'epigraph' itself is either an inscription, as that on a statue or building, or a quotation at the start of a book, head of a chapter, etc. An example of a combined 'epigram' and 'epitaph' is Lord Rochester's lines on Charles II:

Here lies our sovereign lord, the King,
Whose promise none relies on;
He never said a foolish thing,
Nor ever did a wise one.

epigraph see **epigram**

epitaph see **epigram**

epoch see **era**

epos see **epic**

epsilon/upsilon (letter of the Greek alphabet)
'Epsilon', literally 'e simple', is the fifth letter of the Greek alphabet: Ε, ε, 'Upsilon', or 'u simple', is the twentieth letter: Υ, υ. The first corresponds to English short 'e', as in 'epic', the second to 'u' or 'y', as in 'lyric' – as Greek respectively ἐπικός and λυρικός.

equable/equitable (fair, even)
Both words mean 'fair', but in different senses. 'Equable' means 'pleasant', as an 'equable' climate or an 'equable' nature. 'Equitable' means 'just', 'showing fair-mindedness', as an 'equitable' decision or an 'equitable' judge.

equitable see **equable**

era/epoch/aeon (age)

An 'era' is an age when conditions change and a new order begins, as the Christian 'era' or the 'era' of discovery. Geology uses 'era' for a major division of time, as the Mesozoic 'era', which extended for 160 million years. An 'epoch' is properly the start of an 'era', such as an 'epoch' of hostility, although in practice it is frequently used as a simple alternative for 'age'. The original sense still exists in 'epoch-making', however. An 'aeon' or 'eon' is an indefinitely long period of time. In geology it is the largest division of time, comprising two or more 'eras'. ('Epoch' for geologists is one of the main divisions of a geological period, such as the Holocene and **Pleistocene** 'epochs' which make up the Quaternary period.)

ermine see **mink**

erode/corrode (eat away, gnaw away)
'Erode' has the sense 'destroy by slowly eating away', as of rain or a river current on soil or a bank, or figuratively, as of imprisonment 'eroding' a person's will. 'Corrode' implies a more sinister action, and not just eating away at one point but all over. Thus acid 'corrodes' metal and envy can 'corrode', i.e. impair, one's whole outlook on life.

erotic see **exotic**

erratic see **eccentric**

error see **mistake**

eruption/irruption (violent rushing or spreading)
The two are in fact opposites, with the same 'out' and 'in' prefixes as 'emigrant' and **immigrant**. An 'eruption' is an outbreak of something, as lava from a volcano or a rash on one's skin. An 'irruption', literally a 'break-in', is an inrush or invasion of something, as of water through a broken dam or sales shoppers storming a store. Sometimes 'irruption' is wrongly used to mean 'skin-rash' in place of 'eruption', possibly by false association with 'irritation'.

escape/elope (run away)

To 'escape' is to get away in general from something, usually something dangerous or unpleasant, as prison or an accident. To 'elope' primarily suggests running away with a lover in order to marry without parental consent, but it can also mean 'abscond', i.e. 'escape secretly', so that a shop-assistant might be accused of 'eloping' with the day's takings – making off with them.

esoteric/eclectic (superior, 'choosy')
'Esoteric' literally means 'intended for the few or the initiated' and derives from the Greek *esoterikos* (inner). 'Esoteric' poetry is thus written for the chosen or privileged few who can understand or appreciate it. The opposite, an even more 'esoteric' word, is 'exoteric' – 'intended or fit for the public at large'. 'Eclectic' basically means 'selective', the implication being that something has been selected from numerous sources, as an 'eclectic' mind or an 'eclectic' taste in music. Loosely – and inaccurately – 'eclectic' is used to mean 'excellent', with little suggestion that a choice has been made.

especially see **specially**

esplanade see **parade**

essay/assay (try, attempt)
'Essay' is a stylish or semi-technical equivalent of 'try', as when one 'essays' one's strength or climbers 'essay' an ascent up the south face of a mountain. 'Assay' is strictly 'put to the test', 'analyse', in particular with regard to the testing or 'assaying' of metals or coins to establish the quantity of gold or the like that they contain. Unfortunately – or fortunately – one can both 'assay' one's strength as well as 'essay' it. It's a matter of choice, really. 'Assay', in fact, is the older word.

estuary see **mouth**

etching see **engraving**

eternity see **infinity**

Eton crop see **crew cut**

euphemism/euphuism (genteel style or turn of phrase)

A 'euphemism', from the Greek verb 'to speak fair', is a 'toned down' statement, the expression of something regarded as immodest, outrageous or indecent in genteel terms, as 'pass over' instead of 'die' or 'powder room' in place of 'women's lavatory'. 'Euphuism' is a literary term for an affected style of speaking or writing – originally that of the sixteenth-century English writer John Lyly. Euphues was the chief character in Lyly's *Euphues, The Anatomy of Wit* (1579) and *Euphues and his England* (1580), the language of which abounds in alliteration, antitheses and a whole range of similar mannered devices. Today 'euphuism' is virtually obsolete as a style, and 'euphemisms' have been so debased that they are more quaint than genteel.

euphuism see **euphemism**

evade see **avoid**

evening dress see **morning dress**

evening star see **morning star**

exacerbate see **aggravate**

exalted see **elevated**

example/sample/specimen (single unit or part of something designed to show the nature of the whole)
An 'example' is an illustration of something, often to indicate its standard or quality, as an 'example' of someone's painting or of a person's kindness. A 'sample' is an 'example' used for reference, and is usually an extract from something, as a 'sample' of someone's handwriting, of cloth or of a manufacturer's goods. It does not thus primarily denote quality. A 'specimen' is a 'sample' that is usually a scientific or medical one, as a 'specimen' of rock or of blood.

exasperate see **aggravate**

exceed/excel (surpass)
These are occasionally confused. To 'exceed' is to go beyond, with reference to a particular time, extent or quantity, as when a driver 'exceeds' the speed limit. If

someone 'exceeds' in speed, strength, or stamina, for example, he is superior to others – and no doubt it is this sense that leads to confusion with 'excel', which of course means 'outdo', 'be better than'. One can thus 'excel' oneself by doing better than ever before – and by 'exceeding' one's previous limit or record.

excel see exceed

Excellency see Lordship

except/exempt (release from)

To 'except' something is to leave it out, so that if a person is 'excepted' from an invitation, he doesn't get one. To 'exempt' a person, however, is to free him from the obligation of doing something. Conscientious objectors were thus 'exempted' from military service, with the implication that what they did instead counted as military service. Put another way, to 'except' a person is to count him out; to 'exempt' him is not to count him in.

exceptionable see exceptional

exceptional/exceptionable (singular)

'Exceptional' means 'forming an exception', with the implication that the described object is unusual or of high standard, such as an 'exceptional' performance of a play of 'exceptional' interest. 'Exceptionable', meaning 'liable to be excepted to' is virtually the opposite, since it is a term of disapproval. Someone's 'exceptionable' behaviour is such that exception is taken to it, it is regarded as objectionable.

excerpt see extract (quoted passage)

excite/incite (stimulate)

To 'excite' is to stir into action, as a dog, a nerve or envy. To 'incite' has more the idea of encouraging, provoking or stinging to action – although the action itself may not be realised. A person 'incited' to an act of treason, therefore, may be a traitor or may not: it depends if he actually does the deed.

excoriate see excruciate

excruciate/excoriate/execrate (cause suffering to)

'Excruciate' is most common in its adjectival form, 'excruciating'. An 'excruciating' pain is one that causes great discomfort or suffering. To 'excoriate' – literally 'strip the skin from' – is to flay verbally, denounce. To 'execrate' is to curse or abhor, to express strong hatred of. The derived adjective 'execrable' meaning 'deserved to be hated' is common.

execrate see excruciate

exempt see except

exoneration see acquittal

exotic/erotic (romantically exciting)

The two words do get confused. 'Exotic' literally means 'foreign' with reference to something imported from abroad but not acclimatised, as an 'exotic' plant or dish. The sense may be extended to apply to something that may still be abroad, such as the 'exotic' birds of the African jungle or 'exotic' spices of the East. The general overtone of the word is 'exciting because rare and mysteriously stirring'. This appeal to the senses no doubt reinforces its false association with 'erotic' which means, specifically, 'sexually exciting', as an 'erotic' poem or painting. Eros, the Greek god of love, lies behind the word. Both 'exotica' and 'erotica' are terms sometimes used for certain genres of pornographic literature. See also the confusibles eccentric and esoteric.

exploit see achievement

extempore/impromptu (done unprepared)

If you give an 'extempore' speech, you give it unmemorised – possibly referring to notes, but more likely using no notes at all. An 'impromptu' speech, on the other hand, is one not only necessarily unprepared but given at a moment's notice. A musical piece played 'extempore' is an improvised one; a musical 'impromptu' is one composed in such a way that it suggests improvisation. The words derive respectively from Latin terms: *ex tempore* (out of the time) and *in promptu* (in readiness).

extract/excerpt (quoted passage)
An 'extract' is any passage quoted, as an 'extract' from a new novel or a chairman's report. An 'excerpt' implies that the passage has been specially chosen, such as an 'excerpt' from a recently released record or from some important speech. The Latin verbs from which the words derive mean literally 'draw out' and 'pick out'.

extract/extricate (get out)
Two verbs. To 'extract' (see above entry) is basically 'draw out' as a tooth, or payment from an unwilling debtor. To 'extricate' is to get someone or something out of a difficulty, 'set free', as a splinter out of one's finger or, generously, a friend from debt.

extra time/overtime (time beyond that regarded as regular)
Both terms can have an official sense, as the 'extra time' in football, the additional playing time of (usually) fifteen minutes to achieve a decisive result, or the 'overtime' worked, which is usually paid for at higher rates. But 'extra time' can mean 'overtime' in a general sense, as 'I'm going to put in some "extra time" on my drawing this evening'.

extricate see **extract** (get out)

fable see **legend**

facility see **faculty** (ability)

faction see **fraction**

factitious see **fictional**

faculties/senses (power inherent in a bodily organ)
'Faculties' can apply, loosely, to the bodily powers as a whole, or specifically to a particular organ. Usually, however, the word denotes mental power, such as will or reason. One's 'senses' are traditionally the five powers of sight, hearing, smell, taste and touch – together with the so-called 'sixth "sense"' which supposedly gives intuition or some kind of extra-sensory power. Otherwise the word can also denote mental power, but usually means 'mind' as the hallmark of sanity, as in the phrase 'to take leave of one's "senses"'.

faculty/facility (ability, readiness)
'Faculty' is the ability or capability to do something, as a 'faculty' for hard work. 'Facility' is 'provision', in the sense of making something easier, as when one is afforded every 'facility' in some task. It also, however, in its more basic sense, means 'ability to do something easily'. Thus one person may have a 'faculty' for hard work (be able to do it), but another a 'facility' for hard work (be able to do it easily). In this basic sense there is also often a suggestion of readiness.

faculty (section of a university) see **department** (section of a university)

failing see **fault**

falcon see **hawk**

fallacious see **fallible**

fallible/fallacious (false, or liable to be false)
As used of people, 'fallible' indicates a liability to be deceived or mistaken, as a 'fallible' judge or authority, who cannot be relied on. Of things the word means 'liable to be false', as a 'fallible' rule (one that has exceptions). 'Fallacious' is used of things only and means 'containing a fallacy', therefore 'deceptive', as a 'fallacious' argument or 'fallacious' evidence.

familiarity/intimacy (close acquaintance)

97

'Familiarity' and 'intimacy' both denote a close acquaintance or knowledge of something or someone, with 'intimacy' implying, where 'familiarity' does not, a personal interest or sympathy or affection. The words are also used euphemistically for sexual behaviour, 'familiarity' (or 'familiarities') denoting caresses and the like, and 'intimacy' actual intercourse (itself a euphemism, even if one of longer standing). It is to be hoped that such coy usages will soon be mocked out of existence. '"Intimacy" took place on the top of a bus' conjures up an image that is more laughable than shocking.

famished see **ravishing**

fanatic see **frantic**

fancy/whimsy/whim (capricious notion)
A 'fancy' is an attractive, often casual, but usually unreal idea, as a childish 'fancy' or a poetic one. (The word is a contraction of 'fantasy'.) A 'whimsy' is also a fanciful idea, but one that is quaint or odd or possibly amusing or playful. 'His latest whimsy is to paint his car red, white and blue.' A 'whim' may be simply a passing idea or a minor 'whimsy', especially one that is irrational. 'What she has for breakfast depends on the whim of the moment.'

fandango see **flamenco**

farandole see **flamenco**

farce see **comedy**

Far East see **Near East**

farouche/louche (shy or shifty)
Two French words used mostly as vague vogue words. 'Farouche' seems almost to have opposite meanings: 'hostile' and 'shy'. Perhaps the best definition is a compromise – 'sullen', in which sense it is fairly often used. In origin the word goes back to Latin *foras* (out of doors, i.e. foreign or alien). 'Louche' literally means 'squinting', but is most often used in the sense 'shady', 'not straightforward'. As with 'farouche' there is a suggestion of foreignness or 'being on the wrong side'. They are not words to use with

any degree of certainty, but they can on occasions impress.

Far West see **Middle West**

fashion/style/vogue (current or popular method of doing something)
A 'fashion' is what distinguishes the habits or dress or manners of a particular group of people, especially from a historical angle, as the 'fashions' of the 1930s. (Unless qualified, the word usually refers to dress.) A 'style' is close in meaning to a 'fashion', but can indicate a conformity to a general standard, as the Early English 'style' of architecture, or a Queen Anne 'style' chair, both attractively simple and elegant. A 'vogue' is more a passing 'fashion', a prevalent 'style': 'long scarves are the "vogue" this winter.' It is unfortunate that the word suggests 'vague'; it actually derives from Italian *voga*, 'rowing', the reference being to the capricious motion of a boat. In fact 'vogue' and 'vague' *are* related, however, since the latter means 'wandering', 'wavering'. Compare French *vague*, 'wave', which prompts one to recall that the *nouvelle vague* was a special 'vogue' or 'style' of French film-making in the 1950s.

fatal/fateful (causing death or destruction)
The two words are not fully interchangeable. 'Fatal' has the main senses of 'causing death', as a 'fatal' accident, or 'causing destruction', as a 'fatal' mistake (which can result in any kind of downfall or disaster). With reference to time, the adjectives each relate to 'fate' in a different sense. The 'fatal' hour is the one chosen by fate (as an active, usually evil, power) for some kind of catastrophe or inescapable doom. A 'fateful' hour is an important or decisive one, since it determines one's fate (i.e. one's future). However, in popular usage, especially in such phrases as 'the fatal day' (or 'the fateful day'), both words mean the same – 'momentous'.

fate/lot/destiny/doom (predictable, inevitable or predetermined future)
'Fate', which can be a loosely used word – 'what a "fate"!' – implies an inevitable outcome that is irrational and impersonal. 'Lot' is one's personal 'fate', fortune or

'destiny' – what has been apportioned or 'allotted' to one. 'Destiny' is similar to 'fate' or 'lot', but sometimes suggests a favourable outcome, whereas the other two can imply an unpropitious or burdensome future. 'Doom' always implies a final ending that is unhappy or terrible, however, and it is this finality that the word essentially denotes, with a connotation of ruin or death.

fateful see **fatal**

fatigue see **tiredness**

fault/failing/foible (moral shortcoming)
'Fault' is the commonest word, and the strongest: 'His main fault is his lack of patience.' 'Failing' indicates a relatively minor shortcoming, possibly even a temporary one: 'Impatience is one of his failings.' 'Foible' is the mildest word, suggesting a weak point that may even be amusing: 'Giving girls the glad eye is one of his foibles.' (The word is obsolete French for 'feeble'.)

fault see **mistake**

faun/satyr (mythical woodland creature – half beast, half man)
A 'faun' has the ears, horns, tail and quite often the hind legs of a goat. He is not so called because he is fawn-coloured, but because he is identified with the god Pan, who was also called Faunus. (The first word of 'fauna and flora', meaning the animal and plant life of a region, derives from Faunus's sister, Fauna.) A 'satyr' is also part goat, but much more 'bestial' than a 'faun'. 'Satyrs' were the attendants of Bacchus, and made a reputation for themselves by their rioting and lasciviousness. 'Satyrs' differed physiologically from 'fauns', too, in that they had no horns.

feast/banquet (large, sumptuous or formal meal)
A 'feast' is a grand or lavish meal, especially a public one for several guests. A 'banquet' is either an elaborate 'feast' or, more commonly, a formal dinner in celebration of something, often with speeches. 'Feast' is also used metaphorically, as a 'feast' for the eyes, but a 'banquet' is always a literal meal. (The actual word 'banquet' is not used extensively, 'dinner' often being preferred instead.)

feat see **achievement**

feckless see **reckless**

fellow see **don**

felonious see **nefarious**

Fenians see **Sinn Féin**

ferment see **foment**

ferns/bracken (flowerless plants with feathery fronds found in woods)
There are literally thousands of species of 'fern', for example huge tree 'ferns' or ones that float on ponds. The most common British 'fern', however – a large, coarse variety growing abundantly on heaths and hillsides and in woods – is 'bracken', which although dying off in the autumn remains considerately standing, albeit dead, throughout winter, thus offering cover to game. Professor Alan Ross, of 'U and non-U' fame, claims in his book *Don't Say It* (Hamish Hamilton, 1973) that 'fern' is non-U Scots for "bracken"', as in 'Isn't the "fern" lovely?'

ferret/stoat/weasel (small animal with long slender body feeding on small rodents)
The 'ferret' is the domesticated albino variety of the polecat, when used for hunting in the burrows of rabbits and rats (and for the curious north-country sport of maximum time of concealment in trousers). A much rarer 'ferret' is the black-footed 'ferret' (*Mustela nigripes*). This is a wild variety found in the American prairies, especially the plains of Nebraska and Kansas, where it feeds largely on prairie dogs. It resembles the common 'ferret' in its general colouring but has a black mask across the eyes and brownish-black markings on its feet and tail tip. The 'stoat' and the 'weasel' are quite closely related, although the 'weasel' is smaller, with a tail half the length (around two and half inches) of that of the 'stoat'. The 'stoat' has a valu-

able fur, when it is known as the ermine (see **mink**).

fervently/fervidly (ardently)
Both words have the sense 'ardently', but 'fervidly' emphasises the degree of heat or vehemence. Whereas, too, 'fervently' is often used of a mental state or emotion – one can wish, admire or desire something 'fervently' – 'fervidly' usually qualifies a concrete action, such as speaking, writing or pleading 'fervidly'.

fervidly see **fervently**

festal see **festive**

festive/festal (pertaining to a feast or festivity)
'Festive' applies more to something that is fitting for a feast or festival, such as a 'festive' occasion, mood or season. 'Festal' relates directly to the feast or festival itself, so that a 'festal' crowd is one actually present at a feast or festival – at either of which 'festal' music might be played or 'festal' games organised.

fête/bazaar (function with stalls to raise money for some cause)
Broadly speaking, in a 'fête' the emphasis is on entertainment, and in a 'bazaar' the emphasis is on selling. But entertainment and selling are an essential feature of each, and both aim to raise money for charity or some particular cause. Both, too are typically English functions, yet *fête* is a French word, meaning 'feast', and *bazaar* a Persian word, meaning 'market'!

feud/vendetta (lengthy period of hostility between two families)
A 'feud' – related not to 'feudal' but to 'foe' – is a wider term, denoting mutual hostility between not only families but tribes, with murderous attacks in revenge for previous injury or wrongs. A 'vendetta' is a more limited affair: a private or blood 'feud' in which the relatives of a murdered person seek to gain their revenge by killing the murderer or a member of his family. The 'vendetta', as the Italian word (related to 'vengeance' and 'vindictive') suggests, is specially associated with Corsica and particular regions of Italy.

Fianna Fáil see **Sinn Féin**

fib see **lie** (false statement)

fibula see **tibia**

fiction/figment (baseless story)
The two words are sometimes confused in the phrase 'figment of the imagination' (not 'fiction'). Basically a 'fiction' is a story invented with the aim of entertaining or deceiving: 'His account of his visit to Paris was pure fiction.' A 'figment' is a story or statement thought up in order to explain something: is the concept of racial equality a mere 'figment' of the mind, or is it a reality?

fictional/fictitious/factitious (unreal)
'Fictional' means 'pertaining to fiction', so that someone's 'fictional' friends are imaginary ones. 'Fictitious' means 'invented', 'not real', as a 'fictitious' passport with a 'fictitious' name. 'Factitious', a comparatively rare word, means 'artificial', 'not spontaneous', as a person's 'factitious' delicacy of speech – he doesn't normally talk in this way, he is 'putting it on'.

fictitious see **fictional**

field/course/court/rink/pitch/lawn (area of play for a game or sport)
A 'field' usually implies a sizeable area of grass, as for cricket, football or hockey. A 'pitch' normally applies to the 'business' area of a field, where the action really happens. This may be limited, as a cricket 'pitch', or occupy the whole playing area, as a 'football' pitch. A 'course' is a stretch of land set aside for a race, whether over land or water. A 'court' is usually an enclosed area, whether an actual building, as a squash 'court', or in the open air, as a tennis 'court'. A 'rink' normally means an area of ice for skating or curling, but is also the word for the strip of a bowling green that is used for a match. A 'lawn' implies an area of grass, especially a mown one. 'Lawn' tennis is properly played, thus, on a grass 'court', not a hard one, although of course in practice it is played on both. 'Lawn' is also the word often used for the stretch of grass set aside for a game of

croquet, although professionals talk of a croquet 'court'. (Possibly 'lawn' implies a kind of amateurishness?)

field/meadow (enclosed area of grass)
A 'field' is the wider in meaning but not necessarily in size. Apart from denoting an area of farmland set aside for a particular purpose ('hayfield', 'cornfield') it is the word for the region of a natural product, as a 'coalfield', oil-'field' or gas-'field'. A 'meadow' is a piece of grassland, especially one used for hay, or a stretch of low, well-watered ground, as by a river. Not all 'fields' and 'meadows' are enclosed. In some towns meadows are held as common land.

figment see **fiction**

figure see **number**

filly see **colt**

fin/flipper (organ for swimming and propelling an aquatic creature)
'Fins' are usually found on fish, where they are used for propelling, steering and balance. Most fish have one 'fin' on their back – some have more – and all have a tail 'fin' and further 'fins' underneath their body. A 'flipper' is a limb used by a larger creature to swim with, as the 'flippers' of a turtle (its legs) or a penguin (its wings). Circus seals can be trained to clap with their 'flippers', but more conventionally they swim or progress over land with them.

financial/fiscal (relating to money and its management)
'Financial' relates to finance and financiers and people who manage money generally, such as in a 'financial' crisis or when making a 'financial' loss. 'Fiscal' relates specifically to government finance, and in particular tax revenues, so that a 'fiscal' agent will need to know about 'fiscal' policies. Confusingly, what in Britain is called the 'financial' year (beginning on 6 April, of all illogical dates) is in the United States called the 'fiscal' year (beginning much more sensibly on 1 January). See also **Gregorian calendar**, however.

Fine Gael see **Sinn Féin**

finicky/pernickety (fussy)
One sometimes hears the false but attractive blend 'fernickety'. Both words are colloquial, with 'finicky' meaning 'over-fussy', as a 'finicky' old woman or a 'finicky' design, and 'pernickety' having more the sense of 'unnecessarily fussy', as a 'pernickety' old man and 'pernickety' rules. A 'finicky' difference, therefore, but a real one. 'Finicky' is ultimately derived from 'fine'; 'fine'; 'pernickety' may possibly be an alteration of 'particular'.

fir see **pine**

firefly see **glow-worm**

firm/company/corporation (business or commercial or industrial organisation)
'Firm' tends to be used of a smaller, old-established commercial enterprise, as a printing 'firm' or a car hire 'firm'. Strictly speaking, a 'firm' is a partnership business, such as a 'firm' of solicitors. The word is generally used in a wider sense, however. 'Company' usually denotes a larger organisation, especially a business or trading undertaking or a manufacturing plant, as an insurance 'company' or a road construction 'company'. The word very often forms part of the official title of a commercial organisation, especially in the form 'J. Bloggs & Co. Ltd' (meaning that Mr Bloggs's company has a limited liability: he is legally responsible for the company's debts only to the extent of his shareholding). A 'corporation' is technically a business company (in Britain) and likewise treated by law as though it was a single person. In the USA it is an organisation, large or small, chartered under law for doing business, and owned by individuals or institutions who have shares representing fractions of its holdings. It thus approaches the British 'company', and similarly occurs as part of the name of such organisations. Even when it doesn't, many American enterprises have a name ending in 'Inc.', indicating that they have been legally constituted or formed as a 'corporation', i.e. 'incorporated'.

fiscal see **financial**

flagrant see **blatant**

101

flail see **flay**

flair/flare (dazzling display)
It's not simply a confusion of spelling, since both words have an overtone of some kind of brilliance. 'Flair' is discerning talent or aptitude, as a 'flair' for graphic design or improvising a tune on the piano. 'Flare' is literally, of course, a sudden blaze, usually of light or fire. Figuratively it is a burst of temper, zeal, or some other emotion.

flamenco/fandango/farandole (lively dance)
The 'flamenco' is a lively Spanish dance, or the music or singing for it, in the Andalusian gypsy style. It is accompanied by the familiar hand clapping, finger snapping and castanet clacking known technically as *jaleo*. The 'fandango' is a Spanish courting dance in triple time, or the music for it. The movements begin slowly, then gradually increase in ardour and tempo. The 'farandole' is a lively dance of Provençal origin: all the dancers join hands and execute a variety of figures, usually progressing in a chain through the streets to the accompaniment of pipes and tabors. The 'carmagnole', the dance of the French Revolution, was a variety of the 'farandole'. The origin of the name 'flamenco' is explained variously. The *SOED* derives it from the Spanish for 'flamingo', which in turn is from the Portuguese word for 'flaming' – the reference being to the bird's pink or scarlet plumage. Presumably the dance and dancers reflect such a colour, either literally or in fieriness. A more likely derivation, however, would seem to be the Spanish for 'Fleming' or 'Flemish' – not referring to Flanders (whose own name is thought to mean 'Floodland'), but to the Andalusian gypsies known as the 'Flamencos', who are buxom and ruddy. (*They* could link up with the red-feathered bird.) Yet a third explanation sees the origin of the word in the Arabic *felag mangu* (fugitive peasant). There is no doubt that the dance has its roots in both gypsy and Arabic folk song, as well as Andalusian. The 'fandango' may derive from the Portuguese folk song known as *fado* (fate), while the 'farandole' could be a corruption of Provençal *fa* (make) and *roundelo* (round dance).

The whole thing is rather a farrago (Latin for 'mixed fodder') . . .

flammable see **inflammable**

flan see **tart**

flare see **flair**

flaunt see **flout**

flavour/savour (characteristic taste or smell)
A 'flavour' may appeal to smell as well as taste, and is often of something added to food or drink, as a drink with a lime 'flavour' or a spread having a cheese 'flavour'. 'Savour', a less common word, almost always implies a smell as well as a taste, and usually not a sweet one, as the 'savour' of a stew, soup or sauce.

flay/flail (hit or whip severely)
'Flay' has three senses. The basic one is 'strip the skin from', as when a dead animal is 'flayed'. From this comes the figurative meaning 'reprove with scathing severity', 'criticise viciously', as when one critic 'flays' another. A slang sense is 'fleece', i.e. overcharge, extort money from. 'Flail' is basically 'strike with a flail' (an instrument for threshing grain by hand), but is more commonly used today of 'flailing' arms or fists – ones that strike out wildly but do not hit. The two words are not related.

fleece see **fur**

fleet/flotilla (number of ships or boats sailing together)
'Fleet' is a general word, with special reference to a naval force under one commander-in-chief, as the Pacific 'Fleet'. It can also mean a similar force of aircraft – not to be confused with 'flight', which is an RAF term for a group of about six aircraft. A 'flotilla', literally 'little fleet' in Spanish, is either a small 'fleet' or a 'fleet' of small ships or boats, as the 'flotilla' of 'little ships' used for the evacuation of Allied troops from Dunkirk in 1940.

fleeting see **flying**

flinch/wince (draw back hastily with pain or to avoid pain)
If you 'flinch', you do so either when something painful actually happens (someone treads on your favourite corn) or at the thought of pain (the prospect of the dentist's chair). You 'wince', however, only when actually experiencing the pain, mental horror or whatever. 'I have not winced nor cried aloud', wrote W.E. Henley, and so 'My head is bloody, but unbowed.'

fling see **reel**

flipper see **fin**

flock/herd/drove/pack (group or company of animals)
It largely depends on the animal in question. A 'flock' is usually of sheep or goats, or else a company of birds. A 'herd' usually consists of large animals, originally those that were under the charge of someone, as elephants, buffaloes or, in particular, cattle. Animals in a 'herd' are usually thought of as feeding or moving together. A 'drove' – the word is related to 'drive' – is a group of oxen, sheep or pigs, especially when they are being driven. A 'pack' consists either of animals that are kept together, as a 'pack' of hounds, or of animals that hunt or defensively herd together, as a 'pack' of wolves. Some linguistic experts or eccentrics claim that virtually every animal has its special group word, as a watch of nightingales or a covey of partridges. For a whole bevy of these, see Eric Partridge's *Usage and Abusage* (Penguin, 1970) (under the surprising heading 'sports technicalities').

flotilla see **fleet**

flotsam/jetsam (type of wreckage)
'Flotsam', in legal terms is the word for goods that have been lost from a wrecked ship and that are found floating. Such goods belong to the Crown if no owner appears to claim them within a year. 'Jetsam' is the word for goods that have been thrown overboard or jettisoned from a ship to lighten it, and that are usually subsequently discovered washed ashore. Figuratively, the words are used together as a term for vagrants, tramps and the like, the

'"flotsam" and "jetsam" of society'. The terms were also used as the stage names of a team of comic singers popular in the 1930s: 'Flotsam', a tenor, was B.C. Hilliam, and 'Jetsam' was Malcolm McEachern, an Australian bass singer.

flounder/founder (struggle but sink)
To 'flounder' is to struggle, usually in water, but fail to keep afloat or abreast. Figuratively it is to struggle helplessly or hopelessly in some situation, as when 'floundering on' in a speech or stage performance. To 'founder' basically means 'sink or collapse', especially of ships filling with water and going to the bottom, or buildings falling or being razed to the ground. The word is also used in a specific technical sense of a horse going lame. Figuratively it means 'fail utterly', as of a bankrupt. 'Flounder' seems to derive from a combination of 'flounce' and 'founder' – possibly with an additional association with 'blunder'.

flour/meal (sieved or ground grain product)
'Flour' is bolted (i.e. sieved) 'meal', from which the husks have been sifted out after grinding. 'Meal' is the ground product of any grain – of wheat it is familiar as 'wheatmeal' – or pulse (the edible seeds of peas, beans, lentils and the like). 'Wholemeal' bread is made of 'meal' that has not been bolted and thus deprived of some of its constituents. 'Meal' the word is not related to 'meal' meaning 'taking of food' but to 'mill'. (For what happens to the grains that get left behind in the bolting machine see **semolina**.)

flourish/brandish (wave or display vigorously)
One can 'flourish' anything – a sword, a stick, one's arm – by waving it about or, as a flower in the button-hole, by displaying it ostentatiously. 'Brandish', however, is applied exclusively to weapons: to 'brandish' a sword or a knife is to wave it about threateningly.

flout/flaunt/vaunt (treat brazenly)
In a sense, 'flout' and 'flaunt' are opposites. To 'flout' means 'mock', as authority, the rules, etc., by treating them with contempt,

so drawing the attention of others to them. To 'flaunt' means 'parade ostentatiously', as one's views or wealth, with the aim of drawing the attention of others to oneself. To 'vaunt' something is to boast about it, make it known by displaying it. This need not have, as 'flaunt' does, a disparaging sense. The word is, though, related to 'vain'.

fluid see **liquid**

fluorescent/phosphorescent
(luminescent)
In scientific terms, a 'fluorescent' lamp is one in which light is produced by fluorescence, especially that initiated by the radiation of mercury vapour which causes a coating of phosphor on the inside of the tube. 'Phosphorescent' applies to a substance that glows as the result of slow oxidation of phosphorus, or, in particular, to some marine plants and animals that generate light by the oxidation of luciferin (a pigment) in the presence of luciferase (an enzyme).

flush see **blush**

flutter see **wow**

flying/fleeting (rapid)
'Flying' means 'hasty', as a 'flying' visit or a 'flying' trip somewhere; 'fleeting' means 'brief', as a 'fleeting' glimpse or a 'fleeting' farewell.

foal see **colt**

foe see **enemy**

fog/mist (effect caused by water vapour condensing onto particles of dust, soot, etc.) 'Fog', is thicker, of course, and 'mist' thinner. Meteorologically, 'fog' has a visibility of less than one kilometre and 'mist' a visibility greater than one kilometre (but less than two kilometres). 'Mist', too, often occurs in thin bands or layers, while 'fog' is cloud-like.

foible see **fault**

foil/épée/sabre (type of fencing weapon)
The 'foil' is the basic weapon of fencing. It is

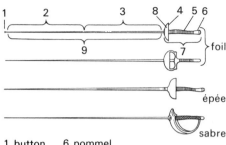

1	button	6	pommel
2	foible	7	mounting
3	forte	8	guard
4	cushion	9	blade
5	handle		

light, with a small bell guard and a square, tapering blade. Hits with the 'foil' are valid only if they are made with the point on the body. The 'épée' is the duelling sword, heavier than the 'foil', with a fluted, triangular blade and a larger bell guard. Hits – with the point only – score when made on the opponent's body, head or limbs. The 'sabre' is the light Italian duelling sword. It has a half-circular guard and a flexible, flattened blade which can score hits with the whole of its front edge, the last third of its back edge, or its point. Such hits are valid on the head, arms, and body down to the waist. 'Épée' fencing is a more open, simpler and athletic game than 'foil', and hits tend to be concentrated on the sword-arm and wrist – as the nearest parts of the target – rather than elsewhere on the body.

folio see **quarto**

foment/ferment (heat up)
'Foment' has two basic senses: 'promote', 'stoke up', as a rebellion or hatred, and 'apply warm water to', as a boil or abscess, to lessen the pain. To 'ferment' has, apart from the sense 'undergo chemical change and give off a gas', the meaning 'cause trouble'. In this latter sense it is virtually synonymous with 'foment', although often applied specifically to political unrest.

foolscap see **quarto**

forage/foray (search)
To 'forage' is to search for food, supplies and the like, or to make a raid in search of

some kind of plunder. To 'foray' is to plunder only, or 'pillage'. The words are related, and derive from French *forayer* (marauder).

foray see **forage**

forceful/forcible (showing force)
'Forceful' is literally, of course, 'full of force', and is used of someone or something acting or behaving with power or vigour, as a 'forceful' speaker making a 'forceful' speech with 'forceful' gestures. 'Forcible' means 'effected by force', as a 'forcible' explosion. It can, however, also mean 'producing a powerful effect', as a 'forcible' argument. There is a difference, therefore, between a 'forceful' performance, which is one made powerfully (with vigour) and a 'forcible' performance, which produces a powerful effect (but itself could be refined or restrained).

forceps/tweezers (instrument for holding something tightly)
'Forceps' are specialised surgical pincers, for anatomical repair work. 'Tweezers' are small, thin pincers for toiletry generally, and are used to pluck hairs, for example, or extract splinters – otherwise cosmetic repair work.

forcible see **forceful**

forest see **wood**

foreword/preface/introduction (material given at the front of a book)
A 'foreword' is a 'word in advance' about what to expect in the book and is always written by someone other than the book's author. The word – sometimes confused with 'forward' and even misspelled as such – was devised in the nineteenth century as an English rendering of German *Vorwort*. A 'preface' is similar but is written by the author of the book. An 'introduction' is a more or less formal preliminary statement or guide to the book, and is often written by the author to explain what he is about. Some books have a sort of epilogue at the end called an 'afterword' or even some notes in the form of a 'postface'. An 'extroduction' is something that so far, mercifully, we seem

to have been spared. See also **preface** for its more general use.

form see **class**

fort/fortress (fortified building)
A 'fort' is any fortified building. A 'fortress' is essentially a military stronghold, especially a strongly fortified town where a large garrison is stationed. The nucleus of such a town was originally the 'fort', which is why many towns, especially in the USA and Canada, have a name that today has 'Fort' as the first element, as Fort Lauderdale, Fort Frances, Fort Wayne. For a similar reason the Scottish Fort Augustus, Fort George and Fort William are so named.

fortress see **fort**

fortuitous see **fortunate**

fortunate/fortuitous (chance)
'Fortunate' means 'lucky', 'bringing good fortune', as a 'fortunate' meeting or discovery. 'Fortuitous' simply means 'produced by chance', so that a 'fortuitous' discovery is not necessarily a good one – or a bad one.

founder see **flounder**

fowl see **chicken**

foyer see **hall**

fraction/faction (militant political or other body)
The basic difference is that a 'fraction' is a deviant or schismatic political group, while a 'faction' is normally a self-interested grouping within the main body. The term 'fraction' – literally a 'break-off' or 'splinter' group – came to be associated in the 1920s with the British Communist Party, and was officially defined as 'a Party (i.e. Communist) organisation inside a representative or delegate body' and also as 'a grouping of all the Communists and their followers inside a trade union or similar organisation'. In this sense it is clearly an approved group, not a schismatic one. 'Faction', however, has almost always been regarded as a

grouping aiming to achieve its goal by unscrupulous methods, usually resulting in party strife. It literally means 'action' group.

fragile/frail (delicate)

'Fragile' implies a liability to break, as literally china or glass or, figuratively, a truce. 'Frail', which is rarely used literally, means 'weak', especially of health or morals.

frail see fragile

Frankenstein/Dracula (fearsome humanoid monster of sinister central European origin)

First, a popular misconception that must be corrected: 'Frankenstein', in the original Gothic novel by Mary Shelley, second wife of the poet, was not actually the monster but the student who created him – and who was eventually killed by his own fiendish creation. So it was 'Frankenstein's' monster – not 'Frankenstein', the monster – who was brought to life from human bones in charnel-houses and inspired loathing in all who beheld it. 'Dracula' actually was a human – that is, a **vampire** by night, but Count 'Dracula' by day. The Count features in the story by the Irish writer Bram Stoker, and his activities begin – and end – in Transylvania, the traditional home of vampires and werewolves. Both owe much of their delectably gory image – or is it the other way round? – to the Hammer horror films. This dedicated company is said to make several versions of its 'Frankenstein' and 'Dracula' films: the bloodiest for Japan, the blandest for Britain.

frantic/frenetic/fanatic/phrenetic (wild, unreasoning)

'Frantic' implies a desperation as well as a wild striving of some kind, as felt in 'frantic' pain or heard in a 'frantic' scream. 'Frenetic' and 'phrenetic' are near-synonyms meaning 'frenzied', although 'phrenetic' suggests 'half-crazed', particularly of religious beliefs or manias. The implication behind 'fanatic' – which produced the 'fan' – is that the enthusiasm or zeal is of unreasonable proportions. The word itself derives from Latin *fanaticus* (pertaining to a temple), while the other three words go back

ultimately to Greek *phren* (midriff – the supposed seat of passions).

freedom/liberty (absence of restrictions)

'Freedom' is the more common word, implying a positive free exercise of one's choice, powers, rights, and so on. 'Liberty' is a more stately or solemn word, and also a more emotive one, since it normally suggests a previous restriction or *lack* of 'liberty'. It can, too, connote unwarranted 'freedom', as when someone takes the 'liberty' of doing something he should not do.

freehold see leasehold

free house/tied house (type of pub)

A 'free house' is not, alas, a pub that provides beer free, but one that sells liquor from more than one brewery. A 'tied house', by contrast, is a pub that is 'tied' to and often owned by one brewery: it is bound to supply that one brewer's liquor only.

freezer see refrigerator

freight/cargo (transported goods)

The difference is mainly in the means of transport used. 'Freight' is normally transported in containers or by water – and in American usage, also by land (hence the American '"freight" train' which corresponds to the British 'goods train'). 'Cargo' is usually carried by ship or aircraft, although again in the USA it can also go over land by motor vehicle. 'Cargo' as a word is nothing to do with cars, but is related to 'charge'.

frenetic see frantic

fresco see mural

friar see monk

frock see dress

frog/toad (tailless amphibian found in fields and gardens)

There are three main differences: 'frogs' like water, are smooth-skinned, and leap; 'toads' are not aquatic (except when breeding), are dry or rough-skinned or warty (though, in

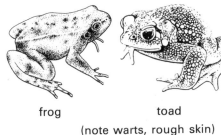

frog   toad

(note warts, rough skin)

spite of superstitions, they do not actually cause warts), and hop. This should be sufficient for the two to be distinguished, but if not, look more closely: a 'frog' has teeth, a 'toad' has none.

frontier see **border**

frown/scowl (as verb: contract the brow)
To 'frown' is to contract the eyebrows to indicate displeasure or deep thought or puzzlement; to 'scowl' is to do likewise – but always angrily or sullenly.

frowsty see **fuggy**

frowzy see **fuggy**

fruit/fruition (awaited or desired product)
Apart from its literal sense, 'fruit' can mean 'the product of an action', as the 'fruits' of one's labours or the 'fruits' of learning. 'Fruition' is the realisation of what is wished for, so that if your hopes are brought to 'fruition' you have an entirely satisfactory outcome. Like 'fruit', 'fruition' can be used both literally and figuratively – meaning 'the bearing of fruit' – although rather surprisingly the two words are not related. 'Fruition' has come to be firmly but wrongly associated with 'fruit'. It in fact derives from Late Latin *fruitio* (enjoyment).

fruition see **fruit**

fuddled see **muddled**

fuggy/fusty/frowsty/frowzy (stuffy, ill-smelling)
'Fuggy' is used of air filled with something fairly dense, as tobacco smoke. 'Fusty' suggests a mouldy, musty smell, or at any rate a stale one. (Figuratively it can mean

'old-fashioned', much as 'stuffy' can.) 'Frowsty' suggests both ill-smelling and musty and, very often, warm, as of a stuffy, heated living-room. 'Frowzy' hints at dirt, as well as an unsweet smell.

fur/fleece (hair of animals used for clothing)
'Fur' is the fine, soft, short hair of certain animals (as such distinguished from longer hair) used for coats, hats, wraps and the like, as of the ermine, beaver, and so on. The term usually applies to the skin of a dead animal complete with such hair. 'Fleece' is the woolly covering of the sheep – and, occasionally, other animals – used for clothing materials. It is usually shorn from a live sheep rather than cut from the skin of a dead one.

furore see **fury**

further education/higher education
(education for those who have left school)
'Further education' is a blanket term usually referring to all post-school education outside the universities. 'Higher education' (post-graduate, first degree and similar level work) is provided at universities and on advanced courses at polytechnics (see **technical college**) and other establishments of 'further education'.

fury/furore (vigorous display of emotion or enthusiasm)
A 'fury' is a rage, a fit of temper, typically as displayed by a single person, so that 'He was in a real fury' means 'He was really furious'. A 'furore' is a public thing, an uproar or expression of scandal because of some injustice or avoidable accident, such as the 'furore' over a popular person's dismissal or the collapse of a famous commercial organisation such as an airline. But it can also be a good thing, a show of enthusiastic admiration, as when a film director produces a startlingly effective film: 'He caused a furore'. The two words are related, with 'furore' coming into English direct from the Italian. (It can be pronounced in three syllables or two, with the latter increasingly common, in line with other words ending in '-ore', such as 'ignore', 'before' and 'restore'.)

fury (annoyance) see **anger**

furze see **gorse**

fuse/fuze (device in electrical or detonating mechanism)
Until quite recently, 'fuze' has been regarded in British English as an American spelling of 'fuse'. Early in 1978, however, the British government announced that NATO would henceforth distinguish between the two: 'fuse' is to be the spelling for 'wire or strip of fusible metal inserted in an electric circuit to prevent current overload', and 'fuze' – 'device designed to initiate an explosion'. The distinction seems a useful one.

fusty see **fuggy**

Futurism/Surrealism (art movement still regarded by some as avant-garde)
Thanks to the rather vague use of the terms 'futuristic' and 'surrealistic' to apply to anything of weird and wonderful (or apparently incomprehensible) appearance or design – a futuristic curtain pattern or a surrealistic TV comedy – the original meanings have become rather blurred. 'Futurism', which evolved in Italy, had its heyday for about five years from 1910 to 1915, and aimed to depart violently from traditional forms in order to plan for a new, dynamic and revolutionary future. 'Surrealism' flourished rather later, at the end of the First World War, and was the conscious expression of an imagination uncontrolled by reason, 'more real than real'. Salvador Dali is one of the best known 'Surrealist' painters. The movements were not, however, restricted to art, but also embraced literature, music, and even, as the 'Futurists' envisaged in their movement, life itself.

fuze see **fuse**

G

gabble see **babble**

gad/gallivant (go restlessly in search of pleasure)
To 'gad' – more often 'gad about' – implies an idle search for pleasure. 'He's always gadding about at the week-end.' To 'gallivant' is to 'gad' with marked merriment or frivolity, even flirtatiously, by gad.

Gaelic see **Celtic**

Gaiety girls/Gibson girls (winsome maidens popular in the Naughty Nineties)
The 'Gaiety girls' were chorus girls at the Gaiety Theatre, London, admired especially in the 1890s. They were famed for their prettiness and knack of charming their way to a title by means of their associations with the nobility. 'Gibson girls' existed only in paper form. They were drawings of willowy, wasp-waisted girls by the American cartoonist Charles Dana Gibson, and were also much in vogue at the turn of the century.

galaxy see **constellation**

gale see **storm**

gall see **bile**

gallant see **valiant**

gallery see **balcony** (section of the auditorium of a theatre)

gallivant see **gad**

gallop see **trot**

gallows/gibbet (structure on which person used to be hanged)
A 'gallows' – the word is actually plural but treated as singular – normally had two uprights and a crosspiece, something like a

goalpost. A 'gibbet' was usually a single upright post with an arm supported on an angle. It was, too, used more for hanging the dead body of a criminal than for actually executing him. It still features in the word-guessing pencil-and-paper game called 'Hangman' or 'Hanging', where the first three guesses are drawn as the upright, the arm and the support.

game/set/match/rubber (portion of play forming a scoring unit in tennis)
A 'game' of tennis can be won with a minimum of four points (with one side always winning and the other never winning a point), the scoring being 15–0, 30–0, 40–0, 'game'. A 'set' is a group of six 'games' won by one side, with a lead of at least two 'games'. A minimum score here would thus be 6–0. A straight 'set' is a result in which the winner does not lose a 'set'. This would be in a 'match', which usually consists of five 'sets' for men and three for women. A 'rubber' is a match of three 'games' in not only tennis, but other sports and games such as cricket, whist and bridge. If you win a 'rubber', you win two out of three 'games'. But in 'tennis', the exciting moment is when the winner eventually reaches his final point – 'match' point – so winning 'game', 'set' and 'match' simultaneously and becoming a triple victor.

game/sport (activity involving play and entertainment)
A 'game' is an individual contest of some kind, usually according to set rules, as a 'game' of football or of hide-and-seek. The word can also refer to the activity or pastime as a whole, so that football is a very popular 'game'. 'Sport' is a more professional word, and can likewise mean a 'game' that is particularly strenuous or tricky, as the 'sport' of boxing (one would hardly say game) or the 'sport' of fishing (which needs guile and patience). Many 'sports', too, are usually played out of doors. 'Games', however, can be played out of doors or in, and for this reason are often qualified as, for example, outdoor 'games', indoor 'games', ball 'games', team 'games', card 'games', board 'games', and the like. People who say that blood 'sports' are no 'sport' at all since they do not give the creatures a

sporting chance may or may not be on the side of the gods. They are, however, over-looking the basic origin of 'sport' as a word: it does not mean an activity that gives the other side a sporting chance, i.e. a fair one, but a diversion. (It is actually a shortened form of 'disport'.)

gamma rays see **X-rays**

gammon see **ham**

gargantuan see **gigantic**

garish see **gaudy**

garret see **attic**

gasoline see **petrol**

gaudy/garish (bright and in bad taste)
'Gaudy' colours are flamboyant ones, regarded as ostentatious and 'flashy'. 'Garish' suggests 'glaring' and a crude vividness. In combination 'garish' colours 'clash', whereas 'gaudy' ones tend to be 'loud'.

gauze see **muslin**

gazebo see **pagoda**

GCE/CSE (school-leaving examination taken at about the age of fifteen)
'GCE' (General Certificate of Education) is run by nine examining boards in England, and held at 'O' or 'Ordinary' level for most pupils and at 'A' or 'Advanced' level for those who stay on at school for a further two years. It can also be taken by adult candidates at **further education** establishments as well as by private candidates. 'CSE' (Certificate of Secondary Education), organised in England by twelve regional boards consisting mainly of teachers serving in the schools that provide the candidates, is designed for pupils at the end of their fifth year of secondary education and is more commonly held in comprehensive schools than in grammar-type schools (which tend to go in for 'GCE'). In Wales, 'GCE' and 'CSE' are both conducted by a single board, while Scotland has its own examination system. 'CSE' is normally but not entirely

correctly regarded as being of a lower standard than 'GCE', although the highest 'CSE' grade (1) is widely accepted as being the equivalent of at least grade C at 'GCE' 'O' level, both of these grades in turn being usually reckoned as qualifying for entry to a further education course of some kind. The system has its defects, however, if only because of the disparity between the two types of examination, and the government is planning to replace both 'GCE' and 'CSE' by a single examination called 'GCSE' (General Certificate of Secondary Education), with the first courses starting in 1986 and first examinations held in 1988.

gelignite see **dynamite**

gem see **jewel**

genie see **jinn**

genius see **jinn**

genus/species (scientific class or category of living things)
A 'genus' (plural 'genera') contains a number of 'species' (plural 'species'). The two are ranks in the hierarchy accepted by zoologists and botanists and based on the system devised by Linnaeus in the eighteenth century. They are the two lowest of the seven ranks, the others being (starting with the highest) kingdom, phylum, class, order and family. Thus man is 'species' *Homo sapiens* in 'genus' *Homo* in family *Hominidae* in order *Primates* in class *Mammalia* in phylum *Chordata* (comprising the vertebrates, or creatures with backbones, and some small groups of invertebrates) in kingdom *Animalia*. Members of a 'genus' have common structural characteristics distinct from those of all other groups, while members of a 'species' can interbreed and differ only in minor details.

gerbil/jerboa (mouselike animal)
'Sir, What *is* a gerbil?' once wrote a puzzled reader to the editor of *The Times* in the course of correspondence on the creature. The animals are related: the 'gerbil' (or 'jerbil'), otherwise 'sand rat', is a rodent belonging to the mouse family found as a native in Asia, Africa and South Russia. It

became popular as a pet in the USA and Britain in the mid-1960s. The 'jerboa', found in Asia and North Africa, is distinguished by its very long hind legs which it uses for travelling. Both animals have long, hairy tails; both are up to six inches long.

German measles see **measles**

Gestapo/SS (Nazi military organisation)
The two can be distinguished. The 'Gestapo', so abbreviated from *Geheime Staats-Polizei* (secret state police), was set up by Goering in Prussia in 1933 and extended to the whole of Germany the following year. In 1936 it merged with the 'SS' or *Schutzstaffel* (protection squad), which was Hitler's personal army, otherwise known as the **Blackshirts**. The 'SS' was originally a section of the *Sturmabteilung* (storm troops), or Brownshirts.

gesticulate see **gesture**

gesture/gesticulate (use part of one's body to express an emotion or idea)
You can 'gesture' with your body, head, arms, hands or face to get your meaning over. If you do so excitedly, you 'gesticulate', usually with waving arms. Both words are sometimes mispronounced with a hard 'g' as in 'guest', instead of a soft one, as in 'gentle'.

ghost/spectre/phantom (disembodied spirit or apparition)
A 'ghost' is the soul, spirit or image of a dead person as seen, or otherwise experienced or sensed, by a living person. A 'spectre' is usually the word for a terrifying or unearthly 'ghost', especially a visible one, otherwise a frightening apparition. A 'phantom' is a 'mere' apparition, one that appears in a dream, in the mind, or even in reality, but not normally a terrifying one. Put another way, from the point of view of 'spookiness' the 'spectre' is positive, the 'phantom' negative, and the 'ghost' neutral.

gibbet see **gallows**

Gibson girls see **Gaiety girls**

giddiness see **dizziness**

gift see **present**

gigantic/gargantuan (enormous)
Strictly speaking, 'gigantic' is 'giant-like' and 'gargantuan' 'like Gargantua', the voracious character in Rabelais's *Gargantua and Pantagruel*. 'Gigantic' is used of anything very large or outsize such as a building, a success or an appetite. Gargantua, whose name originated from the Spanish *garganta* (gorge), had a spectacular capacity for eating and drinking. 'Gargantuan' is therefore an ideal word to describe a large appetite, meal or booze-up, but perhaps not so suitable for other huge objects.

giggle/snigger/snicker/titter (suppressed laugh)
These suggestive words can be distinguished quite usefully. A 'giggle' (as of schoolgirls) is an affected or silly laugh, often at something trivial or 'catty'. A 'snigger' (as of schoolboys) is a secretive, usually 'smutty' laugh, often at something improper, or disrespectful in tone. A 'snicker' (as of fools) is similar to a 'snigger' but has a neighing or whinnying tone to it. A 'titter' (as of a church congregation) is a nervous or restrained or covert laugh, usually made when either one regards it as unseemly to laugh or because one is embarrassed.

ginger group see **pressure group**

girdle see **grill**

glance/glimpse (brief view)
A 'glance' is a quick view or sight of something or someone, so that full recognition is possible but only for a brief moment. A 'glimpse' implies that the object is only barely caught sight of, or partly seen, and that it may not be fully recognisable. One thus may see a 'glimpse' of red or catch a 'glimpse' of the sea (not see it completely).

gleam/ray/glimmer (dim or pale show of light)
A 'gleam' is a light that is not very bright, and which is often intermittent, as from a distant window or a remote star. A 'ray' is a single line of light narrower than a beam, often from a source that is small or, as with a 'gleam', distant. A 'glimmer' is a feeble or unsteady light, as of the moon or a glow-worm (who 'shows the matin to be near, And 'gins to pale his uneffectual fire', as Hamlet's ghostly father remarks before he exits). All three words are used figuratively, often with reference to a hope, a 'gleam' of which is brief or slight, a 'ray' slight but usually optimistic, and a 'glimmer' rather dim and not too promising, although clearly better than no hope at all.

glee see **madrigal**

glimmer see **gleam**

glimpse see **glance**

gloss/lustre/sheen (bright or shining appearance or quality)
A 'gloss' is a superficial 'lustre', and 'sheen' is a 'gloss' on the surface only. In other words, the two are much the same. A 'lustre', therefore, is more of a general term to mean the state or quality of shining by reflecting light, and comprehends a 'gloss' and a 'sheen'. The latter two, though, can be imparted by means other than reflection, as by polishing, say, or by brushing. A 'lustre' tends also to be more long-lasting, with a 'gloss' and a 'sheen' perhaps a temporary state, as of sleeked hair or highly polished shoes. A natural 'lustre', however, as on a butterfly's wings, is not a 'gloss' but a 'sheen'.

glowering/lowering/louring (threatening, angry-looking)
A 'glowering' look is an angry or sullen one. It often hints at a **frown** or scowl. A 'lowering' look – the two words rhyme with 'towering' – is similar but less forceful. A 'lowering' or 'louring' sky is a threatening one, promising bad weather. (The spellings are interchangeable, with 'lowering' unrelated to 'low'.)

glow-worm/firefly (beetle emitting light after dark)
Both creatures emit phosphorescent light, although the 'glow-worm' gives a steady glow, while the 'firefly' produces flashes. The 'glow-worm' is normally the name of

the wingless female beetle (not a worm at all) that emits such a light, although the term 'glow-worm' can also apply to the larvae of 'fireflies', especially ones in the Americas and the tropics. (Unlike 'glow-worms', 'fireflies' are beetles that do actually fly.) The light is usually greenish and at the rear end, although one so-called 'rail-road worm' also thoughtfully has a red headlight. The idea behind this luminescence is to make signals to a likely mate. See also **gleam**.

gnat/midge/mosquito (small, annoying, biting insect)
'Gnat' is rather an imprecise word, since even 'mosquitoes', especially small or young ones, often get called this. At best it is a general word for any small annoying flying insect, as the black fly, fruit fly or, of course, the 'midge'. 'Midges' resemble 'mosquitoes' but their wings have no scales. There are two main kinds: those that bite, and those that don't. The latter are probably the more common ones, found around ponds or streams in late afternoon and evening in swarms. The biting 'midges', which are bloodsucking insects, are usually found along seashores, rivers and lakes. Occasionally they are known as 'no-see-ums', as the female, which is the one with the irritating bite, is difficult to find. The 'mosquito' is the most distinctive and maddening of the trio, with its ominous whining hum and often quite painful bite, but in this case it is fortunately rather easier to find (and catch).

gnome see **goblin**

goblin/dwarf/gnome/elf (small imaginary man-like creature)
A 'goblin' is a grotesque mischievous sprite, usually in human form although also appearing as an animal. A 'dwarf' is a creature from Scandinavian mythology, where he is specially associated with metal-working. In common with several other creatures, he was much popularised – and personalised – by Walt Disney, as one of the seven companions of Snow White. A 'gnome' is fabled to inhabit the interior of the earth and act as guardian of its treasures. He is usually thought of as a shrivelled

malevolent little old man, but in spite of this has for some years now enjoyed popularity in Britain as a garden deity, where he can be seen perpetually angling or otherwise purposefully engaged. (His name looks Greek, and may in fact be related to Greek *gnome*, 'intelligence'; it was directly invented as a neo-Latin word, *gnomus,* however, by Paracelsus.) The 'elf' is closer to the German mountains than the Scandinavian mines. He has magical powers, which he enjoys using to interfere, in the nicest but also naughtiest way, in human affairs. All four, in fact, now that they have been resettled and domesticated, have lost much of their original evil influence on man. (Although if the love of money is the root of all evil, presumably the 'gnomes' of Zurich – those powerful Swiss financiers – must be regarded with more than a little awe and doubt by those who are wary of their great influence in the wicked world of capitalism.)

gold see **platinum**

gorge see **ravine**

gorgon see **dragon**

gorilla/orang-outang/baboon/mandrill (member of ape or monkey family)
The 'gorilla' is the largest of the man-like apes, living on the ground or in trees and

gorilla

orang-utan

baboon   mandrill

a professed vegetarian. Its habitat is west equatorial Africa. The 'orang-outang' (or 'orang-utan') – whose name exotically although erroneously suggests 'orange glutton', but in fact is Malay for 'man of the woods' – is a now quite rare, alas, large, long-armed ape living in trees in Borneo. The 'baboon' is a monkey with a dog-like snout, large cheek pouches, and a short tail. It lives in Africa, south of the Sahara, and in parts of Asia. The 'mandrill' is a monkey that is actually a member of the 'baboon' family, and possibly the most spectacular one, with its huge dog-like teeth, bright red buttocks, and gaudily striped blue and scarlet cheeks. It lives on the ground (but sensibly feeds and sleeps in trees) in west Africa.

gorse/furze/broom/whin (spiny shrub with yellow flowers growing on open land)
'Gorse' and 'furze' and 'whin' are three different names for one and the same plant, otherwise *Ulex europaeus,* with 'whin' more common in the east and north of Britain, and in some cases applied to other prickly or thorny shrubs such as rest-harrow or buck-thorn. 'Broom' is a non-spiny shrub belonging to the pea family, with long slender branches (once used for making besoms, or brooms), having yellow flowers. The name can, however, also be applied to the prickly 'gorse' (or 'furze' or 'whin'), which is perhaps not very helpful.

go-slow see **sit-in**

goulash see **hash**

gourmand/gourmet (one fond of good food)
'Gourmand' smacks of 'glutton' and in fact implies an excessive fondness of good food

and drink. A 'gourmet', however, is a connoisseur of food and drink, otherwise, more refinedly, an epicure. 'Gourmand' derives from some French word of uncertain meaning; 'gourmet', although influenced in its meaning by 'gourmand', derives from a French word meaning 'wine taster' and is related to English 'groom', which in turn originally meant 'boy'. For further gastron-omes, see **bon vivant**.

gourmet see **gourmand**

gown see **dress**

grab/grabble/grapple/grope (grasp, or try to grasp)
To 'grab' is to seize eagerly, usually with the hand. To 'grabble' is to feel or search with the hand, as when one 'grabbles' for something in the bottom of a bag or case. To 'grapple' is to seize something in order to fold it or put it in order, as when 'grap-pling' with the pages of the newspaper. Figuratively it means 'struggle to grasp with the mind', as when one 'grapples' with a problem. To 'grope' is to feel about with the hand, usually when searching for some-thing. One thus 'gropes' one's way in the dark or, figuratively, 'gropes' for the answer – searches for it uncertainly. All four verbs belong to the semantically linked 'grasping' group, as do 'grip', 'gripe', 'grapes' (which are all hooked together) and 'grasp' itself.

grabble see **grab**

Grace see **Lordship**

graceful/gracious (having or showing grace)
'Graceful' means 'showing grace' as a 'graceful' gesture or a 'graceful' leap in the air. 'Gracious' means showing 'gracious-ness', i.e. 'kind', 'benevolent', 'courteous', as a 'gracious' deed. The word can imply a patronising or condescending manner, especially in such phrases as 'honoured by his gracious presence'. A 'gracious' smile, by the same token, can be a kind one or a condescending one. Of royalty, as 'by gracious permission of Her Majesty the Queen', the word is simply a polite epithet.

113

gracious see **graceful**

grain see (1) **corn**, (2) **gram**

gram/dram/grain (small unit of weight)
A 'gram' (or 'gramme') is a decimal measure, formerly defined as one cubic centimetre of water at 4°C, now one thousandth of the International Prototype Kilogram – a cylinder of platinum-iridium kept in Paris. In avoirdupois, one ounce equals 28.35 'grams'. A 'dram' is, other than a 'wee drappie', one sixteenth of an ounce, and was formerly, with apothecaries, one eighth of an ounce. The 'grain' is the smallest British weight – one seven-thousandth of a pound, regarded as the average weight of a plump grain of corn. British and American 'grain' are identical.

grammar school see **comprehensive school**

Grammy see **Emmy**

grampus see **walrus**

grapple see **grab**

grasshopper/locust/cricket (leaping, chirping insect)
All three are members of the order of insects called *Orthoptera* ('straight-winged'), although some insects of this order, such as the house 'cricket', have no wings. The 'grasshopper' is familiar on a hot summer's day for being the opposite of the proverbially well-behaved child: heard but not seen. It is not really a pest. The 'locust' certainly is, although not found in Britain. It is infamous in Africa, for example, where it can swarm in vast numbers and cause serious depredations to crops. The 'cricket' exists in around 900 species, of which two are found in Britain: the field 'cricket' and the house 'cricket', distinguished from the 'grasshopper' by their very long antennae and extra loud 'chirps'.

graticule/reticle (network of fine lines)
Not only are the words similar, but 'graticule' is frequently used to mean 'reticle' in the sense 'network of fine lines in the sight of an optical instrument'. The device is found in telescopes, for example, to enable measurements and accurate observations to be made. 'Graticule', however, has a second sense: 'grid of fine lines on a map indicating latitude and longitude'. Moreover, 'reticule' can be used as an alternative spelling for 'reticle', although more familiarly the '-ule' version applies, in a historical sense, to the small netted bag or purse formerly carried or worn by women and serving, in effect, as a kind of portable pocket – a forerunner of the modern handbag. 'Graticule' derives from Latin *craticula* (gridiron), while Latin *reticulum* means 'little net'.

grave/tomb (burial place)
A 'grave' is primarily an excavation for a dead body, although the word can include, or even exclusively mean, the mound or monument above such an excavation. A 'tomb' is any hole or excavation made for a body, not necessarily below ground, but in rock, say. It also means the structure over a 'grave' or even a monument not over a 'grave' at all, as the many fine 'tombs' seen in some churches. The word 'tomb' generally differs from 'grave' in implying a resting place for the body, whereas 'grave' tends to mean just the place where someone is buried. The words are often used more or less interchangeably, though, and there is hardly any different shade of meaning between 'gravestone' and 'tombstone', for example. Compare both 'grave' and 'tomb' with **vault**.

Great Britain see **England**

greengrocer see **grocer**

Green Paper see **White Paper**

Gregorian calendar/Julian calendar (type of reckoning for a calendar)
The 'Gregorian calendar' is the one prevailing in the vast majority of western countries today. It was devised by Pope Gregory XIII in 1582 in order to correct the 'Julian calendar' which was 'out' by thirteen days. He therefore aimed to restore the vernal equinox to the date (21 March) it had at the time of the Council of Nicaea in AD 325. So in the Italian states, Portugal and certain other countries 4 October 1582

was followed by 15 October. England followed suit in 1752, China in 1912, the USSR in 1918, Greece in 1923 and Egypt in 1928. The earlier 'Julian calendar' had been established by Julius Caesar in 45 BC as a reform of the confused Roman republican calendar. Unfortunately, Caesar's astronomer Sosigenes over-estimated the length of the year by eleven minutes – which by 1582 had accumulated to thirteen days. Hence Gregory's reform. The 'Gregorian calendar' itself differs from the 'Julian' only in that no century year is a leap year unless it is exactly divisible by 400. This means that 1900 was not a leap year, but 2000 will be. A relic of the 'Julian calendar' still survives in Britain in the date of 6 April as the start of the tax year. This date is the 'Gregorian' adjustment (by thirteen days) of the start of the New Year under the 'Julian calendar', which was on 25 March (in turn transferred from 25 December in the fourteenth century).

griddle see **grill**

gridiron see **grill**

grieve see **mourn**

griffin see **gryphon**

griffon see **gryphon**

grill/griddle/gridiron/girdle (utensil for grilling)
A 'grill' is now normally a device on a cooker for grilling or broiling by directing heat downwards onto the food. In its original sense it is the same as a 'gridiron' – a set of parallel metal bars over a flame used for grilling meat and the like. (The 'iron' is by false association with the bars: the word is really a variant of 'griddle'.) A 'griddle' is usually a flat heated surface on the top of a stove for cooking oatcakes, biscuits and the like, and especially, of course, griddlecakes. 'Girdle' is a variant of this in turn – hence the alternative 'girdlecakes'. No doubt 'girdle' proved easier to say and had an obvious association with a circular object: the iron plate itself is normally round.

grisly see **gruesome**

grocer/greengrocer (dealer in household provisions and foods)
A 'grocer' sells such things as tea, butter, flour, sugar, spices, canned foods, and miscellaneous household stores such as matches or soap. He originally was one who sold in the gross, that is, not net. A 'greengrocer' sells mainly fruit and vegetables, although these can also be sold by a fruiterer. Supermarkets, of course, sell all these things, but there are still, thank goodness, a number of high-class 'grocers' and 'greengrocers' left.

grope see **grab**

gross/crass (coarse, thick)
'Gross' has four basic meanings: 'unpleasantly fat' (she looks quite 'gross'), 'coarse' ('gross' behaviour), 'flagrant' (a 'gross' mistake), and 'total' (see **net amount**). 'Crass' overlaps fully with the second of these senses ('coarse') and partly with the first, where it means 'unusually great'. In this last sense its favourite companion word is 'stupidity', possibly since the very sound of 'crass' is expressive of foolishness and one's contempt for it. It conjures up, for a start, 'cretin' and 'ass'.

gross amount see **net amount**

grouse see **pheasant**

grove see **wood**

grudge see **begrudge**

gruesome/grisly (horrible, revolting)
'Gruesome', deriving from the French *grue* (shudder), is used of anything that makes one recoil or react in horror or revulsion, as a 'gruesome' sight or sound. 'Grisly' coincides in meaning with this, but has the additional sense of 'grim', 'formidable', as seen in someone's 'grisly' expression. Both words are commonly used in a semi-humorous sense. 'Rather grisly, you know – we had to stand in the train all the way.'

gryphon/griffon/griffin/wyvern (mythological winged creature)

'Gryphon' and 'griffon' are alternative spellings for the mythical monster that has the head and wings of an eagle and the body of a lion. (The spelling 'gryphon' 'is supposed to be dignified', notes the *SOED*.) It is also a heraldic figure resembling this creature. As a real creature, a 'griffon' is also a breed of toy dog, in particular the Brussels 'griffon', and a species of vulture found in southern Europe. A 'wyvern' (or 'wivern') is purely a heraldic beast: a two-legged dragon whose rear quarters are those of a serpent with a barbed tail. The word is related to 'viper' but the original sense is obscure. 'Gryphon' derives from Greek *grypos* (curved, hook-beaked).

guarantee/warranty (pledge that something is genuine)

Both words are of identical origin, with 'guarantee' coming directly from French and 'warranty' via Middle English. As normally used commercially, a 'guarantee' is an undertaking to repair something free of charge or replace it within a specified period, while a 'warranty' is a pledge as to the reliability or good working order of something (often implying a previous thorough testing or servicing, especially with second-hand goods). A 'warranty' may also overlap to some extent with a 'guarantee' in that the vendor may undertake to repair any faults or to replace parts over a certain period after purchase. This especially applies to more substantial purchases, such as that of a second-hand car.

guerrilla/partisan (irregular or 'underground' fighter)

The chief difference between the two is that 'guerrillas' aim to harass the enemy (by surprise raids, sudden attacks and the like), while 'partisans' seek to form an armed resistance to an invading or conquering power, as the French Resistance in the Second World War. 'Guerrilla', sometimes spelt with one 'r', is Spanish for 'little war', and was introduced into English during the Peninsular War of 1801–14. 'Partisan' is French in origin.

guitar/banjo/ukelele (musical instrument played by plucking its strings)

The 'guitar' has now largely and popularly gone electric, but it still has its traditional six strings and is still played either with the fingers or a plectrum (a small pointed device for plucking the strings). The 'banjo' can have from four to nine strings, although the usual number is five or six. It has the neck and head of a 'guitar' but the body shaped like that of a tambourine. It is chiefly associated with Negro music and entertainment, especially of the seaside sort. The 'ukelele' (also spelt 'ukulele' and known as 'uke' to aficionados) is a small, four-stringed Hawaiian 'guitar' (in fact originally Portuguese) with a very short finger-board. The word is Hawaiian for 'jumping flea', probably from the native nickname of the nine-

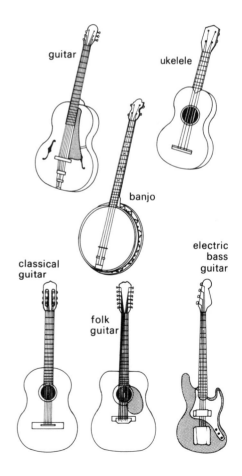

teenth-century British army officer Edward Purvis, who was small and quick and who popularised the instrument. Another, more familiar name associated with it is of course that of George Formby, whose little 'ukelele' was sometimes called a 'banjolele', i.e. an instrument somewhere between a 'banjo' and a 'ukelele'.

gulf see **bay**

gun/cannon (firearm)
'Gun' is a very general word, so that it can apply to a small pistol on the one hand and a mighty howitzer on the other. In Britain 'gun' usually tends to mean a hand arm of the 'shotgun' type. In artillery, 'guns' are distinguished by having flat trajectories, while howitzers and mortars have arching trajectories. A 'cannon' is a large 'gun', howitzer or mortar, as against a musket, rifle or other small arm. Modern 'cannon' usually have rifled bores. From the seventeenth century, the word came to apply to every 'gun' that was fired from a fixed carriage or fixed mount, usually with a bore greater than one inch. In the twentieth century, 'automatic cannon' came to be rapid-firing 'guns' in aircraft, with a calibre of 20 mm or more. In 1952 the United States Army introduced the 'atomic cannon', a 280 mm 'gun' that fired atomic shells. (See also **gun** below).

gun/rifle (portable firearm)
'Gun' is a general word (as mentioned above) that covers most kinds of firearms, such as pistols, revolvers, cannon, artillery 'guns' and the like. For most people, though, who read or hear a sentence such as 'He had a "gun"', the word denotes either a pistol of some kind or perhaps a 'shotgun'. At any rate it means a portable (hand-held) weapon, although not a 'rifle', which is a firearm with a rifled barrel (that is, a barrel with spiral grooves that make the bullet rotate and thus attain the target with greater accuracy), since the term 'gun' is almost always applied to firearms with no rifling. Those who do, however, call a 'rifle' a 'gun' may like to know that in a sense they are not far short of the mark since a 'rifle' was originally called a 'rifle gun'.

gynaecologist/obstetrician (doctor specialising in women's diseases and disorders)
A 'gynaecologist' – a title impressively hard to say and spell correctly – deals with diseases that in women differ from the equivalent in men, i.e. diseases of the urinary and genital organs, and thus subsumes diseases of childbirth – which is precisely what an 'obstetrician' deals with, since he cares for women in, before, and after labour, especially when there may be complications. The terms are respectively of Greek and Latin origin and mean 'one skilled in the study of women' and 'one standing facing' (i.e. like a midwife).

H

haberdasher/milliner (dealer in minor or ornamental items of dress)
A 'haberdasher' formerly dealt in a variety of items, in particular hats, caps and the like. Today he specialises in accessories for clothing and dressmaking, as ribbon, lace and thread. The word suggests 'hatter' but is of uncertain origin. The derivation may be in the name of some fabric. A 'milliner' is usually a woman who makes or sells women's hats or trimmings. She was originally a dealer from Milan. (The male equivalent, less originally, is a hatter.)

hachuring/hatching (drawing of fine, closely-spaced lines to shade in an area)
'Hachuring' is the use of so called 'hachures' on a map to indicate relief, hills and valleys, with the hachures themselves being a series of short, fine, parallel lines drawn in the direction of maximum slope, with the lines thickest where steepest and thinnest where gentlest. Good examples of 'hachuring' can

be seen on the earlier Ordnance Survey maps, where today height differences are shown by contours (with the heights indicated in figures). 'Hatching' is a similar process as 'hachuring', but is used in drawings and engravings, where the heaviness or lightness of the lines (whether drawn or actually engraved) can indicate various degrees of shading or shadow. Again, good examples of traditional 'hatching' can be seen in older prints and drawings, where the technique can be used to great artistic and realistic effect, even in fine portrait work. The two terms are related, with 'hachuring' the more obviously French version. (The French verb *hacher* is literally 'to chop'.)

hack/hackney (type of horse)
A 'hack' is not a breed of horse but a definite type – a refined riding-horse. The term can also mean, however, an old, worn-out horse (hence the literary 'hack' and the tired 'hack' phrase). The word is an abbreviation of 'hackney', which is a harness horse with characteristic high-stepping, long-striding or smart-trotting gait. Its ancestor is the Norfolk trotter. The sense 'worn-out' is shared with 'hack' in such metaphorical uses as a 'hackneyed' phrase, which is a common or trite one. A 'hackney' carriage was the term used for a vehicle plying for hire in the nineteenth century, the predecessor of the modern taxi, which is still technically known thus. The origin of the word is uncertain, although it could derive from Hackney, now a London borough: horses were raised on pasture there and taken through the town to Smithfield Market via (appropriately enough) Mare Street.

hackney see **hack**

hack phrase see **cliché**

haft see **shaft**

halibut see **cod**

hall/lobby/foyer (entrance or other passage in a building)
A 'hall' is usually an entrance passage – although in American English can be any passage or corridor. A 'lobby' is a rather vague word meaning either an entrance

'hall' or any passage, especially one serving as some kind of ante-room. A 'foyer' is either the large entrance 'hall' of a hotel, or the large room or 'hall' in a cinema or theatre set aside for use of the audience in an interval. (The word is French, meaning 'hearth', 'fireside'; originally it was the room in a theatre in which audiences went to warm themselves in between acts.)

hallelujah/hosannah (exclamation of praise to God)
'Hallelujah' – in hymns usually 'alleluia' – goes back ultimately to the Hebrew *hallelu* (praise ye) and *Jah* (Jehovah). Its most famous biblical location is in the opening verses of Revelation, from where come the words of the Hallelujah Chorus that triumphantly closes Part II of Handel's *Messiah*. 'Hosannah' from Hebrew *hōshī'ah nnā* (save, I pray) occurs in both the Old and New Testaments as well as a number of hymns and was originally an appeal to God for deliverance by the Jews.

Hallowe'en see **All Saints' Day**

halter see **rein** (part of horse's harness)

ham/gammon (type or cut of pork)
'Ham' is thigh of pig prepared for food, either fresh, or cured (salted and smoked). It is also the name of the upper part of the leg from which the meat comes. 'Gammon' is always cured and prepared like bacon, although served in thicker cuts than the normally thin rashers of bacon.

Hamitic see **Semitic**

hamlet see **village**

handball see **netball**

handiwork/handwork (work done by hand)
To start with the basics: 'handwork' is work done by hand as distinct from that done by machine, e.g. lace-making. 'Handiwork' is work done or something made by the hands or by the personal agency of someone. In its general sense it is often contrasted with nature or God, that is, 'manmade' as distinct from 'natural' or 'divinely made'.

The word is also used in some junior schools as an alternative to 'handicraft'. However, 'handiwork' is often used in place of 'handwork' in any of these senses, possibly because of the influence of 'handicraft'.

handwork see **handiwork**

harakiri/kamikaze (Japanese form of suicide)
'Harakiri' – sometimes, wrongly, 'harikari' – is a form of suicide carried out by ripping open the abdomen with a dagger or knife. It was notably practised by the higher classes, the *samurai,* when in disgrace or sentenced to death. The Japanese term is self-descriptive (belly cut). 'Kamikaze' became notorious in the Second World War as a form of suicidal crash dive performed by a Japanese aircraft, fully loaded with explosives, onto an enemy target, usually a ship. The word literally means 'god wind', and refers to the supposed divine wind that blew on a night in August 1281 destroying the navy of the invading Mongols.

harbinger see **herald**

harbour see **port** (place where ships can dock)

hard drugs/soft drugs (class of drug)
As popularly divided, 'hard drugs' are the potent, addictive ones, such as cocaine, heroin and LSD, while 'soft drugs' are those not likely to cause addiction, such as marijuana and **cannabis**. The analogy is with 'hard' and 'soft' drinks, the former being powerful and possibly habit-forming, the latter inoffensive. A similar comparison is also popularly made between 'hard' pornography ('hard porn'), which is highly obscene and an offence in law, and 'soft porn' which is legally tolerated, as in '18' films and many 'girlie' magazines.

hardware/software (computer or other technical components)
Both terms were originally computer operators' jargon. 'Hardware' is the actual computer equipment, the physical components, such as the keyboards and paper-tape punches. The 'software', contrasted with it, is the material necessary for operating the computers, that is, the written or printed programs and handbooks. (Instructions in these are followed by the 'liveware', the actual computer operators.) A similar distinction exists in the field of education, where the 'hardware' are devices such as tape recorders, closed-circuit television and other audiovisual equipment used for instruction, as compared with the materials (tapes, films, transparencies, etc.) used in such equipment and being the 'software'. A special type of (computer) 'software' is 'firmware', referring to programs and the like that are processed through a small special-purpose computer memory unit, as a 'read-only' memory.

hare see **rabbit**

harpsichord/spinet/clavichord/virginals (early keyboard instrument)
The names for these precursors of the modern piano are sometimes used rather imprecisely, but the instruments are actually quite distinct. The 'harpsichord' has strings that are technically plucked, not struck (hence 'harp-'), by leather or quill points connected with the keys. The 'spinet', possibly named after the Venetian inventor Giovanni Spinetti, is smaller than the 'harpsichord' and distinguished by its 'leg of mutton' outline. The 'clavichord' has strings that are struck, not plucked, by metal blades projecting from the rear end of the keys. Its name literally means 'key string'. Its tone is less brilliant than that of the 'harpsichord' but more expressive, since the force with which the keys are struck can be controlled by the player, as in a modern piano. The 'virginals' is, or was, the earliest and simplest form of 'harpsichord', with just one string to each note. The instrument, at its most basic, is really just a stringed box on a table. It is so named not because Queen Eliabeth, the Virgin Queen, particularly favoured it but, apparently, because it was regarded as a suitably 'maidenly' instrument for chaste young ladies.

hart see **stag**

harum-scarum see **helter-skelter**

hash/ragout/goulash (type of stew)
All three consist basically of a hot dish of
small pieces of meat and vegetables cooked
by simmering. A 'hash' is a dish in which
the meat has been hashed, or cut up into
small pieces beforehand. It will of course
be eaten with vegetables, but these are not
properly part of the 'hash'. A 'ragout', from
the French *ragoût,* meaning a dish that
'regusts' you or revives your appetite, is
usually a highly seasoned affair: a stew of
poultry or meat and vegetables flavoured
with mushrooms, tomatoes, port wine and
the like. It must not be confused – the two
foreign words look rather alike – with a
'goulash'. This is also a meaty seasoned
stew, but the meat is usually beef or veal
and the seasoning paprika. The dish is
perhaps the most exotic of the three, as its
name suggests: it is derived from the
Hungarian for 'herdsman's meat'.

hassle see **bustle**

hat/cap (item of headwear)
A 'hat' usually has a brim and a fairly
roomy crown, and is normally worn out-of-
doors, as a bowler 'hat', top 'hat' or panama
'hat'. A 'cap' is normally brimless, soft,
close-fitting, and frequently has a peak, as
a cricket 'cap', school 'cap', peaked 'cap' or
forage 'cap'. 'Caps' are mainly intended for
outdoor wear, but some have specific indoor
uses, as a 'nightcap', smoking 'cap' or
awesome black 'cap' worn by a judge when
pronouncing a death sentence. But such
'caps' are today either obsolete or obsolescent, and even the outdoor ones have only
limited uses, notably in the worlds of sport
and military life.

hatching see **hachuring**

haversack see **rucksack**

hawk/falcon/kestrel (bird of prey)
'Hawk' is a word applied fairly generally to
all diurnal (daytime) birds of prey except
the vulture and eagle. The 'hawks' proper,
in Britain, are the 'sparrowhawk' (*Accipiter
nisus,* which preys extensively on sparrows
and other small birds) and the 'goshawk'
(*Accipiter gentilis,* formerly used in falconry,
and one of the larger or 'goose-sized'

falcon

hawk

kestrel

a falcon hooded, cast off and lured
back by the falconer

'hawks'). In general, 'hawks' have short
wings. 'Falcons', by contrast, have long
wings. The name is applied to about sixty
species of 'hawks' that are thus long-winged,
and that formerly were trained – and are
still, by a few dedicated enthusiasts – to
hunt game-birds for sport. In a restricted
sense the name 'falcon' applies to the genus
Falco which has over 35 species, one of them
being the small 'falcon' known as a 'kestrel'
(*Falco tinnunculus*), the only 'kestrel' in
Britain, where it is also known by the name
'windhover' from its distinctive habit of
hovering in the air with its head into the
wind.

hawks/doves (political group advocating a
specific policy)
'Hawks' advocate a hardline policy, even a
militant one, while 'doves' prefer nego-
tiation to violence, especially to terminate

or prevent a military conflict. In the Cuban Crisis of 1962, the 'hawks' favoured an air strike to eliminate the Cuban missile bases, but the 'doves' opposed this policy and favoured a blockade. In the event it was the 'doves' who won the day when a blockade – tactfully called a 'quarantine' – was mounted on Cuba and Khrushchev subsequently backed down. It was this incident, in fact, that introduced the terms to the language at large, in the account of the crisis by the American journalist Charles Bartlett, President Kennedy's confidant.

haws see **hips**

health resort/spa (place visited for the benefit of one's health)
A 'health resort', or just 'resort', is often a place that has naturally beneficial amenities, as one by the sea, in the mountains, or with mineral waters. A 'spa' is specifically the latter of these, named after Spa, in Belgium, which has such a spring. In England Cheltenham was formerly a 'spa' and Bath still is, an association that is still officially recognised in the names of the railway stations of these towns, Cheltenham 'Spa' and Bath 'Spa'. Many visitors to 'spas' today perhaps derive as much benefit from the agreeable surroundings of the resort as directly from the mineral waters themselves.

heart attack see **stroke**

heath/moor (extent of open, flat, uncultivated land covered with shrubs)
A 'heath' properly has the shrub called heath, or heather, growing on it, especially in Scotland. A 'moor' is virtually the same, but the reference is more to the peaty land rather than the shrubs that grow on it. 'Moors' are characteristically found in high altitudes where the drainage is poor, as 'Dartmoor', 'Exmoor' and Bodmin 'Moor', all in the West Country. The former existence of a 'heath' is often indicated (in disguised form sometimes) in place-names such as Heathcote, Hadley and Hatfield, while 'moors' can be similarly detected in places called Morton, Morden, and the two Leicestershire (late lamented Rutland) villages of Morcott and Cottesmore.

heathen/pagan (person who does not belong to an established religion)
The words have certain overtones. A 'heathen' is by implication a barbaric or unenlightened or – at the least – primitive person, who does not believe because he does not understand the prevailing religion, or who *will* not understand it. A 'pagan' is perhaps a more civilised person, especially a Greek or Roman in classical times who was not a Christian. Both words have interesting origins. A 'heathen' is so called because he was, most likely, a heath-dweller, that is, a kind of savage. A 'pagan' was so called because he was a 'civilian' – Latin *paganus* (originally 'country-dweller'): he was called this because he was not a 'soldier of Christ'. (The Roman Christians called themselves *milites*, 'soldiers'.)

Hebrew/Yiddish (language spoken by Jews)
'Hebrew' is both the **Semitic** language of the ancient Hebrews, in which the Old Testament was originally written, and the revived modern version of this language as used in present-day Israel. 'Yiddish' is the vernacular language spoken by Jews in Europe and elsewhere (the latter by emigrant Jews) and is usually written in the 'Hebrew' alphabet. Historically, it is a dialect of standard German, with some 'Hebrew' and Slavonic elements, that developed in central and eastern Europe in medieval times. Its name comes from German *jüdisch* (Yiddish *yidish*), 'Jewish'.

Hebrew (follower of Judaism) see **Jew**

hecatomb see **catacomb**

heel over/keel over (overturn, collapse)
To 'heel over' is to cant or tilt or lean to one side, of a ship. To 'keel over', of a ship, is to turn right over so that the keel is uppermost. Both expressions, especially the second, are applied to any object that leans or overturns; of a person, 'keel over' means 'collapse'. 'Heel over' is not connected with 'heel' but is probably derived from an Old English verb *hieldan*, 'to incline'.

heifer see **calf**

height/depth (measurement to the top – or to the bottom)
The 'height' of something is the distance from its base, where you are standing, to its top, as with a house, tree, cupboard, person or mountain. But it is also the distance of an elevated object above sea-level, such as a cliff-top, where you might be standing, in which case the measurement is in a sense downwards, or from below upwards. In measuring 'height', therefore, you yourself may be at the bottom or top. And if you are on that cliff-top, you could also measure the 'depth' of the rocks below you, since 'depth' is defined as 'measurement from top down' (*Concise Oxford Dictionary*). Normally, however, the 'height' of something is the measurement of a thing that is regularly above you, and the 'depth' the measurement of a thing that is regularly below you, as the bottom of the sea or a pot-hole. 'Depth', too, is the measurement of a thing from its front to its back, as a shelf with a 'depth' of two feet, or from the surface inwards, as (try this for size) a gash in the plaster of the ceiling two inches in 'depth'. Tricky words, therefore – in their spelling, too, since 'height' has gained an 'e' (from 'high') and 'depth' has lost an 'e' (from 'deep'). And those who say – or even write – 'heighth', or an analogy with 'depth' and 'width' and 'length' and 'breadth', are unfortunately wrong.

helicopter/autogyro (type of aircraft propelled by rotating blades)
A 'helicopter' has one or more overhead rotors that turn horizontally around a vertical (or nearly vertical) axis, and it is these rotors that propel it and enable it to take off and land vertically and hover. An 'autogyro' is a form of 'helicopter', not so common now as formerly, whose overhead rotors are, however, non-powered, so that it is propelled by a propeller in front, like a conventional aeroplane. Because of its different type of propulsion it cannot take off vertically like a 'helicopter', although it can land vertically. The word is also spelt 'autogiro' and was originally a trade name meaning 'self-rotating'.

helm see **rudder**

helter-skelter/harum-scarum/higgledy-piggledy (in disorder or confusion)
English loves rhyming jingles like these. (Oddly, many of them begin with 'h', as 'hocus-pocus', 'hoity-toity', 'hurly-burly', 'Humpty-Dumpty'.) 'Helter-skelter' implies disorderly haste, as of an enemy fleeing or crowds hurrying out of a stadium after a soccer match. By comparison the spiral slide known as a 'helter-skelter' is a relatively organised device. 'Harum-scarum' suggests recklessness or wildness, as of a passionate or capricious person or his behaviour. 'Higgledy-piggledy' is descriptive of a number of objects in jumbled confusion, as of objects in a 'glory-hole'. Etymological connections with hares and pigs are only tentative.

hen see **chicken**

herald/harbinger (messenger, forerunner)
A 'harbinger' is not just a poetic word for 'herald'. The word literally meant 'one who provides lodgings for an army' and now has the general sense of 'sign of something to come', as the cuckoo is the 'harbinger' of summer. A 'herald', by comparison, is simply 'one who announces', a messenger – hence the word's popularity as a newspaper title. The 'g' in 'harbinger' is soft, as in 'messenger'.

herd see **flock**

heritage see **inheritance**

herring/bloater/kipper (edible sea fish)
The 'herring' is a versatile fish from the North Atlantic. It can be sold fresh, salted, pickled, smoked, or canned (tinned). When cured and smoked – that is, split open, cleaned, rubbed with salt, and dried in smoke – it is called a 'kipper'. A special 'herring' is a 'bloater' which is one cured by bloating, that is, salted and smoked, but only slightly. (The word is related to 'bloat' meaning 'inflate', 'swell', although the obsolete word 'bloat' meaning 'soft and wet' gives the direct derivation.)

higgledy-piggledy see **helter-skelter**

high commission see **embassy**

higher education see **further education**

high frequency/VHF/UHF (radio and
television frequency band)
A 'high frequency' is one in the range 3 to
30 megacycles a second, i.e. 3 to 30 megahertz, or 10 to 100 metres. (A megahertz is
the same as one million hertz, so that one
hertz equals one cycle per second. The basic
unit is named after the German physicist
H. R. Hertz, who died in 1894.) 'VHF'
(very high frequency) is a frequency
between 30 megahertz and 300 megahertz
(1 to 10 metres), while 'UHF' (ultra high
frequency) is between 300 megahertz and
3000 megahertz (10 centimetres to 1 metre).
(Above this there also exist super high
frequency and extra high frequency, which
are mainly used for satellite broadcasting.)
Below 'high frequency' there is medium
frequency, better known as medium wave,
with a range of 300 kilohertz to 3 megahertz
(100 to 1000 metres), and below this, low
frequency (long wave), ranging from 30
kilohertz to 300 kilohertz (1000 to 10,000
metres). Most radio broadcasts in Britain
go out on both medium frequency and
'VHF', with the 'high frequency' (short
wave) used for broadcasting to Europe and
overseas. Television broadcasts were
formerly made on both 'VHF' (or 405 lines)
and 'UHF' (625 lines) by BBC 1 and ITV,
and 'UHF' only by BBC 2 and Channel 4.
The 'VHF' transmissions have now been
phased out, however, and all four channels
transmit on 'UHF' only. For more about
cycles and frequency, see **alternating
current**.

highway see **motorway**

hill/mountain (elevation of the Earth's
surface)
When is a hill high enough to become a
mountain? In Britain, the traditional definition of a 'mountain' is that it must be over
1000 feet high. However, any large or steep
'hill' can be called a 'mountain', and
conversely, many 'hills' are over 1000 feet
high: the Cheviot 'Hills', for example, rise
to 2676 feet. In other parts of the world
there are 'hills' higher than Britain's highest

'mountain'. The Chagai 'Hills' bordering
Afghanistan and Pakistan, for example, rise
to 2462 metres (8077 feet), while Britain's
top peak, Ben Nevis, manages only 1343
metres (4406 feet). So it's all rather relative.

hind see **stag**

Hindi see **Hindu**

Hindu/Hindustani/Hindi/Urdu (native,
religion or language of India)
A 'Hindu' is a native of India who adheres
to the country's dominant religion,
Hinduism. 'Hindustani' is the standard
language of northern India based on a
dialect of western 'Hindi' spoken around
Delhi. 'Hindi' is the name given either to
one of the modern Indic languages of
northern India, usually divided into eastern
and western 'Hindi', or to the literary
language derived from 'Hindustani' used by
'Hindus'. 'Urdu' is a dialect of 'Hindustani'
used by Muslims: it uses Arabic characters
and much of its vocabulary is of Persian
and Arabic origin. It also is the official
language of Pakistan (together with
English). See also **hoard**.

Hindustani see **Hindu**

hippopotamus/rhinoceros (large,
ungainly, thick-skinned animal)
The scientific names of the animals – more
like those of prehistoric creatures – mean
respectively 'river horse' and 'horny nose',
and this brings out the immediate difference
between them: the 'hippopotamus' lives in
rivers in Africa, the 'rhinoceros' lives in both
Asia and Africa but not in rivers, and moreover has one or two upright horns on its
snout. The wretched rhino is, alas, a
declining species, since its horn is valued as
an aphrodisiac and worth almost half its
weight in gold.

hips/haws (wild berries)
'Hips' are the red, fleshy, edible, berry-like
fruit – not actually a true fruit – of the wild
rose, and in particular the dog-rose. When
there was a shortage of citrus fruits in the
Second World War they were collected in
large numbers by schoolchildren to make
vitamin-packed rose-hip syrup. 'Haws' are
the deep red berries of the hawthorn. They

are also edible, but are eaten more by birds than humans.

historic/historical (relating to history)
'Historic' means 'important in history' as a 'historic' battle or a 'historic' speech. 'Historical' means 'concerned with history', such as a 'historical' novel or a 'historical' costume. A 'historical' map will show 'historic' sites.

historical see **historic**

histrionics see **hysterics**

hoard/horde (collection, multitude of things or people)
Which does a miser have, a 'hoard' of coins or 'hordes' of coins? Possibly both, although 'hoard' is the word meaning 'accumulation', especially of something saved up for the future and hidden away. A 'horde' is a large number of something, nearly always people or animals. The Golden 'Horde' was a troop of Mongol Tartars that overran eastern Europe in the thirteenth and fourteenth centuries. ('Golden' because of the magnificent apparel of their leader Batu Khan, the grandson of Genghis Khan.) The word is related to 'Urdu': both of them mean literally 'camp'.

hobby/pastime (leisure pursuit)
A 'hobby' is a favourite subject or occupation that is not one's main business, as gardening, 'do-it-yourself', or the rather vague 'reading' entered against 'hobbies' by some job applicants in the hope that it will impress as a cultural interest (although it may involve little more than a daily scan of the tabloid press). A 'pastime' is a recreation, something that makes the time pass agreeably, as playing cards, watching television or dining out.

hog see **pig**

Holland/Netherlands/Low Countries
(kingdom in western Europe famous for canals, tulips and windmills)
'Holland' is the popular but not official name of the country – which does, however, have two provinces named North 'Holland' (Noord-Holland) and South 'Holland'

(Zuid-Holland). The official name is thus The 'Netherlands', which formerly included Belgium and Luxembourg as well. The 'Low Countries', which obviously means the same, is more a historic name, in turn once applying to a wider region divided into a number of small states. Opinions seem to be divided about the actual meaning of the name 'Holland': possibly 'hollow' land, i.e. low-lying land, or 'wooded' land (related to 'holt'). One thing is clear: the district of 'Holland' in Lincolnshire (called officially the Parts of 'Holland' until 1974, when most counties in England were reorganised administratively) is, in spite of its tulips, nothing to do with its Dutch cousin. The name means 'heel' land, that is, land by the spur of a hill – which admittedly is surprising as the district is notoriously flat and fenny.

Holy Land see **Israel**

home see **house**

homicide/manslaughter (killing that may be justifiable or excusable)
'Homicide' is usually divided into justifiable, excusable and criminal. Justifiable 'homicide' is carried out: as a legal sentence of death, by an officer of justice as a means of taking a person who assaults or resists him and cannot be taken otherwise, or as a means of dispersing a riot or 'rebellious assembly' or preventing an atrocious crime such as murder or rape. It is excusable when committed by misadventure or in self-defence (when it virtually is the same as justifiable 'homicide' in the third instance mentioned above). Criminal 'homicide' embraces all other forms of killing, and is subdivided into 'manslaughter', murder, and infanticide. 'Manslaughter', as distinct from murder (see **murderer**), is unlawful killing without express or implied malice, especially where a person was provoked to lose his self-control or there was a high degree of negligence (as in a fatal motor accident). The difference between 'manslaughter' and murder is often, in fact, one of degree.

homonym/synonym (word closely associated with another)

A 'homonym' is a word identical in spelling to another, but having a different meaning, as 'bark', 'fair', 'like', and 'till'. (Some people also distinguish 'homophones', which are words pronounced alike but having a different meaning *and* spelling, as 'air' and 'heir', 'right' and 'write'.) A 'synonym' is a word that means approximately the same as another, as 'tired' and 'weary', 'tepid' and 'lukewarm', 'bit' and 'piece'. Not many synonyms have *exactly* the same meaning: there is usually a discernible difference or shade of meaning, if only a very fine one, or at any rate a difference of usage, as in 'little' and 'small', and 'begin', 'start' and 'commence'. The opposite of a 'synonym' is an antonym. Some apparent antonyms are in fact 'synonyms', as 'flammable' and 'inflammable', 'loose' and 'unloose', 'bend' and 'unbend'.

honorary see **honourable**

honorary degree see **honours degree**

honourable/honorary (worthy of, or given for, honour)
An 'honourable' award is one worthy of honour; an 'honorary' award is one given to serve as a token of honour, especially when not actually earned or won directly. Both words are used (with a capital 'H') as titles, the official abbreviation of which is, confusingly, 'Hon.'. 'Honourable' has a number of applications as a courtesy title. Among them, it is used as a prefix:

1 to the Christian names of the younger sons of earls and all children of viscounts and barons;
2 to the names of all justices of the High Court who are not Lord Justices or Lords of Appeal;
3 to the word 'member' or 'gentleman' in the House of Commons, when one MP is addressing or referring to another ('The Honourable Member for Ealing').
As a title, 'Honorary' means 'holding a position without being paid for it', as an 'Honorary' president, treasurer or secretary.

honours degree/honorary degree (type of university degree)
An 'honours degree' is one awarded (usually

as a 'Class 1' or a 'Class 2') to a student who has performed well ('with honour') in a final examination and so has obtained a good **degree** (which see). An 'honorary' degree is one awarded to a person as a sign of recognition for eminence in a particular field such as literature or music. It is 'honorary' since it does not carry the usual privileges and since, basically, the person did not have to pass an examination in order to receive it.

hoodoo/voodoo (spirit bringing bad luck)
A 'hoodoo' is a person or thing that brings bad luck or bad luck itself, a 'jinx'. 'Voodoo' is the genuine article: the 'black magic' rites of Negroes of the West Indies and the American South, involving sorcery and witchcraft and probably of African origin. Hence, too, it is the term used for one who practises these rites or for an object of 'voodoo' worship. The words are possibly related.

horde see **hoard**

hornet see **wasp**

horsebox see **stall**

hosannah see **hallelujah**

hotel/inn/pub (place where guests or customers can eat, drink, be merry, and often stay overnight)
The main purpose of a 'hotel' is to offer overnight accommodation. It therefore also offers, and usually to resident and casual guests alike, meals in a restaurant and drinks in one or more bars. An 'inn', broadly, seems to have two meanings: either a small 'hotel', which in turn may have developed or grown from a 'pub', or a 'pub' itself, especially an 'olde worlde', well-appointed, or simply pretentious one – or just an ordinary 'mine host' 'pub' which happens to have 'Inn' as part of its name, as the New 'Inn' or the London 'Inn'. This leaves us with the 'pub', the Englishman's local social club and serious drinking establishment. Many 'pubs' do, however, offer, if on a more modest scale, the services basically provided by 'hotels', since in a number you can eat as well as drink and also stay the night. Tourists in Britain seeking to eat,

drink or stay overnight somewhere should not, though, seek the place of their choice through the Yellow Pages telephone directory, where all three categories are listed without any clear form of distinction, but should be guided by personal recommendation or a specialist publication!

house/home (place to live in)
The distinction was once more clear-cut than it now is. A 'house' was a building for living in. A 'home' was a 'house' (or flat or any family residence) seen as not just a place to live in but a place of domestic comfort and family happiness. Today the two words are – at any rate in the jargon of estate agents – one and the same thing: 'new show "homes" for sale'. (Not that estate agents do not use the word 'house', they do – extensively. But when they say 'home' they simply mean 'house'.) In senses other than 'house', however, 'home' remains a highly emotive word, as in 'homeland', 'homesick', '"home" town' and even the 'Home' Guard. (For yet another example, see **longing**.)

hovercraft/hydrofoil (vehicle able to travel over the water at speed)
Both vehicles appeared more or less simultaneously, at the end of the 1950s. The 'hovercraft' is the one that has the 'cushion of air' enabling it to travel over any relatively smooth surface. The name was invented by the designer of the craft, Sir Christopher Cockerell, as a 'not altogether appropriate word'. A 'hydrofoil' is a vessel fitted with hydrofoils: surfaces designed to lift the hull out of the water at speed (after 'aerofoil'). Unlike the 'hovercraft', it can travel over water only.

hub/nub (centre of something)
In its literal sense, a 'hub' is the centre of something that rotates, such as a wheel, propeller or fan. Hence its figurative use to mean 'focal point', as in the 'hub' of the universe. A 'nub' is literally a small lump or chunk of something (the word is probably related to 'knob'). This is not the usual meaning, however, and 'nub' is normally used figuratively to mean 'point', 'gist', 'central theme', as the 'nub' of a story or a problem.

hulk see **hull**

hull/hulk (body of a ship)
The 'hull' of a ship is its frame or body, i.e. not including any sails, masts or superstructure. A 'hulk' is the body of an old or dismantled ship or wreck. A 'hulk' is also a term sometimes applied to a big person. (It suggests 'bulk', but that is simply a coincidence.)

humidity see **damp**

humiliation see **shame**

humour/wit (expression of the clever or amusing)
'Humour' usually depends on incongruities of some kind for its effect, whether verbally or visually. 'Wit' is a more intellectual affair, with carefully chosen words or ideas. This is not to say that it depends on careful or lengthy preparation: 'wit' can be spontaneous, and indeed the quickness of a witty response adds to its effectiveness. 'Wit' frequently uses analogy, especially between unlike things, for its impact, especially when such an analogy is expressed vividly or entertainingly. By implication, 'wit' is sharper than 'humour', 'humour' more kindly than 'wit'. 'Humour' can be unintentional; 'wit' rarely is. Furthermore, 'wit' is not necessarily amusing, of course – it can be perfectly serious.

hurdy-gurdy see **barrel-organ**

hurling/curling (Gaelic team game)
'Hurling' is a Gaelic game like Highland shinty, played with a team of fifteen on a field. The game, played in Ireland, resembles hockey, because the hurley, used for hitting the ball, suggests a heavy hockey stick. However, when 'hurling' you can catch the ball, kick it, hit it with your hurley *and* with your hands – a licence not permitted in the relatively more genteel hockey. 'Curling' is a Scottish game with four players on each side. It is played on an ice rink with two 'stones' – rock blocks shaped like a squashed ball with a curved handle on top – as a kind of 'bowls on ice'.

hurricane see **whirlwind**

hustle see **bustle**

hydrofoil see **hovercraft**

hydrogen bomb see **atomic bomb**

hydrometer/hygrometer (instrument for measuring liquid)
A 'hydrometer' is an instrument in the form of a cylindrical glass tube containing a weighted glass bulb. This is immersed in a liquid to measure its density or specific gravity (found by reading a calibration on the neck of the bulb). A 'hygrometer' is a device for measuring the relative humidity of the atmosphere. A number of types exist as e.g. evaporative, mechanical, electrical and dew-point. The French prefer the term *aréomètre* to *hydromètre* since the latter means 'water-spider'.

hygrometer see **hydrometer**

hypermarket see **supermarket**

hyperthermia see **hypothermia**

hypochondriac/dipsomaniac (one suffering from a morbid complaint)
A 'hypochondriac' is a person suffering from acute depression or, more generally, imagined ill-health. The term derives from the Greek, literally 'under the gristle': the reference is to that part of the abdomen that lies under the cartilage of the breast-bone. This region was supposed to be the seat of melancholy or 'black bile'. (For related concepts, see **bile, frantic**.) A 'dipsomaniac' is someone who suffers from a craving for alcohol, literally a 'thirst maniac'.

hypothermia/hyperthermia (condition of having the body temperature unusually cold – or hot)
The prefixes are the cause of the trouble, 'hypo' being 'under' and 'hyper' being 'over'. 'Hypothermia' is the distressing and often fatal condition prevalent among elderly people in cold weather, when the body temperature drops significantly below normal. 'Hyperthermia' is the opposite. The latter condition can be brought on by natural causes, such as intense heat, or induced, for example for therapeutic purposes.

hypothesis see **theory**

hysterics/histrionics (violent emotional display)
'Hysterics', popularly, is a display resembling hysteria, with the familiar crying and/or laughing, gesticulating, babbling and the like. 'Histrionics' is a similar display, but a theatrical one, with vehement speech and exaggerated gestures – 'theatricals', in fact. The word derives from the Latin *histrio* (actor), while 'hysterics' has its origin in the Greek *hystera* (womb). It was originally thought that women were more likely to suffer from the disorder than men; science, subsequently, has proved otherwise.

I

Ice Age see **Stone Age**

ideal/idyllic (perfect, the best imaginable)
'Ideal' is very much a general word to describe something that is the best one can think of, as an 'ideal' picnic spot or 'ideal' timing. 'Idyllic' has a similar meaning, but in an aesthetic sense and often with a poetic flavour, as an 'idyllic' spot (one that is rustic, romantic, picturesque or the like). The essence of the word is in the origin of 'idyll' – Greek *eidyllion* (little picture).

idiot/moron/cretin/imbecile (stupid or mentally subnormal person)
'Moron', 'imbecile' and 'idiot' are terms still sometimes officially used in Britain, in this order, for increasing degrees of mental subnormality, with a 'moron' having an IQ of 50 to 69 (the average is 100) and the mental age of a child of eight to eleven, an

'imbecile' having an IQ of 20 to 49, or a mental age below eight, and an 'idiot' having an IQ of 20 or under. A 'cretin' is specifically a person with a deformity and mental retardation caused by a thyroid deficiency. (Cretinism, this condition, is now usually called hypothyroidism.) The words have interesting origins: 'idiot' comes from the Greek meaning 'private person' (as in 'idiosyncrasy'); 'moron' (perhaps more predictably) is Greek 'foolish'; 'cretin' derives, via French, from 'Christian' (that is, a simple, holy person, 'God's fool'); 'imbecile', from Latin, literally means 'without a stick', that is, for support (the same Latin word, *baculus*, gives 'bacillus' as a term for a rod-shaped bacterium). All four words, of course, are used, viciously or playfully, as terms of abuse for a stupid or foolish person. It is a hard linguistic fact of life that words denoting mental or physical abnormalities or deficiencies often become insults: compare 'spastic', for example.

idle/indolent (inactive, lazy)

The difference lies in the emotiveness: 'indolent' is a derogatory word, 'idle' is not. 'Idle' means 'not working', whether legitimately or not; 'indolent' means 'not working because lazy'.

idyllic see ideal

i.e. see e.g.

illegal/illicit/illegitimate (unlawful, improper)

There are three well-defined shades of meaning here. 'Illegal' means 'not legal', i.e. refers to something that is against the law and known to be forbidden, as 'illegal' entry into a country. 'Illicit' applies to something that is known to be 'illegal' but which is nevertheless deliberately done, usually regularly and secretly, as the 'illicit' import of drugs. (The implication is that, given other circumstances, the act could be legal.) 'Illegitimate' implies that what is done has not been authorised by law, has not been made lawful, as the familiar 'illegitimate' child born outside a lawful marriage.

illegitimate see illegal

illicit see illegal

illness/disease (disorder of the body or a bodily organ)

An 'illness' is often a general disorder, usually not severe, but occasionally grave. A 'disease' is a more specific disorder, especially an active, lengthy or serious one. An 'illness' is a relatively vague word, too, so that it is often qualified, as a slight 'illness', serious 'illness', short 'illness' or long 'illness'. It relates, moreover, to the whole body or state of health, whereas a 'disease' may be in a particular organ *or* the whole body.

illusion see delusion

imbecile see idiot

imbrue see imbue

imbue/imbrue (soak, impregnate)

The root of both words is Latin *bibere* (to drink). 'Imbue' is basically 'fill', especially with reference to feelings: 'My visit to Rome imbued me with a real sense of history.' Similarly a teacher can 'imbue' his pupils with, for example, a regard for safety or a concern for the needs of others. 'Imbrue' is a more forceful word, and a rarer one. Literally, it is usually associated with blood: 'hands imbrued with blood' is a near hack phrase with some thriller writers. 'Imbue' used literally is normally applied to colours and scents, as a handkerchief 'imbued' with perfume.

immeasurable see immense

immense/immeasurable (vast, boundless)

'Immense' is simply 'very great', as an 'immense' size or quantity. 'Immeasurable', logically enough, has the implication that the object described is too great to be measured and often is therefore, by extension, priceless, as a jewel of 'immeasurable' value.

immersed see submerged

immigrant/emigrant/émigré/migrant

(person leaving one country or place to go to another)
The prefixes hold the key: an 'immigrant'

is someone who has come *in* to a country; an 'emigrant' is a person who has gone out of (Latin *ex-*) a country. An 'émigré' is a special kind of 'emigrant'. The original 'émigrés' fled from France at the time of the French Revolution. The word is now most frequently applied to political and religious refugees, in particular Russians and Jews. A 'migrant' is used of anyone or anything that moves regularly from one place to another, as 'migrant' workers, 'migrant' birds and fishes and even 'migrant' plants whose seeds are carried abroad. One person can, of course, be both an 'immigrant' and an 'emigrant', but not at the same time.

immoral/amoral (not moral)
'Immoral' is the opposite of 'moral', i.e. means 'having bad or low morals', 'not conforming to a moral standard'. 'Amoral' means 'having no morals', that is, no moral standards by which one can be judged. 'Immoral' is thus a positive epithet; 'amoral' is negative. Put more basically, 'immoral' connotes 'bad'; 'amoral' is neither good nor bad.

immunity/impunity (freedom from liability or penalty)
To have 'immunity' from something – usually unpleasant or disagreeable – is to be free from it, as 'immunity' from disease, attack or interference. 'Impunity' implies freedom from punishment or undesirable consequences. It is most commonly used in the phrase 'with impunity': 'Go on, criticise him, you can do it with impunity!'

imperial/imperious (domineering)
The basic meaning of 'imperial' is 'pertaining to an empire or emperor', as the 'imperial' palace or an 'imperial' decree. It also means 'commanding', in the sense 'emperor-like'. 'Imperious' implies a dictatorial attitude, but basically means 'domineering', as an 'imperious' voice or an 'imperious' gesture.

imperious see imperial

impersonate/personate (represent in personal form)
To 'impersonate' someone is to pretend to be him in some way. We are all familiar with the 'impersonations' of stage and television comics. More widely, every actor is 'impersonating' once he sets foot on the stage. It also means 'represent in bodily form', 'personify': the aim of many revolutionaries is to 'impersonate' the will of the common people. 'Personate' has the same meaning as 'impersonate' when it comes to acting: go to a local theatre group's production and you could see your bank manager 'personating' an American ranch hand. This sense is extended to mean 'pass oneself off as', often for fraudulent purposes, as when a pickpocket 'personates' a reporter at some public gathering. In the arts, especially painting, 'personate' means 'stand for' in the sense of representing an abstract quality or personal property. The snake usually 'personates' evil.

impertinent see insolent

impetuous see compulsive

impetus see momentum

impinge see infringe

implement see instrument

imply/infer (deduce – or mean)
Two fairly hoary confusibles: the diarist of *The Times* once (15 March 1977) used 'inferred' for 'implied' and caused an excited flutter among his readers. (He subsequently, but not too convincingly, referred readers to the *OED* in his defence.) In fact the two are indeed often used interchangeably, but strictly speaking: 'imply' means 'express indirectly' – almost 'mean' – and 'infer' means 'derive by reasoning', 'deduce'. For some reason 'infer' is frequently used where many would prefer 'imply', but 'imply' hardly ever used instead of 'infer'. So if I 'imply' that you are deceitful, I say so indirectly; if I 'infer' that you are deceitful, I gather that you are from what you say or do, or from what I hear about you.

impracticable see impractical

impractical/impracticable/unpractical/unpracticable (not practical or practicable)

'Impractical' means 'not able to be put into practice although theoretically possible', as an 'impractical' plan (not a good one). Of a person, 'impractical' means 'no good at doing practical things'. 'Impracticable' means 'not manageable', 'not workable', as an 'impracticable' road (it cannot be used) or plan (it will not work). An 'impracticable' person is one hard to deal with, as someone who is stubborn or stupid. 'Unpractical' is not a common word, but it means 'not practical', as an 'unpractical' person (who cannot do practical things). 'Unpracticable' is a rarish alternative for 'impracticable'.

impromptu see **extempore**

impudent see **insolent**

impugn see **infringe**

impulsive see **compulsive**

impunity see **immunity**

inapt see **inept**

incarnadine see **crimson**

incentive see **motive** (inducement)

inchoate see **incoherent**

incident see **accident**

incidental/accidental (fortuitous)
'Incidental' means 'happening or likely to happen in conjunction with something else'; 'accidental' means 'happening by chance', i.e. not in connection with something else. A season ticket is not only cheaper than a number of individual ones, it has the 'incidental' advantage of needing to be purchased only periodically instead of every day, and perhaps the 'accidental' advantage of fitting your inside pocket.

incite see **excite**

incoherent/inchoate (imperfectly expressed or formed)
The two are not synonymous, in spite of the definition of 'inchoate' given by the *Sunday Times* (25 September 1977) – one of those 'words which give you those chilly doubts when you use them' – as 'just begun, incomplete, imperfectly formulated, incoherent'. 'Incoherent' usually relates to thoughts or words with the sense 'not fitting together', 'rambling', as in an 'incoherent' speech or argument. 'Inchoate', something of a vogue word of the 1970s, means 'just begun', 'unformed', as an 'inchoate' mass of gas or the 'inchoate' church of the early Christians. Confusion with 'incoherent' may be due to false association with its near anagram, 'chaotic.'

inconsequent/inconsequential (irrelevant)
An 'inconsequent' remark is one that is not relevant to what has been said before; an 'inconsequential' remark is one that is trivial and that is of no consequence.

inconsequential see **inconsequent**

incumbent/encumbent (holder of a particular post)
Kenneth Hudson, in his *Dictionary of Diseased English* (Macmillan, 1977), points out that 'encumbent' is a 'strange and quite unjustified spelling of "incumbent", now common in the business world, especially in Australia' and suggests, very fairly, that the word has a false association with **encumber**. The term applies chiefly to the holder of a post in industry or commerce, and is possibly too recent – or Australian – to have been recorded in most British and American dictionaries. 'Incumbent', however, is a well documented word. It has the same meaning (in the business sense) as 'encumbent' although its precise definition is 'holder of an ecclesiastical office'. As things stand, therefore, the 'in-' spelling is the 'in' one and preferred in British English. Possibly in time the Australian version may be the one to gain the wider acceptance.

Indian elephant see **African elephant**

indifferent/diffident (showing little or no enthusiasm)
'Indifferent' means 'not caring', 'impartial', even 'apathetic': 'He was quite indifferent

to her pleas'. 'Diffident' means 'lacking confidence', even 'shy'; a 'diffident' suggestion is one made reservedly or without much confidence.

indignation see **anger**

indolent see **idle**

inductive see **deductive**

in effect see **in fact**

inept/inapt/unapt (inappropriate, unsuitable)
There is an overlap between 'inept' and 'inapt', but although an 'inept' remark is usually an absurd or silly one, an 'inapt' remark is simply one that is out of place or inappropriate. The words can apply to people: an 'inept' pupil is one slow to learn; an 'inapt' mechanic is one who lacks skill. 'Unapt' is not a common word, but can be used as an effective emphatic equivalent of 'not apt' or 'unsuitable'.

in fact/in effect (in reality)
'In fact' means 'in actual truth' and is used when explaining the real facts behind something that is false or doubtful: 'He thought he was right, but in fact he wasn't.' 'In effect' is used to mean 'in reality' when clarifying something or explaining it more precisely, especially when such clarification is apparently illogical or unexpected: 'We come now to what is, in effect, the highlight of the performance (you are intrigued or surprised that it is); 'You will start work on the twelfth, but your pay will in effect be from the first of the month' (illogically). From this it can be seen that in effect 'in effect' is basically rather different in meaning to 'in fact'.

infant see **child**

infant school see **nursery school**

infectious/contagious (communicable, 'catching')
Speaking strictly medically: an 'infectious' disease is one spread by germs, as colds or flu or typhoid; a 'contagious' disease is spread by actual bodily contact, or by contact with something that itself has been in bodily contact with the diseased person. Used figuratively, 'infectious' suggests that the 'source' of infection is agreeably irresistible, as 'infectious' laughter; 'contagious' emphasises the rapidity of spreading, as 'contagious' enthusiasm.

infer see **imply**

infinity/eternity (state of continuing for ever)
The two words are rather mind-bending. 'Infinity' is a space, time or quantity that is boundless: no end or limit to it is known or can be envisaged. 'Eternity' relates to time only, where it is not quite the same as 'infinity', since it not only has no end, but – even more awesomely – had no beginning. Something that is thus eternal will exist, and has existed, for ever.

inflammable/flammable (catching fire easily)
The words illustrate the importance of prefixes: the 'in-' does not mean, as it often does, 'not', but simply 'in', i.e. 'in flame'. The two words therefore mean exactly the same, with the older word 'flammable' now revived and commonly used to avoid ambiguity in what could be a matter of life and death. In 1959 the British Standards Institution announced: 'It is the Institution's policy to encourage the use of the terms "flammable" and "non-flammable" rather than "inflammable" and "non-inflammable".'

inflation/reflation/deflation/disinflation (rate of increase, or decrease, in the supply of money in a country's economy)
'The words relating to inflation need to be treated with the greatest care' wrote the Editor of *The Times* in a memorandum on the subject circulated on the paper's staff. Basically, 'inflation' is an increase in the supply of money beyond its proper limits with a consequent increase in prices. The reverse of this is 'deflation', i.e. a reduction in the supply of money, with consequent fall in prices. 'Reflation' (meaning 're-inflation') should logically be used to mean another period of 'inflation' after a period of 'deflation', although it in fact is commonly

defined as 'the supply of money being restored to a higher level after deflation has occurred' ('A memorandum on style', *The Times,* 7 September 1977) – that is, not 'inflation', but a recovery from 'deflation' and a slump, with or without a later stage of 'inflation'. 'Disinflation' is a post-war word used to indicate a slow increase in the supply of money in order to check 'inflation' without producing the disadvantages of 'deflation'. All four words have been vigorously batted around since the mid-1970s.

inflicted/afflicted (having something unpleasant imposed)
To be 'inflicted' with something or someone, as a heavy load of work or a mother-in-law to stay, implies that what is imposed must be borne as a necessary evil. To be 'afflicted' with a thing, usually a disease, implies positive suffering with associated distress or pain. The two are quite often confused: *Collins English Learner's Dictionary* under 'afflict' ('cause pain, disease etc.') gives the example 'afflict somebody with extra work' instead of 'inflict'.

infra-red rays see **X-rays**

infringe/impinge/impugn (oppose, counter, encroach)
To 'infringe' something is to violate or act contrary to it, as when one 'infringes' someone's right or 'infringes' a law. The derivation is not from 'fringe' – as if one was 'edging in' where one had no right to – but from a Latin verb meaning literally 'break in'. To 'impinge' is to make an impact, often so as to spoil or affect adversely. Thus to 'impinge' on a person's spare time is to appropriate it unreasonably, to make unfair demands on it. To 'impugn' a thing is to question the truth of it, so that one can 'impugn' a statement or someone's words, call them in question.

ingenious/ingenuous (artful – or artless)
The confusion, where it exists, is not so much over the meaning of 'ingenious' but over the relationship to it of 'ingenuous'. There is also a similarity of meaning in the qualities the words describe – both 'ingenuity' and 'ingenuousness' (the respective nouns) are personal characteristics to be

admired. Moreover, an 'ingenuous' person, by being sincere and frank and open, may unwittingly be quite 'ingenious', or clever at inventing or discovering things. However, enough no doubt said to establish the difference between the two.

ingenuous see **ingenious**

inheritance/heritage (that which has been inherited)
An 'inheritance' is the property or possessions that pass to an heir, whether actually bequeathed, as a sum of money, or passed down by natural means, as a gift for languages. In a wider, although still personal sense, the word can apply to any quality or attribute passed down by one group of people to another, as the Viking 'inheritance' of English northcountrymen. 'Heritage' is a grander word and applies to some specific quality or possession that is, or can be, inherited – usually something valuable or beneficial, as 'our heritage the sea', but also an undesirable thing, as when poverty is regarded as the 'heritage' of war.

inlet see **bay**

inn see **hotel**

innuendo see **insinuation**

innumerable see **numerous**

inoculation/vaccination (medical process of producing immunity against disease)
An 'inoculation', in general, induces a milder form of the disease and so safeguards against attacks from it. The word is not related to 'innocuous' but derives from Latin *inoculare,* 'to engraft'. A 'vaccination' is an 'inoculation' given specifically against smallpox, when the virus inoculated – the vaccine – is that of cowpox. The word comes from the Latin for 'cow', *vacca.*

inquiry see **enquiry**

insecticide/pesticide (preparation for destroying unwanted creatures)
An 'insecticide' is designed to kill harmful insects. A 'pesticide' kills pests – which are not only harmful insects but animals and

plants that are a threat to man or his interests. Some pests need specialised 'pesticides' such as a *herbicide* for weeds, a *fungicide* for fungus or a *vermicide* for worms. Take your pest, translate him into Latin, add '-cide' to denote the killing agent, and you have a particular 'pesticide'. (Ants? Formicide. Foxes? Vulpicide. Rats? Raticide.) Although take this too far and you tend to get a form of verbicide ('deliberate distortion or destruction of the sense of a word', as *Webster* defines it).

insert/inset (as noun: something inserted) An 'insert' is something placed in a complete entity, as an advertisement in the newspaper, an illustration plate in a book, an enclosure in a letter and the like. An 'inset' usually implies the insertion of something smaller in a larger entity, as a photograph in the corner of a larger one, a short scene in another in a play (for purposes of shifting scenery) and so on. Both words are accented on the first letter.

inset see **insert**

insignia/regalia (badges of honour or of office)
'Insignia' is a general term for distinguishing badges of any kind, as the ebony wand carried by the House of Lords official known as Black Rod, or the crown and three stripes that are the 'insignia' of a staff sergeant in the army. 'Regalia', as the term implies, are the 'insignia' of royalty, especially the 'regalia' used at coronations, such as the crown, orb and sceptre. The word also applies, however, to the 'insignia' of civic dignitaries, as a mayor (his chain of office, for example), or of an order of Freemasons.

insinuation/innuendo/insinuendo
(indirect suggestion)
An 'insinuation', literally something 'brought in by winding', is an artful suggestion or hint, often an unpleasant one, as an 'insinuation' that one is being dishonest. It also has the sense 'ingratiation', applied to someone who has 'wound his way in' to someone else's company, or into a group activity such as a discussion. An 'innuendo', derived from a medieval Latin formula –

literally 'by nodding', indicating a parenthetical explanation, a 'that is to say' – is a derogatory indirect statement about someone attacking his character or behaviour, as an 'innuendo' that someone is a thief. It is thus more positive and forceful than an 'insinuation' which is merely a hint. An 'insinuendo' – the word is a blend of the other two – is a combined derogatory hint and statement. It is condemned by the *OED Supplement* as 'a tasteless word'; it would, moreover, seem to be a superfluous one.

insinuendo see **insinuation**

insipid see **tepid**

insolent/impudent/impertinent/pert
(rude, cheeky)
'Insolent' is the strongest word here, implying an attitude that is insulting or unpleasantly arrogant, as seen in 'insolent' behaviour or heard in an 'insolent' remark. 'Impudent' implies shamelessness, which need not necessarily be insulting, so that an 'impudent' remark is one that is either disrespectful or brazen. 'Impertinent' – literally 'not pertinent', i.e. 'out of place' – is a word that implies intrusion or presumption: an 'impertinent' remark is one that is not called for and one which usually shows lack of respect. 'Pert' almost has the sense of 'engagingly cheeky', with a 'pert' remark suggesting a saucy but at the same time rather clever comment. (The old sense of 'pert' was indeed 'clever'.)

insolvency/bankruptcy/liquidation
(state of being unable to pay one's debts)
'Insolvency' is the inability to settle one's debts when they fall due. It is not the same as 'bankruptcy' since a very rich man can be insolvent if he cannot actually realise his assets at the time he needs the cash. 'Bankruptcy', which may follow 'insolvency', is the state of a person who declares that he is unable to pay his debts, or who by his conduct makes this obvious, and whose property is accordingly distributed by law among his creditors. Such a person will remain bankrupt officially until he has been discharged. He will have certain so called disabilities (such as not being able to be a company director or become an MP or JP)

but he can continue in business. 'Liquidation' is, in effect, the 'bankruptcy' of a company, with two sorts: voluntary and compulsory (which terms are self-explanatory).

insouciant see **nonchalant**

instinctively/intuitively (naturally, innately)
'Instinctively' means 'by instinct', 'by an innate response', as when one 'instinctively' shades or screws up one's eyes when looking towards the sun. 'Intuitively' means that what is done results from the ability of the doer to understand a situation instantly without any reasoning process: 'She intuitively chose the longer route' (she knew it was the right one without being able to explain why).

institute see **institution**

institute of education see **teacher training college**
institution/institute (organisation for promoting or studying something)
The difference is not always clear-cut. On the whole, an 'institution' is an establishment of some sort or its building, usually one of a kind, as a school (an educational 'institution'), hospital (medical 'institution') or charity (philanthropic 'institution'). Its field of activity is thus on the whole a broad one. By contrast an 'institute' concerns itself with a more specific object, frequently one that is studied rather than actively practised, as a cultural or scientific 'institute'. As with 'institution', the word is also used for the building or premises of the body. One thus has, for example, a literary 'institute' but a benevolent 'institution'. The names of a number of specialised bodies contain the word 'institute', as the Scott Polar Research Institute in Cambridge or the British Film Institute in London. In the field of education, the word is used for an establishment that specialises in technical subjects at post-secondary school level, as an 'institute' of technology. Generally, then, an 'institute' is more advanced and specialised in its field of activity than an 'institution'.

instrument/implement (tool, device)
An 'instrument' tends to be more precise or complex than an 'implement', as a musical 'instrument' or an electrical device or mechanism such as a telephone. An 'implement' is basically a tool, utensil or article used for a specific purpose, and usually performs a function that is subordinate or preparatory to the realising of a final product or process. Thus agricultural 'implements' are used for work such as ploughing, sowing and harrowing which is subordinate to the end process of the consumption or marketing of the produce, and kitchen 'implements' are used for the preparing and cooking of food as a process ancillary to the actual eating of the food. 'Implements' are thus a means to an end; most 'instruments' perform a function that is complete in itself.

insure see **assure**

intellect see **mind**

intense/intensive (strong, concentrated)
'Intense' means 'occurring in a high or extreme degree', as 'intense' heat or anxiety. 'Intensive' means 'growing more intense', as an 'intensive' course of 'intensive' treatment, which can be carried to the limit of endurance or safety.

intensive see **intense**

intimacy see **familiarity**

introduction see **foreword**

intrusive/obtrusive (thrusting, prominent)
It's the prefixes again: 'intrusive' is 'thrusting in'; 'obtrusive' is 'thrusting forward or onto'. Both suggest an action performed without permission or reason. An 'intrusive' manner thus forces itself into other people's company; an 'obtrusive' manner forces other people to pay attention to it.

intuitively see **instinctively**

invective/inveighing (violent verbal attack)

'Invective' is usually an abusive verbal attack; 'inveighing' implies a vehement verbal attack, a 'railing'. Both words, as well as 'vehement', ultimately derive from Latin *vehere* (to carry, bear). 'Inveighing' is most common in the verbal form 'inveigh': 'He inveighed heavily against the rising cost of petrol.'

inveighing see **invective**

invention/discovery (making or revealing of something previously unknown)
An 'invention' usually implies the creation of a new device or mechanism by thought, planning and the deliberate application of one's knowledge. A 'discovery' may well result from a planned course of action, but equally it can follow as a pure chance, with no idea of a deliberate search for something new. A 'discovery', too, is often simply the finding or establishing of something that was already in existence, whereas an 'invention' is always something that is new. Hydrogen was thus 'discovered' by Henry Cavendish in 1766; the hydrometer was 'invented' by Hypatia of Alexandria in 400.

inventory see **list**

invoice see **account**

ionosphere see **atmosphere**

iron/steel (tough, heavy metal)
Iron is an element with the atomic number 26 and is a white, magnetic metal. It is rarely found in a pure condition but in its impure form it is used for making a variety of tools, implements, machinery and the like. Pig-'iron' is the impure form of 'iron' obtained from 'iron' ores, wrought 'iron' is the purest commercial form of 'iron' ('iron' nearly free from carbon). 'Steel' is 'iron' containing a small percentage of carbon in the form of cementite. The properties of different 'steels' vary according to their percentage of carbon and other metals and to the method of preparation. 'Steel' with very little carbon, so called 'mild' or 'dead mild', is used for sheets, pipes and plates. Ultra-high-carbon 'steel' is used for the manufacture of chisels, files, razors and other turning and cutting tools. 'Steel' itself is now often blended with alloying elements such as nickel and chromium, and thus 'alloy steel' is used, for example, for tyres and widely for table knives.

irony see **sarcasm**

irruption see **eruption**

Israel/Palestine/Holy Land (country on shores of eastern Mediterranean)
'Israel' is the modern republic formed as a Jewish state in May 1948 out of the former British mandated territory of 'Palestine'. 'Israel' originally extended over approximately eight-tenths of this territory, the remainder being occupied after the Six Day War in June 1967, together with the Sinai Peninsula and Golan Heights in Syria. (In October 1973 these two latter regions became the scene of a new conflict between Arab forces, led by Egypt and Syria, and 'Israel'.) In biblical times 'Israel' was the northern kingdom of the Hebrews, with capital Samaria, the southern kingdom being Judah (Judaea), with capital Hebron. 'Palestine', now a historic region, was an ancient country that for centuries was closely linked to the Jewish people and to Syria. In biblical times it was occupied by these same two kingdoms of 'Israel' and Judah – and in the twentieth century has remained the scene of conflicts between Jews and Arabs. Its age-long religious associations have caused it to be known as the 'Holy Land' and a world centre of pilgrimage. It is a land sacred not only to Christians but, of course, to Jews, for whom it was the 'Promised Land', and to Muslims also, since certain sites are associated with Mohammed. The latter tie has resulted in the keen desire of Arabs, especially members of the Arab nationalist movement, to claim 'Palestine' (as they call 'Israel') as the homeland of the Arab people, who have lived there since the Muslim conquest of the seventh century. Meanwhile, in spite of the initiative of President Carter in bringing about the peace treaty between 'Israel' and Egypt, signed in Washington on 26 March 1979, unrest remains, and rival claims to the territory continue to be made with continuing loss of life.

Israeli see **Jew**

Israelite see **Jew**

iterate see **repeat**

its see **it's**

it's/its (relating to 'it')
Possibly two of the commonest confusibles in the language: 'it's' does not mean 'belonging to it' (i.e. the apostrophe 's' is not a possessive one) but 'it is' or 'it has', as 'It's a long way and it's started to rain'. 'Its', *without* the apostrophe, does mean 'belonging to it'. 'Look at that fledgling – it's lost its mother!'

J

jacket see **coat**

Jacobean/Jacobin/Jacobite (pertaining to James)
All three words relate to a James or Jacques, the Latin for which is *Jacobus*. 'Jacobean' relates to James I of England (reigned 1603–25) or his times, in particular with regard to the style of architecture and furnishings. A fine example of a 'Jacobean' mansion is Knole House, Kent. As a noun, a 'Jacobin' was a member of the society of French revolutionaries set up in 1789 who met in the Dominican convent of Saint-Jacques in Paris. The term came to be applied to an extreme political radical. A 'Jacobite' was an adherent of James II of England after his overthrow in 1688, or of his descendants, and in particular his son the Young Pretender – 'Bonnie Prince Charlie'.

Jacobin see **Jacobean**

Jacobite see **Jacobean**

jade see **emerald**

jaguar see **leopard**

jam/marmalade (kind of fruit preserve)
'Marmalade' is not simply orange 'jam' eaten at breakfast. It is properly a jelly in which small pieces of citrus fruit (as oranges, lemons, or limes), including the rind, have been suspended. The citrus fruit ensures that the taste of 'marmalade' is thus normally sharp and tangy. Jam, on the other hand, is made from whole fruit (not usually citrus) that has been slightly crushed or pulped to make a preserve, as typically (and tastily) from strawberries, raspberries, apricots, plums, blackcurrants and the like. Depending on the kind of fruit, the taste of 'jam' is thus usually sweet and sugary. In spite of its close association with the English (and American) breakfast table, 'marmalade' in fact derives from the Portuguese for 'quince', since this was the fruit that the preserve was originally made from.

janitor see **caretaker**

jargon see **slang**

javelin see **lance**

jazzy/snazzy/natty (colourful and smart – of dress)
'Jazzy' implies bright colours, as perhaps sported in a 'jazzy' tie or scarf. 'Snazzy' really means 'flashily stylish', often with a suggestion of bright or gay patterns or colours (much as 'jazzy'). The origin of the word is obscure – possibly a blend of 'snappy' and 'jazzy'? 'Natty', which may derive from 'neat', means 'smart and trim', usually impressively so, as a 'natty' suit or uniform.

jealousy see **envy**

jeans/denims (type of clothing popular with younger people)
'Jeans', characteristically a faded or blotchy blue in colour, are properly made of a twilled cotton cloth called 'jean' or 'denim'. When 'denim' is used for the fabric of over-

alls or work clothing, however, the garment is usually actually called 'denims'. As such, they are familiar to an older generation as a type of military working trousers, although they are toughish, loose-fitting and khaki-coloured in contrast to the thinnish, tight-fitting blue 'jeans' of today. Both are imports, as materials and words, since 'jeans' – or the fabric called 'jean' – originally came from Genoa in Italy, while 'denim' was once, in French, *serge de Nîmes,* or 'serge from Nîmes', a town in the south of France.

jejune see **juvenile**

jelly/blancmange (sweet or flavoured gelatinous dessert)
A 'jelly' is clearish in consistency, a 'blancmange' opaque, as every child knows. But how does a milk 'jelly' differ from a 'blancmange', since both are opaque? The answer is in the ingredients. A 'blancmange' contains cornflour as a thickening agent, a 'jelly' does not. (What makes a milk 'jelly' opaque is its milk alone, even though milk, too, is present in the 'blancmange'.) Otherwise both contain gelatine or some similar substance, both are sweet or fruit-flavoured, both are made in a mould and both are attractively wobbly. They come in different colours, but originally, because of its cornflour, the 'blancmange' was white only, as its French name indicates.

jerboa see **gerbil**

jeroboam/rehoboam/jorum (large vessel for holding wine)
First the definitions: a 'jorum' is a rarish word for a large bowl or vessel for holding drink, or the contents of such a bowl. A 'jeroboam' is a large wine bottle holding 2½–3 gallons; a 'rehoboam' is a very large bottle, containing 5 or 6 gallons (i.e. two 'jeroboams'). The origins are quaintly biblical: a 'jorum' is said to be named after Joram, who brought vessels of silver, gold and brass to David (II Samuel 8:10). A 'jeroboam' is named after Jeroboam, 'a mighty man of valour' (I Kings 14:16). The same gentleman, some claim, gave his name to that more lowly vessel, the 'jerry'. The 'rehoboam', modelled on the 'jeroboam', is

said to have borrowed the name of Rehoboam, the first King of Judah (II Chronicles 13:7). There are also rich and rare vessels with names on the same lines such as 'methuselah', 'salmanazar', 'balthazar' and 'nebuchadnezzar'.

jersey see **pullover**

jetsam see **flotsam**

jetty see **quay**

Jew/Israelite/Israeli/Hebrew (person whose religion is Judaism)
The word 'Jew' has essentially religious connotations, and applies especially to a descendant of the ancient nation of Palestine (called 'Hebrews' in the Bible) whose present-day representatives have found homes in many countries of the world apart from Israel, the 'true' Jewish homeland. 'Jew' as an appellation has lost most of its former derogatory associations, and is frequently used today as a contrast to 'Christian'. An 'Israelite' was a member of the ancient kingdom of Israel, just as an 'Israeli' is a native or inhabitant of the modern state of Israel. The 'Hebrews' were a Semitic people in ancient Palestine, familiar in Old Testament stories. (The 'Hebrews' to whom an Epistle in the New Testament is addressed were probably Hebrew Christians, that is, 'converted' 'Hebrews' from either Palestine or Rome.) For more about the language, see **Hebrew**.

jewel/gem (precious stone)
A 'jewel' can be three things: an ornament containing a precious stone; a precious (or semi-precious) stone itself, especially a cut and polished one; a special precious stone, or its substitute, used in a watch or some other delicate instrument. A 'gem' coincides with the second of these two definitions (a cut and polished precious stone), but the word is also used of a precious or semi-precious stone that has an engraved design – in other words a cameo.

jig see **reel**

jinn/jinnee/genie/genius (spirit)

Alternative spellings increase the confusion here: moreover 'jinn' ('djinn', 'ginn') is really a plural word, the singular of which is 'jinnee' ('djinnee', 'jinni', 'djinni', 'genie'). The first three words thus are one and the same: a spirit, or class of spirits, influencing men for good or evil in Islam and Arabian mythology. The plural of the variant 'genie' is sometimes wrongly given as 'genii', but this is the plural of 'genius', a Latin word used to denote the attendant spirit that keeps watch over a person – or sometimes simply a demon or spirit in general. (The word 'genus', meaning 'class', 'order', as used scientifically, has the plural 'genera'.)

jinnee see **jinn**

jobber see **stockbroker**

jocose see **jocular**

jocular/jocose/jocund/jovial (merry, convivial)
Distinguishing nicely: 'jocular' is 'always making jokes', 'jocose' is 'playful', 'jocund' is 'cheerful' or 'light-hearted', and 'jovial' is 'hearty and good-humoured'. One might thus have a 'jocular' manner, a 'jocose' air, a 'jocund' companion, and a 'jovial' uncle. The first three relate to 'joke'; but 'jovial' to Jove or Jupiter. Those born under the planet Jupiter are said to be merry and sociable.

jocund see **jocular**

joiner see **carpenter**

jorum see **jeroboam**

journal see **magazine**

journey see **trip**

jovial see **jocular**

judge/magistrate (public officer appointed to hear and try cases in court)
'Judge' is an all-embracing term but as normally used applies to 'judges' of the House of Lords, the Court of Appeal, the High Court, the Crown Court, and county courts. In England and Wales, a 'magistrate' is a minor judicial officer, such as a JP, or a stipendiary 'magistrate' (i.e. a paid one, usually in a large provincial town). In Scotland he is a provost or bailie of a burgh. More basically, 'judges' are major judicial officers, while 'magistrates' deal with less serious or weighty matters – and at the same time are 'judges' in their own right. 'Magistrates' also, however, conduct preliminary investigations into more serious offences. Judging which 'judge' does what is a rather complex business.

judicial/judicious (pertaining to judgment)
'Judicial' means 'pertaining to a judge or court of law', as 'judicial' proceedings or a 'judicial' survey. In a wider sense, the word means 'fair', 'just': a 'judicial' statement is an impartial one. 'Judicious' means 'having sound judgment', 'prudent', 'discreet', as a 'judicious' pause or remark.

judicious see **judicial**

judo/ju-jitsu (type of Japanese wrestling)
'Judo', literally 'soft art', is in fact a refined form of 'ju-jitsu' introduced in 1882 by Dr Jigoro Kano and using particular principles of movement and balance as a sport or form of physical exercise. 'Ju-jitsu' is the basic form of this. Its name has the same meaning, with 'judo' the Japanese adaptation of Chinese *jou tao*.

ju-jitsu see **judo**

jujube see **cashew**

Julian calendar see **Gregorian calendar**

jumper see **pullover**

junction/juncture (point at which two or more things meet)
'Junction' implies a coming together, as a railway 'junction' where the lines meet or a 'junction' box where electric wires unite. 'Juncture' describes either the point where two things are joined, as the 'juncture' of the head and neck, or a particular point in time, as a critical 'juncture' in a football match. One sometimes hears, wrongly, 'At this particular junction . . .'

juncture see **junction**

juvenile/jejune (petty, trivial)
Apart from its literal sense, 'pertaining to young people', 'juvenile' means 'childish', 'immature', as 'juvenile' behaviour or a 'juvenile' attitude to something. The more erudite 'jejune', which literally means 'fasting' (compare French *déjeuner* and its English equivalent, 'breakfast'), means 'naive', 'unsophisticated', 'poor and unsatisfying', and is especially used of speakers and writers, who may have 'jejune' things to say or write in a 'jejune' style. The basic 'fasting' origin points to the general lack of substance or 'goodness' in anything that is 'jejune'.

K

kale see **coleslaw**

kamikaze see **harakiri**

keck see **reach**

keel over see **heel over**

kerosine see **petrol**

kerseymere see **cashmere**

kestrel see **hawk**

kindergarten see **nursery school**

kingdom/monarchy/sovereignty/realm (state ruled by a king or queen)
A 'kingdom' is ruled by a king – or queen, as of course is the case with the United 'Kingdom'. (There *is* a word 'queendom' but it is rarely used.) A 'monarchy' is a state in which the absolute power is vested in a monarch, who is a hereditary sovereign ruler as a king, queen, emperor, tsar, etc. In an *absolute* 'monarchy' the monarch's powers are not limited by laws or constitution; in a *constitutional* 'monarchy', as in Britain, his or her powers are so limited. A 'sovereignty', or sovereign state, is one ruled by a sovereign – a title which more or less equals that of 'monarch' but which implies a recognised supreme head (which is what the word means) of a state, especially from the point of view of authority and overall supervision. ('Monarch', which literally means 'ruling alone', can sometimes virtually mean 'autocrat', especially in an *absolute* 'monarchy'.) A 'realm' is the domain of a king or queen, by implication including his or her subjects. The word is related more directly to 'regal' than to 'rule'.

kinkajou see **cockatoo**

kinky/kooky/quirky (eccentric, bizarre)
'Kinky', of people, often implies some kind of sexual perversion or oddity, in particular a homosexual one; of things the word usually applies to dress that suggests this, notably the so styled 'kinky boots' that came into fashion in the second half of the 1960s. In a more general sense the word means simply 'weird', 'bizarre'. 'Kooky' also means 'eccentric', but the overtones here are of craziness or crankiness. The word is also used with application to clothes, so that a 'kooky' girl might be one who dresses smartly but individualistically. An Australian magazine, the *Melbourne National Revue*, billed the British comedy *No Sex Please, We're British!* as the 'funniest, kookiest night of your life' (31 August 1973). 'Quirky' means 'eccentric' with a suggestion of trickery or duplicity, as found in a 'quirky' book (it tries to dupe its readers) or a 'quirky' speech (a 'devious' one). 'Kinky' derives from 'kink', i.e. 'twist'; 'kooky' is probably a perversion of 'cuckoo'.

kipper see **herring**

knapsack see **rucksack**

knave see **rascal**

knight see **lord**

knot see **mile**

kohlrabi see **coleslaw**

kooky see **kinky**

koruna see **krone**

kraal/laager (type of South African settlement)
A 'kraal' is a native village usually with a stockade and a central area for cattle or other animals. The word can apply to a cattle enclosure in general – in Sri Lanka, to an elephant enclosure. The Afrikaans word ultimately derives from Portuguese *curral* (enclosure), related to 'corral'. A 'laager', from German *Lager* (camp), is essentially an encampment set up inside a circle of wagons. It is commonly used figuratively to apply to a defensive position, especially one that expresses an entrenched policy or viewpoint: White South African advocates of racial segregation are sometimes accused of withdrawing or being driven 'back into their laager'.

kris see **kukri**

krona see **krone**

krone/krona/koruna ('crown' as unit of currency)
The 'krone' (plural *kroner*) is the monetary unit of Denmark and Norway, divided into 100 *øre*. The 'krona' (plural *kronor*) is the unit of Sweden, and the 'króna' (*krónur*) that of Iceland. These are respectively divided into 100 *øre* and *aurar*. The 'koruna' (plural *koruny*) is the unit of currency of Czechoslovakia equal to 100 *haleru* or heller. The 'Krone' (plural *Kronen*) was also formerly a German gold coin worth ten Marks or an Austrian silver coin equalling 100 heller.

kukri/kris (sword with a wavy blade)
A 'kukri' is a Gurkha knife with a short, wavy blade broadening towards the point. A 'kris', earlier sometimes spelt 'creese', is a Malay or Indonesian dagger with a wavy blade that often has two scalloped cutting edges. The 'kukri', however, has a curved blade; the 'kris' a straight one.

kulak see **muzhik**

L

laager see **kraal**

labyrinth see **maze**

lacquer see **varnish**

la-di-da/lardy-dardy (pretentious)
There is a difference: 'la-di-da' relates to speech, to 'talking posh' (the phrase is imitative of the long 'a' sound used by southern or supposedly affected speakers, as in 'grass', or a drawled 'hear!, hear!'), while 'lardy-dardy' denotes pretentiousness of manner, a languid dandyism. It is quite on the cards, however, that someone who has a 'lardy-dardy' manner will also talk with a 'la-di-da' accent. Such speech and manner have long been regarded as typical of the English upper classes, and are the stock devices resorted to by actors to portray a member, or alleged member, of this stratum of society.

lag/laggard/sluggard (idle or slow person)
A 'lag' – often an 'old lag' – is normally a convict, one who has been 'lagged' or sentenced to penal servitude. (The word is not related to 'lag' in the sense 'dawdle'.) A 'laggard' is someone who lags behind or lingers, and a 'sluggard' is a person who is generally slow or slothful – not necessarily with the implication that he is slower than someone else.

lager see **ale**

laggard see **lag**

lair see **den**

laissez-aller see **laissez-faire**

laissez-faire/laissez-passer/laissez-aller (entitlement to free action)
All three terms are French, of course,

meaning respectively 'let do', 'let pass', 'let go'. (The '-ez' in each is sometimes written '-er'.) 'Laissez-faire' encapsulates the theory of government stating that the state should intervene as little as possible in economic affairs, i.e. should pursue a policy of 'non-interference' in trade and industry. A 'laissez-passer' is a permit or pass, usually a diplomatic one, to enter a particular area. 'Laissez-aller' is a general term indicating absence of restraint or unlimited freedom. The phrase 'Laissez-faire, laissez-aller', implying no interference and freedom of movement, is attributed to the eighteenth century French economist and royal physician François Quesnay.

laissez-passer see **laissez-faire**

lake/pool/pond (enclosed body of water)
A 'lake' is the largest of the three, as the 'Lake' District with its fine mountain scenery and fifteen 'lakes', or the Great 'Lakes' of North America. A 'pool' has water that is usually still and often deep. It may not be surrounded entirely by land, but be a still or deep place in a river, as the 'Pool' of London, or reach of the Thames below London Bridge. A 'pond' is a relatively small body of still water normally formed naturally or by hollowing or banking, and an essential feature of rural or village life, still often viewed as picturesque or romantic ('Four ducks on a pond, A grass-bank beyond,' and that sort of thing). A 'lake' is called 'loch' in Scotland and 'lough' in Ireland, although these words can also denote an arm of the sea, as Loch Fyne and Lough Foyle.

lance/javelin (type of spear)
A 'lance' has a wooden shaft and a pointed steel head and was used in war by soldiers on horseback (lancers) in charging. The word is also used for a spear for spearing fish or killing a harpooned whale. The 'lance' is thus an instrument of death and destruction. The 'javelin' is used for more peaceful purposes. It is the light spear thrown in an athletics contest. In the original Greek Olympics throwing the 'javelin' was one of the five events of the pentathlon, so it has an honourable history. It also, however, was originally used for hunting or

in battle, in the days when man was beginning to discover the lethal potential of guided (more or less) missiles.

Landsturm see **Landwehr**

Landwehr/Landsturm (German military reserve)
The 'Landwehr', literally 'land defence', is West Germany's first military reserve force, consisting of men under thirty-nine years of age with seven years of active service. The 'Landsturm' or 'land storm' is a subsidiary reserve comprising all untrained young men, and all ex-servicemen aged between thirty-nine and forty-five, i.e. those who are not in the 'Landwehr' or regular forces. There were no 'Landwehr' units in the Second World War since all servicemen were regulars; the 'Landsturm', however, was a reserve category of all men aged forty-five to fifty-five who were assigned to local defence battalions and later used in occupation duties and even ultimately in front line duties.

languid see **limpid**

larboard see **port** (side of a ship)

larceny see **theft**

lardy-dardy see **la-di-da**

largo/lento (slow musical tempo)
'Largo', literally 'broad', implies a slow dignified tempo, as in the well-known *Largo* by Handel. 'Lento' means just 'slow', as found, for example, in the second movement of some classical symphonies and sonatas.

lariat see **lasso**

larynx/pharynx (part of the throat)
The 'larynx' is the part of the throat at the upper end of the windpipe. It contains the vocal cords, so that laryngitis, or inflammation of the 'larynx', usually involves loss of voice. The 'pharynx' is the cavity connecting the mouth, nose and 'larynx' with the gullet. The 'pharynx' is thus situated above the 'larynx'.

lascivious see **licentious**

laser/maser (instrument for producing a beam of light of high intensity)
The 'maser' came first, around 1955. Originally the 'maser' emitted microwaves, hence its acronym which stands for '*M*icrowave *a*mplification by the *s*timulated *e*mission of *r*adiation'. Later, 'masers' emitted waves in other parts of the spectrum, so that in 1960 the term was modified to 'laser', with the first letter of the acronym standing for '*l*ight'.

lasso/lariat (long rope with running noose for catching animals)
Both implements are used for catching horses and cattle, but the 'lariat' is also used for picketing animals while grazing. 'Lassos' tend to be found mostly in Spanish America, with 'lariats' also in use in Mexico. Both words are Spanish in origin: 'lasso' from *lazo*, 'lariat' from *la reata* (the picketing rope), in turn from the verb *reatar* (to tie again).

Latvian/Lithuanian (native or language of one of Baltic republics)
Latvia is a north-western Baltic republic, officially the Latvian Soviet Socialist Republic, whose population speaks 'Latvian' or Lettish – a language that is similar to 'Lithuanian' but more 'innovating'. Lithuania is slightly larger that Latvia and lies to the south of it. It, too, is a republic of the USSR. The Latvian capital is Riga, the Lithuanian Vilnius. The inhabitants of Latvia are sometimes known as 'Letts'.

laudable/laudatory (deserving or expressing praise)
'Laudable' means 'praiseworthy', so that one can have a 'laudable' deed or effort. 'Laudatory' means 'expressing praise' and applies to a person's work or effort such as a 'laudatory' speech (one given in glowing terms) or a 'laudatory' review (a favourable one).

laudanum see **opium**

laudatory see **laudable**

laurel/myrtle (evergreen plant with dark green shiny leaves)
The most straightforward distinction is that the 'myrtle' has white scented flowers and black berries, both quite conspicuous; the 'laurel' has small, inconspicuous yellowish or greenish white flowers and a rather insignificant green, purple or blackish berry. (The laurel is also known as the bay tree.) There is also a difference in height: the 'laurel' grows 20 to 60 feet tall, the 'myrtle' rarely reaches 20 feet.

lawful see **legal**

lawn see **field** (area of play)

lawyer/barrister/attorney (professional person practising in court of law)
'Lawyer' is a general term for the person who conducts suits in court or gives legal advice and aid. He is usually a solicitor or a barrister. The latter acts for his clients in court, pleading a case or defending it. He does not deal directly with his clients but through a solicitor. Collectively, 'barristers' are called the 'Bar', and individually are known as 'counsel'. An 'attorney' – more correctly, 'attorney-at-law' – is a member of the legal profession who represents a client in court when pleading or defending a case, that is, in his client's absence he takes his place or 'turn'. In the USA 'attorney' applies to any 'lawyer'. Most of us are familiar with the American 'district attorney', or 'DA', who is the prosecuting officer of a district.

lay see **lie** (be horizontal)

leasehold/freehold (type of basis for house purchase)
'Leasehold' gives the purchaser ownership for a limited number of years, traditionally 99. Today most houses, however, are sold 'freehold', so that the purchaser has full ownership for all time.

leave see **let**

lecherous see **licentious**

leeward/windward (exposed to – or protected from – the wind)
Confusible opposites. 'Leeward' means 'in the lee of the wind', i.e. sheltered from it

('lee' meaning 'shelter'); 'windward' therefore means 'exposed to the wind'. There are several groups of Leeward and Windward Islands around the world, with their names indicating their location relative to the wind. The Windward Islands in the West Indies, for example, are in the path of the north-east trade winds, while the Leewards, north-west of them, are relatively sheltered from these winds.

legal/lawful (allowed by law)
The two words are often used more or less interchangeably, but it is possible to distinguish: 'legal' means 'authorised by law' or 'pertaining to the law', as a 'legal' application or the 'legal' profession; 'lawful' means 'permitted or recognised by law', i.e. not contrary to the law, as a 'lawful' act or 'lawful' access. But 'legal' can also mean 'permitted by law', as a 'legal' act. Confusion, therefore, is not general but limited. See also the related **illegal**.

legation see **embassy**

legend/fable/tale/myth (fictitious, traditional or non-historical story)
A 'legend' was originally a collection of lives of the saints, or something similar, such as the Golden 'Legend' of the thirteenth century. Later the word came to be used of a traditional story popularly regarded as historical or mythical, such as the stories about King Arthur. A 'fable' is a fictitious story often involving animals or inanimate things, and one that is designed to teach a moral, as the famous ones by Aesop. A 'myth' usually has an element of the supernatural, with fanciful ideas often based on natural or social phenomena, as the ancient Greek 'myths' (which attempted to explain such phenomena). A 'tale' is any narrative story treated imaginatively, as the *Canterbury Tales* by Chaucer, or the 'tales' of the Crusades, or Dickens's *Tale of Two Cities*.

leitmotiv see **motive** (art theme)

leniency/lenity (mildness)
'Leniency' (or 'lenience') is the more general word, the noun from 'lenient', so that one can show 'leniency' in administering a punishment or in criticising some-

one's faults (by making allowances for them). 'Lenity' means more specifically 'mercifulness': 'The lenity of the judge's sentence was unexpected.'

lenity see **leniency**

lento see **largo**

leopard/panther/puma/jaguar/cheetah (member of the lion or tiger family)
The 'leopard', found in Africa and southern Asia, regrettably in decreasing numbers, is closely related to both lions and tigers and has a pale brown or yellow coat with black spots or 'rosettes'. (It was once thought to be a cross between a lion and a pard, or 'panther' – hence its name.) The 'jaguar', found in Central and South America, rather resembles it but is more thick-set, although on the whole a little shorter. 'Panther' is another name in India for the 'leopard', especially the black variety (the black panther). The 'puma', called, confusingly, 'panther' by early settlers in Peru, where it lives also as the mountain lion, is related to the 'jaguar' but differs from it by its lack of spots. Another distinction between the two is that the 'puma' is timid in the presence of man, but the 'jaguar' is more likely to attack. The 'cheetah', also known as the 'hunting leopard', is found widely in Africa and India – although also in rapidly decreasing numbers – and is distinguished by its long limbs, non-retracting, blunt claws, and its extreme speed when in full chase, even as fast as 60 miles an hour.

let/leave (allow)
Does one 'let a person alone' or 'leave a person alone'? *Partridge* distinguishes: to 'let' a person alone is to stop bothering him, but to 'leave' him alone is to leave him as he is, on his own. However 'let' has its basic sense of 'allow', and 'leave' means 'go away from', so that 'let him alone' can mean 'allow him to stay on his own', and 'leave him alone' can mean 'go away and let him stay on his own' – in other words, there is little if any difference! What has happened is that 'leave' has colloquially come to be used to mean 'allow' – compare the established sense of the noun 'leave' = 'permission' – with the result that the two words,

especially with 'alone', can be used interchangeably without any cause for confusion.

libel/slander (defamation of another in spoken or written form)
Roughly – 'libel' is defamation in written or printed form, and 'slander' is oral defamation only. The scope of 'libel' – the word derives from Latin *libellus,* 'little book' – is more extensive than that of 'slander', however, and can be punished as a criminal offence, whereas 'slander' can be proceeded against only civilly. 'Libel' must in fact consist of matter published in permanent form, and since 1952 this also includes broadcast statements. It seems wiser to steer clear of either, though.

libertarian see **libertine**

libertine/libertarian (one who preaches or practises a form of liberty)
Originally a 'libertine' was a 'freedman' or, more narrowly, a freethinker in religious matters. The word is now used to describe someone who is 'free' in matters of morals, notably one who leads a sexually immoral life. A 'libertarian' is someone who advocates freedom of thought or conduct, or who holds the doctrine of free will. The latter word has thus acquired a noble aura, the former an ignoble one. But then crimes have more than once been committed in the name of liberty.

liberty see **freedom**

licentious/lascivious/lecherous (lewd, lustful)
'Licentious' literally means 'characterised by licence', that is, 'morally unrestrained'. 'Lascivious', from the Latin *lascivia* (wantonness) means 'inclined to lust'. 'Lecherous' – the word is related to 'lick' (compare French *lécher*) with its implied reference to gluttony and debauchery – means 'pertaining to free indulgence of lust'. 'Licentious' thus indicates the attitude, 'lascivious' the potential, and 'lecherous' the nitty-gritty.

lie/lay (be – or put – in a horizontal position)
Basically 'lie' is not transitive, and 'lay' not

intransitive, that is, one can't 'lie' something and one must always 'lay' something. 'Lay' is, however, increasingly frequently used to mean 'lie', and in particular 'lie down'. People sometimes say 'I'll just lay here', for example, or 'Here, come and lay on this seat'. Is this usage incorrect? One might argue that 'lay' has the general sense 'cause to lie', so why can it not mean 'lie' itself? That is, the object pronoun is understood – 'Come and lay (yourself) on this seat'. Not only is 'lay' easier to say than 'lie', but the influence of such terms as 'lay-by', 'layabout' and 'lay-off' is strong. (Of these nouns, only 'layabout' can be objected to on grammatical grounds, since 'lay-by' has the implied object 'vehicle' and 'lay-off' that of 'workers'. A 'layabout' just 'lies about' – or lazes about). However, if the distinction between 'lie' and 'lay', as intransitive and transitive verbs, is to be observed, the correct forms of the present and the past tenses are:

lie		*lay*
	Present	
I lie		I lay
I am lying		I am laying
	Past	
I lay		I laid
I was lying		I was laying
I have lain		I have laid

Neither set of forms should be confused with that of 'lie' meaning 'tell an untruth'. The forms for this verb are: I lie, I am lying; I lied, I was lying, I have lied.

lie/untruth/fib (false or incorrect statement)
A 'lie' is a fairly serious falsehood, usually a deliberate one that is told with the intention of deceiving. An 'untruth' may be deliberate or unintentional, and it is not so grave as a 'lie'. A 'fib' is the least serious type of falsehood – a trivial 'lie', or just a partial 'untruth'. It is almost a pleasant, homely word: 'What a "fib"!' you say in secret admiration of such daring. It's also a rather curious word, in origin an abbreviation of 'fibble-fabble', itself a reduplication of 'fable'. Such an explanation sounds itself like a 'fib' – but it's no 'lie'.

lift-off/blast-off (stage in the launch of a spacecraft)

'Blast-off' is the initial firing of the rocket's motors. This gives the thrust for 'lift-off', the actual launch, when the rocket leaves the ground. The well-known countdown ('Ten, nine, eight, . . .') is actually to 'lift-off', with 'blast-off', or 'ignition', occurring a few seconds before 'zero' or 'launch'.

limerick/clerihew (short, witty, biographical verse)

A 'limerick', which can range from the epigrammatic through the ribald to the downright indecent, has five lines, with the first and second rhyming with the last and the shorter third and fourth lines rhyming. It was popularised by Edward Lear's nursery rhymes (many of which are still very effective, but spoilt by repetitiveness in the last line). The 'limerick' traditionally starts, 'There *was* a blank blanket of blank . . .', as Lear's:

There was an old person of Ealing,
Who was wholly devoid of good feeling
    He drove a small gig,
    With three Owls and a Pig,
Which distressed all the people of Ealing.

The name is said to derive from the chorus, 'Will you come up to Limerick?' sung after each verse as a refrain, Limerick being the town in Ireland. A 'clerihew' is in four lines, with the first two rhyming and the last two, and is a 'potted biography' of some kind, usually with a dig at the subject's reputation or characteristic behaviour. It was devised by the English journalist Edmund Clerihew Bentley, who died in 1956. Some of his classic 'clerihews' are still quite cruel, as the famous:

George the Third
Ought never to have occurred.
One can only wonder
At so grotesque a blunder.

The 'clerihew' obviously offers considerable scope for development (W. H. Auden devised some good ones), but it has never acquired the general popularity enjoyed by the 'limerick'.

limpid/languid (still)

'Limpid' is sometimes falsely influenced by 'limp'. In fact it means 'clear', 'lucid', as 'limpid' water, 'limpid' eyes or a 'limpid' style of writing. 'Languid', which in turn may wrongly suggest 'liquid', actually means 'flagging', 'dull', as 'languid' spirits or a 'languid' manner. A 'languid' wave of the hand, however, could coincidentally be a limp one.

liqueur see liquor

liquid/fluid (non-solid substance)

A 'liquid' is a substance such as water, oil or alcohol that is not solid or gaseous. Very often it is wet. A 'fluid' is anything that *flows* (which is what the word means), either a 'liquid' or a gas, 'liquids' being technically incompletely elastic, and gases completely so. Substances can change, of course, so that water, for example, can be 'liquid', or a 'fluid' (as steam), or solid (as ice), and oxygen, say, can be reduced from a gaseous state to a 'liquid' by intense cold.

liquidation see insolvency

liquor/liqueur (strong alcoholic drink)

'Liquor' usually means spirits, as whisky and brandy, as distinct from wines and beer. In the USA, however, 'liquor' can mean any alcoholic drink, although often the reference is specifically to spirits. A 'liqueur', in Britain often pronounced 'likyure', is a class of 'liquors', especially the strong, sweet, highly-flavoured, after-dinner ones such as chartreuse, curaçao and cherry brandy. The two words are close in spelling and meaning and are sometimes confused.

list/catalogue/inventory (written record or list)

A 'list' is a series of things in order or not, as a shopping 'list' or a laundry 'list' (possibly in no special order) or a price 'list' or school 'list' (presumably in some kind of order). A 'catalogue' is a special 'list' of things, such as books for sale, that are arranged according to some principle, as alphabetically or by subjects. A 'catalogue', too, will often have particulars of the things listed. An 'inventory' is a descriptive 'list' of property, stock, goods or the like. Military 'inventories' are noted for their distinctive, and sometimes curious, word order, as 'Chair, arm, officer's, one' or 'Polish, boot, other ranks, for the use of'. This sort of thing is used by some writers in order to produce laughs, cheap, readers, for the delectation of.

litany see **liturgy**

Lithuanian see **Latvian**

liturgy/litany (form of church service)
The 'liturgy' is the actual form of public worship followed in a particular church, properly that of the eucharistic service of the Orthodox church. The word – from the Greek *leitourgia* (public duty) – is also used to apply to the Anglican *Book of Common Prayer* (see the word used in the Preface to this). The 'litany' – from Greek *litaneia* (an entreating) – is a liturgical form of prayer consisting of a series of requests and responses successively repeated. In the Anglican 'litany', for example, which is often said or sung at the beginning of Lent (the words are not related), the supplication 'Good Lord, deliver us' is repeated eight times, and 'We beseech thee to hear us, good Lord' twenty-one times.

livid/lurid (angry, terrible)
The figurative use of the words is the most common, with 'livid' meaning 'angry' and 'lurid' – 'fiercely intense': a 'lurid' report of a crime could make you simply 'livid'. The basic meaning of both words denotes a colour, with 'livid' being bluish-grey, as the colour of a bruise or a black eye, and 'lurid', strangely, either red or fiery, as a 'lurid' sky, or pale and ghastly, as the 'lurid' glare of snow and ice in the polar regions.

load/burden (something carried)
Originally, both words meant the same: something carried by a person or animal or conveyed in or on a vehicle. 'Burden' – except in the phrase 'beast of "burden"', where the word is still used neutrally – now means an unwelcome or unduly heavy load. In a figurative sense, however, both words imply an unreasonable amount of duties, cares, and the like, as in the 'real "load" on my mind' that is a constant worry. To say that 'children can be a "burden"', though, suggests something of a pun, since 'burden' is related to 'bear', 'born' (and 'borne') and 'birth'.

loadstone/lodestar (natural object used for guiding the way)
A 'loadstone' (or 'lodestone') is a variety of iron ore used as a magnet, and originally a 'way stone' used by sailors to guide ships. Loosely it is anything that attracts or has a magnetic pull, as the 'loadstone' of an exhibition. A 'lodestar' (or 'loadstar') is a star that shows the way, especially the Pole Star, or generally something or someone who serves as a guiding star. According to his contemporary, John Lydgate, Chaucer was the 'lodesterre' of the English language. 'Lode' is here related to 'lead' rather than to 'load' in the sense of 'burden'.

lobby see **hall**

locust see **grasshopper**

lodestar see **loadstone**

loft see **attic**

logistics see **strategy** (science of warfare)

Londoner/cockney (native of London)
A 'Londoner' is any native of London, or someone who has lived there a long time. A 'cockney' is a 'Londoner' who comes from the East End, especially with his distinctive accent and 'rhyming slang' dialect. A true cockney is held to have been born within the sound of Bow Bells – the bells of the church of St Mary-le-Bow in Cheapside. The name might be supposed to derive from 'cocky', which is also fitting, but in fact comes from 'cock's egg' which, although obviously a biological impossibility, was a slang term, a nickname given by country folk, for a small, misshapen egg, and subsequently a townsman. To country people, a townsman, and especially such a blatant one as a 'Londoner', would be regarded as a queer fish, and a strange species of the human race.

longing/craving/yearning (strong desire for something)
A 'longing' is a keen wish for something, especially a thing that is remote but which may one day be attainable, as a 'longing' for peace or for a meeting with a loved one. A 'craving' is a sense of need in spite of

oneself, usually implying a kind of hunger, as a 'craving' for a drink or for affection. A 'yearning' is often a wistful or romantic 'longing', as a 'yearning' for home when one is away from it. It's not for nothing 'yearning' turns up in romantic or nostalgic songs to rhyme with 'burning', 'turning', 'spurning' and the like. Perhaps the *locus classicus* is the First World War song, 'Keep the home fires burning'. (The word 'yen' is apparently not related to 'yearn', in spite of the closeness in meaning.)

loosebox see **stall**

loot/booty (stolen goods or possessions)
'Loot' and 'booty' are both some kind of spoil and plunder, as from an enemy, but 'booty' nearly always implies a common acquisition, a plunder that is to be divided. In addition, 'loot' is also the word for a burglar's haul, and a slang term for money. The term 'booty' suggests a haul of old boots, as in the stock cartoons of incompetent anglers, but actually derives from the French *butin*, with the same meaning, itself apparently coming from a German word meaning 'share'.

lord/peer/knight (high-ranking title of the nobility)
'Lord', as a rank or title, has several applications. It is used for any 'peer' for certain high officials as a 'Lord' Mayor, 'Lord' Commissioner or 'Lord' Lieutenant, for a bishop or archbishop, less formally for a marquis, earl, viscount or baron, as a courtesy title for the younger sons of a duke or marquis (before his Christian name), and or a legal official or dignitary as a 'Lord' of Appeal in Ordinary or the 'Lord' Chief Justice. 'Peer' is the title for the member of any of the five degrees of nobility; duke, marquis, earl, viscount and baron. A 'peer' of the realm is one entitled to sit in the House of 'Lords'. A 'knight' is a man on whom a special honour or 'dignity' has been conferred by the sovereign for personal merit or services to the country. In Britain he holds the rank next below that of a baronet, with 'Sir' before his Christian name. The title is not hereditary, and not so high-ranking as many suppose.

Lordship/Excellency/Grace/Worship

(title or form of address for member of the nobility or other high-ranking person. preceded by 'Your', 'His', etc.)
'Lordship' is used of any holder of the title Lord, as well as of a judge or woman sheriff; 'Excellency' is the title of a governor or ambassador; 'Grace' applies to a duke, duchess or archbishop; 'Worship' is the word for a mayor and for most magistrates. Both 'Lordship' and 'Worship' can be used ironically for any 'superior' person, especially one who fancies himself: 'I'll have a word with His "Lordship"', 'Oh, yes, Your "Worship"', three bags full, Your "Worship"!'

lot see **fate**

louche see **farouche**

loudspeaker/amplifier (instrument for increasing the volume of sound)
A 'loudspeaker', or simply 'speaker', is either an individual instrument, as one for boosting the volume of speech, music, and so on in a hall or the open air, or an instrument that is an integral part of a record player, music centre, radio, TV set or the like. It will be actuated by an 'amplifier', which is a device that accepts a small input signal which it 'converts' to a large output signal by means of a circuit containing transistors or valves. An 'amplifier' thus amplifies the electrical charge, not the sound. 'Loudspeaker' is a word which in several languages has been literally translated from the English, as French *haut-parleur*, German *Lautsprecher*, Italian *altoparlante* and Russian *gromkogovoritel'*.

louring see **glowering**

Low Countries see **Holland**

lowering see **glowering**

loyalty/allegiance (devoted or dedicated attachment to a person or thing)
'Loyalty' is a lofty but usually personally motivated sense of dedication, as to one's country, family or friends. 'Allegiance' is more an impersonal sense of duty, as that of a citizen to his country or ruler, or a party member to a cause.

lumbago see **sciatica**

lumber see **encumber**

lunch/dinner (one of regular meals of the day)
Most people have a meal at or shortly after midday. What they call it depends rather on their eating habits and social (and even regional) background. Those who call it 'lunch' may regard it as the main cooked meal of the day, in which case they will have a lightish supper (or tea) in the evening. Those who take a light 'lunch' may do so because their main meal of the day will be in the evening, when it will be called 'dinner'. (A formal 'lunch' is called a 'luncheon'. This rather strange word probably derives from the equally strange 'nuncheon', which originally meant a 'noon drink'.) But for many people, in particular manual workers and children, the main midday meal is called 'dinner', and the evening meal will be either tea or, perhaps less often, supper. Such manual workers, especially those active out of doors, may additionally have a mid-morning snack which they call 'lunch', which more or less corresponds to other people's 'elevenses'. So depending how they regard their midday meal, people have either a 'lunch' break or a 'dinner' break half-way through their working day. Household pets, incidentally, always have 'dinner' as their main meal. Exactly when they have it depends on their boss.

lure/allure (as verb: to attract, entice)
To 'lure' is to attract deliberately, especially to something dangerous or sinful, as a decoy 'lures' a prey to a bait or trap, or the attractions of life in a city 'lure' people to come and live there. To 'allure' is to attract, not necessarily deliberately, by offering something really or apparently good: one can thus be 'allured' to the delights of music or into mistakenly confiding in someone. Both words are common as nouns.

lurid see **livid**

lustful see **lusty**

lustre see **gloss**

lusty/lustful (full of lust or lustiness)
'Lusty' means 'vigorous', 'hearty', as of a 'lusty' bull or a 'lusty' appetite. 'Lustful' means 'full of sexual desire', as seen in a 'lustful' look (a lecherous one). In fact 'lusty' meant 'lustful' as late as the seventeenth century, although 'lustful' had already established itself in its present sense a hundred years earlier.

luxuriant see **luxurious**

luxurious/luxuriant (rich, abundant)
The second of these is sometimes wrongly used instead of the first. 'Luxurious' means 'characterised by luxury', as a 'luxurious' hotel (a comfortable well-appointed one) or a 'luxurious' life (one full of luxury). 'Luxuriant' means 'growing or producing abundantly', as 'luxuriant' grass (thick and dense) or 'luxuriant' soil (rich and fertile). Both ultimately derive from Latin *luxus* (abundance). The noun of 'luxurious' is 'luxuriousness'; of 'luxuriant' it is 'luxuriance'. The association between 'luxuriant' and 'lush' is purely fortuitous.

lynx see **minx**

macaque see **macaw**

macaroon/meringue (light sweet cake made of sugar and eggwhites)
A 'macaroon' – from a French word surprisingly related to 'macaroni' – is more of a cake or biscuit, and is often almond-flavoured. A 'meringue' – some trace the name back to the German town of Mehringen, where the cake was said to have been first made – is white, light, crumbly and

either hollow or containing cream. The interesting false blend 'maroon' is sometimes heard, possibly inspired by 'marron' or the colour of chocolate.

macaw/macaque (exotic animal)
A 'macaw' is a large, long-tailed, brightly feathered parrot, a native of tropical and sub-tropical America. A 'macaque' (occasionally 'macaco') is a smallish monkey with cheek pouches and a short tail, found chiefly in Africa.

machismo see **sadism**

macho see **sadism**

Mach one see **Mark one**

mackerel sky/mare's tail sky (type of cloud formation)
A 'mackerel sky' is one almost covered with bands of high, small, white, fleecy clouds (altocumulus or cirrocumulus) resembling the markings on a mackerel's back. Such a sky usually indicates the end of an unsettled or stormy period of weather, so is a good sign. A 'mare's tail sky', one with 'mare's tails', has thin wisps of long, flowing, grey clouds (cirrus) whose streaky appearance, caused by strong winds, resembles a horse's tail. A sky like this usually means bad weather since it indicates an approaching depression.

mackintosh see **raincoat**

madam/madame (title or form of address for a woman)
'Madam' is the polite term of address, especially to a married lady or an elderly one. 'Madame', accented on the second vowel, is sometimes similarly used, especially to impress. More regularly, however, 'madame' is a conventional title of respect for any woman who is not English-speaking, either on its own or prefixed to her name, as Madame Giroud, the former French Minister of Culture. Both forms can be used to mean 'brothel-keeper' (as a noun). 'Madame' as a title is also used, or assumed, by certain women who claim to be non-English-speaking, for example,

'palmists, milliners and musicians', as *Chambers* classes them. A 'madam-shop' is a small one which sells ready-to-wear clothes to 'fashionable women of mature taste'. A 'madam', or 'proper little madam' is a derogatory term sometimes applied to a pert young woman or girl – otherwise a **minx**. Both words derive, of course, from the French *ma dame* (my lady).

madame see **madam**

madrigal/glee (musical composition for unaccompanied voices)
These charmingly dated yet often romantic forms of music originated two or three hundred years ago and still have a small but loyal and enthusiastic following. A 'madrigal' is a part-song for several voices sung properly with elaborate contrapuntal imitation and without instrumental accompaniment. It originated in Italy and came to England in the sixteenth century, where such composers as Byrd, Orlando Gibbons, Weelkes, Wilbye, Morley and Tomkins brought it to a fine and popular art. A 'glee' is a composition for three or more voices – strictly, adult male ones – with one voice to each part and words grave or gay and, as the 'madrigal', without instrumental accompaniment. The heyday of the 'glee' was the eighteenth century with its 'glee' clubs, such as the famous Noblemen and Gentlemen's Catch Club founded in 1761 and still in existence. The chief difference between the two is in the words: 'madrigals' are mostly musical love poems; 'glees', which may be gleeful (the latter word comes from the former), have as their themes a range of more or less poetic or fanciful subjects. They are also a purely English form, whereas, as mentioned, the 'madrigal' was an import.

Mafia see **Maquis**

magazine/journal/periodical (publication appearing regularly)
A 'magazine' is a general term for a popular publication of some kind, often a weekly or monthly one, usually thought of by contrast with a newspaper, published daily. A 'journal', in spite of its name, which means 'daily', is normally a monthly or even quar-

terly publication on a specialised or learned topic, especially a scientific one. (As a specific example of the difference, compare the *Geographical Journal*, the learned quarterly of the Royal Geographical Society, and the *Geographical Magazine*, the popular monthly.) A 'periodical' is a general but rather formal word, usually seen in public reading rooms, for any regular publication, including newspapers.

magenta/magnolia (shade of red)
'Magenta' is a reddish purple colour – that of the aniline dye discovered shortly after the French defeated the Austrians at the battle of Magenta (1859) in northern Italy. 'Magnolia' is the colour of the large fragrant flowers on the shrub named after the French botanist Pierre Magnol – strictly speaking white, yellow, pink or purple. On paint charts, however, 'magnolia' is used for a nondescript shade of pale pink.

magician see **conjuror**

Maginot Line/Siegfried Line (line of fortification in Europe built before the Second World War)
The 'Maginot Line', named after the French minister of war, André Maginot, was built in the 1930s on the north-east border of France, along the French-German frontier (but not the French-Belgian frontier, which the Germans broke through in 1940). The 'Siegfried Line' was constructed, also in the 1930s, as the German answer to the 'Maginot Line', and in fact faced the latter along the German western frontier. The Germans used it when retreating from France in 1944. The name was also used in the First World War of a fortified line occupied by German troops in France, although the Allies knew this as the Hindenburg Line. The Second World War 'Siegfried Line', named after the legendary German hero (whose own name, perhaps ironically, means 'victory-peace'), became well known from the British song of the late 1930s, 'We're gonna hang out the washing on the Siegfried Line'. When the Canadians broke through it in the spring of 1945 they hung a number of sheets on it with a large notice, 'The Washing'.

magistrate see **judge**

magnificent/munificent (lavish)
'Magnificent' means generally grand or fine, as a 'magnificent' sunset or a 'magnificent' gesture (which could be a generous one). No doubt the latter sense leads to an association with 'munificent', which really does mean 'generous' or 'liberal' – the basis is Latin *munus* (a present).

magnolia see **magenta**

maharajah see **rajah**

mahatma see **rajah**

mahdi see **mufti**

malachite/marcasite (mineral used for making ornaments)
'Malachite' is a green mineral – basic copper carbonate – used for making ornamental objects such as vases. 'Marcasite' is a common mineral, known sometimes as white iron pyrites, that forms pale yellow crystals. It was used in the eighteenth century for making ornaments, notably costume jewellery. The origin of the words is, respectively, Greek *malache* (mallow) and Arabic *marqashītha* (of Markhashi – a region thought to have been located in north-eastern Persia).

malevolent/malignant (malicious, harmful)
'Malevolent' is literally 'wishing ill', as a 'malevolent' look or tone of voice. 'Malignant', a more powerful word, means 'wishing to cause harm', as a 'malignant' delight in someone else's misfortunes. With reference to diseases it means 'causing death', as a 'malignant' growth – contrasted with a 'benign' one which is not normally fatal.

malice see **spite**

malignant see **malevolent**

mambo see **tango**

mammal see **animal**

mandarin see **tangerine**

mandrill see **gorilla**

manège see ménage

manslaughter see homicide

manzanilla see amontillado

map/chart (representation of surface of earth or of the sky)
A 'map' is a graphic or pictorial representation of a particular area, with conventional symbols. A 'chart' can be an outline 'map' or a special 'map' for navigators in water or air. Distinguishing another way, a 'map' is more for passive use (fact-finding, study), while a 'chart' is for active use (calculating one's route, estimating distances, exploring territory).

Maquis/Mafia (secret militant organisation)
The 'Maquis' was the collective term for the French Resistance forces who counterattacked the Germans in the Second World War. Their name derives from the Corsican Italian word *macchia* (thicket); the dense scrub of Corsica was used originally as a refuge by fugitives from German conscription in 1942. The 'Mafia' is a criminal secret society of Sicilians or Italians, active either at home or in other countries, particularly the USA (where they also have the title Cosa Nostra, Italian for 'our thing'). The name originates from the Italian dialect word *mafia* (boldness), which probably goes back to the Arabic *mahyah* (boasting).

marabou see cockatoo

maraca see marimba

marathon/pentathlon/biathlon/decathlon (sporting event, especially an Olympic one)
The 'marathon' is the great long distance race of the Olympic Games, since 1924 standardised at 26 miles 385 yards (42.195 kilometres). Its name comes from the story of the Greek messenger, possibly one Pheidippides, who ran some twenty-five miles from Marathon to Athens to bring news of the Greek victory over the Persians in 490 BC. (On arrival, he is said to have gasped, '*Chairete, nikomen*' – 'Rejoice, we win' – before dropping dead). The race did not figure in the original ancient Olympic Games. The 'pentathlon' (Greek for 'five contests') did, however, and comprised the long jump, running, throwing the discus, throwing the spear, and wrestling. The modern 'pentathlon' consists of riding, fencing, pistol-shooting, swimming and cross-country running, while the women's 'pentathlon', introduced in 1964, includes the shot-put, high jump, hurdles, sprint or dash and long jump. The 'decathlon' ('ten contests') is a two-day contest of ten track and field events: the sprint or dash, running long jump, shot put, high jump, 400-metre race, 110-metre hurdles, discus throw, pole vault, javelin throw and 1,500-metre race. The 'biathlon' ('two contests') figures in the Winter Olympics and is a combination of cross-country skiing and rifle marksmanship – the competitor stops every five kilometres to fire five rounds at a target 100-250 metres away. The term 'marathon' has come to be applied to any long-distance race or endurance contest, notably the dance 'marathon', and has engendered such hideous halfbreeds as 'talkathon', 'walkathon' and 'moviethon' (monstrous talks, walks and movie shows).

marcasite see malachite

marchioness see marquis

mare's tail sky see mackerel sky

margarine see butter

marijuana see cannabis

marimba/maraca (South American percussion instrument)
The 'marimba' is a sort of xylophone consisting of strips of wood of various lengths struck by hammers or sticks. The 'maraca' is basically a gourd filled with pebbles, seeds or other rattling objects and shaken to mark the rhythm. Both instruments feature in Latin American folk bands.

marionette see puppet

Mark one/Mach one (designation used for military equipment)
A 'Mark one' aircraft (for example) is the

first of a number of successive types or modifications. A 'Mach one' aircraft is one that flies at a speed of 'Mach number one', i.e. at the speed of sound (about 760 m.p.h. at sea level). The term gets its name from the Austrian physicist and philosopher Ernst Mach (1838-1916). 'Mark one', 'mark two' etc., is not restricted to military usage, but can designate the first or subsequent model of virtually any manufactured product or piece of equipment. The confusion, when it arises, is more perhaps aural than visual. The usual abbreviated forms for the terms are Mk-1, Mk-2 (or Mk-I, Mk-II), etc., and M 1, M 2.05, etc.

marmalade see **jam**

maroon see (1) **mulatto**, (2) **violet**

marquess see **marquis**

marquetry see **parquetry**

marquis/marquess/marchioness
(high-ranking member of the peerage)
A 'marquis' ranks between a duke and an earl in Britain; in other countries between a duke and a count. A 'marquess' is not the wife of a 'marquis' – this is a 'marchioness' – but a form of 'marquis' used by some peers who hold this rank. The spelling 'marquess' is an official one, as used in the Roll of the House of Lords and as favoured by *The Times*. Some Scottish 'marquesses', however, prefer the spelling 'marquis', since this is the French spelling, which reminds many Scots of their particular French connection – the 'Auld Alliance' between Scotland and France that dates back to the thirteenth century. See also **lord**.

marriage see **wedding**

marsala see **amontillado**

marsh/swamp/bog/slough (tract of wet or soggy land)
A 'marsh' is a tract of low, wet land in general. A 'swamp' is wet ground that is also soft and unfit for cultivation even though certain trees may be growing in it. A 'bog' is wet, spongy ground with soil mainly composed of decayed vegetable matter (see

turf). A 'slough' is a piece of soft, muddy ground in Britain; in Canada and the USA it is a marshy or reedy pool, pond or other stretch of water. The word is not now commonly used in Britain, but still exists in the place name Slough, the industrial town in Berkshire, of which John Betjeman wrote, in jaunty but characteristically jaundiced vein, 'Come friendly bombs and fall on Slough, It isn't fit for humans now'.

martin see **swallow**

mascot see **charm**

maser see **laser**

masochism see **sadism**

mason see **builder**

mass see **weight**

mast/spar/yard (pole on a ship to which sails are attached)
The 'mast' is the general pole set up vertically to support the sails. The 'spar' is the word for the actual pole that serves either for the 'mast' or for a 'yard', which is a cylindrical 'spar' slung horizontally (a so called square 'yard') or slantwise (a lateen 'yard') across the 'mast' to hold the sails. The word derives from 'yard' – 'branch', 'stick', not 'yard' – 'enclosed piece of ground'.

masterful see **masterly**

masterly/masterful (superior)
'Masterly' means 'done like a master', so 'clever', 'skilful', as a 'masterly' touch, stroke or performance. 'Masterful', means 'acting like a master' in the sense 'imperious', 'commanding', as a 'masterful' tone of voice or manner. But 'masterly' is occasionally used as an exact equivalent of 'masterful'.

matador/toreador/picador (bullfighter)
The 'matador' is the one who actually kills the bull, from Spanish *matar* (to kill). The 'toreador', famous from his song in Bizet's *Carmen*, is a more general term for a bullfighter, usually one that is mounted,

from Spanish *torear* (to fight bulls). A 'picador' is a horseman who, however distastefully, pricks the bull with a lance early on in the fight to irritate it and weaken it, from Spanish *picar*, 'to prick'.

match see **game** (portion of play forming a scoring unit)

mate see **check**

maudlin/mawkish (distastefully sentimental)
'Maudlin' is 'tearfully emotional' or 'weakly sentimental', the reference being to Mary Magdalene, who is often represented in art as weeping. 'Mawkish' – from an Old Norse word meaning 'maggot' – means 'sickly', 'slightly nauseating'. A 'mawkish' film might thus arouse a 'maudlin' sympathy for the hero/heroine/animal star or whatever.

Mauritanian/Moorish/Moresque
(pertaining to the Moors or their land)
'Mauritanian' pertains to Mauritania, the west African republic situated mainly in the Sahara desert, or to Mauretania, the ancient kingdom in north-western Africa that included the territory now held by Morocco and part of Algeria. 'Moorish' pertains to the Moors, Muslims living in north-western Africa in what was Mauretania, or formerly a group of these people who invaded and conquered Spain in the eighth century. 'Moresque' or 'Mauresque' is the term applied to the 'Moorish' style of ornamental design (of architecture, furniture, etc.) associated in the West with films starring Rudolph Valentino. 'Mauritanian' should not, in turn, be confused with 'Mauritian', which relates to Mauritius, the island state east of Madagascar in the Indian Ocean.

mausoleum see **mortuary**

mauve see **violet**

mawkish see **maudlin**

maxim/axiom/aphorism (saying)
A 'maxim' is a saying expressing what is generally held to be a general truth, especially a neatly phrased one, often even a proverb, such as 'He who laughs last,

laughs best.' An 'axiom' is not really a saying but the expression of a clearly established principle, such as 'More haste, less speed'. An 'aphorism' is very similar to a 'maxim' and is essentially, too, a terse saying embodying a general truth, such as 'Time is money' or 'People need people'. 'Axiom' and 'aphorism' derive from the Greek words meaning respectively 'requisite' and 'definition'. 'Maxim' originates from the Latin phrase *maxima propositio* (greatest proposition).

maze/labyrinth (confusing pattern of paths or routes)
The two words are more or less completely synonymous, with 'maze' perhaps being the commoner word, as the famous one at Hampton Court. Possibly a 'maze' is a less convoluted thing, such as one cut out of the turf, or merely with low hedges, while a 'labyrinth' applies more to a mass of confusing passages, a 'rabbit-warren', as in a large building. The original 'labyrinth' was the one in Crete, where the mythological Minotaur was confined. A 'maze' is designed to amaze, or bewilder, confuse and confound. 'Mazes' may well have been originally built as defences, designed to baffle the enemy.

meadow see **field** (enclosed area of grass)

meal see **flour**

meander see **wander**

meaning/sense (what is expressed, indicated or intended)
'Meaning' denotes what is – or is intended to be – actually expressed, as the 'meaning' of a word or the 'meaning' of a pictorial sign. 'Sense' tends to mean a particular 'meaning', as 'knave', which used to mean 'boy', but has become obsolete in this 'sense'. 'Sense' is used rather more loosely to mean 'intelligible "meaning"', as 'I don't see the "sense" of it'. This dictionary is concerned not only with the 'meanings' of words but their differing 'senses'.

measles/German measles (infectious disease with red spots)
The popular names for the two diseases are

as alike as their medical names, respectively *rubeola* and *rubella*. 'Measles' is the contagious virus disease with fever and a blotchy rash commonly contracted by children. 'German measles' is shorter and milder, although it has a longer incubation period. It is more common in older children and young adults, for whom it is a minor inconvenience. It is a more serious thing for a pregnant woman, however, since it may lead to a defect of the foetus. One attack of 'German measles' gives lasting immunity. Oddly enough, there is no cross-immunity between 'measles' and 'German measles', so that many supposed second attacks of 'measles' are in fact of 'German measles'. Why 'German'? The name derives from the close study of epidemics of the disease made in Germany in the nineteenth century.

medicine man see **witch doctor**

meistersingers/minnesingers (medieval German singers and poets)
The 'meistersingers' (master singers), immortalised by Wagner, were members of one of the guilds, chiefly working men, established in the fourteenth, fifteenth and sixteenth centuries in Germany for the cultivation of poetry and music. The 'minnesingers' (love singers) were a class of German lyric poets and singers who wrote and sang of love in the twelfth, thirteenth and fourteenth centuries, i.e. the German counterpart of troubadours. Thanks again to Wagner, the 'minnesinger' lives on in the figure of Tannhäuser and his opponent Wolfram of Eschenbach, who represent the lower and higher types of 'minnesinger' character.

Melanesia see **Micronesia**

melodic see **melodious**

melodious/melodic (pertaining to melody)
'Melodious' means 'tuneful', 'producing a pleasant melody', as a 'melodious' voice. 'Melodic' is sometimes used in this sense, but technically means 'pertaining to melody', i.e. to the musical succession of single notes distinguished from harmony and rhythm in musical composition. The

word is used in such expressions as 'melodic sequence', meaning the more or less exact repetition of a melody at a higher or lower level, as the third and fourth bars of *Three Blind Mice*. See also **tune**.

melody see **tune**

ménage/menagerie/manège (home for animals or people)
A 'ménage' is a household or domestic establishment, the French word deriving ultimately from Latin *mansio* (mansion). In Scotland the word is used to apply to a kind of benefit society or an arrangement for selling on an instalment plan. The notorious 'ménage à trois' (household of three) is a household consisting of a man, a woman, and the lover of one of them. A 'menagerie' is now a collection of wild animals, sometimes by implication strange ones. The term originally meant 'management of a household'. 'Manège' – related to 'manage' rather than 'ménage' – is primarily the art of training and riding horses, and by extension the actual premises of a riding-school. 'Menagerie' is a useful word to describe, in a transferred sense, a set of weird or unusual people: 'The doctor's waiting-room was a real menagerie.' Both 'ménage' and 'manège' are often written without the accents.

menagerie see **ménage**

menhir see **cromlech**

meringue see **macaroon**

message/missive (something sent)
A 'message' is the common word for anything communicated, whether in writing, by speech, or by signals (perhaps in code). A 'missive' is a much more formal word (unless used humorously) for a written communication, such as a letter or note. Both words ultimately derive from Latin *mittere*, 'to send' (past participle passive *missus*), but 'missive' is a direct borrowing into English from French *lettre missive*, 'letter waiting to be sent'.

metacarpus see **tarsus**

metaphor see **simile**

metatarsus see **tarsus**

meteor see **comet**

meteorite see **comet**

meter see **metre**

metre/meter (measure or measurer)
The spelling of these two is frequently confused, doubtless because the American spelling of 'metre', and of all words that in the British spelling end in '-metre', is consistently 'meter'. As a basic word, 'metre' is the unit of length and the poetic measure; 'meter' is 'instrument that measures', as a gas, electricity, water or parking 'meter'. The ending '-metre' is used for all units of length based on the 'metre', as 'kilometre', 'millimetre', 'centimetre', so that all other words, mainly measuring devices such as 'speedometer', 'thermometer' and 'altimeter', but including such mathematical terms as 'parameter', 'perimeter' and 'diameter', will end in '-meter'. The two words have the same basic derivation: Greek *metron* (measure), although 'meter' is more directly from the English verb 'mete', as 'mete out' (measure out).

Micronesia/Melanesia/Polynesia (Pacific island group)
'Micronesia' comprises a number of island groups to the east of the Philippines, the main ones being the Marianas, the Caroline Islands and the Marshall Islands. 'Melanesia', which includes Fiji, New Caledonia, Vanuatu and Solomon Islands, among others, is in the south Pacific, northeast of Australia. 'Polynesia', which includes Hawaii, Samoa and Tonga, lies east of 'Melanesia' and 'Polynesia', and extends southwards to New Zealand. The three island groups form the three principal divisions of Oceania. The names are composed of Greek elements: 'Polynesia' – the first to be named – meaning 'many islands', 'Micronesia' – 'small islands', and 'Melanesia' – 'black islands' (either because the islands have a dark outline when seen from sea level, or because the natives are black-skinned).

middle/centre (location of something furthest from the edges or sides)

The difference is in precision: the 'middle' is somewhere *near* the 'centre' – which is the exact 'middle'. Thus the 'middle' of the night is at some time during it, and if you find yourself in the 'middle' of an argument you are simply engaged in one. The 'centre' of a square, however, is right in the 'middle', and a person who is the 'centre' of attraction is the focus of everyone's attention.

Middle East see **Near East**

Middle West/Far West/Wild West (area of the USA)
The 'Middle West', or Midwest, is the northern portion of the central USA covering the states of Ohio, Indiana, Illinois, Missouri, Michigan, Wisconsin, Iowa, Minnesota and parts of Kansas, Nebraska and North and South Dakota, which is one of the world's most fertile farm regions. The term 'Middle West' came into use with the settlement of the 'Far West' – the area of the Rocky Mountains and Pacific Coast – in the late eighteenth and early nineteenth centuries. The 'Middle West' is sometimes also known as the Heartland of America. The 'Far West', however, is not the same as the rootin', tootin' 'Wild West', home of cowboys and westerns, which was the western frontier region of the USA before the establishment of a stable government.

midge see **gnat**

midget/dwarf/pygmy (very small person)
Thinking here of real human beings: a 'midget' is a perfectly formed, normally functioning person, but very small; a 'dwarf' is a person whose growth has been checked and who is of stunted appearance, perhaps with a large head or improperly formed in some way; a 'pygmy' is a member of one of the naturally small-sized peoples of Africa and Asia, as some of the Bushmen of the Kalahari Desert. (The latter word wrongly suggests 'piggy'; it actually derives from Greek *pugme*, the name of a measurement – the length from a person's elbow to his knuckles.) For mythical 'dwarfs' see **goblin**.

migrant see **immigrant**

mild see **ale**

mildew see **mould**

mile/knot (unit of distance or speed)
There are 'miles' and 'miles'. The statute 'mile' is 1,760 yards in length, or about 1.609 kilometres, and the standard unit of distance in both Britain and the USA. In Britain there is also an admiralty, air, geographical, nautical, and sea 'mile'. These are all different names for the 'mile' that is approximately 2,025 yards in length, or more precisely, one minute of the great circle of the earth. A 'knot' can also be this (the nautical 'mile' especially), but properly it is a unit of speed equal to one nautical 'mile' per hour. This speed was originally measured by knots on a log-line that ran out from a moving ship: the number of knots that ran out in a certain time, measured by a running sandglass, was the 'rate of "knots"'. Thus 'knots', because of the difference in length between a statute and a nautical 'mile', seem slower to the landlubber than his customary m.p.h.

militate see **mitigate**

millenary/millennium (period of one thousand years)
A 'millenary' is any period of a thousand years. A 'millennium' is also this, but more often the term is used in one of two specific ways: either to denote the period of a thousand years when Christ will reign on earth after his second coming, as foretold in Revelation 20, or to apply to a general lengthy period of happiness, good government or – ironically, perhaps – to a future 'golden age'. For similar confusibles see **centenary**.

millennium see **millenary**

milliard see **million**

milliner see **haberdasher**

million/billion/milliard (high number – 1 followed by six, nine or twelve noughts)
A 'million' is a thousand thousands, i.e. 1,000,000. The word literally means 'big thousand', and is said to have been invented in the fourteenth century by Marco Polo to describe the vast wealth of the East. The much travelled traveller dictated the tale of his journeyings to a fellow-prisoner in Genoa, and the subsequent somewhat far-fetched account came to be known, when in book form, as *Il milione*. A 'billion' was formerly a million millions in Britain (1,000,000,000,000), but today, as in the USA, it is normally a thousand millions (1,000,000,000). A 'milliard' is the word used in France and a number of other European countries to mean a thousand millions, i.e. the same as the modern 'billion'.

millipede see **centipede**

miminy-piminy see **namby-pamby**

minced meat see **mincemeat**

mincemeat/minced meat (finely chopped meat or fruit)
'Mincemeat' is normally thought of as a mixture of minced apples, candied peel, suet and the like used with currants and raisins for filling mince pies. 'Minced meat' is simply meat that has been minced. However, 'mincemeat' is also sometimes used to mean 'minced meat' – and even 'minced' pies have been spotted on sale (although this seems to suggest that the pies themselves have been minced).

mind/intellect/brain/brains (mental faculties)
'Mind' is that which thinks, feels and wills, and is usually contrasted with 'body' and occasionally with 'soul' or 'spirit'. Part of one's 'mind' is the 'intellect', which thinks or reasons, as distinct from feeling or willing. It is often contrasted with emotions, 'head not heart'. 'Brain' – other than the bodily organ – is virtually synonymous with 'intellectual capacity' or simply 'intellect', so that one can talk of a fertile 'brain' or a lively 'brain'. 'Brains' tends to mean shrewd or practical intelligence, so that you can pick someone's 'brains' – if he has the 'brains', that is. 'Brain' also, of course, means 'brainy person', as in 'brain' drain and the brains trust.

Ming/Tang/Ch'ing (Chinese dynasty)
The 'Ming' dynasty ruled from 1368 to 1644 and is famed for the association with fine

porcelain, especially vases, produced by the imperial factory. The 'Tang' dynasty was much earlier, from AD 618 to AD 907, and is associated with the considerable territorial expansion of China (in particular the contact with Central Asia), the first development of printing, the political as well as religious importance of Buddhism, and the peak of Chinese poetry. The 'Ch'ing' was China's last dynasty, from 1644 to 1911, the one founded by the Manchus. Under it, the Chinese empire increased to three times the size of the previous 'Ming' dynasty, the population more than doubled to 450 million, and an integrated national economy was established.

minister/priest/pastor (person authorised to conduct religious worship)
'Minister' is normally the title assumed by a Nonconformist clergyman, as a Methodist 'minister'. Strictly speaking, the title can apply to any clergyman, even an Anglican one. (See various rubrics in the Book of Common Prayer, where, for example, 'the Minister shall read with a loud voice', or 'Then shall the Minister kneel'.) In practice, in the Church of England, a 'minister' is normally regarded as the conductor of a religious service – whether a 'priest' or not – with a 'priest' in turn often being regarded as one appointed, and ordained, to represent the people before God. According to the *OED,* the word minister was used 'at first chiefly by those who objected to the terms "priest" and "clergyman" as implying erroneous views of the nature of the sacred office'. A 'pastor' – the word deliberately evokes a shepherd – is used in some churches (non-Anglican ones) as an alternative to 'minister'.

ministry see **department** (division of government)

mink/sable/ermine (precious fur)
'Mink' is a brown fur from the mink, a small animal like a stoat. 'Sable' is not a black fur, as might be supposed, but a dark brown one. It comes from the Arctic or Subarctic marten, an animal like a weasel. Weasel-like too is the 'ermine', an animal that has brown fur in summer, and white, except for a black-tipped tail, in winter. It's the white,

winter fur that is used for the robes of judges, peers and other dignitaries. The name is said to derive from Latin *mus armenius,* 'Armenian mouse', which is a reminder that the richest and best 'ermine' still comes from Russia. For the distinction between stoats and weasels see **ferret.**

minnesingers see **meistersingers**

minnow/tiddler/stickleback (small fish traditionally caught in streams by small boys with jam-jars)
The 'minnow' can rise to the scientific name of *Phoxinus phoxinus.* It is a small fish up to three inches long found in streams and rivers. The 'tiddler' is the name of any small fish, in fact, but especially the 'stickleback', which is distinguished by the sharp spines on its back. In length it is from two to four inches, and it is found in both fresh and salt water. All three small fry have names that suggest their diminutiveness: the 'minnow' seems to be related to 'minute', the 'tiddler' is probably a combination of 'tiddly' and 'tittlebat', a childish name for the 'stickleback', while the 'stickleback' itself has the little spines ('stickles') on its back in front of its dorsal fin.

minor see **child**

Minotaur/centaur/bucentaur (mythical creature – half beast, half man)
The (one and only) 'Minotaur' was the monster with the head of a bull and body of a man who was confined in the Cretan labyrinth and fed with human flesh. The creature was the offspring of Pasiphaë, wife of Minos, the king of Crete, and a bull. According to the Greek classic tale the 'Minotaur' – the name means 'bull of Minos' – was killed by Theseus with the help of Minos's daughter Ariadne, who guided Theseus out of the labyrinth with a thread after the deadly deed had been done. A 'centaur' was one of a race of monsters in Greek mythology who had the head, trunk and arms of a man and the body and legs of a horse. Chiron is one of the best-known 'centaurs', whose name has not been satisfactorily explained. The 'bucentaur' was not really a beast. It was the title of the state barge of Venice from which the doge

and other officials performed annually, on Ascension Day, the ceremonial marriage of the state with the sea by dropping a ring into the Adriatic. The name is said to derive from Greek *bous* (ox) and *kentauros* (centaur), with reference to the figure-head of the barge which represented a mythical creature that was half bull, half man. The word could, however, originate from the Italian *buzino d'oro* (barque of gold). The last 'bucentaur' was destroyed by the French in 1798.

minster see **cathedral**

minstrel/troubadour (medieval musician who sang or recited to the accompaniment of a musical instrument)
A 'minstrel' was rather more than just a singer or reciter; he was really a professional itinerant entertainer, who could tell stories, juggle and do acrobatics, much welcomed in castle households in the winter months, when hunting was not possible and there was a dearth of distractions. A 'troubadour' was more of a specialist; he sang songs of chivalry and courtly love, and he notably sang them in southern France. (The word comes from Provençal *trobador*, meaning 'one who finds', that is, seeks out, invents and composes.)

minute/moment (short period of time)
Apart from the exact sense of 'minute' (60 seconds), which denotes the briefer time? If I say 'Wait a "minute"', am I likely to be longer than if I say 'Wait a "moment"'? On the whole, the answer is yes. Compare such expressions as 'in a "minute"', meaning you must wait while I complete what I am doing (which may even take more than the 60-second 'minute'), or 'just a "minute"', meaning I want to object and wish you to pause while I do so. However, the difference is certainly a fine one, and many people use the words interchangeably. The *Concise Oxford Dictionary* does in fact define 'minute' as 'short time', though, and 'moment'· as 'very brief portion of time' as well as 'short period of time'.

minx/lynx (bright-eyed creature)
A 'minx' is not a quadruped but a pert or flirtatious girl, deriving from 'minikin',

meaning 'diminutive person' (in turn not related to 'manikin' but formed on the basis of the Old Dutch *minne*, 'love'). A 'lynx' is the animal sometimes known as a wildcat, which has lent its name to the expression 'lynx-eyed' – 'sharp-sighted'. Possibly the association with 'mink' aids the confusion: the fur of the 'lynx' has come to be used commercially, though not to the same extent as that of the mink.

Miocene see **Pleistocene**

miracle play/morality play/mystery play (type of medieval religious drama)
A 'miracle play' is one that sets a religious subject in dramatic form, such as a Bible story or the life of a saint, and presents the material in a series or cycle, as performed by the medieval craft guilds. York, Chester, Coventry and Wakefield are cities where famous 'miracle plays' were, or are said to have been, performed. A 'morality play', as its name implies, is an allegorical drama – rather later than the 'miracle play' – in which the characters are personifications of virtues and vices. The most famous 'morality play' is *Everyman*, which dates from about 1500. A 'mystery play' is often used as an alternative name for a 'miracle play'. In his *English Dramatic Literature*, however, Sir A. W. Ward makes the distinction that 'mystery plays' deal only with Gospel stories, while 'miracle plays' deal with the lives of the saints. This distinction is rather too fine, though, and rarely observed in general use.

misanthropist/misogynist/misogamist (one who hates his fellow men – or women)
The three are haters, respectively, of mankind, women and marriage. The 'mis-' element denotes the hating, the other halves of the words are the same as those in 'anthropology', 'gynaecologist' and 'bigamy'.

misogamist see **misanthropist**

misogynist see **misanthropist**

missive see **message**

mist see **fog**

mistake/error/fault (incorrect or wrong act)

A 'mistake' is usually caused either by bad judgement or by disregard of some rule – in which case, of course, it is deliberate. An 'error', by contrast, although an infringement of a similar nature, is unintentional, as an 'error' of judgement or an 'error' in calculating. A 'fault' is a 'mistake' made because of some kind of defect or imperfection or moral shortcoming. The word often implies an offence, as a 'fault' at tennis.

mistrust see **distrust**

misuse see **abuse**

mitigate/militate (have an effect or influence on)

The two words are frequently confused by those who are trying to use one or the other to impress or to sound more 'official' or authoritative. To 'mitigate' is to lessen, decrease or moderate, as in the familiar 'mitigating' circumstances, which enable a punishment or penalty to be reduced, since evidence has been produced that encourage or enable a judge or jury to be less severe. To 'militate' is to have an effect on, to have weight or influence. The word is almost always used with 'against', as in a sentence such as: 'His youthful appearance militated against his promotion.' The verb comes from Latin *militare*, 'to be a soldier', and indeed that was what the word originally meant in English before it acquired its present sense.

module see **probe**

Moguls see **Mongols**

mohair/moire/moiré/moygashel (type of fabric)

'Mohair' is the fleece of the Angora goat, used in plain weave for draperies and pile weave for fabrics. The association with 'hair' is a false one – the word comes from Arabic *mukhayyar* (select choice), as applied to a cloth made of goat's hair. 'Moire' is a watered fabric, originally watered 'mohair' but now commonly watered silk or wool, and 'moiré' is a fabric of silk, rayon or the like which has a wave-like pattern pressed

on it. Both words are a French borrowing of English 'mohair'. 'Moygashel' is a type of Irish linen used mainly for suits and costumes, as originally woven in the village of Moygashel in County Tyrone, Northern Ireland.

Mohammedan see **Muslim**

Mohawks/Mohicans (North American Indian tribe)

The 'Mohawks', whose name relates not to hawks but comes from an Indian word meaning 'they eat animal things' (the tribe was formerly supposed to be man-eating), are the most easterly of the Iroquois Five Nations and once lived along the Mohawk river, in New York state. The 'Mohicans' – their name is Algonquian for 'wolf' – were formerly concentrated in the upper Hudson Valley and are now a confederacy of North American Indians whose native tongue is Algonquian. They are famous largely thanks to Fenimore Cooper's novel *The Last of the Mohicans,* in which the 'last of the Mohicans' is Uncas who, with his father Chingachgook and their friend Natty Bumppo, frustrates the attempts of Magua, the evil Indian Huron leader, to block the efforts of Alice and Cora Munro to join their father, who is the British commander of Fort William Henry, near Lake Champlain.

Mohicans see **Mohawks**

moire see **mohair**

moiré see **mohair**

moisture see **damp**

molasses see **treacle**

mollusc/crustacean (class of shellfish)

These are the two broad categories of shellfish, of which altogether there are more than 90,000 varieties. Among 'molluscs' are oysters, mussels, clams, scallops, whelks and snails; among 'crustaceans' are lobsters, crabs, crayfish, shrimps, prawns and barnacles. Neither category – technically a phylum – has a backbone. 'Molluscs' have a soft body (Latin *mollis*, 'soft') inside a shell that builds up in layers and becomes hardened with calcium carbonate from the water; 'crustaceans' have a crusty shell that they periodically shed as they grow.

molto/mosso (musical direction)
Both words, of course, are Italian. 'Molto' means 'much', 'very', as in *'molto vivace'* – 'very lively'. 'Mosso' means 'fast' (literally 'moved') as in *'più mosso'* – 'faster', and *'meno mosso'* – 'slower' (literally 'more moved' and 'less moved').

moment see **minute**

momentum/impetus (moving force)
Two rather technical words, or at any rate imposing ones. The simplest distinction is: 'momentum' is the force *of* something moving; 'impetus' is the force *with which* something moves. Otherwise, 'momentum' is the 'impetus' of something that is gained by movement.

monarchy see **kingdom**

monastery/abbey/priory (residence of a religious community)
A 'monastery' is usually a community of monks – as a nunnery is of nuns. An 'abbey' which is or was centred on an 'abbey' church or cathedral, is a community of monks or nuns under an abbot or abbess. Many 'abbeys' disappeared with the dissolution of the 'monasteries' under Henry VIII, and all that was left was the 'abbey' church. This is what happened with Westminster 'Abbey' in London. The status of an 'abbey' is that of an important 'monastery'. A 'priory', thus, is normally a smaller 'monastery' or nunnery governed by a prior or prioress respectively, and may also be subordinate to an abbey. (A prior belongs to a mendicant or 'begging' order, as does a prioress. Apart from being the head of a priory or nunnery, a prioress may be the title of a 'second-in-command' in an 'abbey', where her superior will be the abbess.)

money order see **postal order**

Mongols/Moguls (Asian rulers and conquerors)
'Mongols' are properly natives of Mongolia, but historically – the more familiar usage –

were members of the Mongol Empire that in the thirteenth century extended over the larger part of Asia, reaching the Dnieper river in the west. The 'Moguls' were the 'Mongol' conquerors of India ruling from 1526 to 1857 (nominally from 1803) when the last of the emperors was dethroned. The 'Great Mogul' or 'Grand Mogul' was the title, as used by Europeans, of the emperor of Delhi. In modern use a 'mogul' is a 'king', 'baron' or 'boss' of some kind of commercial empire, as a 'movie mogul'. The historical 'Moguls' were noted for their rich works of art and jewellery, which were produced in India during the 'Mogul' empire.

monk/friar (member of male religious order)
A 'monk' is properly a member of a monastery, where under a superior he is bound by vows of poverty, chastity and obedience. The female equivalent is 'nun'. A 'friar', strictly, is not attached to a monastery, but a member of a so-called mendicant order (who originally worked or begged for a living), such as the Franciscans, Augustinians, Dominicans and Carmelites. If he lives, as he probably does, in a religious house, it will be a friary. He will, however, be bound by the same vows as a 'monk'. There are female equivalents, as the Poor Clares who form the Second Order of Franciscans. They are simply called 'sister'. The title 'friar' originates from Latin *frater*, 'brother'.

monologue/soliloquy (scene in a play in which one person alone speaks)
In origin, the words are exact doublets: Greek 'monologue' and Latin 'soliloquy' both meaning 'single speech'. They are now carefully distinguished, however. A 'monologue' is a speech made by one person in the company of others; a 'soliloquy' is spoken by one person on his own. Dramatically, Hamlet's 'To be or not to be' speech is thus a 'soliloquy', since no one else is on the stage. (For definition purposes, the audience doesn't count!) Henry V's 'Once more unto the breach, dear friends' is a 'monologue', therefore.

monsoon/simoom/sirocco (strong, hot wind)

The 'monsoon' is a seasonal wind of the Indian Ocean and southern Asia that blows from the south-west in summer and the north-east in winter. The summer 'monsoon' is the notorious one, with its heavy rains. The 'simoom' or 'simoon' is a hot, sand-laden, suffocating wind that blows over the deserts of North Africa and Syria in spring and summer. The 'sirocco' is a hot, dry, dust-laden wind, a 'simoom' in fact, blowing from North Africa and affecting parts of southern Europe, or a warm, sultry, south or south-east wind with rain in the same regions.

Montilla see **amontillado**

mooch see **moon**

moon/mooch/mope (move about aimlessly or listlessly)
If you 'moon' about, you wander around dreamily or idly, as if moonstruck. If you 'mooch' about you are acting rather furtively, whether hanging about or slouching along somewhere. If you 'mope' – the only verb of the three not colloquial – you may not be moving at all, but sunk in a listless apathy (the word comes from the obsolete verb 'mop', meaning 'pull a wry face').

moor see **heath**

Moorish see **Mauritanian**

moot see **move**

mope see **moon**

moped see **motorcycle**

morality play see **miracle play**

Moresque see **Mauritanian**

morgue see **mortuary**

morning dress/evening dress (formal clothes worn on a special occasion)
'Dress' here is used in the sense 'men's costume', not 'garment worn by women'. 'Morning dress', worn typically at weddings, consists of black morning coat with grey or lavender waistcoat and striped trousers. Accessories are: white shirt, white stiff collar (wing or turned down), grey tie and grey top hat. 'Evening dress', as worn at an official dinner or special theatre performance, comprises black tail coat with silk lapels, black trousers, white waistcoat, stiff-fronted white shirt, white wing collar and white bow tie. In place of the tail coat the more popular alternative today is the dinner jacket (the American tuxedo), which is a black (occasionally, white) jacket with silk lapels and without tails. This is worn with black trousers and with a waistcoat or cummerbund, a plain or pleated white or coloured shirt and a black bow tie. On like occasions women can also wear 'evening dress', and this is usually in the form of an evening gown, especially a long, floor-length one. A form of 'evening dress' with tails is still worn traditionally by pianists, waiters – especially wine waiters and head waiters – and, where they exist, butlers.

morning star/evening star (heavenly body brightly visible in the morning or evening)
These two names are poetic but misleading – they are both used as names of Venus, which is a planet, not a star! At certain times of the year, Venus can be seen in the east before sunrise or in the west after sunset. (For the characteristics of Venus, see **star**.) The name 'morning star', the political press apart, is sometimes also given to other planets, such as Mercury, or even to a real star, so long as it is one prominent in the morning. The name is also sometimes used figuratively for the precursor of the dawn of a new age of some kind: Wycliffe was thus the 'morning star' of the Reformation. The 'evening star' is a name also sometimes extended to other planets or stars, but not so readily to people.

moron see **idiot**

morpheme see **phoneme**

morphine see **opium**

Morrison shelter see **Anderson shelter**

mortgagee/mortgagor (one who mortgages property – or to whom property is mortgaged)

The confusion lies perhaps more in the process of mortgaging than the suffixes, with '-ee' denoting the person to whom something is done, sold, given, sent, etc. (as 'addressee', 'employee', 'internee', 'examinee') and '-or' used for the person who does, sells, gives, etc. ('donor' 'dedicator', 'vendor', 'consignor'). In practice the 'mortgagee' is usually a building society (to whom the property is mortgaged), and the 'mortgagor' the house buyer (who is mortgaging the property). That is, the 'mortgagor' must repay the 'mortgagee' the loan he has been given.

mortgagor see **mortgagee**

mortification see **shame**

mortuary/morgue/mausoleum (place for the dead to lie)
A 'mortuary' is a place where the dead are temporarily kept before being buried or cremated. A 'morgue', more common in American than British usage, is a place where the bodies of people found dead, whether or not in suspicious circumstances, are laid out for identification. A 'mausoleum' is a grand tomb of some kind – originally the one erected at Halicarnassus in Asia Minor around 350 BC for Mausolus, the ruler of Caria. (It was one of the wonders of the ancient world; fragments of the original frieze are in the British Museum). The original 'Morgue' was a building in Paris used for the same purpose as a modern 'morgue', with the actual name itself of uncertain origin. Both 'morgue' and 'mausoleum' are used figuratively to mean a large, dreary room: 'My hotel bedroom was a real morgue'; 'The waiting room at the station is a proper mausoleum of a place'.

Moslem see **Muslim**

mosquito see **gnat**

mosso see **molto**

moth see **butterfly**

Mothering Sunday see **Mother's Day**

Mother's Day/Mothering Sunday (day when traditionally presents are given by children to their mothers)
The former, which is relatively recent, and American, has commercially ousted the latter, which is quite old, and of English origin. An Act of Congress of 1913 in the USA set aside the second Sunday in May for remembering mothers. In the Second World War, American troops introduced 'Mother's Day' to Britain, where it subsequently became confused with 'Mothering Sunday'. This in the church calendar is the fourth Sunday in Lent, otherwise Mid-Lent Sunday, Refreshment Sunday or Laetare Sunday (and any date from 1 March to 4 April) when traditionally the mother church (the principal or oldest one in the district) was visited and school-children and apprentices were given a day's holiday to be at home with their parents. 'Father's Day', celebrated on the third Sunday in June, is a similar import from America.

motif see **motive** (art theme)

motion see **resolution**

motive/incentive (inducement to action)
A 'motive' is what actually 'moves' you to take some action, as an inner urge or the desire to see a satisfactory completed result. An 'incentive' is what stimulates you to action, as the prospect of a bonus, a prize, or a promotion. A 'motive' is thus more from within, and an 'incentive' from without.

motive/motif/leitmotiv (subject or theme of a work of art)
The basic meaning of 'motive', of course, is 'what induces a person to act', but the term is used in the arts as an alternative to 'motif', which is the distinctive feature or theme in an artistic, literary or musical composition. (In music the word applies specifically to a brief passage from which longer passages are developed – otherwise a 'figure'.) In design, a 'motive' or 'motif' is a particular repeated figure, as a lace ornament sewn on a dress or a pattern printed on wallpaper. A 'leitmotiv', from the German (leading motive), is a term used

in musical drama for a theme associated throughout the work with a particular person, situation or idea. Wagner made the 'leitmotiv' his speciality.

motorcycle/moped (two-wheeled motor-driven road vehicle)
A 'moped' is not simply a small or low-powered 'motorcycle', but specifically one that has pedals (which a 'motorcycle', even a low-powered one, never has). Basically the 'moped' is a form of motorised bicycle, usually one with a cubic capacity of 50 c.c. or less. It was extensively developed in Germany in the 1950s, although the word 'moped' is itself, rather unexpectedly, of Swedish origin: the abbreviation of *tramp-cykel med motor och pedaler*, 'pedal cycle with engine and pedals'.

motorway/trunk road/highway/clearway (type of main traffic road)
A 'motorway' is a specially constructed road designed for fast motor traffic and mainly running between large cities, as the M1 London to Yorkshire 'motorway' or the M6 from Birmingham to Carlisle. Distinctive features of a 'motorway' are its lanes (as a dual carriageway), its special signals and signs, and its service stations. It cannot be used by pedestrians, learner drivers, cyclists, and riders of small motorcycles. The world of 'motorways' is one that has attracted its own jargon of 'slip-roads', 'hard shoulders' and 'central reservations'. A 'trunk road' is the first of three categories of road in Britain (the other two are 'classified' and 'unclassified' roads) and caters for long-distance traffic. It includes most 'motorways'. A 'highway' is a semi-legal or technical term for a main road in general – in full, the 'Queen's highway', which is regarded as protected by the power of the monarch. In its strictest sense, a 'highway' is a public road which all the subjects of the realm have a right to use (as distinct from a private road). It is also maintained and improved at public expense. A 'clearway' is a British term for a stretch of road on which vehicles must not stop, the aim being to keep the road *clear* for moving traffic. A special sort is an 'urban "clearway"', on the main roads into a large town or city, where

stopping is allowed but only on certain days or between certain times.

mould/mildew (growth of minute fungi associated with disease or decay)
The main distinction is that 'mould' grows on vegetable or animal matter, especially food, while 'mildew' forms on plants and fabrics such as paper and leather, when exposed to moisture. The words are not related: 'mildew' is a form of Old English 'honeydew'.

mountain see **hill**

mourn/grieve (feel great sorrow at a death)
To 'mourn' is to express one's grief or sorrow generally, either involuntarily, as by weeping or withdrawing from society, or more formally by the wearing of dark clothes, for example, as 'mourners' do at a funeral. To 'grieve' is to feel great sorrow, to lament, implying pain and distress, whether expressed or not. Although both words usually refer to a death or bereavement, they need not necessarily do so. One can 'mourn' one's lost childhood, for example, or 'grieve' at all the violence in the world.

mousse/soufflé (light sweet or savoury dish)
A 'mousse' – from the French for 'moss' or 'froth' – is a light, sweet pudding with cream, beaten eggs, gelatine, etc., served chilled. A 'soufflé' – French 'puffed' – is a light, savoury, baked dish made fluffy with beaten eggwhites and containing fish, cheese or other ingredients. There exist savoury 'mousses' and sweet 'soufflés', but with these it's usually a casual or careless extension of the name.

mouth/estuary (place where river enters the sea)
'Mouth' is a rather vague word for the 'sea end' of a river, thought of as the opposite of its source. An 'estuary' is the 'tidal mouth' of a river, or any part of the lower reaches of a river where its current meets the tides of the sea and is affected by them. This means for example, that the 'estuary' of the Thames is strictly speaking 92 miles long, and extends not just from below

London Bridge to the sea but upstream to Teddington Lock, a further 19 miles, where the first lock from the sea (apart from the one at Richmond) is situated. An 'estuary' is generally regarded as the seaward rather than the landward stretch of a river, however, so that at high tide the 'estuary' virtually *is* the sea.

move/moot (raise or propose)
To 'move' a point or matter is to make a formal request or application. 'Mr Briggs then moved that the meeting be adjourned.' To 'moot' a point is to raise it for discussion. 'Mrs Jones mooted the question of the subscription' (she wanted it to be discussed). The second verb becomes an adjective in the fixed phrase 'moot point', meaning a debatable one and by implication a doubtful one. The phrase is sometimes spoken as if it was 'mute point', by false association with this more common word. (This would mean a point that was not spoken, and presumably one that might therefore be in doubt. The legal phrase 'to stand mute' means not to plead in court.) 'Moot' has its origins in the Old English *gemōt* (meeting, assembly).

moygashel see **mohair**

mucus see **phlegm**

muddled/fuddled/addled (mixed, confused, bemused)
'Muddled' is the general word. 'Fuddled' has the specific sense 'muddled by drink', while 'addled' means 'mentally confused' – the word usually occurs in such phrases as 'addle-brained' or 'addle-headed'. There is an association with 'addled' eggs – ones that are bad or spoiled.

muffin see **crumpet**

mufti/mahdi (Muslim leader)
The 'mufti' is the Muslim legal adviser who is consulted on religious matters. Under the Ottoman empire the word was used as a title of the official head of the state religion, or of one of his deputies, with the 'Grand Mufti' being the head of the Muslim Arab community in Jerusalem. 'Mufti' in the sense 'plain clothes' derives from the fact that the official is a civilian. The 'mahdi', with Muslims, is the title of the expected spiritual and temporal ruler who, it is believed, will set up a reign of righteousness throughout the world. There have been a number of claimants to the title, notably Mohammed Ahmed (died 1885) who established in the Egyptian Sudan an independent government that lasted until 1898. The titles mean, respectively, 'one who delivers a judgment' and 'the guided one'.

mulatto/maroon (Negro or part Negro)
A 'mulatto' is the offspring of one white parent and one Negro, i.e. a half-breed. The word, which is Spanish, goes back ultimately to Latin *mulus* (mule), with reference to the person's hybrid origin. (A mule is a cross between an ass and a horse.) A 'maroon' was a Negro – originally a runaway slave – living in the wilder parts of the West Indies in the seventeenth and eighteenth centuries. The derivation is not from 'maroon' meaning the dark brownish red colour, but the verb meaning 'strand on an island'.

mule see **donkey**

multiple store see **chain store**

munificent see **magnificent**

munitions see **ammunition**

mural/fresco (type of wall painting)
A 'mural' is any painting executed on a wall, whether inside a building or out. A 'fresco' – sometimes thought, by association with 'fresh air' or 'al fresco', to be an exclusively external painting, which it is not – is a wall painting (or ceiling painting) done before the plaster is dry, that is, while it is fresh (so called 'true fresco', or *buon fresco*), or when the plaster is partly dry ('dry fresco', or *fresco secco*). The technique is a complex and ancient one: many famous Greek 'frescoes' were executed several hundred years BC. The Italian word indicates, however, that some of the finest 'frescoes' since the Middle Ages are to be found in Italian churches, such as the ones by Michelangelo in the Sistine Chapel.

murderer/assassin (killer)

A 'murderer' is one who kills unlawfully, legally known as 'with malice aforethought', i.e. express malice (where the person intends to kill or cause grievous bodily harm), or implied (where he does not intend to do either, yet intentionally does an act which he knows will lead to death). An 'assassin' is one who kills treacherously, often for political motives. The unusual word comes from the Arabic for 'hashish-eater'; in Muslim history the 'assassin' was a fanatic sent by the founder of his sect, the so-named Old Man of the Mountain, to murder either Crusaders or the leaders of rival Muslim sects. He did this in a hashish-drugged state.

musical/revue/music hall/cabaret/ vaudeville (light dramatic entertainment with music)

The 'musical' – properly 'musical comedy' – is a development of the operetta (see **opera**) and today is a fairly general word for a light play or film with songs, dialogue and dancing and a rather insubstantial plot. The songs and dialogue are not necessarily comical, but are almost invariably light-hearted and reasonably undemanding. Two well-known traditional 'musicals', both box office hits, are *West Side Story* and *My Fair Lady*, and two rock 'musicals', a development of the 1970s, *Hair* and *Jesus Christ Superstar*. A 'revue' is composed of a rapid series of short items, such as songs, dances and sketches, with a vaguely tropical or satirical basis. *Beyond the Fringe* was a 'revue' of the early 1960s that has since been emulated but rarely equalled. 'Music hall' was a variety entertainment, mainly of songs and comic turns, at which the audience could buy drinks. It flourished in Britain from roughly 1880 to the First World War, and developed out of the earlier tavern entertainments. The keynote of the 'music hall' was precisely its variety, with a succession of artistes – unlike a 'revue', where the same artistes perform in different items – and even with interludes of ballet dancing, for example. Licensing laws banned drinking in the auditorium from 1902 and the popularity of the 'music hall' began to fade with the increasing competition of films and, later, radio. (Some might

say, though, that a number of radio variety shows are in fact an extension of 'music hall'. Certainly television, with such programmes as 'Sunday Night at the London Palladium', has proved that the genre of 'music hall', when transferred to this particular medium, is as popular as ever.) 'Cabaret', an offshoot of the traditional 'music hall', is an intimate entertainment – 'intimate', so that individual performers can establish a close relationship with the audience – in a club, bar or restaurant, usually while patrons are wining and dining. 'Cabaret' in pre-war Germany was linked with political and artistic groups, and the film *Cabaret* (1972) was one of the Broadway 'musicals' so named which was based on the play *I am a Camera* by John Van Druten that in turn was based on Christopher Isherwood's sketches of Berlin life in the 1930s (including the role of 'cabaret'), *Goodbye to Berlin*. 'Vaudeville' is variety entertainment, approximately the American equivalent of the British 'music hall', with the same heyday (1890s to 1920s) and the same fate — ousted by the cinema.

music hall see **musical**

Muslim/Moslem/Mohammedan/Mussul-man (follower of Islam or of Mohammed)

Mohammed was the founder of Islam, so that the four terms are closely related and in many ways overlap. The distinction is chiefly one of preference and usage. 'Muslim' is currently the preferred form, with 'Moslem' being obsolescent, 'Mohammedan' relating more to Mohammed than the Islam religion as a whole, and 'Mussulman' (plural strictly speaking 'Mussulmans') decidedly archaic. 'Moslem' survives in such proper titles as the 'Moslem League' – the Muslim political organisation founded in India in 1906 whose demands in 1940 for an independent Muslim state led to the establishment of Pakistan. The name 'Muslim' comes from the Arabic *muslim* (he resigned himself, i.e. to God), to which 'salaam' is also related.

muslin/gauze/cheesecloth (thin cotton fabric)

'Muslin', originally from Mosul, a city in Iraq, is a fine cotton fabric of plain weave

165

used for curtains and the like. It is frequently printed or embroidered in patterns. The word has a much more specific meaning than 'gauze' – originally from Gaza, in the Middle East – which is the name for any thin transparent fabric made from any fibre (for example, cotton or silk) in a plain or so-called leno weave (in which the warp threads are arranged in pairs). Cotton 'gauze' is used for surgical dressings, for example, and silk 'gauze' for dress trimmings. Similar to it is 'cheese-cloth', which is made of cotton – originally as a wrapping for pressed cheese – and used commercially for book bindings, dustcloths and the like. The actual difference between 'gauze' and 'cheesecloth' is in the finishing: 'cheesecloth' may be bleached and stiffened, when it is called 'scrim'; 'gauze' is usually very fine on account of its use for delicate applications.

mussel see **cockle**

Mussulman see **Muslim**

mutiny see **revolt**

muzhik/kulak (Russian peasant)
A 'muzhik', often still spelt 'moujik', is the basic word for the Russian peasant, seen as a rustic countryman as opposed to a more or less sophisticated town-dweller. The word now has a distinct pre-revolutionary flavour. A 'kulak', literally 'fist', was a special sort of 'muzhik' – a rich and often hard-fisted 'exploiting' peasant who employed hired labour or owned machinery. 'Kulaks' were also largely pre-revolutionary, although a number were still in existence after 1917, and many of these organised a grain strike in 1927–8 as a protest at the uncompetitive prices offered them by the state. By 1934, when three-quarters of all Soviet farms had been collectivised, most remaining 'kulaks' had either been resettled in remote parts of the USSR, or arrested and their property and lands confiscated.

myrtle see **laurel**

mystery play see **miracle play**

myth see **legend**

nabob/nawab/nizam (official of India)
A 'nabob', properly the title of certain Muslim officials in the Mogul empire, was the term that came to apply to an Englishman who had grown rich in India, or, by extension, to any wealthy person. The word is a variant of 'nawab', which is closer to the Urdu (literally 'deputy governor'). The 'nizam' was the title of the ruler of Hyderabad, India, from about 1700 to 1950, and was also used to apply to a soldier in the regular Turkish army.

naiad see **dryad**

namby-pamby/niminy-piminy/miminy-piminy (affected)
'Namby-pamby' usually means 'weakly sentimental'. It was originally the nickname, Namby Pamby, invented by Henry Carey for the English poet Ambrose Philips (died 1749). Carey – who among other things wrote 'Sally in our Alley' – used the name as the title of a poem he composed in 1726 to ridicule Philips's verses. 'Niminy-piminy' means 'affectedly refined', with the phrase a meaningless imitation of mincing speech. 'Miminy-piminy', no doubt influenced by it, means 'absurdly affected', 'ridiculously finicky'.

narcissus see **daffodil**

natty see **jazzy**

naturalist/naturist (one who studies things in a natural state)
One term can sometimes be misread or misunderstood for the other. A 'naturalist' studies natural history, and is often a specialist such as a zoologist or botanist. A 'naturist' is an alternative term for a nudist. Many nudists prefer this word, regarding 'nudist' as emphasising the wrong aspect of what they think of as 'social nakedness'. But

'naturist' as a semantic cover-up is rather transparent.

naturist see **naturalist**

nawab see **nabob**

Nazarene/Nazarite (member of religious group)
A 'Nazarene' is basically a native or inhabitant of Nazareth, while 'The Nazarene' was one of the titles of Christ. The term is used to mean 'Christian' by some Jews and Muslims, and the 'Nazarenes' were also a sect of early Jewish Christians who retained the Mosaic ritual. The name was also adopted by a group of early nineteenth century German artists. Among the ancient Hebrews, a 'Nazarite' was a religious devotee who had taken certain vows of abstinence (see Numbers 6 for what they were). Here the derivation of the name is not 'Nazareth' but Hebrew *nāzar* (consecrate).

Nazarite see **Nazarene**

Near East/Middle East/Far East (region to the east of Europe)
The regions are rather imprecise and in some cases their names are used interchangeably. The 'Near East', now more often called the 'Middle East', is thus an indefinite term for the countries from Egypt to Iran, that is, from the eastern shores of the Mediterranean and Aegean to (but not including) India. Formerly the 'Middle East' included not only Iran but also Afghanistan, India, Tibet and even Burma, while the 'Near East' was restricted to Turkey and the Balkan countries. The 'Far East' is a similarly wide-ranging term which embraces 'the Orient', that is, the countries of east and south-east Asia, such as China, Japan, Korea and Thailand. For the occidental opposite, see **Middle West**.

nebula see **constellation**

nefarious/felonious (wicked)
'Nefarious' means 'very wicked', 'iniquitous', as 'nefarious' deeds or practices. 'Felonious' means 'pertaining to a felony', i.e. a grave crime such as murder or burglary. (Felonies were, until 1967, officially distinguished from misdemeanours, which were lesser offences.)

neglectful/negligent (careless, disregardful)
'Neglectful', which means 'characterised by neglect', refers to the actual act of neglect, so that if one is 'neglectful' in one's duty one does not do something that should be done. 'Negligent' means virtually the same, but refers to the *habit* of neglect. Someone who is 'negligent' in his duties, therefore, fails to do, in general, what he ought to do. A 'neglectful' person shows 'neglect'; someone who is 'negligent' shows 'negligence'.

negligent see **neglectful**

neigh/whinny (characteristic cry of a horse)
A 'neigh' is the word for any 'speech' by any horse. By a 'whinny' is usually meant a pleasant-sounding or happy 'neigh', especially a low, gentle or joyful one (or any combination of these). Both words are ultimately imitative in origin, with 'whinny' related to 'whine'.

net amount/gross amount (measure of a financial quantity)
The 'net (or "nett") amount' is the amount after deductions or expenses have been paid, so that a 'net' profit is an actual gain, a 'net' price has no discount, and 'net' pay is 'take-home' pay, after tax and other deductions. 'Gross' is thus the opposite – before deductions, so that to 'gross up' is to increase the 'net amount' to its value before tax, or whatever, was deducted. People who complain that they earn 'only £80 a week' may tactfully neglect to add that this is the 'net amount' they receive, whereas normally a pay or salary figure is quoted in 'gross' terms since the deductions will to a large extent depend on the individual and will vary. (The £80-a-week man may, too, be in receipt of certain benefits, which he also overlooks when making his claim for a pay increase.) The term 'net' relates not to 'net' as in fishing – as if the deductions had slipped through and were not 'caught' –

but to 'neat', that is not liable to (further) deduction, 'clear'.

netball/volleyball/basketball/handball (team game in which a ball is struck by the hand)

Perhaps 'basketball' is the best known. This is essentially an American game played usually indoors by two teams of five men or women. Points are scored by throwing the ball through baskets located high on a stand at the end of each court. 'Netball' is similar to it, but mainly played by (English) women or girls, with seven players in each team. The game is played with the ball entirely in the air, whereas in 'basketball' it frequently rebounds against the floor. 'Volleyball' is really a sort of hand tennis played with a football. The game is played outside or in a gym, with six players a side, and has the object of preventing the ball from touching the ground by banging it from one side to the other over a net. 'Handball' with eleven players a side, is also played with a football. In fact, the rules are similar to those of football, so that the ball can be caught, thrown, passed back or forward or 'dribbled' (by being 'caressed'). It can be struck not only with the hand but with any part of the body except below the knee (although the goal-keeper can kick it). The game is popular on the continent, especially in Germany.

Netherlands see Holland

neuralgia/neuritis/neurosis/neurasthenia (nervous disorder)

Possibly the first two are confused the most. 'Neuralgia' is pain along the course of a nerve, especially in the areas round the nose and mouth (so-called trigeminal neuralgia, or tic douloureux) or the throat and ear (glossopharyngeal neuralgia). Authorities differ as to whether the '-itis' of 'neuritis' really does mean 'inflammation' (in this case, of a nerve) as it normally does. The *Encyclopaedia Britannica*, defining 'neuritis' as a 'degenerative, non-inflammatory disease of nerve tissue', recommends 'nerve disease' as a more accurate term. The disease can be experienced anywhere in the body, with pain and a pricking or burning numbness in the affected part. 'Neurosis' is an emotional disorder, with obsessions, compulsions, and often associated physical complaints that, however, show no objective evidence of disease. (The '-osis' denotes a verbal noun.) 'Neurasthenia' is nervous debility or exhaustion, as from overwork or prolonged mental strain, its symptoms being vague complaints of a physical nature. The 'asthenia' is Greek 'weakness'.

neurasthenia see **neuralgia**

neuritis see **neuralgia**

neurosis see **neuralgia**

neurotic see **psychopath**

nexus see **plexus**

niche see **nook**

niminy-piminy see **namby-pamby**

ninepins see **bowls**

nitrate/nitrite/nitride (chemical compound of nitre or some related substance)

The suffixes tell all: a 'nitrate' is the salt of nitric acid (HNO_3), and also a fertiliser consisting of potassium nitrate or sodium nitrate; a 'nitrite' is the salt of nitrous acid (HNO_2); a 'nitride' is a binary compound of nitrogen. The suffixes thus denote, respectively, 'salt of an acid with name ending in -ic', 'salt of an acid with name ending in -ous', and 'binary compound'.

nitride see **nitrate**

nitrite see **nitrate**

nizam see **nabob**

noise see **sound** (thing heard)

noisome see **obnoxious**

nonchalant/insouciant (casual, unconcerned)

'Nonchalant' means 'coolly unconcerned', 'indifferent', as a 'nonchalant' air or attitude. The word is the participial form of the archaic French verb *nonchaloir*, with *chaloir* in turn deriving from Latin *calere* (to be hot). 'Insouciant' means 'free from concern', 'carefree', being *'sans souci'*, as an 'insouciant' whistle.

nook/niche (recess)

Although similar, the two words do not seem to be related. A 'nook' is a corner or any small recess, especially one that is obscure, remote or cosy. An 'inglenook' is a chimney corner. The word is often used in the phrase 'every nook and cranny', where 'cranny' is a small narrow opening or chink or **crevice**. A 'niche', going back ultimately to Latin *nidus* (nest), is either an ornamental recess for a statue or something similarly decorative, or a place or a position that is just right for someone or something: 'At last he's found a niche for himself' (he's found a good job, a secure position, a role in life, or the like).

Nosy Parker/Paul Pry/Peeping Tom

(unduly inquisitive or prying person)
A 'Nosy (or Nosey) Parker' is one who pries or meddles, a real busybody who minds everyone's business except his own and who sticks his nose in everywhere. A 'Paul Pry' is similar, but perhaps more of an interferer than a busybody, and less of an active meddler than a 'Nosy Parker'. A 'Peeping Tom' is a furtive observer, especially a voyeur, who gets a kick out of the naughty things he sees. Did this unholy trinity actually exist? Was there actually a prying Mr Parker? In his *Words and Names* (John Murray, 1932), Ernest Weekley quotes an 'amateur philologist' who boldly states that the original 'Nosy Parker' was Matthew Parker, Queen Eliabeth's first archbishop of Canterbury, who was a 'human ferret' and, moreover, had a long nose. Perhaps. (The female equivalent, incidentally, is sometimes called Rosa Dartle.) 'Paul Pry' is of surer origin: he was the hero of a play of this name written in 1825 by the English dramatist John Poole. (He is said to have been based on a real person, one Thomas Hill.) 'Peeping Tom' was, according to the story, the man who took a sneaking look at Lady Godiva as she rode naked through the streets of Coventry.

notable/noticeable (significant, appreciable)

A 'notable' difference is a big one, and 'notable' progress is great or considerable progress. A 'noticeable' difference may well be a small one, but one that can nevertheless be discerned or appreciated; 'noticeable' progress is progress that can clearly be seen. These two confusibles are surprisingly common.

notary see **solicitor**

noticeable see **notable**

nourish see **nurse**

noxious see **obnoxious**

nub see **hub**

number/figure/numeral (word or sign used for counting)

A 'number', the commonest word of the three, is a symbol or 'figure' that stands for a count or sum or total, especially when identifying one of a series, as a telephone 'number', house 'number', or car 'number' (which also includes letters as well as 'figures'). A 'figure' is a numerical symbol, especially one of the Arabic notation (1, 2, 3, 4, 5, etc.), so that one talks of a 'figure' of eight, double 'figures' (10 to 99) or a three-'figure' number'. The term 'numeral' is used for a word expressing a 'number', as a cardinal 'numeral', or a letter or 'figure', or group of letters or 'figures', that expresses a 'number', as a Roman 'numeral', which is expressed as a letter or letters.

numeral see **number**

numerator/denominator (mathematical term expressing the figure in a fraction)

The 'numerator' is the number written above the line in the fraction, showing how many parts of a unit are taken; the 'denominator' is the number below the line, showing the number of equal parts into which the unit is divided. The words are Latin ones meaning respectively 'counter' and 'namer'. Thus in $2\frac{3}{8}$, the 'numerator' is 3 and the 'denominator' is 8.

169

numerous/innumerable (very many)
'Numerous' simply means 'of great number'. 'We have been there on numerous occasions' thus means that we have been there very often. 'Innumerable' is literally 'countless'. It is a more forceful word than 'numerous' and means in effect 'of very great number'.

nurse/nurture/nourish/cherish (tend carefully)
To 'nurse' somebody or something implies a constant tending or fostering. One can literally 'nurse' a person back to health or 'nurse' a grievance (foster it by brooding over it). To 'nurture' a person suggests training him as well as supporting him in some way. It is often used of children or young people generally. The word is related to 'nourish', wich has an implication of the provision of food or nutriment, especially to promote healthy development. To 'cherish' is to hold dear, used of a person or thing: if you 'cherish' a close friend you will presumably 'cherish' his friendship. There is a certain overlap of meaning of almost all the words, with 'nurse' the predominant idea behind them.

nursery school/play school/kindergarten/day nursery/play group/infant school (school or centre for young children)
A 'nursery school' provides a combination of informal, simple teaching and play activities for children aged two to five. It exists independently or as part of a primary school. A 'play school' and a 'play group' are the same thing, in effect. They are the paying equivalent of the (free, state-run) 'nursery school' and are run by a voluntary organisation or a group of parents. They differ from a 'nursery school', however, in that – as the name suggests – the emphasis is on play rather than any kind of formal education. A private school corresponding to the state 'nursery school' where education *is* provided on a formal or informal basis is a 'kindergarten', which may also exist separately or be part of a preparatory school or a pre-preparatory school (which would take over at the age of five). This latter school has a state equivalent, too: the 'infant school', which, as before, may also be a department of a primary or 'first' school.

This leaves the 'day nursery', which partly corresponds to a 'nursery school' or 'play group'. It is not really, though, an educational establishment proper, but more a place where parents can park their children while they are at work. For this reason the 'day nursery' does not operate in 'terms' but is open virtually throughout the year. The odd name out of all these, 'kindergarten', owes its German origin (literally, 'children's garden') to the deviser of schools of this type, the nineteenth century educator Friedrich Froebel.

nursing home/convalescent home/rest home (special type of hospital)
A 'nursing home' is not a home for nurses but a private hospital where both medical and surgical treatment are obtainable (for payment). A 'convalescent home' is a rehabilitation centre, either a state one (National Health, non-paying) or a private one. A 'rest home' is a residential centre for old and/or frail people, usually one run by a voluntary organisation or privately. A number of 'rest homes' are, however, also provided by local authorities, and are non-paying.

nurture see **nurse**

nylon/rayon/Dacron/Orlon/Bri-Nylon (name of a synthetic fibre)
'Rayon' came first, with its final '-on' spawning the endings of all the other names, as well as West German perlon, East German dederon, Japanese niplon and Russian kapron. The 'ray' may be arbitrary but, more likely, the word is simply the French *rayon* (ray), with reference to the fibre's thin strands or filaments. 'Rayon' is basically any textile made from cellulose, and is what used to be known as artificial silk. The term originated around 1924. It was followed by 'nylon' in 1938, which was the word used to describe, more specifically, a synthetic polyamide capable of extrusion when molten into fibres, sheets, etc. The name was based on both 'cotton' and 'rayon' with the 'ny-' an arbitary element. The letters of 'nylon' do not stand, as is sometimes thought, for 'New York' and 'London', and still less are they the acronym of '*Now you, lousy old Nipponese!*', an excla-

mation said to have been made by one of the material's inventors. (The name was in fact chosen out of 350 words as the result of a competition. It may be no coincidence that '-ny-' also occurs in 'vinyl', a basic ingredient of many artificial fabrics.) 'Dacron' is an American form of Terylene made by Du Pont. One of its chief attributes is its combined resilience and crease-resistance. 'Orlon', also made by Du Pont, is mainly used as a wool substitute in knitwear. 'Bri-Nylon' is a type of 'nylon' manufactured by British Nylon Spinners.

nymph/sylph/sibyl (bewitching woman)
A 'nymph', in Greek mythology, is a minor goddess – a beautiful maiden inhabiting the sea, rivers, woods, trees, mountains, meadows and the like, and often attending a more important deity. Greek *nymphe* means 'bride'. A 'sylph' is one of a race of imaginary beings supposed to inhabit the air, that is, one of the four 'elements' (with salamanders inhabiting fire, undines water, and gnomes – the only males – the earth). The word was probably invented by the sixteenth century Swiss-German physician and alchemist Paracelsus, perhaps based on a blend of Latin *sylvestris* (of the woods) and 'nymph'. Both 'nymph' and 'sylph' are extended to describe a beautiful woman or girl in general, with 'sylph' perhaps being a more graceful or 'airy' female. A 'sibyl' was a woman in ancient Greece or Rome who was said to possess powers of prophecy or divination, with her name derived from Greek *Sibulla,* of uncertain meaning (perhaps *theosoulle,* 'divinely wise'). She is the old maid of the three. The word should not be confused with the female forename, of the same origin, that is now usually spelt Sybil.

o see **oh**

obbligato/ostinato (special part in musical piece or score)
Strictly speaking, 'obbligato' applies to a part that must be played – it is obligatory (as opposed to 'ad lib.'). The term can also be used, however, for an extra part, such as a violin 'obbligato', with the meaning 'violin ad lib.'. So what should mean 'obligatory' can on occasions mean 'optional'. 'Ostinato' – the Italian for 'obstinate' – refers to a constantly recurring melodic fragment, as often found in a 'basso ostinato' or ground bass – which is 'obbligato' in the literal sense of the word.

obdurate see **obstinate**

object/subject (thing or person to which attention is directed)
Why an 'object of interest' but a 'subject of conversation'? The difference lies in the concept: 'object' implies an end or goal, as an interesting 'object' or an 'object' of study; 'subject' implies a means to an end, as a school 'subject' or the 'subject' of a portrait. Furthermore 'object' implies an aim that can be short or long term. There is thus a difference between the 'object' of one's research (the purpose of it), and the 'subject' of one's research (what one is actually studying).

obnoxious/noxious/noisome (offensive)
'Obnoxious' means 'objectionable', usually highly so, as 'obnoxious' behaviour or an 'obnoxious' remark. 'Noxious' means 'injurious', as a 'noxious' gas. Both words are related to Latin *noxa* (hurt). 'Noisome', which is related not to 'noise' but to 'annoy', means 'offensive', 'disgusting', usually of a smell. In a figurative sense, however, both it and 'noxious' can mean 'harmful', as a 'noisome' or 'noxious' task – one that is sickening.

obscure/abstruse/obtuse (hard to understand, difficult)
'Obscure', from Latin *obscurus* (dark) means 'not clear' or 'not expressing meaning clearly' as an 'obscure' remark or an 'obscure' text. 'Abstruse' means 'difficult to understand', from Latin *abstrusus* (concealed), as an 'abstruse' statement or idea. The bogus blend 'obstruse' is sometimes heard, perhaps by false association with 'obtuse', itself meaning 'dull-witted', 'slow to understand'.

observance see **observation**

observation/observance (act of observing)
'Observation' is the noun of 'observe' in the sense 'watch carefully' and 'remark', as 'He was kept under constant observation' and 'That's an interesting observation.' 'Observance' is the noun of 'observe' in the sense 'keep (a law)' or 'celebrate' (e.g. a festival), as in Shakespeare's 'custom more honour'd in the breach than the observance' and the Lord's Day Observance Society.

obstacle/obstruction (hindrance or impediment)
An 'obstacle', whether material or not, is something that stands in the way of literal or figurative progress. It usually can be overcome with an effort, ingenuity, or patience. An 'obstruction' is something that more or less completely blocks a passage of some kind, making progress difficult or even quite impossible. The word is not used so frequently in the figurative sense, although in Parliament an 'obstruction' is the use by an MP of his right to speak and move motions for the purpose of delaying or preventing the passing of some measure to which he objects – usually strongly.

obstetrician see **gynaecologist**

obstinate/obdurate (persistent, stubborn)
The words derive from the Latin for, respectively, 'determined' and 'hardened'. 'Obstinate' means 'not yielding', often perversely so, as an 'obstinate' child who refuses to obey, and 'obstinate' resistance which is difficult to overcome. 'Obdurate' means 'not easy to influence or change', with the suggestion of a hard line being

taken – a hardened offender may well have an 'obdurate' conscience.

obstruction see **obstacle**

obtrusive see **intrusive**

obtuse see **obscure**

obverse/reverse (side of a coin)
Somehow, 'obverse' suggests the less important or secondary side, until you realise that it cannot be, since that is the 'reverse' side. The 'obverse' side of the coin must thus be the main one, or 'heads', so that the 'reverse' is 'tails'. Doubtless the 'ob-' suggests the second word in such pairs as 'subject and object' (in grammar) or 'acute and obtuse' (of angles, in mathematics), as well as 'belittling' words such as 'obliterate', 'obscure', 'obsolete', 'obstruct' and 'obstacle'. 'Obverse', too, can itself actually mean 'serving as a counterpart or complement', especially of a fact or truth, so that the 'obverse' of the science of medicine, for example, could be said to be witchcraft (as if it was the 'other side of the coin'). However, 'obverse' literally means 'turned towards'. Hence its use in numismatics. On some older coins it is often quite difficult to determine which side actually is the 'obverse' and which the 'reverse', not because the coin is worn, but because the devices and inscriptions are similar on both sides. Not all coins, for example, have a head on the 'obverse', which is usually the distinguishing characteristic.

occidental see **oriental**

occupation/business/profession/trade
(one's regular work or employment)
'Occupation' is the general word, usually a more or less formal word for 'job'. 'Business' usually implies a commercial 'occupation', especially one that renders an essential or useful service, as a car sales 'business'. 'Profession' denotes a specialist or highly qualified 'occupation', as the legal 'profession' or the nursing 'profession'. 'Trade' generally suggests an 'occupation' that involves craftsmanship or manual skills, as the building (or, as it is now more often called, construction) 'trade'.

occupied/preoccupied (engaged, busied)
'How will you preoccupy yourselves?' a television reporter asked a couple facing a two days' wait at an airport. To 'occupy' oneself is to busy oneself, to be engaged in doing something. To be 'preoccupied' – one does not normally 'preoccupy' oneself as a conscious process – is to be engrossed in something, to be occupied to such an extent that one is oblivious to everything else.

ocean see **sea**

ochre see **amber**

octavo see **quarto**

octopus/squid/cuttlefish (mollusc noted for its ability to eject a type of inky substance)
All are mutually related. The 'octopus' has eight arms (literally 'eight feet') and lives on the seabed, where it ejects an inky substance when threatened. The 'squid', whose name is not a Lewis Carroll-type portmanteau blend of 'squirt' and 'fluid' but is of obscure origin, has ten arms and ejects ink as a characteristic cigar-shaped object as long as itself, the aim being to leave a 'dummy' so that it can escape. The 'cuttlefish' is actually used as a source of ink called sepia, which is brownish in colour and can serve for drawing with brush or pen. Both the 'octopus' and the 'squid' are edible, but not the 'cuttlefish'. The latter's shell, however, is popular when dried with budgerigars, who peck it and so 'manicure' their beaks.

oculist see **optician**

odium/opprobrium (reproach)
The two Latin words mean 'hatred' and 'infamy'. Public 'odium' is general public dislike or hatred of someone or something. 'Opprobrium' is disgrace or reproach incurred by conduct that is regarded as shameful. The respective adjectives 'odious' and 'opprobrious' are also confused, with 'odious' sometimes falsely conjuring .up 'odorous' – which can mean bad-smelling as well as fragrant – and the phrase 'be in bad odour' (be disliked).

offence see **crime**

official/officious (pertaining to an office)
'Official' is 'authoritative', as an 'official' announcement made by someone in his 'official' capacity. 'Officious' means 'fussily dutiful', especially ostentatiously so, as an 'officious' waiter. In diplomatic circles, however, an 'officious' statement is the opposite of an 'official' one – it is informal, or unofficial, in fact.

officious see **official**

oh/o (exclamation preceding a word or beginning a phrase or sentence)
'Oh' is easily the commoner, and is used to express a wide range of sudden emotions or reactions, such as joy ('Oh, how lovely!'), regret ('Oh dear!'), sorrow ('Oh, how sad!'), surprise ('Oh, look!'), pain ('Oh – don't!'), desire ('Oh yes!') and many more. It can also be used on its own in a variety of ways to express understanding, acknowledgement, interest, uncertainty and simply 'thinks...' Before a name, it usually draws a person's attention ('Oh, Graham, did you get the tickets?'). 'O' is much more rarefied and poetic, and can either be used to address a person or thing, especially in worship or veneration (as Chaucer's 'O chaste goddesse of the wodes grene', or the now forgotten line in the National Anthem, 'O Lord, our God, arise!'), or express a longing or approval, especially when followed by 'for' or 'that' (as Shakespeare's 'O! for a muse of fire' and the Christmas carol line 'O, that we were there').

ohms see **volts**

older see **elder**

onyx/sardonyx/sardius/sardine (type of precious stone)
An 'onyx' is a kind of chalcedony (a type of quartz) with different colours in layers or bands. It is used for cameos in particular. A 'sardonyx' is a type of 'onyx' containing layers or bands of sard, which is the yellow or orange-red kind of chalcedony known as cornelian. 'Sardonyx' is used mainly in jewellery – it is the 'sardine stone' mentioned in Revelation. 'Sardius' is an alternative word for sard, but it was also the name of the precious stone in the breast-

plate of the Jewish high priest, in fact thought to have been a ruby.

op-art/pop-art (art form of the mid-twentieth century)

'Op-art' – or 'optical art' – is an international form of art that uses optical illusion as its basis, especially so as to produce emotional or visual stimulation and to create the illusion of movement. This is achieved by the careful arrangement and manipulation of colours and geometric forms, particularly repetitive ones. 'Pop-art', which is mainly of British and American inspiration – names such as David Hockney, Roy Lichtenstein and Andy Warhol have become internationally famous through their association with it – essentially reflects the mass media oriented society of the West, with representations of everyday objects such as typewriters and canned goods. The 'pop' is 'popular', but also suggests the explosive effect, or 'pop', produced on the viewer by many of the form's works. One definition of 'pop-art' by Richard Hamilton, an English exponent of it, is 'Popular/Transient/Expendable/Low-Cost/Mass-Produced/ Young/Witty/Sexy / Gimmicky / Glamorous / Big Business. . . .' By the end of the 1970s both 'op-art' and 'pop-art' had lost much of their sense of immediacy and iconoclasm. See also '**pop**' itself.

opera/operetta (musical dramatic composition)

In general, an 'operetta' is a short, light 'opera', usually with a considerable proportion of spoken dialogue. More specifically, it is either a light 'opera', such as one by Johann Strauss or Suppé (but not, say Mozart's *Così fan tutte,* which is a comic 'opera'), or a musical comedy, that is, a comedy with plenty of music in it. (This is more familiar today as a musical.) Whether the much-loved Gilbert and Sullivan 'operas' are really 'operettas' is rather a subjective matter: they are certainly quite far removed from 'grand' 'opera', yet not slight enough, or consistently comic or light-hearted enough, to be called 'operettas'.

operative see **operator**

operator/operative (one operating a machine or piece of equipment)
In industrial terms, an 'operator' is someone operating a specialised piece of equipment, whether sophisticated, as a computer, or reasonably complex, as a copy lathe. An 'operative' is a factory worker, quite often a skilled one, who operates fairly standard machinery, as a loom 'operative'. The greater the skill, however, the more likely the 'operative' will become an 'operator'.

operetta see **opera**

ophthalmologist see **optician**

opium/morphine/laudanum (soporific drug)
'Opium' is made from the juice of the poppy (*Papaver somniferum*). It may (usually illegally) be smoked or eaten as a stimulant, intoxicant or narcotic, or (normally legally) be used in medicine as a sedative, when it is called 'laudanum' – a tincture of 'opium'. (The name 'laudanum' was invented by that mostly unappreciated genius, the Swiss alchemist and physician Paracelsus.) 'Morphine' is the name of the principal alkaloid in 'opium', used in medicine to deaden pain or as a hypnotic. The highly addictive narcotic heroin is derived from it.

opossum see **possum**

opponent see **enemy**

opprobrium see **odium**

optician/oculist/ophthalmologist/optometrist (one specialising in eyes)
To the myopic man in the street, an 'optician' is a man who makes or sells spectacles. In fact 'opticians' also sell, reasonably enough, optical instruments, and are divided into 'ophthalmic', who can test sight if registered by the General Optical Council, and 'dispensing', who can make up prescriptions. The term 'oculist' is now rather dated. It used to apply to a doctor of medicine who was skilled in examining and treating the eye. An 'ophthalmologist' is a professional title of either an eye specialist or eye surgeon or, at a less exalted level, an 'ophthalmic optician'. The term

derives from the Greek *ophthalmos* (eye), with Latin *oculus* (eye) giving 'oculist'. An 'optometrist' is a specialist in optometry, the examination of the eye for defects and faults of refraction and the prescription of correctional lenses and exercises. Unlike an 'ophthalmologist' he does not use drugs or surgery.

optometrist see **optician**

orang-outang see **gorilla**

oration/orison (special address)
An 'oration' is a formal speech, especially on an occasion such as a funeral or the presentation of academic awards. It is a grand word that suggests stylishness and a considerable display of rhetoric. An 'orison' is a prayer, public or private. The word, which is related in origin to 'oration', is rather archaic and usually used in the plural. 'Nymph, in thy orisons Be all my sins remembered', Hamlet entreats Ophelia in his 'To be or not to be' speech.

oratorio/cantata (dramatic musical composition for chorus, soloists and orchestra)
The 'oratorio' has its origin in the musical services held in the church of the Oratory of St Philip Neri, in Rome. It has come to be the term for a rather 'grand' or extended musical composition, with a more or less dramatic text, based on a religious theme – although with no action, costume or scenery, as in an opera, say. Handel's *Messiah* is one of the best-known examples of an 'oratorio'. A 'cantata' (Italian for 'something sung') is a form of short 'oratorio', either sacred or secular, especially a lyric work. Bach's *Christmas Oratorio* is in reality a series of 'cantatas' designed to be performed on six days successively at Christmas-tide.

orchid/orchis (rare, exotic plant and its flowers)
The 'orchid' is a member of the large family *Orchidaceae*, and typically (and familiarly) the exotic plant with brilliant flowers, with one petal usually larger than the other two, that traditionally is born to blush unseen in an inaccessible wood somewhere. The

'orchis' is an 'orchid' that is wild (as distinct from the hothouse variety) or that, more narrowly, belongs to the genus *Orchis*, which has a tuberous root and an upright fleshy stem with a spike of purple or red flowers. The names are often used interchangeably, however, since all 'orchises' are 'orchids'. Both words derive from Greek *orkhis*, 'testicle', from the appearance of the root tubers in some of the genus *Orchis*. One wonders whose fertile imagination invented the name. (Compare 'porcelain' under **china**.)

orchis see **orchid**

order/command/direction (instruction)
An 'order' is usually an instruction given by a superior to an inferior, with the relationship between the two marked by rank, standing or age, for example. A 'command' is similar, but is a more formal word – and possibly a less specific one – and emphasises the authority of the one who commands. A 'direction' is simply a general instruction what to do in order to carry out some task, as the 'directions' for use that accompany several commercial products.

ordinal/cardinal (class of numbers)
'Ordinal' numbers state the order (first, second, third, etc.); 'cardinal' numbers are the basic ones (one, two, three, etc.). Latin *cardinalis* means 'pertaining to a hinge'.

ordinal/ordinary (order of church service)
An 'ordinal' is a directory of church services in general, or a book containing the forms for the 'ordination' of priests. An 'ordinary' is a book containing the order for divine service, especially the mass or, specifically, the service of the mass exclusive of the canon (that part of the service between the Sanctus and the communion). While in ecclesiastical circles, it might be useful to note that an 'ordinary' is also a bishop or archbishop or his deputy regarded as a legal authority. Such a dignitary should not, of course, be confused with a 'cardinal', one of the officials who elects the Pope. All the terms are more widely used in the Roman Catholic church than the Anglican, although the 'ordinary' is an official long

established in both Anglican and Common law.

ordinary see **ordinal** (order of church service)

ordinary shares/preference shares (types of shares on the stock market)
'Ordinary shares' are ones which have no special right to a dividend but entitle their holder to all the profits after prior demands, such as loan interest or 'preference' dividends. By implication, therefore, 'preference shares' have a preferential right to dividends, that is, the holder is entitled to his profits before anything is paid to the holders of 'ordinary shares'. On a more technical level, holders of 'ordinary shares' are regarded as the true owners of the company, while the voting rights of the holders of 'preference shares' are strictly limited.

organdie/organza/organzine (type of fine fabric)
'Organdie' is a thin, translucent, usually stiffened muslin with a lasting crisp finish and in colour white, dyed or printed. It is used chiefly for dresses and curtains and any suitable 'display' of fabric. 'Organza' is made from a mixture of silk or nylon with cotton – it's similar to 'organdie' but not as fine. 'Organzine' is a silk yarn used in weaving silk fabrics. 'Organza' may be an alteration of the trade name 'Lorganza' but the origin of 'organdie' and 'organzine' is a mystery. (*Webster* traces 'organzine' back to the town of Urgench in the Soviet Union, where it was said to have been first manufactured.)

organza see **organdie**

organzine see **organdie**

oriental/occidental (Eastern – or Western)
'Oriental' is 'Eastern', and 'occidental' is 'Western'. The 'Orient' is a rather vague geographical term applied to either the countries of Asia generally – and especially Japan – or the countries to the east of the Mediterranean, such as Iran. The 'Occident', a less common word, is ʳhe countries of Europe and the USA – by contrast with those of the 'Orient'. The *SOED* notes that

'Orient', in modern American usage, can occasionally be used to mean Europe. This may increase the confusion over the words. Americans, too, can reach the Far Eastern 'Orient' more rapidly by travelling west!

orison see **oration**

Orlon see **nylon**

orotund see **rotund**

orthopaedic/paediatric (pertaining to children's diseases)
'Orthopaedic' relates to the correction of diseases and deformities of the skeletal system, notably the spine, bones, joints and muscles, especially, although not exclusively, in children. The two Greek elements making up the word are 'right' and 'child'. 'Paediatric' relates, simply, to the study and treatment of children's diseases in general.

ostensibly see **ostentatiously**

ostensively see **ostentatiously**

ostentatiously/ostensibly/ostensively (characterised by showing or demonstrating)
'Ostentatiously' means 'in the manner of a pretentious display', 'so as to deliberately draw attention': 'He ostentatiously straightened the picture on the wall.' 'Ostensibly' means 'outwardly appearing as such', 'professedly': 'He borrowed some money, ostensibly to pay the rent' (but really to back a horse that he hoped would be a winner). 'Ostensively', a rarer word, can be used as an alternative to 'ostensibly', but is primarily a term confined to logic meaning 'in a manner that is immediately demonstrative', 'proving directly'.

ostinato see **obbligato**

outrageous/outré (shocking)
'Outrageous' means either 'very bad' or 'very offensive', as an 'outrageous' crime (which could be either, or both). The word is not, unfortunately, related to 'rage', but derives from an Old French verb, *outrer* (to exceed). It is the past participle of this verb that gives *outré*, meaning 'exceeding the

bounds of what is regarded as usual and proper', or simply 'eccentric', 'bizarre' as 'outré' clothes or an 'outré' remark. The word is usually pronounced 'ootray'.

outré see **outrageous**

oven/stove/cooker (apparatus for cooking, usually in the kitchen)
An 'oven' is an enclosed heated compartment for baking or roasting, as for example in a gas 'stove' or electric 'stove'. A 'stove' itself is a wider term to mean an apparatus that provides heat for any purpose, as heating (oil 'stove') or cooking (gas 'stove' – complete with 'oven') or some mechanical process. Loosely, 'stove' can mean 'cooker' – 'Put the saucepan on the "stove" would you?' – but 'cooker' is the general purpose cooking appliance, portable or fixed, and usually heated by gas or electricity, that contains an 'oven', cooking rings and often a grill, and stands in most kitchens.

overtime see **extra time**

overtone see **undertone**

ox/bull/bullock/steer (male bovine animal found on farms)
An 'ox' is a fully-grown castrated 'bull', used either as a draught animal or for its beef. More generally, it is any bovine animal. A 'bull' is an *un*castrated 'ox', used in particular for breeding. A 'bullock' is either a young bull or an 'ox', especially one that has never been used for breeding. A 'steer' is a young 'ox', although in the USA the word is used for male beef cattle of any age. The word seems to be related to 'steer' meaning 'guide the course of' rather than be derived from Latin *taurus*, 'bull'.

Oxford Group/Oxford Movement
(religious movement)
The 'Oxford Group' was an early nickname for Moral Rearmament, or Buchmanism. (Buchanan won support for his ideas at Oxford University in 1921, but the movement has no special association with the city.) The 'Oxford Movement' was the one started in the Church of England by J. H. Newman (later Cardinal Newman), John Keble and others at Oxford University in 1833 with the aim of guiding Anglicanism towards High Church principles or Anglo-Catholicism.

Oxford Movement see **Oxford Group**

P

pace see **vice**

pack see **flock**

package see **packet**

packet/package/parcel (something packed and wrapped)
A 'packet' is basically a small 'package', a 'pack-ette', while a 'package' is a bundle or collection of things that are packed, but not necessarily wrapped. A 'parcel' is the word for goods that are normally wrapped in a single 'package', and especially such a 'package' wrapped in paper and designed to be sent through the post. The British Post Office regards its mail as consisting of letters and 'postal"packets"', with the latter including 'parcels'.

paediatric see **orthopaedic**

pagan see **heathen**

pagoda/pergola/portico/gazebo (exotic structure)
The 'pagoda' is well known as the many-storeyed temple or sacred building in India, China, Burma, etc., constructed over the relics of the Buddha or a saint. A 'pergola' is an arbour, or a construction resembling one, formed out of horizontal trellis-work on columns or posts over which vines or other plants are trained. A 'portico' is a kind of porch over the entrance to a temple, church

177

or other building, consisting of a roof supported by columns or piers. A 'gazebo' is a belvedere – a construction such as a turret, pavilion or summerhouse that commands an impressive view. One tentative etymology of the word – a blend of 'gaze' and Latin *videbo* (I shall see) – is as whimsical as the structure itself.

pain see **ache**

palate/palette (potential artistic vehicle)
Confusion is not normally found in the true sense of the words, respectively 'roof of the mouth' and 'board on which artist mixes his colours', but in the transferred or metaphorical sense, especially as used by wine writers and music critics. Thus a wine with a 'well-rounded palate' is one which has a full-bodied (or whatever) taste. But what did the music critic of *The Times* mean when he wrote of Prokofiev seeming to represent 'a clean palette and a breath of fresh air' (4 March 1976)? In other words, was his metaphor from painting or wine drinking? Both a 'clean palette' and a 'clear palate' would represent a latent vehicle for some kind of artistic experience. The use of 'palate' to mean 'sense of taste' is, of course, incorrect, since the taste buds are on the tongue, not on the roof of the mouth.

Palestine see **Israel**

palette see **palate**

palimpsest see **papyrus**

palmy see **barmy**

palsied see **paralysed**

pampas see **prairie**

pamphlet see **brochure**

pan see **track** (movement of camera)

panacea/placebo (type of medicine)
A 'panacea' is a remedy for all diseases, a cure for all ills, both physical and figurative. (The word comes from the Greek meaning 'all healing'.) A 'placebo' is a medicine given more to please or placate than to benefit, since the drug that the patient supposes it contains has been replaced by an inactive substance such as sugar. Its application is thus entirely psychological. 'Placebo' is Latin for 'I shall please', this being the opening word of the Latin rite of Vespers for the Dead.

panama/boater (type of straw hat)
A 'panama' hat is a soft one, made by hand-plaiting strips of leaves from a South American plant, the screw-pine. The hats were not made in Panama but widely marketed and distributed there: their country of origin is in fact Ecuador. The 'boater', correctly worn in boating, especially at the turn of the century and also between the wars, has a hard, stiff brim. It is still worn in some sections of society for certain occasions, and also regularly, as part of the uniform, at some boys' and girls' public schools, such as Harrow and the Godolphin School.

pandemic see **epidemic**

panoply see **canopy**

panorama see **view**

panther see **leopard**

pants see **trousers**

papyrus/palimpsest (ancient document)
A 'papyrus' is an ancient document or manuscript written on sheets made from the 'papyrus' or paper reed, formerly abundant in Egypt. (The word is actually related to 'paper'.) A 'palimpsest' is a parchment on which the writing has been partially or completely rubbed out to make room for another text. The term is also used of a monumental brass that has been turned and engraved on the reverse side with a new text. The origin of the word is the Greek *palin* (again) and *psestos* (rubbed smooth).

parade/promenade/esplanade (public place or road designed for walking or driving)
A 'parade' can be a 'promenade' or a place for walking for pleasure or display, although as the name of a street a 'Parade' is usually short, with a row or block of shops. A 'prom-

enade' is usually associated with a seafront at a resort, where it is a road for strolling or driving that runs beside the sea. An 'esplanade' is either a level space between a fortress and a town such as the one at Edinburgh Castle, where the Tattoo is held, or a term used in much the same sense as 'promenade' to apply to a road running along a seafront. The word comes from Latin, via Spanish, with the basic meaning 'levelled'.

paraffin see **petrol**

parakeet/paroquet/popinjay (kind of parrot)
A 'parakeet' is a kind of small, slender parrot, usually with a long, pointed tail, such as the Australian, or grass 'parakeet'. The word is the anglicised variant of 'paroquet', which is the Old French form. 'Popinjay' means 'parrot' only in an archaic sense. It was also used to apply to the figure of a parrot used as a target for shooting practice. In modern use a 'popinjay' is either a fop or dandy or, in some regions, an alternative name for the green woodpecker. All words are probably related to 'parrot', which in turn may derive from the proper name 'Pierrot' – although one theory traces 'parakeet' and 'paroquet' back to the Italian *parchito* (little parson).

paralysed/petrified/palsied (unable to move)
To be 'paralysed' is to have no power to contract one's muscles; to be 'petrified' is literally to be turned into stone. To be 'paralysed' or 'petrified' with fear, say, means to be unable to move as a result of being terrified. If there is any difference in the shades of meaning it is that a 'paralysed' person cannot make the necessary movements to escape, but a 'petrified' one is rooted to the spot by his rigidity. 'Palsied' means 'affected with palsy' – a paralysis accompanied by tremulous movements – and hence 'paralysed', although in a secondary sense 'palsied' means 'trembling' or 'tottering'.

parameter see **perimeter**

parcel see **packet**

parka see **anorak**

parochial see **provincial**

parody/pastiche/skit/burlesque (literary or theatrical composition mocking an author or his work)
A 'parody' is a humorous imitation, designed to make the author's work or words seem ridiculous. A classic example is Stella Gibbons's *Cold Comfort Farm* (1932), which is a 'parody' on the novels of Mary Webb. A 'pastiche' is a medley or patchwork of words, sentences or complete passages from one or several authors, so is also a type of imitation. If this is intentional, it will also be a 'parody'. A 'skit' comes close to both a 'parody' and a 'burlesque'. It aims to caricature a person or his style of writing by a kind of 'guying'. As such it is common in musical revues, where famous people are 'taken off' by humorous impersonation. A 'burlesque' is a derisive imitation, an exaggerated 'send-up' of a person or his work, and usually stronger and broader in style than a 'parody'. It chiefly occurs in stage plays. An example of 'burlesque' is the rendering of the play 'Pyramus and Thisbe' performed by Bottom and company in Shakespeare's *Midsummer Night's Dream*. (The word is not related to 'burly' or 'hurly-burly' but comes from Italian, through French, meaning 'mockery'.)

paroquet see **parakeet**

parquetry/marquetry (mosaic work in wood)
'Parquetry' is essentially mosaic woodwork in floors or wainscoting. 'Marquetry' is inlaid work of variously coloured woods or other materials mainly in furniture. French *marqueter* means 'to chequer', 'to inlay'.

parsnip see **turnip**

parson see **vicar**

part/piece/portion (section of the whole)
A 'part' is a general word to mean any division or section or bit of something, as 'part' of the road or a spare 'part'. 'Piece' suggests a 'part' that is a complete unit on its own, as a 'piece' of cake or a 'piece' of

advice. 'Portion' is the word for something given or allotted to a person, as a 'portion' of ice cream or the 'portion' of an estate.

partially see partly

particular/peculiar (special)
The 'particular' advantages of something are the specific or exceptional ones; the 'peculiar' advantages are the distinctive or exclusive ones – possibly even rather unusual or unexpected ones. 'A particular advantage of this job is that I can be home by 4.30.' 'A peculiar advantage of this job is that I can work on Sunday and have Monday off.' A similar distinction exists between the words when used with such nouns as 'interest', 'difficulty', 'problem', 'liking', 'influence'.

partisan see guerrilla

partly/partially (not wholly)
'Partly' is the opposite of 'wholly', meaning thus 'in part', 'to some degree'; 'partially' is the opposite of 'completely' and means 'not fully'. A 'partially' blind person crossing the road might thus be 'partly' responsible for a car having to brake suddenly: he cannot be fully blamed as his sight is not perfect.

partridge see pheasant

pash see crush

passage/corridor (way through)
In a building, a 'passage' is any way, not necessarily particularly narrow or lengthy, that gives access to another room or area. The word does imply, however, an intermediate or linking part through or along which one must pass to get from A to B. A 'corridor', thus, is a main passage in a large building, giving access to several rooms and usually fairly narrow and straight, as the 'corridors' in a hotel that lead to various bedrooms. The word came to English from Italian, via French: Italian *correre* means 'to run'. Schoolchildren forbidden from running in the 'corridor' must feel the word to be rather a misnomer.

passe-partout/en-tout-cas (type of frame or border)
'Passe-partout' – French for 'passes everywhere' – is the term used for the strips of adhesive paper fastening the two pieces of glass that contain a photograph. (The word can also apply to the whole frame made with such strips.) 'En-tout-cas' – French for 'in any case' – is the term, properly a trade name, used for a type of all-weather hard tennis court. The phrase is also sometimes used to mean a combined umbrella and parasol.

pastiche see parody

pastime see hobby

pastor see minister

pastry/pasty/patty/pâté (kind of pie or cake)
'Pastry' is the baked crust of pies and tarts, made of paste or dough; a 'pastry' is a small individual cake, such as a fancy cake. A 'pasty' is a pie filled with anything savoury, or sweet, such as a meat 'pasty', fish 'pasty' or apple 'pasty'. (For more about its contents, see **tart**.) A 'patty' is a small pie or 'pasty', or a small flat cake of minced beef or some other food – there are even peppermint 'patties'. 'Pâté' is a paste or spread of finely ground liver, meat or fish, usually served as a starter or hors d'oeuvre. 'Pâté de foie gras' – literally 'pastry of fat liver' – is goose liver paste filling, regarded by some gourmets as a worthy rival to caviare. All the words are basically related to 'paste'.

pasty see (1) pastry, (2) tart

pâté see pastry

paten see platen

pathos/bathos (sad or sentimental sensation)
'Pathos' is that quality of speech or music that evokes a feeling of pity or sympathetic sadness: 'The tale was told with a pathos that drew tears from all those present.' 'Bathos' is at best insincere 'pathos'; at worst it is a descent in speech or music 'from the sublime to the ridiculous'. Pope illustrates 'bathos' with the lines:

Ye Gods! annihilate but Space and Time
And make two lovers happy.

Both words are Greek, meaning respectively
'suffering' and 'depth'.

patty see **pastry**

Paul Pry see **Nosy Parker**

peach/apricot (soft luscious fruit)
The 'peach' is a large, round fruit, with a
downy white or yellow skin flushed with
red – the model of a 'peaches and cream'
complexion – a sweet, juicy flesh, and a
rough stone. Its name rather unexpectedly
comes from Latin *persicum malum*, 'Persian
apple', but then the best 'peaches' came
from Persia, and 'apple' can be used of fruit
other than apples (as the pineapple, which
is neither an apple nor grows on pine trees).
The 'apricot', which is smaller, is related to
both the 'peach' and the plum. Its skin
when ripe is orange-pink and not 'flushed'
in quite the same way as a 'peach', which
otherwise it resembles. It, too, has something of an exotic name, which comes from
Arabic *al-birqūq*, 'the early-ripe', in turn
from Latin *praecox* (which gives
'precocious') under the influence of Latin
apricus, 'ripe', via several other languages.
(Dictionaries get quite excited about the
origin of 'apricot': in the 'big' dictionaries,
such as the *Oxford English* and Wyld's
Universal Dictionary of the English Language,
the etymology of the word takes up
considerably more space than the actual
definition of the fruit.)

peal/chime (ring of bells)
A 'peal' is normally the word for a series of
changes rung on a set of bells. A 'chime'
describes the melodious or tuneful sound
produced by bells rung harmoniously, as
the carillon played on the church bells in
Belgium, for example. It is the method for
ringing, in fact, that signifies the real difference between the words: bells that 'chime'
are usually struck with an external hammer
(as in many striking clocks) or by the mechanical movement of a clapper (as in the
carillon); bells that 'peal' are swung by
means of ropes, as church bells – although
church bells can in fact be sounded both
ways.

peat see **turf**

peculiar see **particular**

pedagogue see **pedant**

pedant/pedagogue (unduly dogmatic or
'serious' person)
Both can be rather a bore, especially when
both simultaneously, like a humourless
classics teacher. In fact, they both *are*
teachers, or at least were, with 'pedant'
having this meaning when the word first
entered English in the sixteenth century
(from French), and 'pedagogue' also used
in this sense earlier and later. But soon both
became derogatory words for a person (not
necessarily a teacher) who insists on
displaying his detailed knowledge, or who
attaches undue importance to minor aspects
of it, or who is dogmatic or unreasonably
'bookish'. Today, 'pedant' is the more
common word for such a person, with 'pedagogue' still retaining its 'teaching' connotation. Nor are the epithets confined to men
only, as Mary Russell Mitford reminds us
when in a letter of 1812 she refers to 'learned
young ladies – pedants in petticoats'. No
doubt girls' schools have produced and
nurtured just as many 'pedants' (among the
students) and 'pedagogues' (among the
staff) as boys' schools have, with the same
applying to universities. The words may
actually be related, with 'pedant' perhaps
deriving, via Italian, from Latin *paedagogus*,
itself a word of Greek origin meaning literally 'boy leader'. In ancient Greece, a 'pedagogue' was a slave who escorted his master's
son to school and back.

**pedestrian crossing/zebra crossing/
pelican crossing** (place where pedestrians
have the right to cross the road)
A 'pedestrian crossing' is a general term for
a place where the road can be crossed. A
'zebra crossing' is a common form of
crossing where the black and white stripes,
compared to those of a zebra, indicate that
pedestrians, once on the crossing, have right
of way over vehicles. Points where such
crossings are located are indicated by
flashing Belisha beacons. 'Pelican crossings'
are the ones where pedestrians have their
own lights, which they can control – the

'green man' – to tell them when it is safe to cross (many 'pelicans' also have a bleeper as an audible signal), and motorists have a conventional set of traffic lights with, however, a flashing amber light following the red to indicate that they must give way to any pedestrians who may be on the crossing. 'Pelican crossings' bear little resemblance to the ungainly bird that stores fish in its pouch: the name comes from (near enough) the first letters of 'pedestrian light controlled crossing'. Such crossings were introduced in 1966.

Peeping Tom see **Nosy Parker**

peer see **lord**

Peke see **Pom**

pelican crossing see **pedestrian crossing**

pellagra/podagra (disease)
'Pellagra' – possibly from Italian *pelle agre* (rough skin) – is a non-contagious disease caused by a deficient diet and marked by skin changes, nervous dysfunction, and diarrhoea. 'Podagra', from the Greek meaning 'foot seizure', is gout – properly in the feet.

pendant/pennant/pennon (type of flag)
A 'pendant' is anything hanging, as an ornament, chandelier, length of rope or . . . 'pennant', which is properly a long triangular flag used for signalling, with its widest end next to the mast. In practice a 'pennant' can be any flag used as an emblem. In the USA it is a flag awarded for success in athletics. The sense also coincides to a large degree with 'pennon', which is a distinctive flag having various forms, such as tapering, triangular or swallow-tailed. Originally it was the flag on the lance of a knight. There is thus little difference between the latter words, although a 'pennon' is usually longer and narrower than a 'pennant'.

pennant see **pendant**

pennon see **pendant**

pentathlon see **marathon**

perceptive/percipient/perspicacious/perspicuous (intelligent, clear, lucid)
'Perceptive' means 'understanding readily or quickly', as a 'perceptive' remark. 'Percipient' means simply 'showing understanding', as, again, in a 'percipient' remark. 'Perspicacious' means 'having the ability to see and distinguish', 'discerning', as a 'perspicacious' mind or wit. 'Perspicuous' means 'clear', 'easily understood', as a 'perspicuous' reason, or 'expressing clearly': 'He is quite clear and perspicuous'. Both 'perceptive' and 'percipient' are commonly used of people: 'He is very perceptive' means 'He understands things well'; 'He is a percipient arguer' means 'He argues with understanding.' The nouns of these adjectives are: of 'perceptive' – 'perceptivity', of 'percipient' – 'percipience', of 'perspicacious' – 'perspicacity' (or less commonly 'perspicaciousness').

percipient see **perceptive**

percolate see **pervade**

peremptory see **perfunctory**

perennial see **annual**

perfume/scent (fragrant cosmetic product)
In common usage, the words are hardly differentiated. However, 'perfume' is basically the substance – either natural, as the oil from leaves, trees or flowers, or artificial – from which 'scent' is made, 'scent' being the commercial product. But 'perfume' is the term also used for a natural substance used commercially outside cosmetics, as for example in toothpaste, tobacco, plastic wrappings and so on. Thus 'perfume' is more wide-ranging, and 'scent' is almost always, too, a liquid product.

perfunctory/peremptory (brief)
'Perfunctory' means 'performed merely as a routine or an uninteresting duty', 'casual', as a 'perfunctory' inspection (a brief, superficial one) or a 'perfunctory' piece of work (done half-heartedly or carelessly). 'Peremptory' means 'dictatorial', and implies a command that is absolute. Such commands or orders are given in a 'peremptory' tone, i.e. an abrupt one.

pergola see **pagoda**

perigee see **apogee**

perimeter/parameter/periphery
(mathematical term defining length or
quantity)
A 'perimeter' is the outer border of a two-
dimensional figure or the length of such a
border. 'Parameter' has a number of precise
and vague senses. Of these, two precise
meanings belong to mathematics and statistics. One mathematical definition is 'the
line or quantity serving to determine a
point, line, figure or quantity in a class of
things'. From this evolved the statistical
usage: 'a quantity which determines the
distribution of a random variable, and
which can be estimated from sample data.'
(An example of this might be 'fertility and
mortality parameters', meaning approximately 'the extent to which people give birth
and die'.) This sense has itself given birth
to a vogue word of vaguest meaning, as in:
'By the parameters of her upbringing, she's
a very well educated person.' In this loose
usage 'parameter' simply means 'standard',
'limit', 'condition', 'criterion'. A 'periphery'
is much more precise; it is the external
boundary of any surface or area, especially
a rounded one.

periodical see **magazine**

periphery see **perimeter**

permeate see **pervade**

pernickety see **finicky**

perquisite see **requirement**

perry see **cider**

perseverance see **persistence**

**persistence/perseverance/pertinacity/
tenacity** (resoluteness, stubbornness)
'Persistence' can be a favourable or
unfavourable word, implying either dogged
resolve or prolonged annoyance. 'Perseverance' implies an activity maintained in spite
of difficulties. 'Pertinacity' suggests an
essentially unfavourable doggedness,

although the word can also be used in a
favourable sense ('They fought with
considerable courage and pertinacity').
'Tenacity' means 'the quality of holding
fast', as the 'tenacity' of the attack of an
enemy or, more literally, of a firmly binding
glue.

persistently see **consistently**

personate see **impersonate**

perspicacious see **perceptive**

perspicuous see **perceptive**

pert see **insolent**

pertinacity see **persistence**

perturb see **disturb**

pervade/permeate/percolate (spread,
extend, penetrate)
To 'pervade' is to extend an activity,
influence, presence or the like, as the wit
that 'pervades' a new novel, or the scent of
spring flowers that 'pervades' a room. To
'permeate' is to penetrate or pass through,
literally or figuratively, as water that
'permeates' the soil or the new teaching
methods that have 'permeated' the schools.
To 'percolate' is to 'permeate', but slowly,
especially of liquids, as water that 'perco-
lates' through the sand or the new ideas that
are beginning to 'percolate' into people's
minds. The word is from the Latin with
literal meaning 'strain through'.

peseta/peso (unit of currency of Spanish-
speaking countries)
The 'peseta' is the basic currency of Spain,
equal to 100 *céntimos*. The 'peso' is the unit
of Mexico, Cuba, the Philippines and
Spanish American countries (equal usually
to 100 *centavos*) The 'peso' was also a former
Spanish gold coin with a value of eight *reales*.

peso see **peseta**

pesticide see **insecticide**

petrified see **paralysed**

**petrol/paraffin/petroleum/gasoline/
kerosine/diesel oil** (type of liquid fuel)
'Petrol' is refined 'petroleum' and the most
familiar to the man in the car on the street.
So what is 'petroleum'? It is the hydrocarbon oil found in the upper strata of the
earth, known also as crude oil. This is the
'oil' found in the North Sea. 'Paraffin' –
more fully, paraffin oil – is also got from
'petroleum', by distillation, and is
commonly used for lamps, domestic heaters,
and as a fuel for jet aircraft. 'Gasoline' is
the American equivalent word for 'petrol'
(hence 'step on the gas' and similar
phrases), while 'kerosine' is American
parlance for 'paraffin', as it also is in
Australia and New Zealand. (The spelling
is the commercial one; formerly it was 'kero-
sene'.) This leaves 'diesel oil', or diesel fuel,
which is a heavy 'petroleum' fraction used
in diesel engines. A special form of this is
derv, used in heavy road vehicles such as
buses and lorries. The word is made up
of the intitial letters of '*d*iesel-*e*ngined *r*oad
*v*ehicle' – rather oddly, since one would
expect the name to be based on the fuel
rather than the type of vehicle it is intended
for.

petroleum see petrol

phantom see ghost

Pharisee see Philistine

pharmacist see chemist

pharynx see larynx

phase see phrase

pheasant/partridge/grouse/ptarmigan
(game bird found in fields or on moors)
The male 'pheasant' is rather a striking
bird, both in colouring and often literally,
alas, in its inability to avoid speeding cars
as it is crossing the road. The bird has a
long tail, lives mainly in open fields and
woodlands, and is larger than the
'partridge', by an average of three feet in
length to one. The 'partridge' is thus rather
a squat bird, often living on farmland (and
seasonally in pear trees). The 'grouse' is
sometimes wrongly called by the name of

phrase/phase (unit of a whole)
The two words are surprisingly often
confused, with 'phrase' often used for
'phase'. A 'phrase' – from Greek *phrasis*
(speech) – is a group of words in speech,
notes in music, or motions in dancing that
acts as a unit and, with other such units,
makes a complete work. In this sense the
meaning is thus close to 'stage', which is the
basic meaning of 'phase'. A 'phase',
however, is not necessarily a repeated or
like unit but normally a unit of change or
development, such as a 'phase' of the moon
(e.g. first quarter or full moon). Doubtless
the temptation to say 'phrase' instead of
'phase' was formerly increased by the
association of the Government's 'Pay Code'
or 'Phase Four', introduced in 1978 to
control inflation, with a 'wage freeze', i.e. a
jumble of 'pay', 'stage', 'wage', 'freeze' and
'phrase'.

phrenetic see frantic

physician see doctor

pianola/piano-player/player-piano (type
of mechanical piano)
The 'pianola', originally a trade name
apparently intended to be a kind of diminutive of 'piano', was an American invention
of the end of the nineteenth century and to
begin with was just a contrivance pushed
up to an ordinary piano, on whose keys
it played with felted fingers. Later it was
physically incorporated in the body of the
piano. The piano music produced by it
came about by air from a 'tracker-bar'
passing through the little perforations of an
unrolling paper roll and striking the
necessary hammers against the strings.
Such music was mostly of the tea-time
variety, and essentially Victorian. The
'pianola' was generically a 'piano-player',
otherwise a 'player-piano', the first of these
being a device that plays the piano, and the
second a piano that can be played automati-
cally, i.e. one and the same instrument.
'Pianolas', like certain other Victoriana, had
a revival in the 1950s, with even several new
instruments being built.

piano-player see pianola

piazza see **plaza**

picador see **matador**

piccalilli see **pickles**

pickles/piccalilli/chilli (seasoned relish)
'Pickles' are vegetables such as cucumbers, onions and cauliflowers that have been preserved in vinegar, brine and the like. 'Piccalilli' – which word is probably a blend of 'pickle' and 'chilli' – is a highly seasoned 'pickle' of East Indian origin made of chopped vegetables and hot spices, the whole usually yellowish in colour. 'Chilli', originally an Aztec word, is the pod of a species of capsicum used in 'pickles' and sauces and, in dried form, as the chief ingredient of Cayenne pepper. 'Chilli con carne' – Spanish for 'chilli with meat' – is a Mexican dish made from meat and finely chopped red pepper, usually served with beans, and 'chilli' sauce is made of tomatoes cooked with 'chilli', spices and other seasonings. The preferred American spelling of the word is 'chili'.

pie see **tart**

piebald see **dappled**

piece see **part**

pier see **quay**

pig/hog/boar (animal noted for its bacon, bristles and boorishness)
'Pig' is the generic word, of which the feminine is 'sow'. A 'hog' – the word is used more widely and generally in the USA – is a domesticated 'pig', and especially a castrated male raised for slaughter. By contrast a 'boar' is an *un*castrated male, especially one used for food. ('Boar''s head – traditionally served up with an apple in its mouth – was long a Christmas dish, as witness pubs and inns so named.)

pigeon/dove (wild or tame bird associated with pies or peace)
All 'doves' are 'pigeons', and all 'pigeons' are 'doves', since these names are used for any member of the family *Columbidae*. However, 'pigeon' usually means a larger 'partridge', especially in the USA. The 'grouse', about twice the length of the 'partridge', often has a heather habitat, in particular on the Scottish moors. Among the special kinds of 'grouse' are the capercaillie (or capercailzie), also called the wood 'grouse', and the 'ptarmigan', the fourth of this game bag. This is a bird that has black or grey plumage in summer and white in winter and is decidedly small rather than large. In Britain it is confined to northern Scotland. It differs from other members of the 'grouse' family in having toes covered with stiff feathers, a distinguishing feature almost as original as its Greek-looking name. This is actually derived from Gaelic *tarmachan*, with an initial classy 'p' added by association with such scientific zoological names as 'pterodactyl' or Greek words in general beginning 'pt-'.

phial/philtre (small bottle – or the drug it contains)
Two rather archaic confusibles. A 'phial' is a small glass vessel for liquids, usually medicine or some kind of potion. A 'philtre' is the potion or drug itself, especially one supposed to arouse amorous feelings, or any magic potion. The 'phil-' element means 'love', as in 'philanthropic' or 'Francophile'.

philanderer see **philanthropist**

philanthropist/philanderer (one who loves his fellow men – or women)
A 'philanthropist' loves all mankind. The word is usually used to apply to a benefactor of some kind. A 'philanderer', from the Greek meaning literally 'man lover', is not one who loves men, but a man who loves women, otherwise a male flirt. Philander was, in an old ballad, the lover of Phillis, and in Beaumont and Fletcher's *Laws of Candy* the lover of Erota. Hence a 'philander-er', or 'Philander-like' person.

Philistine/Pharisee (nickname for a despised person)
The original 'Philistines' were the warlike people who occupied the southern coast of Palestine and harassed the Israelites. The term is now applied to anyone looked down on as lacking in culture or aesthetic refinement, or any 'boor' in general. The 'Phar-

isees', from a Hebrew word meaning 'separated', were the Jewish sect who observed the religious law strictly and claimed a consequent superior sanctity. The word is now used of any self-righteous or hypocritical person.

philtre see **phial**

phlegm/mucus (viscous substance secreted by a mucous membrane)
'Mucus' is the general word for the viscid secretion, acting as a lubricative or to moisten the passages, found in the digestive system, nose, windpipe, bladder and other organs. 'Phlegm' is the thick, morbid form of this, especially in the lungs and throat passages, which is normally discharged by a cough or nose-blowing. 'Phlegm', ultimately from the Greek for 'flame', was originally one of the four so-called humours or bodily fluids, the others being blood, choler (yellow bile) and melancholy (black bile). 'Phlegm' was regarded as the clammy humour that caused sluggishness or apathy.

phoneme/morpheme (linguistic unit)
A 'phoneme' is the basic sound unit in a language. In English it is often, but by no means always, represented by a single letter. In 'phoneme', for example, there are six 'phonemes': one for 'ph', two for 'o' (which is really, in standard speech, something like 'er' followed by 'oo'), one for 'n', one for 'e' and one for 'm'. 'Phonemes' in English are ususally represented not by conventional letters but by special symbols such as those of the International Phonetic Alphabet, in which 'phoneme' appears as *fəuni:m*. (The colon indicates a long vowel sound.) A 'morpheme' is a minimal linguistic unit, often a prefix, root, suffix or ending in a word. In 'confusible', for example, there are three 'morphemes': the prefix 'con-', the root '-fus-' and the suffix '-ible'. The terms derive respectively from the Greek words for 'sound speech' and 'form', with 'morpheme' based on the word 'phoneme'. Both words are quite recent: 'phoneme' was first used in the 1920s, and 'morpheme' followed shortly after.

phosphorescent see **fluorescent**

bird, either those found in squares and railway stations, or the ones bred by fanciers or for racing. This means that 'dove' normally applies to the smaller bird, especially a particular variety, as the turtle-'dove', stock-'dove', ring-'dove' (otherwise wood 'pigeon', which is a menace to crops) and rock-'dove', from which many breeds of domestic 'pigeon' are derived. The 'dove', too, is the more poetic or symbolic bird, in particular representing peace (in politics) or innocence, gentleness and tenderness (in literature). In this connection see **hawks.**

pilchard see **sardine**

pile/pyre (heap of wood on which a dead body is burnt)
The confusion is mainly due to 'funeral pile' (or 'funeral pyre'). A 'funeral pile' is a heap of wood on which a dead *or* living person or a sacrifice of any kind is burnt. A 'funeral pyre' is a 'pile' of wood for burning a dead body. The first word is basic 'pile'; the second derives from Greek *pyr* (fire).

pill/tablet (small piece of prepared medical substance for swallowing whole)
A 'pill' is usually round or flat and normally regarded as a capsule containing a drug or medicinal substance. A specific type is 'the pill', the colloquial term for an oral contraceptive. A 'tablet' is normally flat and round, and usually homogeneous, and with no outer casing, so that it consists of a solid or compressed substance, such as aspirin.

pillar/column (upright support)
The general word is 'pillar'. A 'column' is an individual or special kind of 'pillar', in particular one that is architecturally interesting or otherwise noteworthy, as Nelson's 'Column' in Trafalgar Square. A 'column', too, is often thought of as consisting of three parts: base, shaft and capital.

pillory see **stocks** (old instrument of punishment)

pimento/pimiento (strong-tasting fruit)
A 'pimento' is the dried fruit of the *Pimenta officinalis*, otherwise known as all-spice, or the name of the tree itself. A 'pimiento' is a red Spanish pepper with a sweet, pungent

flavour. The 'pimento' berry is used in baking and is often an ingredient of mincemeat. 'Pimento' is often used for 'pimiento', but not the other way round. The confusion is the fault of early Spanish explorers, who seeing the 'pimento' thought it was a type of pepper and called it *pimienta* (pepper).

pimiento see **pimento**

pimp see **poof**

pinafore see **apron**

pincers see **pliers**

pine/fir (evergreen tree with needle-like leaves)
The difference is in the leaves and their arrangement: on a 'pine', leaves grow in clusters of two or more, on a 'fir' the needles are placed singly on the shoots. To complicate matters, however, a Scots 'pine' is the same as a Scotch (*sic*) 'fir', otherwise *Pinus silvestris*, the only British native 'pine' grown for its valuable timber.

pink see **carnation**

pip see **stone**

piquant see **pungent**

pistol/revolver/automatic (firearm fired from the hand)
'Pistols' are divided into single-shot 'pistols', 'revolvers' and 'automatics'. 'Revolvers', as the name indicates, have an element that revolves, in modern 'revolvers' a multi-chambered cylinder, turned by pulling the trigger. This is the weapon for playing Russian roulette: insert one cartridge, spin the cylinder, and you may or may not have a round to fire when you pull the trigger. 'Automatics' have a magazine in the butt, and a mechanism that is actuated by the energy of the recoil when the bullet is fired. The US police force is armed with 'revolvers', although the police in many other countries are issued with 'automatics'.

pitch see (1) **field** (area of play), (2) **tar**

piteous see **pitiful**

pitfall see **trap**

pitiable see **pitiful**

pitiful/pitiable/piteous (causing pity)
'Pitiful' implies that the person or thing excites pity or is contemptible, as respectively a 'pitiful' sight or a 'pitiful' display of knowledge. 'Pitiable' means 'lamentable', 'wretched', as a 'pitiable' old man living in a 'pitiable' shack in a 'pitiable' condition. 'Piteous' implies an exhibition of suffering and misery, as heard in a 'piteous' groan or seen in a 'piteous' sight. (A 'pitiful' sight itself need not necessarily imply a condition of suffering: a field of flattened corn after heavy rain might be a 'pitiful' sight since one would pity the farmer rather than the corn).

pizzazz see **razzmatazz**

placebo see **panacea**

plaice/sole (edible flatfish)
The 'plaice', or *Pleuronectes platessa*, is a European flatfish around fifteen inches long, with red or orange spots on a brownish skin, found in the North Atlantic and around British coasts and popular for its equally palatable partner – chips. The 'sole' can be one of a number of flatfish, but especially the genus *Solea* which gives the well-known Dover 'sole', *Solea solea*. It is under two feet in length, of a more or less uniform brown colour (no orange spots), and found chiefly in the eastern Atlantic and Mediterranean. The lemon 'sole' is not a 'sole' at all but a kind of 'plaice' that resembles one. Moreover, it may be eaten with a slice of lemon, but its name has nothing to do with lemons in origin: it is a corruption of French *limande*, of unknown origin.

plaid see **tartan**

plain see **plane**

plait see **pleat**

plan/project/design (proposed method of doing something)

'Plan' is the general word to denote something thought out in advance with the aim of putting it into effect. A 'project' is a more complex or tentative 'plan', which may perhaps not be realised. A 'design' is a cunning 'plan' – in the good or bad sense of the word – and usually hints at the actual objective, which is why literally it is often a drawing or sketch of some kind, as in the design for a new theatre. See also **scheme.**

plane/plain (flat or level surface)
The confusion is not between 'plane' = 'smoothing tool', 'aeroplane' and 'plain' = 'flat stretch of land' but between 'plain' and 'plane' in the sense 'flat or level surface', either as a mathematical term or in extended use (e.g. a moral 'plane'). It's a matter of spotting the spelling: 'plain' means only the flat stretch of land. All the other senses are 'plane'. (There is of course the noun 'plain' in knitting, as the opposite of 'purl', but this comes direct from the adjective 'plain' meaning 'ordinary', 'simple'.) The two words are in fact of identical origin – Latin *planus* (plain), with the spelling 'plane' differentiated only in the seventeenth century.

planet see **star**

plangent see **pungent**

platen/paten (special kind of plate)
A 'platen' is a flat metal plate that is used to exert pressure of some kind, especially in a printing press. (In a typewriter, it is the technical term for the roller.) A 'paten' is a plate, often one of precious metal such as silver or gold, used to carry the bread or wafers in the Communion service (while the 'chalice' holds the wine).

platinum/gold/silver (special record or disc awarded for high sales)
The whole system of awards for sales of pop or rock records (or albums) tends to vary as values change, but here is the current basis for Britain and America. In Britain, the awards are based on sales figures, so that sales of £250,000 for a record earns a 'silver', £500,000 earns a 'gold', and £1 million gains a 'platinum'. This is only for singles, however, and for LPs (albums)

awards are based on units, as in the United States, so that 60,000 copies sold earns a 'silver', 100,000 gets a 'gold', and 300,000 wins a 'platinum'. In the United States there are no 'silvers'. A single that sells a million copies earns a 'gold', and one that manages two million gains a 'platinum'. However, an LP needs to sell half a million copies in America to gain a 'gold', and a million to deserve a 'platinum'. In Britain, the awards are made by the BPI (British Phonographic Industries Association); in America by the RIAA (Recording Industry Association of America). The actual awards are replicas of the winning record, stamped in the appropriate metal.

platitude see **commonplace**

platoon see **corps**

player-piano see **pianola**

play-group see **nursery school**

play school see **nursery school**

playwright see **dramatist**

plaza/piazza (square on the continent)
The words are respectively Spanish and Italian, and related to 'place'. Both are used for a public square or open space in a town or city, although a 'piazza' can also be an arcade or covered walk, for example round a square or running along the front of a building.

pleat/plait (material folded in a special way)
A 'pleat' is a flattened fold in cloth made by folding the material over itself and fastening it at the top, as in a skirt or a Scotsman's kilt. A 'plait' *can* also be this, but more usually the word means a length of material, especially hair, that has been 'plaited', i.e. intertwined in (mostly) three strands into a pattern. A popular example of a 'plait' is a pigtail (really a misnomer, since a pig's tail is hardly 'plaited'). Both words are related, and in fact 'pleat' developed as an altered spelling of 'plait'.

Pleistocene/Pliocene/Miocene
(geographical epoch)
In chronological order the epochs are 'Miocene', 'Pliocene', 'Pleistocene', their Greek names meaning 'less recent', 'more recent', and 'most recent'. The 'Pleistocene' epoch includes the Ice Age, which was roughly a million years ago, immediately preceding historic times. The 'Pliocene' epoch was around fifteen million years ago, and the 'Miocene' thirty-five million.

plexus/nexus (type of interconnecting network or chain)
A 'plexus' is a complicated network of something, especially of nerves or blood vessels in the body, such as the solar 'plexus', the network of nerves behind the stomach (so called since the network is radial, resembling the rays of the sun). A 'nexus' is a system of linking people or things in a series, such as a social 'nexus'. Both words are from Latin, respectively from the nouns of *plectere'* 'to plait' and *nectere,* 'to bind'. The English words owe something of their popularity or vogue to Henry Miller's trilogy of the 1950s, the *Rosy Crucifixion* series, comprising *Sexus, Plexus* and *Nexus.* (The first of these is not an English word, but the Latin for 'sex', characterising the generally frank treatment of the autobiographical theme of the trilogy and even influencing the subsequent connotation of the English words 'plexus' and 'nexus' themselves.)

pliers/pincers (tool with pivoted limbs forming a pair of jaws)
'Pliers' are small 'pincers' used for bending (plying) wire, holding small objects, and the like. 'Pincers' are used for gripping (pinching) things. Unlike 'pliers' the jaws are rounded, with a sizeable circular area between them. The jaws of 'pliers' are straight, or slightly tapering.

Pliocene see Pleistocene

plutocrat see autocrat

podagra see pellagra

poetry/verse (metrical compositions)
'She writes "poetry", you know.' 'Yes, and he writes "verse".' What is the difference?

The trouble is, that 'poetry' actually *is* 'verse', often as not. The word implies lofty feelings, though, and an inspired passion. 'Verse', on the other hand, is usually contrasted with prose, and is the expression of something in words which conform to accepted metrical rules and structure as a literary form. As an art form, 'verse' is more lowly than 'poetry', which is why one has light 'verse', not light 'poetry'.

poignant see pungent

politeness/courtesy (observance of considerate behaviour)
'Politeness' is the general word, implying a habitual 'courtesy' as a result of one's upbringing – otherwise 'good manners'. 'Courtesy' is a positive show, possibly a rather old-fashioned one, of consideration for others, especially on a specific occasion, such as 'an act of courtesy'.

politician/statesman (one skilled in politics or diplomacy)
The difference perhaps lies in the connotations of the words. 'Politician' can be used disparagingly to imply the scheming of small politics for party ends or one's own advantage, although more usually the word means someone who is professionally engaged in politics, such as an MP. 'Statesman', on the other hand, can never be used disparagingly. Indeed, it suggests a wise, far-sighted 'politician', one who is unselfishly devoted to the interests of his party or country. In the everyday sense, however, the words are almost equal – with 'statesman' nevertheless always having the edge as an important or senior or experienced 'politician'.

polyester see polythene

Polynesia see Micronesia

polystyrene see polythene

polytechnic see technical college

polythene/polystyrene/polyurethane/polyester (plastic or similar artificial product)
All terms refer to a type of polymer, which

is a chemical compound of high molecular weight derived either by a combination of many smaller molecules – Greek *polymeres* means 'of many parts' – or by the condensation of many smaller molecules so as to eliminate water, alcohol, etc. 'Polythene' is a plastic polymer of ethylene, used for containers, electric insulation, packaging and the like. 'Polystyrene' is a clear plastic polymer of styrene having good mechanical properties and, among other things, the ability to resist moisture and chemicals, so that it is used for the housings of such large domestic appliances as refrigerators and air conditioners. 'Polyurethane' is a polymer of urethane best known as a flexible foam for upholstery material, mattresses and the like. 'Polyester' is a term used for a number of polymerised esters (compounds formed by the condensation of an alcohol and an acid with the elimination of water) familiar in a wide range of clothing and home furnishings.

polyurethane see **polythene**

Pom/Peke/pug (breed of toy dog)
The 'Pom' or Pomeranian is said to have been bred down to its present five pounds or less from a thirty-pound sheepdog in Pomerania, a region now mostly in Poland along the Baltic coast. A toy dog with erect ears, it has a thick coat standing out around its neck and shoulders. The breed was a favourite with Queen Victoria. The 'Peke' or Pekinese came to Britain from China in 1860 after the sacking of the Summer Palace in Peking when three Allied officers brought back five of the Imperial pets. Most of today's 'Pekes', however, are descendants of those smuggled out of China at the end of the last century. Their distinctive feature is their wide, flat head and short, wrinkled muzzle. The 'pug' also originated in China and became especially popular in the Netherlands in the sixteenth century (the name of the breed is of Dutch origin). This is the dog, rather bigger than a 'Peke', with a wrinkled face, upturned nose and tight curled tail. The breed is neither noticeably 'pugnacious' nor unduly 'pygmy', in spite of the suggested association with these words.

pomade/pomander (scented medicinal substance)
'Pomade' is a scented ointment for the scalp and hair – originally for the skin and perhaps made with apples (French *pommes*). 'Pomander' is, or was, a blend of aromatic substances, often in the form of a ball, carried on the person as a perfume or guard against infection. Apples come in here, too, as the name derives from Old French *pome d'ambre* (apple of amber). The present form of the word is a corruption of earlier 'pomeamber'.

pomander see **pomade**

ponce see **poof**

pond see **lake**

poof/ponce/pimp (sexually or morally suspect person)
A 'poof' is a slang term – either from 'puff' meaning 'braggart' or the disdainful interjection 'poof!' – for a male homosexual or effeminate man. Confusion with 'ponce' is largely due to the verb 'ponce' meaning 'move or walk about effeminately'. Properly a 'ponce' – the origin may be in 'pounce' – is someone who lives off a prostitute's earnings. This sense links the word with 'pimp', who is a man that solicits for a prostitute or a brothel, in other words a procurer. The term is also used of any contemptible person, especially a tale-bearer. The suggestion that 'pimps' originated in the Dorset village of Pimperne, near Blandford, seems a little unrealistic.

pool see (1) **billiards**, (2) **lake**

pop/rock (type of music having a general appeal to most young people)
The two words are respectively the short forms of 'popular music' and 'rock 'n' roll', although 'rock' now suggests a contemporary individual image, not that of the historically dated (although still popular) rock 'n' roll of the 1950s. To a large extent, especially in casual or 'blanket' usage, the two words overlap, so that a 'rock' band may well be a 'pop' band, and vice versa. However, 'pop' is now largely taken to refer to music that is commercially motivated,

fairly undemanding to listen to and appreciate, and aimed mainly at teenage audiences. It comes over particularly successfully on radio and at discos. It is 'pop' records, too, that are likely to reach the 'top ten' of the charts, and thus to win commercial awards such as a 'gold disc' (see **platinum**). 'Rock', by contrast, is much more 'serious', at least to its devotees, and is not all-embracing as 'pop' is but comprises a number of individual music styles, among them the obviously derivative folk 'rock' and punk 'rock' as well as rhythm-and-blues ('R & B'), so called 'heavy metal', and reggae. The history of 'rock' music is thus more complex than that of 'pop', and in itself it is generally much more 'gutsy' and passionate, with considerable depth of feeling emotionally and sexually. It is also fair to say that it is the type of music most disliked (because least understood) by older people, who may quite like 'pop'.

pop-art see **op-art**

popinjay see **parakeet**

poplin/Crimplene/Terylene (strong fabric used for clothing)
'Poplin' is a finely-ribbed mercerised cotton material used chiefly for dresses, blouses, children's wear and the like. It is said to have been originally made either in the Belgian textile town of Poperinge or in the papal city of Avignon, in the south of France. If the latter, it is possible the word came to English from Italian *papalina* (papal) via French *popeline*. 'Crimplene' is a crimped form of 'Terylene', which itself is a synthetic polyester fibre made from *tereph*thalic acid and eth*ylene* glycol.

porcelain see **china**

porpoise see **dolphin**

port/harbour (place where ships can dock or shelter)
Up to a point the two words are synonymous. A 'port', however, is normally thought of as a seaside or riverside town with a busy or extensive 'harbour' and very likely docks as well. A 'harbour' itself was originally a place of shelter for ships, as its relationship with the word 'haven' suggests. More generally, it is a naturally or artificially protected stretch of water which, while providing a safe and secure anchorage, also has facilities for the loading and unloading of ships, landing and boarding of passengers, and the like. Strangely, this second but wider sense of the word – that is, as more than just a place of shelter – is not given in many standard dictionaries. Yet surely the general definition is the way most people regard it?

port/starboard/larboard (side of a ship or other craft)
When facing forwards, 'port' is the left side of a ship or aircraft, and 'starboard' the right side. Why these strange terms, and what is 'larboard'? 'Port', perhaps, because this side was usually next to the shore when the ship was in port. 'Starboard', since this is the 'steering side': boats were originally steered by a paddle over the right-hand side. 'Larboard' was formerly – and still is, in the USA – a term for 'port'. It was replaced by 'port' to avoid confusion, especially in shouted orders. ('Larboard' itself may have derived from 'loading side', with the word assimilated to 'starboard'.) 'Port' exists as a verb in the phrase '"port" the helm'. This originally meant 'turn the tiller to "port"', so that the ship turns to "starboard"'. Since 1933, however, the meaning has nautically been redefined as 'turn the ship to "port"'. The slang word 'posh' ('elegant', 'upperclass') is popularly supposed to derive from the acronym of '"port" out, "starboard" home', these being the desirable sides of the ship for cabins when sailing to and from the East in the days before air-conditioning, but no evidence has been found to support this. (Perhaps a slang word 'posh' meaning 'money' or 'dandy' is the origin.)

porter (carrier or gatekeeper)
It is sometimes not realised that the two types of 'porter', the carrier and the gatekeeper, are words of different origin. Latin *portare*, 'to carry', gave the 'porter' who works on railway stations, in hotels (both carrying luggage), and in hospitals (transporting patients). Latin *porta*, 'door', gave the other 'porter' who is the doorman or

gatekeeper, typically the one in an office ('porter's lodge') at the entrance to a university or college, or who is in charge of the maintenance of a building such as a block of flats. The dark sweet ale called 'porter', now better known by its commercial name of Guinness (which is stout, a strong form of 'porter'), was popular with the 'carrying' 'porters', hence its name.

portico see **pagoda**

portion see **part**

pose/propose/propound (suggest, put forward)
To 'pose' is to put or set a problem or question, often a difficult or embarrassing one. The word was originally 'appose', a variant of 'oppose'. To 'propose' something is simply to offer it for consideration or acceptance, and this is the basic meaning of 'propound', which is, though, a considerably more bookish word.

possum/opossum (kind of animal with a pouch and distinctive toes)
'Possum' can be simply a colloquial term for 'opossum', although the phrase 'to play possum', meaning to pretend to be unconscious, as the animal itself does to escape danger, is a fixed one. If a distinction is made, however, the 'opossum' is the North American animal, properly *Didelphis virginiana*, that lives in trees or close to water, is about the size of a large cat, and has a pouch and a thumbed hind-foot. Its name derives from a Virginian Indian word meaning 'white beast'. The variant 'possum', on the other hand, is often reserved for one of a number of Australian animals – all phalangers, i.e. having webbed toes – that resemble the true American 'opossum'.

postal order/money order (Post Office order to pay money)
'Postal orders' provide a way of transmitting reasonably small sums of money safely through the post. They are currently (1987) issued in values from 25p up to £20, on which a fee ('poundage') is extra. 'Money orders' were similar but for larger amounts (up to £50). They ceased to exist in 1974.

postulate see **stipulate**

potash/potassium (chemical element or its compound)
'Potash' – originally 'pot ashes', a translation of the early Dutch *potasschen* – is 'potassium' carbonate (K_2CO_3), a crude impure form of which was got from wood *ash* evaporating in *pots*. Caustic 'potash' is 'potassium' hydroxide (KOH). 'Potash' is thus always a compound of 'potassium', which itself is a silvery white metallic element with chemical symbol K (from Latin *kalium*, related to 'alkali'). Compounds of 'potassium' are used as fertilisers and for manufacturing specially hard glasses.

potassium see **potash**

pottery see **china**

pragmatic see **empirical**

prairie/pampas (extensive grassy plain in America)
'Prairies', from French *pré* (field, meadow), are tracts of treeless grassland with fertile soil as found, typically, in the upper Mississippi valley (in the USA) and in Canada. The 'pampas' are in South America. They are vast grassy plains in the rain shadow of the Andes, in Argentina, with the word originating in the Quechua *pampa* (plain). Similar plains north of the Amazon are known as 'llanos' – Spanish for 'plains'.

prawn see **shrimp**

precede see **proceed**

precipitately/precipitously (hurriedly)
The basic distinction is between 'precipitate' meaning 'rash' and 'precipitous' meaning 'steep'. To leave a room 'precipitately' is thus to hurry out of it without regard for the consequences of your action; to leave it 'precipitously' is to rush headlong out of it for some reason.

precipitously see **precipitately**

précis see **summary**

predestined see **designed**

predicament/dilemma (difficult or awkward situation)
A 'predicament' is an unpleasant or even crucial situation which one is faced with. If you run out of petrol or break down on the M1, you are in a 'predicament', you have a difficult situation that you must somehow cope with. A 'dilemma' is a situation in which you are faced with two equally awkward or undesirable alternatives. Wedding presents often cause a 'dilemma': your second favourite aunt gives you a tea-making machine, but you have one already – do you accept it (and wonder what to do with it), or tell her (and run the risk of offending her)? It's a 'dilemma'. The alternatives are the 'horns' of a 'dilemma' on which you, the victim, are likely to be impaled, as a matador on the horns of a bull.

predicate see **predict**

predict/predicate (state)
To 'predict' a thing is to foretell or prophesy it: 'An easy win for the home team this afternoon is predicted.' To 'predicate' something is to state that it is real or true: 'I think we may predicate that his motives are sincere' – that is, we may confidently say that they are. In American usage, 'predicate' can mean 'base': 'We are predicating our plans on those assumptions.' In general English usage, too, 'predicate' can mean 'imply', 'connote': 'Grass predicates greenness.' The words literally mean 'say before' and 'state before'.

predominate/preponderate (prevail)
To 'predominate' is to dominate over all others, to be more widely prevalent or noticeable, as a forest in which pine trees 'predominate'. To 'preponderate' is literally 'to exceed in weight', hence to 'predominate' in power, force or influence. 'These reasons preponderate over all others'. In practice, however, the terms are often used to mean exactly the same: 'to prevail' or 'to exceed'. Even so, 'preponderate' has a definite connotation of weight or authority.

preface/prelude/prologue (preliminary part of something)
A 'preface' is a preliminary statement by the author of a book explaining its aim and range. See **foreword** for more about this. In a general sense it is anything preliminary or preceding. A 'prelude' is literally something 'played beforehand', and is a preliminary event, act or performance of some kind that hints of something greater to come. In musical terms a 'prelude' is either a piece preceding an important movement, such as the 'preludes' that precede the fugues in Bach's *Forty-Eight,* or an independent piece, as Chopin's twenty-four piano Preludes which are complete in themselves. Both 'preface' and 'prologue' have the same original sense, in, respectively, Latin and Greek – 'spoken beforehand'. A 'prologue' is usually found in a play, where it is an introductory speech drawing the attention of the audience to the theme of the play. More loosely it is the 'preface' or introduction to any poem or novel. One of the most famous 'prologues' in English is the one to Chaucer's *Canterbury Tales.*

preface (of a book) see **foreword**

prefatory see **preparatory**

preference shares see **ordinary shares**

prejudice/bias (strong inclination for or against something)
A 'prejudice' is often an unfavourable view or opinion of a thing, as seen in racial 'prejudice' or a 'prejudice' against democracy. Where sides can be taken, however, over a specific issue, a 'prejudice' can be favourable or unfavourable, for or against, as a 'prejudice' in favour of younger applicants for a job. Either way, the word implies a literal 'prejudging' of a case, with a consequent lack of fairness or impartiality. A 'bias' can be favourable or unfavourable, perhaps rather more subjectively, resulting in a tendency to lean the wrong way, as a political 'bias' (a lack of objectivity) or a 'bias' against a new proposal (not giving it fair consideration). The word suggests a 'two-way' idea, and derives from Latin *bifax,* 'two-faced'.

preliminary see **preparatory**

prelude see **preface**

premonition see **presentiment**

preoccupied see **occupied**

preparatory/prefatory/preliminary
(introductory)
A 'preparatory' remark at the beginning of a speech is one that 'prepares' those present for the speech as a whole – virtually an introduction, in fact. A 'prefatory' remark is one that explains the theme or aim of the speech – one that acts as a preface. A 'preliminary' remark might well not relate directly to the speech at all, but simply be one that precedes it. 'Preliminary' notices or examinations, however, are ones that precede more important notices or exams – the ones before the real thing. The word literally means 'before the threshold'.

preponderate see **predominate**

prerequisite see **requirement**

prerogative see **privilege**

prescience see **presentiment**

present/gift (something given freely,
usually to mark an occasion)
A 'present' is a less formal, more personal thing, as a birthday 'present' or a Christmas 'present'. A 'gift' is more formal, and is often given with a degree of ceremony. It is more impersonal, too, as a free 'gift' (so-called) given with the purchase of a particular merchandise – from a remote firm to an anonymous individual. Similarly, 'gift' vouchers or 'gift' tokens are frequently used as prizes or for some kind of presentation. Perhaps rather surprisingly, the Old English word 'gift' has come to be used for the more formal thing, while the Norman 'present' is the homely, everyday object. Usually when there are Anglo-Saxon and French doublets like these, the 'homely/formal' sense is the other way round (as 'freedom' and 'liberty', 'holiday' and 'vacation', 'fire' and 'conflagration').

presentiment/prescience/premonition
(a feeling beforehand)
A 'presentiment' (not, incidentally, a 'presentment', which is an act of presenting or a legal statement) is a feeling that something evil or unpleasant is going to happen – a foreboding. 'Prescience' is knowing or seeing something beforehand, literally or figuratively – in other words foreknowledge or foresight. A 'premonition' is similar to a 'presentiment', but has the implication that the feeling is more of a warning, and therefore that possibly the unpleasantness or evil to come can perhaps be avoided or at least mitigated.

preserve see (1) **conserve**, (2) **reservation**

president/chairman/secretary/director
(head or important official of a company or body of some kind)
A 'president', who presides, or literally 'sits in front', is the head of a permanent or temporary body of people, especially an academic, literary or scientific one, as the 'President' of the Royal Society. As such, the word is in effect a title, as it also is for the heads of some colleges in Britain, as at Queens' College, Cambridge, or most universities in the USA, as at Harvard. A 'president', too, is the title of the presiding officer of a legislative body, especially a government one, as the 'President' of the Board of Trade, and, in an honorary capacity, of a retired member of a board of 'directors', when he acts as their head. At the same time the 'president' of a board of 'directors' in the USA is not retired, since the title corresponds to the British 'chairman'. (Thus an American vice-'president' in a company virtually corresponds to a British 'director'.) Also, of course, the word is used for the head of a republican state, as notably the USA and France. (In 1977 Mr Brezhnev, already General 'Secretary' of the Communist Party of the Soviet Union, and therefore fairly and squarely in the driving seat, was also elected 'President' of the USSR, otherwise 'Chairman' of the Presidium of the Supreme Soviet.) A 'chairman' is therefore a person chosen to 'chair' or preside over a meeting, but not a regular body, although here again the word is used for the permanent head of a committee,

company or board of 'directors', and may indeed preside over the meetings of the latter but otherwise be little but a figure-head. (An active company chairman is often both 'chairman' and managing 'director' of his firm). A 'secretary' in the world of companies – apart, of course, from the essential lady stenographer and typist – is the man who generally keeps the books and supervises the administration of affairs. It is a responsible position and regarded in most companies as a senior post. 'Secretaries' exist, too, in politics as the title of the principal assistant of a government minister, while the 'Secretary' of State in Britain is the head of a major government department, as the 'Secretary' of State for Energy. (In America this title is the equivalent of Foreign 'Secretary'.) Finally, a 'director' is a member of the managing board of a commercial company, the head of this board being the Managing 'Director', and is elected to control or govern its affairs. In many cases he has a special field of responsibility, as Sales 'Director'.

pressure group/ginger group (group aiming to stir others to action)
A 'pressure group' has the aim of persuading others, especially politicians or the authorities ('them'), to implement certain policies, and does this by lobbying and other forms of 'pressure'. A 'ginger group' has the aim of persuading others to take action rather than remain inactive. They thus strive to 'ginger things up' by a form of harassment, usually directed at any body that could have a tendency to be passive rather than active, as a political party, a local authority, or even an individual, such as their MP.

presume/assume (suppose, take for granted)
'You'll come, I presume?': the implication is that I'm taking it for granted that you will, and I would be surprised if you didn't. 'You'll come, I assume?': the implication is that I am expecting you to because I have so decided or because it is your duty or obligation to. 'Assume' thus almost hints at an already completed action or a precondition, while 'presume' relates to a simultaneous action or one in the future. To use

'assume' for 'presume' can seem presumptious, as well as being incorrect.

pretension/pretentiousness (claim)
Both words can mean 'state of pretending to be more important or clever than one really is', but in addition 'pretension' has the basic meaning 'claim', as in 'I have no pretensions to being an expert on this'.

pretentiousness see **pretension**

preternatural see **supernatural**

priest see **minister**

prim/prissy/sissy (fussy, 'old-maidish')
'Prim' means 'formal and correct', 'demure', although applied to a woman it implies prudishness: 'a prim little miss'. 'Prissy' is used more of men in much the same sense: 'prudishly prim', with a hint even of effeminacy. 'Sissy' or 'cissy' is a favourite children's word for 'coward' although it, too, can be used of a man or boy to mean 'effeminate or girlish person'. The origin of 'prim' is not clear – there may be a connection with 'prime', i.e. 'excellent'. 'Prissy' seems to be a combination of 'prim' and 'sissy', with 'sissy' itself probably derived from 'sister'.

primary see **prime**

prime/primary (first)
'Prime' has the implication of 'first in importance or quality', as the 'Prime' Minister or 'prime' beef. 'Primary' relates mainly to being either first in time or great (but not first) in importance, as a 'primary' cause or a 'primary' consideration.

primeval/primordial (primitive, elementary)
'Primeval' means 'belonging to the first or earliest times', 'very old', as a 'primeval' forest. 'Primordial' relates to the very earliest times, the real beginning, as 'primordial' life or matter. The origin of the word is in Latin *primus* (first) and *ordiri* (to begin).

primordial see **primeval**

primp see **prink**

195

prink/primp (dress carefully)
To 'prink' oneself up is to smarten oneself up, especially fussily or showily. To 'primp' – sometimes used as an equivalent for 'prink' – properly means to dress or deck with nicety or affectation. The senses are thus very close. Possibly the difference can be effectively expressed by the associated words 'prank' and 'prim', to which the verbs are apparently respectively related.

priory see **monastery**

prissy see **prim**

pristine/crystalline (pure and clear)
It is probably the first word here that is the most misused. In fact, its misuse is now so general that it has virtually become the accepted sense. Properly, however, 'pristine' really means 'belonging to the earliest period', 'original', such as a 'pristine' landscape, unchanged and unaltered since earliest times, or a person's 'pristine' innocence or 'pristine' vigour (not for nothing is the word related to 'prime'). In modern use, however, where it may have been influenced by 'crystalline' or some similar word, 'pristine' means 'pure', 'clean', 'immaculate', as 'pristine' snow or the 'pristine' pages of a new book. 'Crystalline' itself more obviously means 'like crystal', and applies to something that is bright and clear and probably transparent, like crystal. So one can talk of a 'crystalline' sea or even a 'crystalline' style of writing, that is 'sparkling' and easy to appreciate.

privilege/prerogative (special right or advantage)
A 'privilege' is a benefit or advantage that has been conferred or attained, whether justly or not – the latter being an unfair 'privilege'. A 'prerogative' is a particular or official 'privilege' that has been granted as a right and that is regarded as fitting for a certain rank, status or position, as a royal 'prerogative' (the rights of a sovereign, which in theory are unrestricted).

probe/module/capsule (type of spacecraft)
A 'probe', as a lunar 'probe', is a (complete) spacecraft designed to make preliminary investigations, for example into the atmosphere of a planet. A 'module' is the detachable section of a spacecraft which can be used independently, as is the case with a lunar 'module' which lands on the Moon and later rejoins the parent craft which is still orbiting. A 'capsule' is similar, but is specifically the detachable nose-cone of a spacecraft which can carry an astronaut or astronauts, scientific instruments and the like. It may be manned or unmanned, recoverable or non-recoverable. In early usage, and still loosely, 'module', and 'capsule' are used without distinction, and 'capsule' on occasions means simply 'rocket' or 'spacecraft', without any idea of a detachable section.

procedure/proceedings (course of action)
'At this point in the procedure' one sometimes hears, instead of 'proceedings'. A 'procedure' is the way of doing something, as a special 'procedure' for booking seats. The word has a legal or parliamentary ring to it. The 'proceedings' are the action itself with a specially defined sense in 'record of the transactions of a society' and 'legal action in court'.

proceed/precede (go ahead)
To 'proceed' is to go ahead, especially after stopping. To 'precede' is to *be* ahead, whether moving or not, in either time or importance. Barons 'precede' baronets in rank, and both could 'proceed' in a procession. The trouble is caused by the prefixes, since both 'pro-' and 'pre-' can mean 'before'.

proceedings see **procedure**

proclaim see **announce**

proclivity see **propensity**

procure see **secure**

prodigy see **progeny**

producer/director (person responsible for the realisation of a play, film or radio or television programme)
The two carry out complementary and often overlapping work, with the 'producer' basi-

cally responsible for the overall production and the 'director' specifically for the direction of the acting. But, to complicate things, in Britain 'producer' is the term often used for the 'director', especially on the stage (and in a radio or television production), where he personally manipulates the actors and 'runs the show', and whose authority is therefore respected. In the film world this person is actually called the 'director', and moreover, according to his authority, also supervises the script, casting and editing as well as overseeing the shooting of scenes in the studio. This means that for films the 'producer' has another role to play, and this is usually a financial one, since he is the man in charge of the budget and the person ultimately responsible for the film's commercial success or failure. He thus is responsible for all personnel involved in the making of the film, including the 'director', as the film itself will probably have been his personal brainchild. He normally, however, delegates his various responsibilities, although remaining in overall charge. The distinction is therefore largely between the jargon of stage, radio and television on the one hand, and the film world on the other.

profession see **occupation**

profligate see **prolific**

progeny/prodigy/protégé (special kind of child)
'Progeny' is a general word for offspring. It is a singular word with a collective meaning. A 'prodigy' is a child – or any person – who has special gifts or talents: Mozart, giving public recitals of his own works at six, was a musical 'prodigy'. (The word is related to 'prodigious' in the sense 'unusual', 'wonderful'.) A 'protégé' is a person, either a child or someone older, who is under the protection or patronage of another. The term, which is French for 'protected', was first used in English in the late eighteenth century. No doubt the exclusive association of all three words with children is partly due to the biblical story of the Prodigal Son – but 'prodigal' here means simply 'wasteful', 'extravagant'.

project see **plan**

prolific/prolix/profligate (abundant, excessive)
'Prolific' is the commonest word of the three, meaning 'producing abundantly' as a 'prolific' writer. 'Prolix' means 'excessively or tediously lengthy', especially of a person who reads or writes. Marcel Proust was perhaps a 'prolix' writer as well as a 'prolific' one. 'Profligate' means 'utterly immoral' or 'recklessly extravagant'. Some people regard Proust as having been both.

prolix see **prolific**

prologue see **preface**

promenade see **parade**

prone see **prostrate**

pronounce see **announce**

propensity/proclivity (tendency)
Both words mean 'natural or habitual inclination', but 'proclivity' has the implication of an innate predisposition, especially towards something undesirable or unwholesome. One might thus have a 'propensity' for exaggerating but a 'proclivity' for extravagance. This 'bad' connotation is reflected in the word's Latin origin: *clivus* is a slope. 'Propensity', on the other hand, is literally merely a 'hanging forward'.

propitious see **auspicious**

proposal/proposition (offer, suggestion)
A 'proposal' is any plan put forward for acception or rejection. A 'proposition' is specifically an advantageous offer, as a business 'proposition' or a paying 'proposition'. However, 'proposition' does not have this connotation in some specialised senses; in mathematics and music, for example, 'proposition' means simply 'statement'.

propose see **pose**

proposition see **proposal**

propound see **pose**

prorogation see **abolition**

prostrate/prone/supine (lying flat)
Both 'prostrate' and 'prone' means 'lying face downwards', with 'prostrate' having the implication of doing so as a sign of humiliation or submission. 'Supine' means 'lying on one's back'. Where 'prostrate' means 'overcome by illness or grief', however, one may be lying in any position – or not lying at all.

protagonist see **antagonist**

protectorate see **colony**

protégé see **progeny**

proverb see **saying**

provided see **providing**

providing/provided (if, on condition that)
'Providing' implies the fulfilment of a condition: 'Providing he's not late we can leave at seven', i.e. 'If he is not late, we shall be able to leave at seven'. 'Provided' implies a stipulation: 'Provided he's not late, we can leave at seven', i.e. 'If he does as he should, and arrives on time, we can leave at seven.' But in practice the words are frequently used interchangeably. A distinction can be made, however, provided one is careful.

provincial/parochial (narrow-minded)
The references are to the inhabitants of, respectively, a province and a parish, both limited areas. When used to mean 'narrow-minded', 'provincial' has a connotation of the rustic or 'country-bumpkin', and 'parochial' the implication that the outlook or opinion is not only narrow but limited. These nuances are brought out in phrases such as 'provincial manners' and 'parochial interests'.

psychiatrist see **psychologist**

psychologist/psychiatrist (one who has made a scientific study of the mind)
'Psychologist' is the broader term, for one who is trained in psychology, the study of the mind, or of mental states and processes in general. A 'psychiatrist' actually treats mental diseases or disorders. The '-iatrist' ending is Greek *iatros* (physician), as in 'paediatrician' (doctor specialising in the treatment of children's diseases).

psychopath/schizophrenic/psychotic/ neurotic (mentally or emotionally deranged person)
A 'psychopath' is a person afflicted with a personality disorder characterised by a tendency to commit antisocial and sometimes violent acts and a failure to feel guilt for these acts. A 'schizophrenic' is a person who suffers from psychotic disorders characterised by progressive deterioration of the personality which include withdrawal from reality, hallucinations, delusions, social apathy, emotional instability, etc. A 'psychotic' is a person who suffers from psychosis which is any form of severe mental disorder in which the individual's contact with reality becomes highly distorted. The cause of a 'psychotic's' derangement may be a physical one, such as brain damage, and in this respect, he differs from a 'neurotic', whose neurosis, a mental discord that is also milder than that of a 'psychotic', has an emotional cause, not a physical one. A 'neurotic' will therefore display such symptoms as anxiety, hysteria or obsessive behaviour and will often be aware of his condition. A 'psychotic's' derangement is total, and the sufferer will not appreciate that his behaviour is abnormal.

psychotic see **psychopath**

ptarmigan see **pheasant**

pub see **hotel**

pug see **Pom**

puke see **reach**

pullover/jersey/sweater/jumper (woollen outer garment for top half of body)
A 'pullover' – 'pulled over' the head, as indeed are the others – has long or short sleeves or none at all. It is normally regarded as a male garment. A 'jersey' is a type of 'pullover' that is close-fitting and warm, typically as worn by sailors and fishermen. It, too, is usually a male item of clothing, quite often thought of as giving a

'rugged' air to the appearance of the wearer. A 'sweater' is a 'jersey' (thick, close-fitting) chiefly associated with games and sports, either for wear before or after exercise to prevent chills – or even during exercise to induce sweating – or as part of a traditional costume, as worn by cricketers. In general use it often has a V-neck and is normally designed for informal wear. The garment can be worn by males or females – indeed, a 'sweater' girl, now something of a rare breed, is one who wears it to emphasise her bust. A 'jumper' is essentially a woman's garment, usually of soft wool and quite light. All four can be knitted by machine or hand, and many are not made of wool at all but of some artificial fibre such as acrylic.

pulsar see **quasar**

puma see **leopard**

pun/riddle/conundrum (verbal joke or puzzle)
A 'pun' is a play on words. Shakespeare has dozens of them, and *Romeo and Juliet* kicks off with three:

Sampson	Gregory, o' my word, we'll not carry coals.
Gregory	No, for then we should be colliers.
Sampson	I mean, an we be in choler, we'll draw.
Gregory	Ay, while you live, draw your neck out o' the collar.

(Ones more bawdy than this follow.) They are also favourites with journalists ('Smashing trip' the staid *Times* once headed a news item describing a particularly rough crossing of the Atlantic on board a passenger liner, when all the crockery was shattered) and with children ('Opened the window and influenza', and many more, to a greater or lesser degree ribald or ghoulish). A 'riddle' is a question, or sometimes a statement, that expects an ingenious reply or response. It may itself involve a 'pun' ('What are cows in the Arctic called? Eskimoos'), and this, specifically, is called a 'conundrum' – a strange, learned-looking word, whose origin is unknown (and therefore a 'riddle').

pungent/poignant/piquant/plangent (sharp, painful)
'Pungent' means 'sharp to the taste or smell', 'biting' or, figuratively 'powerful', as 'pungent' criticism. 'Poignant' shares the literal sense of 'pungent' but is more commonly used figuratively to mean 'painful' or 'moving' as a 'poignant' remark (which could be either). 'Piquant' means 'agreeably pungent', as a 'piquant' sauce or 'piquant' wit. 'Plangent' means either 'resounding noisily' as 'plangent' waves, or 'resounding mournfully' as the 'plangent' sound of a violin. The word's association with 'plaintive' is justified, since both senses derive from Latin *plangere* (to beat – in the latter case, the breast).

puny/pusillanimous (feeble)
'Puny' means 'of less than normal size and strength', hence 'weakly', 'petty', as a 'puny' fellow or a 'puny' excuse. It derives from 'puisne', which spelling, pronounced the same way, is still in legal use for a junior judge in the High Court. The word is French: *puis* (after) *né* (born). (The belief was that a child born later would be more frail than those born before him.) 'Pusillanimous' means literally 'petty-spirited', that is, 'cowardly', 'faint-hearted'.

puppet/marionette (small figure of person or animal manipulated to provide dramatic entertainment)
The difference between the two is mainly one of manipulation or motive power. 'Puppet' is the general word for a figure that can be operated by wires, rods, strings, or directly by hand (as a 'glove puppet'). Punch and Judy are among the best known. 'Marionettes' are 'puppets' worked by strings (only). The name is a French one, ultimately from holy figures of biblical personages and in particular the Virgin Mary. A blend of 'marionette' and 'puppet' gave the name of those famous (or infamous) television stars of the 1970s, the Muppets.

purple see **violet**

pusillanimous see **puny**

pygmy see **midget**

pyre see **pile**

python/boa constrictor (large snake that crushes its prey)
Both are tropical snakes, with the 'python' found from West Africa to China, Australia and the Pacific Islands, but the 'boa constrictor' chiefly in South and Central America. There is also an anatomical difference: 'boas' have teeth in their premaxillae (the bones in the front of the upper jaw) and no bones supra-orbitally (above the eye); 'pythons' do not have premaxillary teeth, and do have supra-orbital bones.

Q

Quadragesima see **Quinquagesima**

quail see **quiver**

quake see **quiver**

qualmish see **queasy**

quantum see **quota**

quarksee **quasar**

quarto/octavo/folio/foolscap (book and paper sizes)
The first three are sizes of bound books, the names deriving from the number of times a sheet of paper is folded to give the finished size. Traditionally three finished sizes – crown, demy and royal – obtain for each division, though other sizes also exist.

For 'folio' the sheet is folded once (giving two leaves, thus four pages), crown folio measuring 15 by 10 inches, demy folio 17½ by 11¼ inches and royal folio 20 by 12½

inches. For 'quarto' the sheet is folded twice (giving four leaves, thus eight pages), crown quarto measuring 10 by 7½ inches, demy quarto 11¾ by 8¾ inches and royal quarto 12½ by 10 inches. For octavo the sheet is folded three times (giving eight leaves, thus sixteen pages), crown octavo measuring 7½ by 5 inches, demy octavo 8⅜ by 5⅝ inches and royal octavo 10 by 6¼ inches. These imperial measurements have now been superseded by metric equivalents but the names and principles remain the same.

'Foolscap' is a standard size of paper, originally measuring 17 inches by 13½ inches, a useful size to twist into a dunce's cap in schools and also called after the old watermark of a fool's cap-and-bells. This and other paper sizes have again been largely superseded by new metric paper sizes, of which the most common in general use are A4 (210mm by 297mm) and A5 (148mm by 210mm).

quasar/pulsar/quark (scientific phenomenon of unknown or uncertain origin)
The three are relative newcomers to the scientific scene. 'Quasars' were discovered in 1963. They are starlike objects with a high-energy electromagnetic radiation of unknown constitution or structure. The most common theory to explain a 'quasar' is that of the 'black hole': a dense cloud of gas in the centre of a galaxy collapses under its own weight to form a 'black hole' which then becomes the nucleus of a 'quasar'. The word derives from '*quasi*-stell*ar* source'. A 'pulsar', or '*puls*ating st*ar*', is a source of pulsed radio signals detected within a galaxy but outside the solar system, now thought to be a rapidly rotating neutron star. The 'pulsar' made its debut in the astronomical field in 1968. A 'quark' is the term used for one of three (or more) hypothetical particles with three (or more) corresponding anti-particles (antiquarks) which have been postulated on the basis of all other particles in the universe. The 'quark' was first propounded in 1964 and owes its name to the 'three quarks for Muster Mark' in Joyce's *Finnegans Wake*.

quaver see **quiver**

quay/jetty/pier (projecting landing-place or loading-place for ships)
A 'quay' may not in fact always project into the sea but be part of a harbour, where the 'quayside' is the area where passengers embark and disembark or where ships load and unload. A 'jetty' does run out to sea, and although it can double up as a landing pier, it is usually there to protect the harbour or coast, and so is fairly stoutly made for this purpose. 'Quay' was originally spelled 'key' (ultimately from a Celtic word), meaning a low reef or sandbank. Later it was respelled after the French word for this sandbank, but retained its 'key' pronunciation. 'Jetty' is direct French, however: literally something 'thrown out'. For more about the functions of seaside structures, see **port** (place where ships can dock). A 'pier' is a raised and fairly spacious structure built out over water, traditionally at a seaside resort, where it serves not only as a landing place for boats and ships but as a promenade for holidaymakers, with a variety of entertainments ranging from coin-operated amusement machines to a theatre.

queasy/qualmish/squeamish (sickened, nauseated)
To feel 'queasy' is to feel sick. A 'queasy' stomach is upset by 'queasy' food. The origin of the suggestive word is uncertain – possibly a blend of 'queer' and 'uneasy'. 'Qualmish', of course, relates to 'qualms', which are momentary feelings of nausea or sudden misgivings. 'Squeamish' means 'easily nauseated or sickened' or 'easily shocked'. 'There's no need to be squeamish: any man should be able to change a baby's nappies.'

quiff/coif (type of covering for the head)
A 'quiff' is a lock or curl of hair on the forehead, especially a single, oiled one. A 'coif', from which 'quiff' may derive, is a hood-shaped cap worn under a veil, as by nuns or, as a historical garment, an ecclesiastical or legal headdress worn by men from the twelfth to the sixteenth century. Later, it was a close-fitting white or coloured cap worn by women (from the sixteenth to the eighteenth century.)

Quinquagesima/Quadragesima (Sunday in the church calendar)
'Quinquagesima' is the Sunday before Lent. Latin *quinquaginta* means 'fifty' and this Sunday is fifty days before Easter, reckoning inclusively. 'Quadragesima' is the following Sunday, i.e. the first in Lent. Although *quadraginta* means 'forty', the Sunday is not forty days before Easter, however reckoned. Possibly the name was given on an analogy with 'Quinquagesima', or refers to the forty days of Lent. See also the even more illogical **Septuagesima.**

quire see **ream**

quirky see **kinky**

quiver/quaver/quake/quail (tremble, show fear)
To 'quiver' is to shake with a slight but rapid motion, as with fear or excitement. To 'quaver' is to shake tremulously, as with apprehension or weakness. To 'quake' is to shake or shudder, as with cold, weakness, fear or anger. To 'quail' is not to shake at all, but to shrink or flinch with fear.

quorum see **quota**

quota/quorum/quantum (required amount)
A 'quota' is the fixed or due amount or number of something, or the proportional part of a whole. The word comes from medieval Latin *quota pars* (how great a part). A 'quorum' is the term used for the required number of people needed for business to be transacted, as at a meeting. For Parliament to sit, for example, there must be a 'quorum' of forty MPs, i.e. a minimum number of forty. Latin *quorum* (of whom) was a word used in commissions in a sentence translating as: 'of whom we will that you . . . be one'. A 'quantum' – Latin 'how great' or 'how much' – is a required, desired or permitted amount. The term is used in physics to apply to a unit quantity of energy proportional to a frequency of radiation.

quote/cite (repeat the words of another)
To 'quote' is to repeat someone else's words by way of illustration or as an authority. To 'cite' is either to 'quote' or simply to name

someone or something, but specifically as an authority. Unexpectedly, the two words are not related: 'quote' derives from Latin *quot* (how many) – the reference being to marking a text or passage with numbers, i.e. dividing it into chapters and verses – and 'cite' comes from Latin *ciere* (to set moving).

R

rabbit/hare (brown-furred animal with longish ears)
Both animals are members of the same family, *Leporidae,* with 'hare' in the USA often used to designate a 'rabbit'. The general differences are these: 'rabbits' are naked, blind and helpless at birth and are usually gregarious. They are also smaller than 'hares', with shorter head, ears, hind legs and feet, are greyer in colour, and lack the black tips to the ears that 'hares' have. They live in burrows. 'Hares' at birth are (there is no other word for it) well-haired, and soon able to hop, and are normally solitary. They have long ears and hind legs, short upturned tails, and a characteristic divided lip. They live in 'forms' – that is, they do not burrow like 'rabbits' but make shallow nests on the surface of the earth in the grass.

rabbit (talk rapidly) see **babble**

rabble see **babble**

rabid see **avid**

racialist/racist (person who believes in racial superiority)
The words are quite often used interchangeably. In careful use, however, a significant

distinction can be made. A 'racialist' thus often means a person who shows racial prejudice or discrimination, typically to local people who are seen either as 'inferior' or who represent a cultural or economic threat to the objector's wellbeing. 'Racialists' can therefore be found in areas of large immigrant population. A 'racist', however, is a person who believes in 'racism', that is, in the theory that race is what determines a person's characteristics and abilities, and that as a result of this, some races are superior to others. Used in these ways, a 'racialist' can be seen more as a 'grass roots' activist, and a 'racist' as a theorist, who may not actively protest about his neighbours when they are of a race that he regards as inferior to his own. In popular and practical terms, of course, both 'racialists' and 'racists' are white people protesting about coloured people or blacks.

racist see **racialist**

radar/sonar/Asdic (direction-finding navigation system for ships or aircraft)
All are acronyms, respectively: *r*adio *d*etection *a*nd *r*anging, *s*ound *n*avigation and *r*anging, *A*nti-*S*ubmarine *D*etection *I*nvestigation *C*ommittee. 'Radar' is the best known. Basically, the system involves sending out short radio waves and detecting them or measuring them when they have been reflected by some object. 'Sonar' (the word is analogous to 'radar') is a similar system, but used under water, mainly by ships and submarines, but also by aircraft who can 'dunk' a device in the water for example, when flying over it. 'Asdic' was the early form of 'sonar', officially superseded by the latter name in 1963 to conform with NATO practice. All three systems were widely used in the Second World War.

radial tyres/cross-ply tyres (types of vehicle tyre)
'Radial' – really, radial-ply – tyres have a number of inner cord layers running at right angles to the crown of the tyre, that is, running in a direction that is 'radial' to the centre of the wheel. These are braced together below the tread by a band of additional cords, called breaker cords, that are set at different angles, usually diagon-

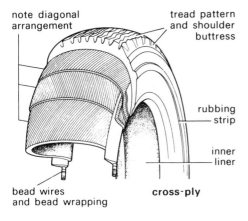

note diagonal arrangement

tread pattern and shoulder buttress

rubbing strip

inner liner

bead wires and bead wrapping

cross-ply

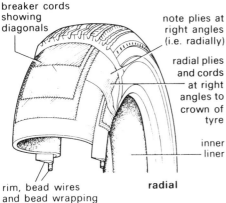

breaker cords showing diagonals

note plies at right angles (i.e. radially)

radial plies and cords at right angles to crown of tyre

inner liner

rim, bead wires and bead wrapping

radial

ally. 'Cross-ply' tyres have inner cord layers that run crosswise or diagonally, that is, they criss-cross one another. 'Cross-ply' tyres are the conventional kind, with 'radial' tyres more suitable for high speeds. As more and more cars are designed for fast travel, so 'radial' tyres are rapidly superseding 'cross-ply' ones. (An alternative American name for 'cross-ply' tyres is 'bias-ply' tyres.)

radius/diameter (straight line on a circle or its length)
The 'radius' of a circle runs from its centre to any point on the edge. The 'diameter' runs right across a circle, passing through its centre, thus in length being the same as two 'radii'. In fact any figure can have a 'diameter', so long as the line passes through the figure's centre.

rage see **anger**

ragout see **hash**

raincoat/mackintosh/burberry
(waterproof coat)
A 'raincoat' is the general word for the light overcoat that is normally proof against moderate rain only, or even just shower-proof. A 'mackintosh' or 'mac' (or 'mack'), is either an alternative word for any 'raincoat' or, more accurately, a rather heavier waterproof overcoat (or sometimes not so heavy) made of impervious material such as the rubberised cotton invented by the Scottish chemist Charles Macintosh. A 'burberry' – properly Burberry, since it is a trade name – is also occasionally used loosely as a word for any type of 'raincoat', although strictly it is one manufactured by Burberrys Ltd. This English firm, founded in the late nineteenth century, aimed to 'substitute overcoats made of self-ventilating materials for "macintoshes" proofed with rubber, which for nearly a hundred years were regarded as the only possible safeguards against getting wet' (*The Royal Warrant Holders Who's Who*, 1921).

raise see **rise**

raise the anchor see **weigh anchor**

raisin/sultana/currant (small sweet fruit used in the making of puddings and cakes)
A 'raisin' is a partially dried grape (compare French *raisin*, 'grape' and *raisin sec*, 'raisin'). It is usually dark brown and larger than a 'currant'. Most 'raisins' are exported from the shores of the Mediterranean, or from France or California. A 'sultana' is a light golden brown seedless 'raisin', which can be eaten raw or cooked. 'Sultanas' originally came from Smyrna, now Izmir, in Turkey, which was ruled over by a sultan. A 'currant' – the dried sort, not the fresh, which is an entirely unrelated fruit – is a small dried grape, also seedless – a small seedless 'raisin', in fact – coming from the same regions as the 'raisin' itself. Originally the 'currant' came from Corinth, in Greece – hence its name.

rajah/maharajah/mahatma (title of Indian ruler or leader)
'Rajah', which is ultimately related to Latin

rex (king), is the title of an Indian king or prince or a Malay chief. 'Maharajah', meaning 'great rajah' is the title of certain of the greater Indian princes. 'Mahatma', meaning 'great-souled', was the title given to a wise and holy Buddhist leader in India. The most famous of the 'Mahatmas' in recent times was Gandhi, whose title connoted his great spiritual reputation.

rallentando/ritardando/ritenuto (musical direction to decrease tempo)
The words are Italian, meaning respectively 'abating', 'retarding', and 'restraining'. 'Rallentando' implies a slackening of the tempo, 'ritardando' a gradual slowing down, and 'ritenuto' a holding back, i.e. an immediate slowing, not a gradual one. The usual abbreviated forms of the words, as encountered in musical parts, are 'rall.', 'rit.', and either (confusingly) 'rit.' or 'riten.'.

rambler/rover/ranger (wanderer, or title for member of sports or other organisation)
The words literally mean 'one who rambles' (wanders in a leisurely or aimless way), 'one who roves' (wanders in search of something), and 'one who ranges' (explores or searches over a wide area). In sporting terms, 'rambler' is usually used by members of walking or cycling clubs, and 'rover' and 'ranger' by members of football clubs, e.g. Blackburn, Bristol, Doncaster and Tranmere 'Rovers' and Queens Park 'Rangers'. 'Ranger' in American usage is a warden or member of the mounted police, and in Britain the keeper of a royal forest or park. In the scout movement 'Rover' Scouts are now Venture Scouts (senior scouts aged sixteen to twenty), but the guides still have 'Rangers' or 'Ranger Guides' (senior girl guides aged fourteen to eighteen).

ranch/range (type of farm in America for grazing and rearing cattle)
A 'ranch' is, at its loosest, any farm in the west of the USA, or Canada and Australia, especially if a large one. A 'range' is, properly, a region in which cattle or sheep can graze. With 'ranch', however, the association is primarily with the buildings of the establishment; 'range' suggests more the animals and pasture land.

rancid see **rank**

randy/raunchy/rangy (uninhibited, fast and loose)
All three words suggest a type of animal zeal. 'Randy' is most commonly used in the sense 'lustful', 'lecherous', although on a Scottish tongue can mean either **lusty** or **boisterous.** Doubtless this is the preferred sense of males bearing the forename Randy (properly an abbreviated form of Randolph), although the *double entendre* is really no *entendre* at all. 'Raunchy', a word of American origin, has the basic connotation of something that has fallen below standard. The word thus has two main meanings: 'slovenly', 'sloppy' – this in fact is the only sense given in the *Dictionary of Misunderstood, Misused, Mispronounced Words* edited by Laurence Urdang (Nelson, 1972) – and, more commonly, 'earthy', 'lewd', especially of speech or style of writing. 'Rangy' is defined by the *Concise Oxford Dictionary* (1982 edition) as 'tall and slim' (of a person), although *Chambers* prefers 'long-legged and thin', which is perhaps rather closer to the sense of the word as it is commonly used. ('Tall and slim' suggests gracefulness, but a 'rangy' person is actually on the ungainly side.) 'Randy' may be related to 'rant', but 'raunchy' is of uncertain origin: it can hardly be a blend of 'randy' and 'paunchy', say, although the combination certainly conjures up the required degree of coarseness and grossness. 'Rangy' is connected with 'range': the image is of long limbs covering a wide area.

range see **ranch**

ranger see **rambler**

rangy see **randy**

rank/rancid (strong, sour)
'Rank' means 'offensively strong', especially of a smell or taste, as 'rank' cheese or a 'rank' cigar. 'Rancid' has basically the same meaning, but an additional implication that what is producing the smell or taste has gone bad or become stale, as 'rancid' butter or fat.

rapacious/voracious (greedy)

'Rapacious' means 'inordinately greedy', especially with regard to money. Of an animal it means 'feeding on living prey'. 'Voracious' means 'devouring, or inclined to devour, a large amount', as a 'voracious' appetite or a 'voracious' reader.

rascal/rogue/scoundrel/knave (dishonest or 'naughty' person)
Most of these words are now used facetiously or even affectionately. In their proper senses, however, they can be distinguished. A 'rascal' is a dishonest person who is also shrewd or sly. (The word 'rapscallion' is related to it.) A 'rogue' is basically a cheat or a fraud. The term seems to be a blend of 'roamer' and 'beggar'. A 'scoundrel' – the word is of unknown origin – is a particularly nasty or selfish 'rogue'. A 'knave', more a historic term, on something of a par with 'villain' or 'varmint', is essentially a constantly dishonest person and a worthless one. Originally the word simply meant 'boy' or 'servant': compare modern German *Knabe*, 'boy'. For the 'Knave' of Hearts to steal the tarts was absolutely in character. In cards, too, the 'knave' many be a courtier but he is the lowest of his kind – a jumped-up jack, in fact. See also **varlet.**

raunchy see **randy**

ravage/ravish (seize violently)
To 'ravage' is to destroy, damage badly or plunder, as a wind that 'ravages' a wood, waves that 'ravage' the shore and an enemy that 'ravages' a town. To 'ravish' is basically 'seize and carry off by force', hence 'carry a woman off by force', hence 'rape'. But 'ravish' also means 'fill with delight', 'enrapture', as a 'ravishing' scene. For more on these lines see **ravishing.**

ravaging see **ravishing**

raven see **crow**

ravening see **ravishing**

ravenous see **ravishing**

ravine/gorge/canyon (deep cleft or cutting in rocks)

A 'ravine' is a long, deep, narrow valley, a mountain cleft worn by fast-flowing water. A 'gorge' is narrow above all else, and usually has a stream at the bottom and steep, rocky walls. A 'canyon' by contrast, is deep first and foremost, although it, too has steep sides and usually a stream at the bottom. All three are technically valleys, and all three, whether actually containing a stream or not, are the result of a fast flow of water over resistant rock.

ravish see **ravage**

ravishing/ravenous/famished/ravening/ravaging (showing pangs of desire)
'My dear, I'm absolutely ravished!' mistakenly exclaimed an elderly maiden lady as she prepared to go out with a friend to lunch. Possibly even 'ravishing' would have been little better. 'Ravishing', apart from its verbal sense (see **ravage**), means 'delightful', 'charming'. 'Ravenous' means 'very hungry', as 'ravenous' beasts in search of prey. (The word has no link with the bird 'raven', in spite of the creature's greedy, predacious nature.) 'Famished' means also 'very hungry', with the strict sense 'suffering from a famine'. 'Ravening' (also not connected with the bird) means 'seizing and devouring', as 'ravening' wolves. The adjective is related to the verb 'to raven' meaning 'plunder'. 'Ravaging' is the adjective of **ravage** and in fact related to 'ravine' – not directly the English word but the Old French *ravine* meaning 'rush of water'.

ray see **gleam**

rayon see **nylon**

razzmatazz/pizzazz (lively activity or display)
These jazzy words with four z's apiece are very much of the twentieth century. 'Razzmatazz', which may be a variant of 'razzle' or 'razzle-dazzle', means 'to-do', 'noisy fuss': 'After all the razzmatazz of last week's visit I'm quite glad to have a quiet evening at home.' 'Pizzazz' (also spelt 'pizazz' and 'pazazz') is an expressive word, of apparently arbitrary origin, used to denote the quality of being exciting or

attractive or spirited. (Many words starting with or containing 'z' themselves have 'pizzazz', such as 'zap', 'zing', and 'zip'. see also **jazzy**.)

reach/retch/keck/puke/cat (vomit, or make effort to vomit)

Five colourful if rather nauseating words. Only 'puke' and 'cat' actually mean 'vomit'; the other three mean 'attempt to vomit'. 'Reach' is a variant of 'retch'. Possibly it is an assimilation to a more acceptable word, with its incidental but apposite suggestion of 'reach over'. 'Retch' itself comes from an Old English verb *hrǣcan* (to clear the throat). 'Keck', which is related to 'choke', has the same meaning, but also is used in the sense 'be disgusted', 'feel loathing': 'His servile manner makes me keck.' All the verbs are partly or wholly imitative in origin, although 'cat' is directly derived from the phrase 'sick as a cat'.

realm see kingdom

ream/quire (large quantity of paper)

A 'ream' equals twenty 'quires' and contains 480 sheets (or more, to allow for waste). (A printer's ream contains 516 sheets.) A 'quire' thus contains 24 sheets. 'Quire' has the original sense of 'four sheets of paper folded to form eight pages', deriving from Latin *quaterni*, 'set of four'. 'Ream' is also used in a general way to express a large quantity of something, especially on paper: 'reams and reams of writing'. There is no connection between 'quire' here and 'quire' the affected spelling of 'choir'.

reap/wreak (endure – or cause)

A writer in the *Times Higher Educational Supplement*, no less, talked of implications that had a 'potential to reap havoc in our universities' (13 February 1976). He meant 'wreak', or course. Similarly, a summary of a television play (*The Reaper*, by Nigel Hinton) described (perhaps deliberately misleadingly or punningly?) how the main character 'reaps his revenge' (*TV Times*, 16 March 1979). To 'reap', in its figurative use, is to suffer as a consequence, as in the following two proverbs, which are both of biblical origin, 'As you sow, so shall you

reap' and 'Sow the wind, and reap the whirlwind'. Possibly the association with disaster causes the confusion, since 'wreak' – which in common use means simply 'cause' – usually applies to something damaging, as when one 'wreaks' havoc or 'wreaks' one's vengeance on someone.

rear see **back**

rebellion see **revolt**

rebuff see **refute**

rebuke see **reproach**

rebut see **refute**

recall/recollect (remember)

To 'recall' is to remember something specifically, and usually clearly, as one 'recalls' an occasion, someone's face, or a promise made. To 'recollect' is to 'recall' with an effort, the implication being that one has to 'collect' or 'muster' one's thoughts. The two verbs are often used indiscriminately as mock-bookish alternatives for 'remember': 'I don't recall the occasion.'

recant see **retract**

recital see **concert**

reckless/feckless (irresponsible, careless)

To be 'reckless' is to be quite careless of the consequences of one's actions. To be 'feckless' is literally to be without 'feck', a Scottish variant of 'effect'. The word thus means 'futile', 'ineffective'.

recollect see **recall**

reconcile/conciliate (placate, make agree)

To 'reconcile', of people, is to bring them together after they have disagreed. Of things, it is to make them compatible. Of people and things, it is to make the people come to terms with the things (or person with the thing). All three of these meanings are brought out in: 'She reconciled the friends who had quarrelled'; 'I can't reconcile the two points of view'; 'He reconciled me to accepting his case.' To 'conciliate' somebody is to placate him by soothing or pacifying, to win him over by doing or saying something to please him: 'I conciliated Fred by telling him that his hollyhocks were much taller than mine.' Or it is simply to 'reconcile'. The context or situation should tell which sense is intended.

recourse see **resource**

recreant see **refugee**

rector see **vicar**

redoubted see **undoubted**

redound see **resound**

reed/rush (type of grass growing in marshy places)
The 'reed' is the name of a number of tall grasses, especially the genus *Phragmites*, growing in marshy places. More precisely, it is the stem of such a grass. The 'rush' is properly the leaf of a grasslike herb, especially the genus *Juncus*, whose stems, more commonly called 'rushes', as is the plant itself, are pithy and hollow and used for making chair-bottoms, mats and the like. A particular type of 'rush' is the bullrush, which has as little to do with bulls as cowslips have to do with cow's lips: 'bull' probably means 'coarse', 'large', as in 'bullfrog'. The biblical bulrushes that hid the infant Moses, incidentally, were not this sort but stems and leaves of the papyrus plant, or paper 'reed'.

reel/jig/fling (lively Scottish or Irish dance)
The 'reel', with music in 2–4 or 4–4 time, is traditionally and chiefly a Scottish dance performed by two or more couples in line and basically consists of the execution of circular figures – which will indeed make your head reel. There are also Irish and English 'reels', but in these the music is usually smoother and the action more 'flowing'. A 'jig' has music in 6–8, or sometimes 3–8, 9–8 or 12–8 time, and is found in Ireland and England as well as in Scotland. It originated as a dance for one or more people, with the English morris-dancing 'jig' being a solo dance executed with raised arms. The 'fling', or 'Highland fling', is a Scottish dance, that is a vigorous 'reel', performed with 'flinging' movements of the arms and legs – hence its name.

referee/umpire (judge or arbitrator in a game, sport, or dispute)
The most straightforward distinction is by the particular sport. 'Referees' officiate in football, boxing, ice hockey (two of them), tennis and rugby football, among others, while 'umpires' operate in cricket (two), hockey (two), tennis, lacrosse (three), and baseball (one or more – four in major league games). Tennis, it will be noted, has both: the 'referee' is in charge of the tournament; the 'umpire', who is the one in the public eye, especially on the Centre Court at Wimbledon, is in charge of a match. In an industrial dispute, according to the provisions of the Arbitration Act, 1950, a 'referee' is a person to whose judgment the disputed matter is referred, with all matters in the dispute being submitted to arbitrators. When two such arbitrators cannot agree, the 'referee' who is called in to decide the matter is often known as an 'umpire'. 'Umpire' as a word falls into the category of 'adder' and 'apron': 'an umpire' should really be 'a numpire', since he is a 'non-peer', that is, a person not equal with the others.

reflation see **inflation**

Reformation see **Renaissance**

refrigerator/freezer/deep-freeze
(appliance for cooling and storing food and drink products)
The 'refrigerator' or 'fridge' is the general word, of course. The temperature in the main compartment of a 'refrigerator' is usually a few degrees above freezing. 'Freezer' has three meanings: a refrigerated room, a compartment for freezing in a 'refrigerator', or a 'deep-freeze', which itself is an appliance for storing a reasonable quantity of food for a long time at a very low temperature, conventionally 0°F ($-18°C$). The word was originally an American trade name (DeepFreeze), with 'deep' referring to the temperature, not the actual depth of the container.

refugee/renegade/runagate/recreant
(escaper or deserter)

A 'refugee' is someone seeking refuge by fleeing to another country. A 'renegade' is one who deserts some party or cause for another. The word comes from the Spanish *renegar* (to renounce, renege). A 'runagate' is an archaic word for a fugitive or runaway especially one who has become a vagabond. The word may be influenced by 'renegade' but 'agate' still exists as a northern dialect word meaning 'away'. A 'recreant' – no doubt falsely influenced by 'miscreant' – is a coward.

refurbished see **refurnished**

refurnished/refurbished (renewed, restored)

'Refurnished', of course, is 'furnished again', 'fitted with new furniture', 'resupplied'. It's the domestic association that supplies the link. 'Refurbished' is thus 'furbished again', with 'furbish' itself meaning 'polish', 'make bright and new again'. One 'refurbishes' much more often than one 'refurnishes', though, since one 'furnishing' lasts a long time but things have to be polished and brightened up repeatedly.

refute/rebut/rebuff (oppose)

To 'refute' – not related to 'refuse', although this suggests it – is to prove someone or something to be in error. One can thus 'refute' a statement or the person who made the statement. To 'rebut' – literally 're-butt' (as if with the head) – is to 'refute' by means of evidence or argument, repel a blow by giving a blow, as it were. To 'rebuff' is to check or snub, usually abruptly: 'She rebuffed his advances.' Here, too, the origin is a 'blow back', but in this case from the Italian *ribuffo* 'reproof' – literally 'puff back'.

regal see **royal**

regalia see **insignia**

regiment see **corps**

regret/remorse (sense of sorrow or guilt)

'Regret' is distress or sorrow for a wrong-doing – not necessarily one's own. 'Remorse' is a more complex thing, and deeper altogether. It implies qualms of conscience, guilt, repentance – and 'regret', and is usually experienced for a grave wrong that one has oneself committed. In origin the word means 'bite' (as in 'morsel'), since the feeling of deep regret seems to bite into one. (Compare the modern slang phrase 'What's eating you?')

rehoboam see **jeroboam**

Reichsrat see **Bundeswehr**

Reichstag see **Bundeswehr**

Reichswehr see **Bundeswehr**

reign/rein (control)

The confusion in not so much between what kings and queens do on the one hand and coachmen and cabbies do (or did) on the other, but in turns of phrase such as 'give free rein (?reign) to one's imagination'. Surely, it might be argued, if one gives something its 'reign' one allows it to take charge in some way, have control, hold sway – in short, reign. The correct confusible in the phrase is in fact 'rein', the metaphor being that of slackening the **rein** (which basically checks or limits) of a horse and allowing it a free head. In passing, the 'rein' of 'reindeer' is nothing to do with a horse's 'rein': it is the Old Norse *hreinn* (reindeer) (with English 'deer' added).

rein/bridle/halter (part of a horse's harness, usually made of leather)

The 'rein' is a long strap fastened to the 'bridle' or bit, usually one of two, designed for restraining or guiding the horse. The 'bridle' is that part of the harness that goes round the horse's head, usually consisting of a headstall, the bit, and the 'reins'. The 'halter' is a rope or strap, with a noose or headstall, used for leading a horse or tying him up to something.

rein (control) see **reign**

reiterate see **repeat**

relation/relative (member of one's family)
Both words really mean exactly the same to refer to a person to whom one is related by ancestry ('blood'), marriage or adoption. It is thus possible to say either 'We went to stay with some relatives' or 'We went to stay with some relations'. If there is any difference, it is that 'relative' is perhaps the more formal word. But really it is a matter of choice. Perhaps older people may prefer 'relative' and younger people 'relation'.

relative see **relation**

relegate see **delegate**

relic/relict (remains of something valuable)
A 'relic' is an interesting or valuable memento of the past, as a 'relic' of the Stone Age, or a custom which is a 'relic' or survival of the past. 'Relics', in a religious sense, are the holy remains of a saint or venerated person. 'Relict' is usually found in the plural in the sense 'remains', 'remnants', as the 'relicts' of a once glorious city. In the singular it can mean 'survivor' in much the same sense as 'relic' although this form of the word has a rarefied aura. In ecology, a 'relict' is a plant or animal species living in an environment that is not typical for it. Such a plant might well be a 'migrant' (see **immigrant**).

relict see **relic**

remand home/borstal/detention centre/attendance centre (centre for young offenders)
A 'remand home' is now a dated term for what is properly a 'community home', where young offenders under the age of seventeen are committed to the care of a local authority as an alternative to being placed with foster parents or, for lesser offences, simply left at home but kept under supervision. A 'borstal' is a now similarly obsolete word for what today is officially a 'youth custody centre'. It is a place of detention for young offenders of either sex aged seventeen to twenty. A 'detention centre' proper, therefore, is something different. In fact there are two kinds: a 'junior detention centre' is for boys aged fourteen to sixteen, and a 'senior detention centre' for young male offenders aged seventeen to twenty. A similar highly disciplined regime exists in both, but the terms of detention (from three weeks to four months) are not as long as in a 'youth custody centre'. Finally, an 'attendance centre' is a place for juvenile offenders of either sex (aged seventeen to twenty, as for a 'youth custody centre'), where they may be ordered to spend up to a total of twenty-four hours of their spare time on Saturdays following a strictly disciplined regime, which includes, however, physical education and instruction in practical subjects.

remonstrate see **demonstrate**

remorse see **regret**

Renaissance/Restoration/ Reformation/Risorgimento (historical period and turning point)
Four great 'come-backs' in European history. The 'Renaissance', or 'rebirth' was the revival in the arts, letters and learning generally throughout Europe in the fourteenth to sixteenth centuries, marking the transition from the medieval to the modern world. The movement began in Italy, with the 'rebirth' regarded as that of the classical world. The 'Restoration' was the re-establishing or 'restoring' of the monarchy in England after the Commonwealth (1649–53) and Protectorate (1653–60) of Cromwell. It was marked by the return of Charles II, and his subsequent reign (1660–85). (The term sometimes extends to the reign (1685–8) of James II.) The name has a cultural significance as well, especially in the field of literature: the period produced such famous writers as Dryden, Congreve, Pepys, Samuel Butler and Sir William Temple. 'Restoration' comedies, or comedies of manners, were a notable feature of the age. Their wit, elegance and stylishness marked a resurgence of theatrical life after the years of Puritanism. The 'Reformation' was the religious sixteenth century movement which had as its aim the 're-forming' of the Roman Catholic church and which led to the establishment of the Protestant churches and to that of the Anglican

church in particular. The 'Risorgimento', literally 'resurrection', was the movement for the liberation and reunification of Italy in the nineteenth century after the end of French rule in 1815.

renegade see **refugee**

repeat/reiterate/iterate (say again)
'Repeat'is the general word – 'do or say again'. 'Reiterate' is 'do or say again repeatedly', a word often used for emphasis, and also where 'iterate', which has exactly the same meaning, would do just as well. Possibly it is felt that a word beginning 're-' expresses a repeated action more effectively.

repel/repulse (drive back)
'Repulse' is the stronger word, often implying discourtesy or denial. To 'repel' an attack is to ward it off; to 'repulse' an attack is to drive it back by force. Used figuratively, 'repel' usually means 'cause disgust in' as in 'His appearance repelled me'. 'Repulse' is less frequently used in this sense, although the noun 'repulsion' is common enough. For the shades of meaning of related words, see **repulsive**.

repellant see **repulsive**

repository see **depository**

repress see **suppress**

reproach/reprove/rebuke (censure)
'Reproach' is a fairly neutral word: 'I reproached her for her forgetfulness', i.e. I charged her with it with the aim of slightly shaming her. 'Reprove' is the mildest word, often meaning simply to correct a fault. One might 'reprove' a child who fails to pass the salt and pepper unprompted to granny. 'Rebuke' is the strongest of the three, usually implying a stern or official 'reproof', a real 'telling off'.

reprove see **reproach**

Republican/Democrat (member of one of the two major American political parties)
The divisions are not clear-cut, and there is no obvious 'right' and 'left' as there is in Britain. The 'Republican' party is in fact regarded as 'right of centre' and the party of 'big business', but it is really a coalition of changing interests and sectional groups, as indeed is the 'Democratic' party. The latter, however, tends to be the party of the 'small man' and has its stronghold in the Southern states, the 'solid south'. Broadly speaking, also, the 'Democratic' party – which came to be caricatured in the form of a donkey in the late nineteenth century – is now identified with social welfare, economic regulation, and civil rights, while the 'Republicans' are largely associated with state rights. The 'Democrats' have thus won the support of a number of industrial workers and, because of their initiative on the racial question, have gained the support of most black voters. Over recent years the 'Democratic' party has become more liberal than the 'Republican'. The 'Republican' party arose in 1854 to combat slavery. Among noted 'Republican' US presidents have been Theodore Roosevelt, Eisenhower, Nixon and Ford. The 'Democratic' party originated in 1792 as a group of voters who supported Jefferson to defend the rights of the individual states against the centralising policy of the Federalists. (It was originally called the 'Democratic-Republican' party, and adopted its present name in 1830.) Well known 'Democratic' presidents have been Jackson, Woodrow Wilson, F. D. Roosevelt, Truman, Kennedy, Lyndon B. Johnson and Jimmy Carter.

repugnant see **repulsive**

repulse see **repel**

repulsive/repugnant/repellant (causing aversion)
'Repulsive' is the strongest adjective, and can be used of anyone or anything, as a 'repulsive' idea or the 'repulsive' appearance of someone. 'Repugnant', from the Latin *repugnare* (fight against), is simply 'distasteful', 'objectionable', so a fairly mild word. A 'repugnant' appearance is one that puts you off, not one unpleasant enough to make you feel sick. 'Repellant' – very often spelt 'repellent' – has essentially the basic

idea of 'off-putting' and is usually applied to people, their faces, expressions, ideas, demands and the like. The word is rather stronger in tone than 'repugnant' but not as strong as 'repulsive'.

requirement/requisite/perquisite/ prerequisite (something needed)
'Requirement' is the general word, meaning 'condition', 'essential', as the 'requirements' of military service or compulsory education. A 'requisite' is something that is indispensable, especially a concrete object, as toilet 'requisites' (what one has to have to wash, dress, do one's hair, etc.) A 'perquisite' is something that is regarded as one's due by right, an incidental or 'fringe' benefit or 'perk' (its accepted colloquial abbreviation). A 'prerequisite' is something that it is essential to have before one can have or do something else. 'A' levels are a 'prerequisite' for university entry, and good eyesight for passing a driving test.

requisite see **requirement**

reservation/reserve/preserve (tract of land set apart for special purpose)
The meanings sometimes overlap, although on the whole it's a question of what the tract of land contains. 'Reservation' is particularly associated with Indian tribes in America; 'reserve' with animals, especially wildlife, trees and plants; 'preserve' with game or fish that must be protected and/or propagated, usually for sport. From this last sense comes the idea of poaching or trespassing on someone else's 'preserves', literally or figuratively.

reserve see **reservation**

resin/rosin (substance used in medicine or for making plastics)
'Resin' is the solid or semi-solid substance secreted by most plants, especially pine and fir trees, used chiefly in medicine and for making varnishes, printing ink and plastics. Synthetic 'resin', made by the polymerisation of simple molecules, is essentially used for plastics, but also for varnishes and adhesives. 'Rosin' – related to 'resin' with an unexplained change of vowel – is the hard, brittle 'resin' left after the oil of turpentine has been distilled off from the crude oleo-resin of the pine tree. It is also used for making varnish, but a more direct application is its use for rubbing on violin bows. In non-scientific usage the two words are often interchangeable.

resolution/motion (proposition at an assembly passed, or to be passed, by voting)
The two words overlap, but strictly: a 'resolution' is the expression of an opinion on which it is proposed to take action – which may in the event, however, not be taken, even if the 'resolution' is passed. A 'motion' is the same – except that passing it *will* result in action being taken.

resort see **resource**

resound/redound (indicate fame or success)
To 'resound', literally 're-echo', is to be famed or celebrated: the name of Shakespeare 'resounds' through the ages. To 'redound' is to bring something as a result. The word is usually heard in the phrase 'redound to one's credit', i.e. make a contribution to it, although things can also 'redound' to one's discredit or disadvantage. Crimes, too, can 'redound' on those who commit them, 'fall on their own heads' as it were. The word has an echo of 'rebound', certainly in this last usage, although it is not related to it. The origin is in Old French *redonder* (to overflow) with the possible influence of 'renown'.

resource/resort/recourse (a turning to, falling back on)
A 'resource' is an action or measure that one can turn to in an emergency. There is no verb 'resource'. A 'resort' is somebody or something actually turned to for help, especially in the phrase 'as a last resort'. The verb 'resort to' means 'turn to', 'use', when all else fails. A 'recourse' has the same meaning as a 'resort', and this is where the confusion lies, together with the corresponding verbal phrase 'have recourse to' and 'resort to'. (Thus there are no forms, 'have resource to' or 'have resort to'.) So 'flight was his only resource' means virtually

the same as 'flight was the only thing he could have recourse to.' The confusion is perhaps more in the usage of the words than the meaning.

rest home see **nursing home**

restive see **restless**

restless/restive (uneasy)
'Restless' means 'showing an inability to remain at rest', as a 'restless' mood or a 'restless' night (one with little sleep). 'Restive' means 'impatient at having to stay at rest', 'uneasy at being restricted', as a 'restive' horse, which usually means a disobedient one. The word is not so much related to 'rest' = 'repose' as to 'rest' = 'remain', a sense apparent in the phrase 'to rest assured'. 'Restive' is not normally the word used in the catch phrase 'The natives are restless.'

Restoration see **Renaissance**

retch see **reach**

reticle see **graticule**

retinue see **suite**

retire/retreat (withdraw)
In military terms, to 'retire' is to withdraw for tactical or strategic reasons, almost on the lines of the French *reculer pour mieux sauter* (draw back in order to jump better). To 'retreat', on the other hand, implies an obligatory withdrawal.

retort/riposte (sharp reply)
A 'retort' is a sharp reply; a 'riposte' a reply that is sharp. In other words a 'retort' is a quick reply, a 'riposte' a smart or witty one. Both the nouns are used as verbs.

retract/recant (take back)
To 'retract' a statement or opinion or promise is to withdraw it, so that things stand as they were before it was made. To 'recant' a statement is to go back on it, or be forced to go back, i.e. to deny one's own words. The word literally means 'unsing', with the prefix 're-' not meaning 'again' but

a negative, as in 'resign' (= 'unsign'). The 'singing' reference is to the Greek palinode, which was an ode or song in which the author 'retracted' something he had said in a former poem. The Greek word *palinōidia* means 'singing over again'.

retreat see **retire**

revenge see **avenge**

reverse see **obverse**

revolt/revolution/uprising/rebellion/ mutiny (form of active resistance against authority)
A 'revolt' normally takes the form of a vigorous outbreak against authority that arises either from general turbulence or from opposition to tyranny or oppression. A 'revolution' is a successful 'rebellion', especially one that having overthrown a government or political system establishes another. Two famous 'revolutions' in this respect were the ones in France (1789) and Russia (1917), which both overthrew the monarchy and replaced it with a radically different type of government by the people. An 'uprising' is really the same as a 'revolt', denoting perhaps more the actual insurrection than the violent outcome that results as a protest against authority. A 'rebellion', thus, is a large-scale 'revolt' that aims to secure independence or bring down the government. A 'mutiny' is normally thought of as a 'revolt' or 'rebellion' by soldiers or seamen (as the famous 'mutiny' on the *Bounty*). When in 1789 news was brought to Louis XVI of France that the Bastille had fallen, he asked, 'C'est une révolte?' 'Non, Sire,' replied the Duc de la Rochefoucauld-Liancourt, 'c'est une révolution.'

revolution see **revolt**

revolve/rotate (turn, go round)
The basic difference is that 'rotate' implies the turning of something around its own centre. Thus the Moon 'revolves' round the Earth, and the Earth 'rotates' on its axis. 'Rotate' is derived from Latin *rota* (wheel). However, 'revolve' is frequently used where 'rotate' should properly be.

revolver see **pistol**

revue see **musical**

reward/award (prize)
A 'reward' is given in recognition of merit, as a recompense. In other words it gives something in return. 'Rewards' are almost always for something good – only rarely is a 'reward' given for something evil. An exception might be an ironic use, as: 'The gallows was his reward for desertion.' An 'award' is something assigned or ordered, as by a judge, for both good and evil, as, respectively, a payment or a penalty. In practice a 'reward' is usually given for a single, specific action and an 'award' for a more general, continuous service or contribution.

rheumatism/arthritis (disease with pain and inflammation in the joints)
'Rheumatism' ('rheumaticks') is a popular word for vague or ill-defined aches and pains in various parts of the body, whether the joints or not. 'Arthritis' is a more precise term for the inflammation specifically of a joint. It has the three forms 'septic arthritis', which results from infection via the bloodstream, 'rheumatoid arthritis', whose cause is unknown, and 'osteoarthritis', which is a degenerative disease of the joints (and not so widespread as 'rheumatoid arthritis', notorious as a chronic disease that affects the whole body).

rhinoceros see **hippopotamus**

rhomboid see **rhombus**

rhombus/rhomboid (mathematical figure in the form of an oblique-angled parallelogram)
A 'rhombus' must be equilateral. The figure has the basic shape of a lozenge. A 'rhomboid' – the '-oid' suffix means 'resembling' – has oblique angles but unequal adjacent sides. The figure is often shown with upper and lower sides longer than the others, i.e. (in unmathematical terms) as an obliquely but uniformly half-squashed cardboard box.

rice/sago (starchy foodstuff)

'Rice' consists of the starchy seeds or grain of the grass botanically known as *Oryza sativa*. 'Sago' is not from a grass at all, but a starchy food from the soft interior or the trunk of various palms, but especially the attractively named *Metroxylon rumphii* and *Metroxylon sago*, that are native to Indonesia.

rick see (1) **stack,** (2) **wrench**

riddle see **pun**

rifle see **gun** (portable firearm)

rigid/turgid/turbid/tumid/torrid (swollen)
'Rigid' means 'stiff', 'hard', 'strict', as a 'rigid' branch or 'rigid' discipline. 'Turgid' means 'swollen', 'distended', as the 'turgid' udder of an unmilked cow. 'Turbid' means 'opaque', 'muddy', especially of liquids, as a 'turbid' river. 'Tumid' means 'swollen', as a 'tumid' stomach. 'Torrid' means 'oppressively hot', 'passionate', as a 'torrid' climate or a 'torrid' kiss. Both 'turgid' and (to a lesser degree) 'tumid' can be used of speech or written work, as verse, to mean 'pompous', 'bombastic'. Moreover, 'turbid', applied to running water, is often wrongly associated – although correctly etymologically – with 'turbulent' and even 'tumultuous'. No doubt, too, an overall Freudian link sometimes inhibits the precise distinguishing of the meanings.

rigorous see **vigorous**

rim/brim (edge or boundary of a circular or curved area)
'Rim' is the word for the edge or border of a hollow vessel, as the 'rim' of a cup or a glass. 'Brim' is usually the word for the inside of the 'rim', especially at the top of a full vessel, as a glass that is filled to the 'brim'. The 'brim' of a hat, though, is its projecting edge, while the 'rim' of a wheel is the outer ring of its framework (not including the tyre). The words are related respectively to 'ridge' and 'border'.

ring road see **by-pass**

rink see **field** (area of play)

riposte see **retort**

rise/arise/raise (move, or be moved, into an upright or higher position)
The verb 'rise' never has a direct object, i.e. you cannot 'rise' something. The verb is used of something or someone moving up, so that hot air 'rises', an audience 'rises' to its feet and on a hill the land 'rises'. 'Arise' also has no object. Its use is largely figurative, meaning 'come into being', 'turn up', as a question that 'arises' or doubts that 'arise'. In a literal sense it is normally used poetically or archaically, as a cloud that 'arises' over the horizon or the pseudo-historical 'Arise, Sir Galahad!' 'Raise', by contrast, must always be followed by an object, that is, it does not mean 'rise'. So one can 'raise' an anchor, one's hat, a question, a child and a thousand and one other things. The verbs sometimes present problems in their different tenses, present and past:

rise:	I rise	I rose	I have risen
arise:	I arise	I arose	I have arisen
raise:	I raise	I raised	I have raised

Risorgimento see **Renaissance**

ritardando see **rallentando**

rite/ritual (ceremonial act or series of acts)
A 'rite' is very often a religious ceremony, as the 'rites' of baptism or the last 'rites'. A 'ritual' is an established procedure for a religious or any ceremony, or simply a social custom – letting the dog out into the garden before breakfast could be a daily 'ritual'. The word does have religious connotations, however, if only because of its use to mean a book containing a prescribed order of service – a book of 'rites', in fact.

ritenuto see **rallentando**

ritual see **rite**

road/street (public way for vehicles)
A 'road' usually runs between two distant points, such as two towns. 'Roads' (and 'streets') leading out of a town are often named after the town to which they lead, as the Bath 'Road' out of Bristol, the London 'Road' out of Leicester (and numerous other towns), and the Woodstock 'Road' out of Oxford. The word is a general one, too, and can apply to a 'street', which is thus a 'road' in a village, town, city or other populated area, especially one lined with houses, shops, and other buildings and having a pavement. The implication here is that if a 'street' does not have these things, it will probably be a 'road'. For this reason, when a town expands, what was formerly a 'road' will become a 'street'. This happened with Oxford 'Street' in London, which was the Oxford 'Road' before – if one can imagine it – it acquired its present wealth of shops. But, again, many 'streets' (by the above definition) are actually named 'road', often because of their importance as a recognised through route for traffic, as London's Bayswater 'Road', Vauxhall Bridge 'Road', and North Circular 'Road'.

road fund licence see **driving licence**

robbery see **theft**

rock see **pop**

rococo see **baroque**

roedeer see **stag**

rogue see **rascal**

roll see **bun**

roller see **billow** (wave at sea)

rook see **crow**

rosin see **resin**

roster see **rota**

rostrum/dais (raised platform)
A 'rostrum' is a platform primarily intended for public speakers, although the word is also applied to an orchestral conductor's podium. The word is actually Latin for 'beak', the explanation being that the platform or elevated place for speeches in the ancient Roman forum was decorated with the beaks of captured galleys or warships. A 'dais' – also (via French) from Latin,

discus meaning 'table' as well as 'disc' – is more of a lecturer's desk, or a platform at the end of a hall for a high table.

rota/roster (list of persons on duty)
The two words are almost interchangeable. Strictly speaking, though, a 'rota' – the word is Latin for 'wheel' – is the actual round, as the early 'rota', and a 'roster' is the list which shows who does what and when. The original 'Rota' was a political club, founded in 1659 by the English political theorist James Harrington, which advocated rotation in the offices of government. 'Roster' is in fact from the Dutch *rooster*, originally 'gridiron' (i.e. 'roaster') and later 'list'. The reference is to the ruled paper used for lists. The word was first recorded in English in 1727.

rotate see **revolve**

rotund/orotund (round)
'Rotund' is wider in meaning, with the general sense 'round' or 'circular' but also with two specific senses: 'plump' or 'podgy', of a person, and 'sonorous', 'grandiloquent', of speech or literary style. 'Orotund' applies only to speech, or more precisely, to utterance, where it means either 'imposing' or 'dignified', or else 'pompous' or 'pretentious' – 'magniloquent', in fact, rather than 'grandiloquent'. The word derives from the Latin phrase *ore rotundo* (with round mouth), found in Horace's *Ars Poetica:*

> Grais ingenium, Grais dedit ore rotundo
> Musa loqui.

('It was the Greeks who had at the Muse's hand the native gift, the Greeks who had the utterance of finished grace.')

round/volley/salvo (firing of a shot or shots)
A 'round' is a single shot by one or each of a number of guns, rifles or the like. A 'volley', directly related to French *voler*, 'to fly', is in the narrow sense the flight of a number of missiles together; of shots it is a simultaneous discharge. A 'salvo', often fired as a salute (to which word it is related), implies a firing of shots in regular succession, although applied to bombs dropped from

an aircraft it means much the same as a 'volley', that is, a simultaneous (and single) release. All three words are used of applause, with 'round' thought of as a plural, since several people are clapping at once. (This is in fact the correct or original sense, since 'round' implies the distribution of something – everybody or everything has or does something, it 'goes round'; 'round' meaning 'single shot' is thus a secondary and strictly speaking inaccurate sense.)

rouse/arouse (stir)
To 'rouse' is to waken or stir, as strong indignation. To 'arouse' – from 'rouse' on the lines of 'arise' and 'rise' – is to excite to action or put into motion. The difference is a fine one. 'Arouse' is more common with emotions and feelings, as 'arousing' someone's curiosity or suspicion. The implication is that 'rousing' stirs from basic inactivity to activity, and that 'arousing' excites something latent or known to be present. Compare 'The sight aroused my pity' (which I had anyway) and 'The sight roused my interest' (which earlier was non-existent).

rover see **rambler**

royal/regal (of or like a king or queen)
The basic difference is that 'royal' pertains to the person of a monarch and 'regal' to the office of a monarch. Thus one talks of the 'royal' family or a 'royal' salute (for an actual member of the 'royal' family), but 'regal' splendour (like that of a king or queen) or a 'regal' bearing. There are certain phrases, however, where 'royal' equals 'regal', as a 'right royal welcome' and 'to have a right royal time', and similar turns of phrase where 'royal' simply means 'magnificent', 'splendid', 'first-rate'.

rubber see **game** (portion of play forming a scoring unit)

rucksack/knapsack/haversack (bag carried on the back)
The three words are ultimately German for, respectively, 'back sack', 'eat sack' and 'oat sack'. 'Rucksacks' are mainly used by hikers and ramblers; 'haversacks' by soldiers for provisions; 'knapsacks' also by soldiers but

not so much for food as for clothes. A 'haversack', moreover, is usually slung over one shoulder rather than carried on the back.

ruckus see **rumpus**

ruction see **rumpus**

rudder/tiller/helm (instrument for steering a boat or ship)
A 'rudder' is a flat wooden or metal piece fastened to the stern-post under the water. It can deflect the water so as to steer the boat in a particular direction, and it does this by being moved by the 'tiller', a horizontal bar fitted to its head. A 'helm' is a 'tiller', too, but also can be a wheel, especially in larger craft. If you take the 'helm', you are literally or figuratively in control.

rude see **coarse**

rugby league see **rugby union**

rugby union/rugby league (form of rugby football)
'Rugby union' is the standard and most widespread form of the game, with fifteen players a side and always an amateur game. 'Rugby league', played largely in the north of England, Wales and southern Scotland, is a chiefly professional game with thirteen players (there are no wing forwards). There are some differences in the rules and scoring. In both games a try scores three points, but in 'rugby league' a successful kick at goal only scores two. If the ball goes into touch, the game is restarted in 'rugby union' with a line-out, in 'rugby league' with a scrum. Furthermore, in 'rugby league' a player can stand up when he is tackled and play the ball back with his foot. He can't do that in 'rugby union'. The two varieties are the result of a split in 1893, when the Rugby League broke away from the Rugby Union. The game still sometimes called 'rugger' is 'rugby union'. Both games are a development of football initiated at Rugby School, when one William Webb Ellis 'with a fine disregard for the rules of football as played in his time, first took the ball in his arms and ran with it, AD 1823'

(commemorative plaque in Rugby School Close).

rumba see **tango**

rumple see **crumple**

rumpus/ruction/ruckus (row, disturbance)
All the terms are colloquial. A 'rumpus' is a disturbing noise or commotion or uproar. A 'ruction' is usually a quarrel: 'There'll be ructions soon, shouldn't wonder.' A 'ruckus', more an American word, is a violent disagreement. 'Rumpus' is of unknown origin – could it be related fancifully to 'rumbustious'? 'Ruction' relates to 'eructation', i.e. belching. 'Ruckus' seems to be a blend of both words.

runagate see **refugee**

rural/rustic (pertaining to the country)
'Rural' is a straightforward adjective meaning 'of the country' (as opposed to the town or 'urban') or 'of country people and their life', as a 'rural' setting or 'rural' studies. 'Rustic' has the overtone of 'unsophisticated', even 'uncouth', as the 'rustic' charm of a country cottage (with few mod cons) or 'rustic' manners or speech (uneducated, coarse). 'Rustic' suggests 'rusty', i.e. behind the times, but this is fortuitous since both words derive from Latin *rus, ruris* (country).

rush/dash (hurry)
'I must rush!' 'I must dash!' 'Rush' usually implies both haste and clumsiness, as when one 'rushes' down the stairs (quickly and noisily) or 'rushes' out of the house (tempestuously). 'Dash' implies enthusiasm or 'go' and a short distance, as when one 'dashes' to the shops (keen to get there before they close) or 'dashes' across the road (impatient to get over).

rush (type of grass) see **reed**

rustic see **rural**

S

Sabaoth see **Sabbath**

Sabbath/Sabaoth (religious name
mentioned in the Bible)
The 'Sabbath' was, and is, the seventh day
of the week (modern Saturday) as a day of
rest and religious observance among Jews –
'remember the Sabbath day to keep it holy'.
The name came subsequently to be given
to the Christian equivalent, Sunday, in
commemoration of the Resurrection, which
occurred three days (counting inclusively)
after the Crucifixion on the Friday (the day
before the 'sabbath', when killing was
forbidden). A witches' 'sabbath' was a
midnight meeting held in medieval times as
a kind of orgy or festival supposedly
presided over by the Devil. The name refers
not so much to the day on which such orgies
took place as to the fact that they were
alleged to be held by Jews. 'Sabbath' ultimately goes back to the Hebrew *shābath* (to
rest). 'Sabaoth' actually means 'armies' or
'hosts' but is left untranslated in the Bible,
the *Te Deum* in the *Book of Common Prayer*
and some hymns, in the phrase 'Lord (God)
of Sabaoth'. The words are classic confusibles: Spenser got them entangled in *The
Faerie Queene* where he has the line:

> O that great Sabbaoth God, grant me
> that Sabbaoth's sight.

The confusion is reinforced by the chain
association: 'Sabbath Day' = 'Lord's
Day' = day of the 'Lord of Sabaoth'.

sable see **mink**

sabre see **foil**

sacristan see **sexton**

sadism/masochism/machismo/macho
(sexually-motivated show of strength)
'Sadism' and 'masochism' are virtually
opposites: the sexual gratification of
'sadism' is derived by causing pain and
humiliation to others, and that of 'masochism' obtained from the pain and suffering
inflicted on oneself. The terms derive
respectively from the names of two novelists
who described the phenomena: the Comte
Donatien Alphonse François de Sade, otherwise the 'Marquis' de Sade, an eighteenth
century Frenchman, and the Austrian
writer Leopold von Sacher Masoch, who
lived in the nineteenth century. 'Machismo'
is a word unrelated to either. It describes
the quality of being manly and virile,
especially when overtly expressed, as in
'tough guy' sports and he-man roles. The
word originates from the Mexican-Spanish
macho (male, masculine). 'Macho' can in
fact be an alternative word for 'machismo',
but commonly it now means 'aggressively
male', as in 'Have you seen the new soccer
manager? He's really macho'. The word
became popular from the 1970s.

safety/security (condition of being free
from danger)
The words are sometimes used interchangeably, although there is a distinction. 'Safety'
implies that danger, threatening or actual,
is now past, and one has nothing to fear.
'Security' relates more to the future and
suggests an absence of worry or concern
about what will come or could come.

sago see **rice**

sailing/yachting/boating (sport or
pastime of racing or moving over water in
a boat)
'Sailing' usually implies a leisure sport, even
a leisurely one. 'Yachting' with its yacht
clubs and high-power sailing craft, is essentially a professional affair, and especially
applies to racing contests. 'Boating' is the
use of boats in general for pleasure, whether
sailing boats (or yachts) or not. And of
course there is absolutely nothing half so
much worth doing as messing about in
boats.

sally see **sortie**

salon see **saloon**

saloon/salon (public room set aside for a specific purpose)

The general image behind the words is that of masculinity (drinking, driving) for 'saloon' and femininity (hairdressing, hostessing) for 'salon'. 'Saloon' is the term for the better class bar in a pub, the dining-hall (and certain other public cabins) on a ship, and, in the USA, a bar in general. A 'saloon' car is one with a solid roof with seats for four or more (including the driver). 'Salon' – the French word (hall) from which the solid English 'saloon' derives – was primarily the word for a reception or drawing room in a large house, and, by extension, the assembly of guests in such a room, especially of leaders in the world of art, fashion and politics, during the seventeenth and eighteenth centuries. Today the word is used either for the gallery or place where art exhibitions are held, or, more extensively, for a fashionable shop, such as a beauty 'salon'. The male/female distinction is also evident in hairdressing: barbers or hairdressers have – or had – 'saloons', but hairdressers (the word is ambisexual) or stylists have 'salons'.

salubrious see **sanitary**

salutary see **sanitary**

salvo see **round**

samba see **tango**

sample see **example**

sanitary/salutary/salubrious (healthy)

'Sanitary' means 'pertaining to health', especially with reference to cleanliness and precautions against disease, as 'sanitary' ware (porcelain for lavatories) and a 'sanitary' engineer (expert on water supply, sewage disposal and the like). 'Salutary' means 'conducive to health', both literally and figuratively, as a 'salutary' swim in the sea or a 'salutary' reminder (one that has a good effect). 'Salubrious' means 'favourable to health', as a 'salubrious' climate. One still hears, though: 'She gave him a good, sanitary warning.'

sapajou see **cockatoo**

sarcasm/irony (expression of scorn or derision)

'Sarcasm' which is essentially harsh or cutting, may be expressed directly or ironically. Direct sarcasm occurs in such a remark as, 'You *would* miss the train, wouldn't you!' With 'irony' there is a contradiction between the literal and the intended meaning, at an elevated or merely a playful level. 'Lovely weather for ducks!' is an example of the latter, as are most remarks concluding ' . . . I *don't* think!' 'Ironical sarcasm' is thus of the kind: 'Of course, you wouldn't know what it's like to spend all day cleaning and cooking, would you!'

sarcastic/sardonic (bitterly ironical)

'Sarcastic' has the implication of making a sneering or cutting remark. It has its origin in Greek *sarkasmos* (flesh-tearing). 'Sardonic' has basically the same meaning of 'scornful' but is usually applied more to a person's nature or features – a 'sardonic' wit or 'sardonic' smile – than to the actual ironical remark. The origin is in Greek *sardanios* (bitter) from the name of a Sardinian plant which, when eaten, was said to bring on convulsions resembling bitter laughter.

sardine/pilchard (small fish sold canned in oil)

The 'sardine' in most European countries is the name for a young 'pilchard' (*Sardina pilchardus*), especially a one-year-old one. 'Sardine', too, is sometimes also used as a name for brislings or young sprats (*Clupea sprattus*) in Norway, where the 'pilchard' is unknown. The 'pilchard' itself is related to the herring, although smaller, thicker and rounder. The name of the 'sardine' may ultimately derive from the Mediterranean island of Sardinia, although the fish itself comes from a much wider catchment area, including the English Channel. The origin of the name of the 'pilchard' is not certain.

sardine (precious stone) see **onyx**

sardius see **onyx**

sardonic see **sarcastic**

sardonyx see **onyx**

sari/sarong (oriental garment)
The 'sari' or 'saree' is the outer garment worn by Hindu women, consisting of a lengthy piece of cotton or silk worn loosely round the body with one end over the shoulder. The 'sarong' is a loose skirt-like garment made of a long strip of cloth wrapped round the body and held or tucked in at the waist, as worn mainly by men and women in the Malay Archipelago and Pacific Islands. Both garments have to some degree become fashionable with Western women, with the 'sarong' being an outer garment usually draped in front.

sarong see **sari**

sat see **sitting**

sated/satiated/saturated (fully supplied or satisfied)
'Sated' means 'satisfied to the full', with particular reference to appetites and desires. 'Satiated' means 'supplied to excess', now – but not originally – with the implication that the recipient is sickened or weary of the abundance. One can be 'satiated' with anything from a strawberry ice-cream to sensational journalism. 'Saturated' means 'thoroughly soaked', 'charged to the utmost', as a tablecloth 'saturated' with spilled tea or a literary style 'saturated' with affectation. The noun of 'satiated' is 'satiety' (rhyming with 'sobriety') or 'satiation'; of 'saturated' it is 'saturation' and of 'sated' – 'satedness'.

satiated see **sated**

satsuma see **tangerine**

saturated see **sated**

satyr see **faun**

savour see **flavour**

sawfish see **swordfish**

saying/proverb (popular quotation embodying a familiar truth)
A 'saying' is an everyday, fairly homely thing, which may be colloquial and not even a complete sentence. Most **clichés** are 'sayings'. A 'proverb' is less colloquial and normally a complete sentence, and is often of considerable antiquity, even to the extent that its original meaning may have been lost, or the original wording altered. This happened with, 'More haste, less speed', which is now loosely used as a cliché to mean, 'If you unduly hurry or skimp something, it will take you more time, not less'; originally it was, 'More haste than good speed', implying that something was done unnecessarily quickly.

scamp/skimp/scrimp/stint (do or act sparingly or less than fully)
Take breakfast, for example. If you 'scamp' your cornflakes you eat them hurriedly or carelessly. If you 'skimp' them you eat them inattentively – reading the paper, say. If you 'scrimp' them you are niggardly with them. If you 'stint' the flakes you unduly restrict the amount you take. 'Scrimp' may be related to 'shrimp' and 'stint' to 'stunt'. 'Skimp' seems to be a blend of 'scamp' and 'scrimp'. English has a generous supply of words beginning with 's' and another consonant to denote meagreness: see, for example **scarce**.

scant see **scarce**

scanty see **scarce**

scarce/scant/scanty/sparse (not abundant, meagre)
'Scarce' has the suggestion of not being enough: 'Many foodstuffs were scarce in wartime.' A 'scarce' book is one that perhaps ought to be more readily available. 'Scant' means 'barely sufficient'. It tends to be used more with abstract nouns, as 'scant' praise or 'scant' justice. 'Scanty' means 'very small' with a hint of not being enough, as a 'scanty' crop of barley or a 'scanty' dress (so short or revealing as to be considered immodest by some). 'Sparse' means 'thinly distributed or scattered' as 'sparse' hair or a 'sparse' population.

scare/scarify (frighten)
To 'scare' is of course to frighten, even frighten away. There should be no problem here. To 'scarify' is often used in something like the same sense, although often with

more of a mental or emotional 'scaring' than a physical one. You can thus be subjected to someone's 'scarifying' gaze or have a 'scarifying' feeling that something has gone terribly wrong. This current sense of the word probably developed under the influence of both 'scare' itself and 'terrify'. Yet 'scarify' does not properly mean 'scare' or 'frighten' at all. Its true sense is 'make scratches in', 'break up the surface of', hence, figuratively, 'criticise severely' (compare 'flay'). In the literal sense, therefore, a doctor or nurse will 'scarify' your skin when giving you an inoculation, or a harrow can 'scarify' the soil when passing over it. If you say this is all a lot of nonsense, you may feel like 'scarifying' me. But this original meaning is now used only rarely, or in technical senses, and we must accept that the word has now acquired a new sense similar to 'scare'.

scarify see **scare**

scent see **perfume**

sceptical see **cynical**

schedule see **scheme**

scheme/schedule (programme, plan)
The words overlap, although 'scheme' is more the actual plan as drawn, displayed or written out, and 'schedule' is often the timetable for the procedure or order of operations of a project. One might thus have the 'scheme' of a town's bus routes but the 'schedule' for a conference. Significantly one has a colour 'scheme' but one is behind, or ahead of, 'schedule'. The two words are quite unrelated in origin. 'Scheme' comes from the Greek *schema* (form), and 'schedule' from Latin *scedula* (small strip of papyrus). Whether one pronounces 'schedule' with 'shed' or 'sked' is a matter of choice. Americans say 'sked'. See also **plan**.

schizophrenic see **psychopath**

school see (1) **department** (section of a university), (2) **shoal**

sciatica/lumbago (pain in the muscles of the back or leg)

'Sciatica' (from the Greek word for 'hip-joint') is a pain down the back of the leg, from the hip down, originating from exertion that puts a strain on the lumbar or loin portion of the spine, where the sciatic nerve has its roots. 'Lumbago' is a fibromuscular injury in the small of the back caused by a sprain, sudden exertion or the like. Both therefore have either a painful or an etymological connection with the small of the back, the lumbar region.

scone see **bun**

scorn/spurn/shun (reject, avoid)
To 'scorn' is to treat with **contempt,** especially when rejecting or refusing. To 'spurn' *is* to reject, but with disdain. To 'shun' is to keep away from someone or something out of dislike or caution, or to take pains in general to avoid him/it.

Scotch see **Scottish**

Scots see **Scottish**

Scottish/Scotch/Scots (pertaining to Scotland or its people or language)
A much-discussed and tricky trio. When does one use which? It's worth quoting *Chambers,* itself a Scottish (?Scotch) dictionary, on the subject: '**Scotch,** adj. a form of **Scottish** or **Scots**, in common use even among Scottish dialect speakers, though disliked or resented by many Scotsmen: applied esp. to products or supposed products of Scotland: having the character popularly attributed to a Scotsman – an excessive leaning towards defence of oneself and one's property.' That is just 'Scotch', of course. What about the other two? Broadly speaking, 'Scottish' and 'Scots' are applied to both people and things, but 'Scotch' is usually used of things rather than people. It's largely, too, a matter of convention. One traditionally has 'Scotch' broth, 'Scotch' eggs, a 'Scotch' mist, 'Scotch' tape (a proprietary brand of adhesive tape made by 3M), 'Scotch' whisky (otherwise just 'Scotch'), 'Scotch' woodcock (egg and anchovies on toast), a 'Scotch' bonnet, a 'Scotch' fir (which, teasingly, is the same as a 'Scots' pine), a 'Scotch' – also 'Scottish' – terrier and a

'Scotch' thistle, Scotland's national emblem – '(not native)', snaps *Chambers*. Apart from such fixed terms, it seems more correct to use 'Scottish' when referring to the country of Scotland and what is native to it, as the 'Scottish' Highlands and the 'Scottish' character, and 'Scots' for an individual person, as a 'Scots' girl. But 'Scotch' is a frequent alternative to 'Scots' in such cases. Thus one can distinguish between a 'Scots' miner, who is a native Scot, and a 'Scottish' miner, who is one working in Scotland and who may or may not actually be a Scot. To the Romans the *Scotti* were a Gaelic race of northern Ireland: it was only around AD 500 that this people came to what was then the Pictish kingdom of Caledonia to give it its present name.

scoundrel see **rascal**

scowl see **frown**

scream/screech/shriek (piercing cry)
These similar-sounding words can be distinguished. A 'scream' is a loud, piercing cry, as of pain or fear, or a startled, high-pitched cry, not so loud (as when one is suddenly surprised by a hand placed on one's shoulder or the unexpected appearance of a mouse). A 'screech' is a disagreeably shrill or harsh cry, as of an old crone or a 'villain of the piece' on the stage. A 'shriek' is sharper, briefer and usually louder than a 'scream', and is usually the prerogative of women and girls. It does not necessarily denote pain or fear, however, but more or less any sudden strong or uncontrollable emotion, as pleasure, surprise, joy, or amusement.

screech see **scream**

scrimp see **scamp**

scrub see **bush**

scrumpy see **cider**

sculpture/statue/torso/bust
(representation in stone or other material of human or animal)
A 'sculpture' is in fact *any* sculptured object in the round or in relief, whether representational or abstract. A 'statue' is a sculptured figure – or a cast or moulded one – of a person or animal, usually one that is lifesie or larger. (Small 'statues' are statuettes or simply models.) Whereas a 'statue' is the figure of a complete person, a 'torso' is much more limited – it is the sculptured figure of a nude human trunk, especially one without the head or limbs. A famous example is the Belvedere 'Torso' in the Vatican. A 'torso' must in turn be distinguished from a 'bust', which is a 'sculpture' of the head, shoulders and upper chest of a person. Good examples are the 'busts' of Roman emperors at the British Museum in London.

scupper see **scuttle**

scurf see **dandruff**

scurry/scuttle (move hastily)
Both words suggest the rapid movement of something small, as mice or ants. 'Scurry' refers more to the movement, which is hurried; 'scuttle' to the steps taken, which are rapid and hasty. Further, 'scurry' is perhaps, under the influence of 'flurry', used of a light, flittering movement, as of snow, leaves or birds.

scuttle/scupper (sink a ship)
To 'scuttle' a ship is to cut holes through the bottom and/or sides for any purpose, but usually in order to sink it, or, alternatively, to do this by cutting holes below the water line or opening the seacocks. A 'scuttle' is more familiar to most landlubbers as a porthole. To 'scupper' a ship is to sink it deliberately in any way. As a noun, a 'scupper' is an opening in the side of a ship or just below the level of the deck to allow water to run off. As a slang verb, which may be connected with it, to 'scupper' is to ruin or 'do for': 'That scuppered all my plans.' This is not the same as to 'scapa' or 'scarper' which is to leave without notice. (This verb is more likely to derive from Italian *scappare* than be rhyming slang – Scapa Flow/go.)

scuttle (move fast) see **scurry**

scythe/sickle (implement for cutting corn or grass)

The 'scythe' is the long one, with a curving blade on the end of a slightly crooked pole having two short handles at right angles. It is used – or was used – chiefly for mowing and reaping. The 'sickle' is the short-handled, short-bladed implement which is used either for cutting corn or, more commonly, for lopping overhanging branches, trimming shrubs, and hacking weeds generally. The 'scythe' has come to be regarded as the symbol of Father Time, who morbidly uses it to mow down the living when their hour has come. The 'sickle', by contrast, has become one of the two symbols of Soviet Russia, where it represents the rural farmworker. (The complementary hammer stands for the urban industrial worker.) Traditionally, too, the 'scythe' has become familiar as an implement used by a man standing, while the 'sickle' is mainly associated with a woman bending – see the paintings of Millet. Both words come from a root meaning 'cut', as in 'section'; 'scythe' should really have no 'c', but it probably acquired it by association with the name of a kindred cutting implement, 'scissors'.

sea/ocean (region of salt water, usually defined and named geographically)
A 'sea' can be three things: a partially enclosed body of salt water, such as the Mediterranean 'Sea'; a definite part of an 'ocean', as the Sargasso 'Sea' (part of the Atlantic); a large body of inland water, when this is saline, as the Caspian 'Sea'. 'Oceans' are larger, of course, and fewer. For many years, the world was regarded as having five 'oceans': Atlantic, Pacific, Indian, Arctic, and Antarctic. Today, however, only three of these are recognised: the Atlantic, Pacific and Indian. (The Arctic is now regarded as belonging to the Atlantic, of which it is a marginal 'sea', while the Antarctic is the Southern 'Ocean', divided into three portions – one for each of the three regular 'oceans'.) 'Seas' and 'oceans' in fact form a single integrated unit and are sometimes known collectively as the World 'Ocean'.

seamy see **steamy**

seasonable see **seasonal**

seasonal/seasonable (pertaining to a season)
'Seasonal' means 'dependent on a season', as 'seasonal' work, e.g. work done only in the summer. 'Seasonable' means 'suitable for a season', as 'seasonable' weather, i.e. weather one would expect for a particular season. 'Seasonable' also means 'timely', as a 'seasonable' reminder.

seated see **sitting**

secondary modern school see **comprehensive school**

secretary see **president**

section/segment/sector (portion of a whole)
A 'section' is a part that is cut off or divided in some way from something, or regarded as a separate unit, as a military 'section' (see **corps**) or the final 'section' of a journey. The 'section' of a society or community is the part of it seen as having distinctive interests or functions of some kind. A 'segment' may also be cut off or separated, but is usually one of a number of pieces or parts that are marked off somehow, as the 'segments' of an orange or the divisions of a limb or the rings of a worm: the common or garden earthworm has up to 150 'segments'. A 'sector' of a society, as distinct from a 'section', is seen as having a single leader or controller, as the private 'sector' of industry, while in military terms a 'sector' is the portion of a front that is under the charge of a single commander. In geometry, a 'segment' is a part cut off from any figure, but especially a circle, by a line or plane, and a 'sector', more precisely, is the part of a circle that lies between two radii (see **radius**, if necessary) and the arc that joins them, like a slice of cake.

section (military formation) see **corps**

sector see **section**

secure/procure (obtain/get)
To 'secure' something is to obtain it for certain, as when one 'secures' seats for a particular performance. To 'procure' some-

thing is to obtain it by care or effort, as a book that is difficult to 'procure'.

security see **safety**

sedate see **solid**

sedulous see **assiduous**

segment see **section**

self-deprecation/self-depreciation (the understating of one's worth)
'Self-deprecation' is modesty, expressed by saying or doing something that makes oneself seem less important, talented or whatever, than one really is. 'Self-depreciation' is the act of humiliating or debasing oneself, usually for the wrong reason.

self-depreciation see **self-deprecation**

Semitic/Hamitic (family of languages spoken in North Africa and the Mediterranean region)
As applied to languages, 'Semitic' is the family that includes, among others, Hebrew and Arabic. Applied to people, 'Semitic' usually means 'Jewish'. 'Hamitic' is a family of languages, related to 'Semitic', that includes ancient Egyptian and modern Berber. The names are those of the peoples who are supposed to be descended from the sons of Noah – Shem, Ham and Japheth, who, with their families (listed in Genesis 10), lived before Babel, when 'the whole earth was of one language, and of one speech'.

semolina/tapioca (floury food used for making milk puddings)
'Semolina' is the name of the large, hard parts of wheat grains that are left behind in the bolting machine after the fine flour has passed through. 'Tapioca' is a grainy food-stuff prepared from cassava starch by drying it on a heated plate while it is still moist. Puddings made from one or the other are notorious for turning up in nutritious school dinners, where they are usually regarded as having the same degree of palatability as **rice** pudding. (For what happens to the grains that pass through the bolting machine see **flour**.)

señor see **signor**

señora see **signor**

señorita see **signor**

sense see **meaning**

senses see **faculties**

sensibility see **sensitivity**

sensitivity/sensibility/susceptibility (capacity for being affected or touched)
'Sensitivity' relates to being sensitive, either of people, as someone who lacks 'sensitivity' or awareness, or of things, as the 'sensitivity' of a nerve or radio receiver. 'Sensibility' relates to 'sensible' – not in the sense 'having good judgment' but 'having delicate feelings'. A man of 'sensibility' would thus feel pity or some other emotion where another man would not. In Jane Austen's *Sense and Sensibility*, Elinor Dashwood represents the 'sense' and her sister Marianne the 'sensibility'. Both sisters have been deserted by their young men; Elinor bears her disappointment with restraint, but Marianne expresses her grief violently. 'Sensibility' also means 'delicacy of emotional or intellectual perception', as a painter of great 'sensibility'. 'Susceptibility' is close in meaning, but the emphasis is on the degree of impressionability. To offend a person's 'susceptibilities' is to upset or disturb his feelings, which by implication are delicate and easily affected.

sensual/sensuous (giving pleasure to the senses)
'Sensual' has an unfavourable connotation. Referring to the enjoyments of physical sensations it usually suggests grossness or lewdness, as a 'sensual' pleasure in eating or taking cold showers. 'Sensuous', by contrast, has a favourable overtone – that of experiencing and enjoying through the senses, as 'sensuous' poetry or the 'sensuous' music of Wagner. The suggestion of 'sexual' in 'sensual' is apt, although the similarity of the words is a chance one.

223

sensuous see **sensual**

sentiment/sentimentality (refined
sensibility)
'Sentiment' is sincere, refined sensibility
(see **sensitivity**), or a tendency to be
influenced more by the heart than the head.
One can thus appeal to someone's loyal or
other 'sentiments'. (The word also, of
course, means 'opinions' as in 'Them's my
sentiments.') 'Sentimentality' is affected or
mawkish 'sentiment', as displayed by
someone in a 'sentimental' manner: 'I can't
stand his weak sentimentality.'

sentimentality see **sentiment**

sentinel see **sentry**

sentry/sentinel (soldier or person on
watch)
Both are stationed to keep watch and chal-
lenge or prevent the passage of unauthorised
persons. A 'sentinel' is, however, more of a
watchdog, in both a literal and a figurative
sense. A 'sentry' is essentially a military
man, and the word is rarely used outside a
military context. Possibly by association
with 'citadel', 'sentinel' has in addition the
suggestion of someone not merely watching
but defending or protecting. The words are
related, deriving ultimately from Latin
sentire (to perceive).

sepia/sienna (brown pigment)
'Sepia' is a brown pigment from the ink-like
secretion of the cuttlefish, or a drawing done
in it. 'Sienna' is an earth used as a yellow-
ish-brown pigment (raw 'sienna') or, after
roasting in a furnace, a reddish-brown one
(burnt 'sienna'). 'Sepia' comes from the
Greek for 'cuttlefish', 'sienna' is Italian *terra
di Sienna* (earth of Siena).

Septuagesima/Sexagesima (Sunday in
church calendar)
'Septuagesima' is the third Sunday before
Lent, 'Sexagesima' the second before. The
names derive from Latin *septuaginta*
(seventy) and *sexaginta* (sixty). This cannot
refer to the number of days before Easter,
since 'Septuagesima' is sixty-three days
before Easter. Possibly the words were
formed on an analogy with **Quinqua-**

gesima. Or, as the *SOED* points out,
perhaps the reference is to the seventy days
between 'Septuagesima' Sunday and the
octave of Easter – the Sunday next after it.
But that would throw 'Sexagesima' out. . . .

seraphic see **chubby**

serf see **slave**

serial/series (set of successive articles or
episodes)
A 'serial' is normally a story, play or the
like that is told, written or broadcast in
separate parts, which together make up the
whole work. The word is actually the adjective of 'series', that is, a 'serial' story – one
told in a 'series' of parts. A 'series', thus, is
a set of individual articles or parts, each of
which is complete in itself. In broadcasting,
a 'series' is a set of programmes on a
particular subject, so that there will be a
common theme, but designed so that each
one can be seen or heard either on its own
or as part of the whole set. There may even
be a number of 'series' on a topic.

series see **serial**

serpent see **snake**

set see **game** (portion of play forming a
scoring unit)

settee see **couch**

sewage/sewerage (waste matter – or the
system that removes it)
The stuff itself is 'sewage', which passes
through sewers. A 'sewage' farm is thus one
that treats the matter so as to be used as
manure – or that uses it itself as fertiliser.
'Sewerage' is the system by which 'sewage'
is removed, including the actual sewers.
'Sewerage' is sometimes used to mean
'sewage', but never the other way round.

sewerage see **sewage**

Sexagesima see **Septuagesima**

sexton/sacristan (church officer)
Both words are from Latin *sacrista*
(sacristan), though 'sexton' less obviously

so. A 'sexton' is, or was, more of an all-rounder, since in addition to looking after the sacred vessels in the sacristy, which is the responsibility proper of the 'sacristan', he takes general care of the church, its contents and graveyard, and also rings the bell, digs graves and the like. 'Sexton', however, is today found more frequently as a surname than a title of office, since his tasks are often performed by others.

shade see **shadow**

shadow/shade (dark area on the ground or elsewhere cause by an opaque or semi-opaque object intercepting the light)
A 'shadow' is either a single dark figure or image, as the 'shadow' or a man, or else an area of relative darkness, as the 'shadow' of a building – the area which the building darkens by intercepting the light. Such an area will be fairly clearly defined. A 'shade' – usually the 'shade' – is a comparatively dark area with no particular form or limit, often regarded as providing shelter or relief from a light or heat that is too fierce, as the 'shade' of an old apple tree, where it is pleasant to sit. Of course, the 'shade' of a tree might also be its well-defined 'shadow'. 'Shade' is usually used with reference to the light of the sun, whereas a 'shadow' can be cast by any bright object, as a fire, a torch, or a candle. In some cases, however, the two words can be used more or less interchangeably, so that one can sit in the 'shadow' or sit in the 'shade'. Don't misunderstand someone, incidentally, when he says, 'Let's move a "shade".' He doesn't mean, 'Let's move into the "shade"', but, 'Let's move a little.'

shaft/haft (handle of long implement)
'Shaft' is used to apply to the pole or 'body' of a long weapon such as a spear, lance or arrow; to the handle of a hammer, axe, golf club or other long implement; to one of the two bars of wood between which a horse is placed for drawing a cart. A 'haft' is the handle of a shorter implement such as a knife, sword or dagger.

shallow/callow (trivial)
As applied to people 'shallow' means 'superficial', as a 'shallow' mind or character.

'Callow' means 'immature', 'inexperienced', as a 'callow' youth. Oddly it derives from Latin *calvus* (bald). The sense is that of 'unfledged', and the word is still used in this literal sense of young birds that are not yet covered with feathers.

shame/humiliation/mortification (feeling of guilt and embarrassment)
'Shame' implies a feeling of guilt mixed with regret: 'I did it, and I shouldn't have.' 'Humiliation' is the sense of being humbled, disgraced or shown up: 'I did it, I shouldn't have, and they let me know it; now I feel a real heel.' 'Mortification' – rather an impressive word – describes a sense of deep embarrassment with possible confusion: 'I did it, I made a proper mess of it, and now I feel terrible.' The word in its origin implies a 'death' or 'killing', as of one's pride or ego.

shares see **stocks** (divisions of a company's capital)

sheen see **gloss**

shilly-shally see **delay**

shindig see **shindy**

shindy/shindig (row, commotion)
There is a slight but discernible difference. A 'shindy' is a 'rumpus', with the hint of people having a rowdy but enjoyable time. A 'shindig' can also mean 'noisy party' but, as well, 'disturbance', 'quarrel': 'There was a real shindig when I said I wanted my money back'. One kicks up a 'shindy', however. 'Shindy' may derive from the kind of hockey known as 'shinty'; 'shindig' may, possibly, derive from a 'shin dig' – a dig on the shin. For further clamorous confusion see **rumpus.**

ship see **boat**

shoal/school (group of fish swimming together)
A 'shoal' is used of any fish, whereas a 'school', although also applicable to fish, tends to be reserved for marine mammals such as porpoises and whales. The word 'shoal' is not related to 'shoal' meaning

225

'submerged sandbank' but derives from the other half of this pair, 'school' which in spite of the fact that porpoises are intelligent creatures and can be trained in captivity – they can imitate human voices as well as locate a variety of objects – comes not from the familiar educational establishment but from an old Dutch word meaning 'troop'.

shoe see **boot**

shore/beach/coast (edge of land beside a sea or lake)
'Shore' is a general word, often with an implied contrast to 'sea'. A 'beach' is a stretch of the shore with sand or shingle, especially at low tide, and is usually associated with swimming and bathing and seaside leisure activities generally. There are a number of shingle 'beaches' on the Sussex coast, but Beachy Head, the famous headland in East Sussex, is not so called because of the 'beach' below but because its name is French in origin: *beau chef*, meaning simply (but attractively) 'beautiful headland'. 'Coast' more or less equals 'shore', but the word applies to seas or oceans only, and is not used of a lake, however large it is. The 'coast' too, is normally regarded as the natural border or frontier of a country, which may have to be defended or protected, for example, from enemy attack, as implied in 'coastguard' and the name 'Coastal' Command for the RAF section which operated against enemy shipping in the Second World War.

shriek see **scream**

shrimp/prawn (edible crustacean)
The common 'shrimp' (*Crangon vulgaris*) is the smaller of the two, with a semi-transparent body, fanlike tail, and long whiplike antennae. The antennae of the 'prawn', however (by which is usually meant the *edible* 'prawn', *Leander serratus*), are much longer – one and a half times its own body length – and its largest pair of claws are on its second pair of legs, whereas the 'shrimp' has its largest pair of claws on its first pair of legs. Yet another difference is that 'shrimps' like to burrow in the sand between tides, whereas 'prawns' prefer rocky pools.

In the USA, a jumbo 'shrimp' is about three inches long.

shrub see **bush**

shun see **scorn**

sibyl see **nymph**

sick humour see **black humour**

sickle see **scythe**

sideboard/dresser (piece of furniture containing or holding plates and dishes)
A 'sideboard', as its name suggests, is a table or flat-topped chest standing at the side of the dining-room with dishes, plates, decanters and the like either on it or in it. The word essentially means a table placed at one side in a room where meals or dishes can be served or taken. A 'dresser' is a type of 'sideboard' specifically for the kitchen, also with shelves for dishes and plates. It sounds something like an item of furniture for the bedroom, but the connection is not with dressing but French *dresser*, 'to prepare' (i.e. food). A Welsh 'dresser' has a tall backboard with open shelves above its lower cupboard, and as a fine piece of furniture has come to be promoted not only to the dining-room but even to the sitting-room for the display of its own workmanship and the dishes ranged along its shelves.

sidesman/churchwarden (church official)
A 'sidesman' is an assistant 'churchwarden', whose special duty is usually that of taking the collection – when he may literally stand by the side of the 'churchwarden'. The 'churchwarden' is one of two officials elected annually – one by the parish priest, the other by the parishioners – to represent the lay members of the parish and to have special responsibility for the movable property in the church.

Siegfried Line see **Maginot Line**

sienna see **sepia**

sieve see **sift**

sift/sieve (as verb: sort out smaller things from larger)

Used figuratively, to 'sift' is to examine closely, as when one 'sifts' the evidence, i.e. analyses it minutely. The idea is that what is being examined has been scattered into fine particles by means of a sieve. To 'sieve', used figuratively, is to search for something smaller among something larger, as when one 'sieves' for clues by looking for them against the much wider background of the scene or circumstances of the incident.

signor/signore/señor/signora/señora/ signorina/señorita (title or form of address of Italian or Spanish man or woman)
The ones with 'gn' are Italian, and those with the tilde (˜) Spanish. 'Señor' and 'signore' mean 'gentleman', 'Mr' or 'sir', with, however, the shorter form 'signor' used in Italian before a name, e.g. 'il signor Lavatelli'. 'Señora' and 'signora' are used for married women, i.e. correspond to 'lady', 'Mrs' or 'madam', and 'signorina' and 'señorita' for unmarried, usually young, women ('young lady' or 'Miss'). Note that 'señorita' is the only one to have a 't' – there is no word 'señorina'. It is worth remembering that 'signore' is also the plural of 'signora' (i.e. could mean 'ladies'). The plural of 'signore' is 'signori'. There exists a 'signorino' as the male equivalent of 'signorina', approximating to English 'master' as applied to a boy.

signora see **signor**

signore see **signor**

signorina see **signor**

silver see **platinum**

simile/metaphor (figure of speech comparing one thing to another)
A 'simile' uses a direct comparison, however hackneyed, bizarre or inept, usually with the word 'as' or 'like', so 'cool as a cucumber' and 'like a bat out of hell' are both 'similes'. A 'metaphor' (from the Greek for 'transfer') is rather more subtle: it is saying that something *is* another, although of course it literally is not, so to speak of your mother-in-law (or whoever) as 'a real old gas-bag' or to call someone a 'red-bellied

son of a yellow-livered caterpillar' (children are experts in the genre) is to indulge in 'metaphors'. A sustained form of this (a gas-bag filled with laughing gas, a caterpillar who will never turn into a butterfly, and more) is an 'extended metaphor'. A specially enjoyable form of it is a 'mixed metaphor', when two or more elements of the comparison are absurdly incongruous – often quite unintentionally so – as to 'set the ship of state on its feet', or the much quoted specimen allegedly perpetrated by the Irish politician, Sir Boyle Roche: 'Mr Speaker, I smell a rat: I see him forming in the air and darkening the sky; but I'll nip him in the bud.' Mixed 'metaphors' can, however, be used most effectively, with no comic effect, as 'take arms against a sea of troubles' (instead of 'host of troubles'), in Hamlet's famous 'To be or not to be' speech. Many 'metaphors' are proverbs, as 'Time flies', or **clichés**, as 'out of the frying-pan into the fire'.

simoom see **monsoon**

simulating see **dissembling**

sinecure/cynosure (something attractive or desirable)
A 'sinecure' is a position or office that requires little or no work, especially a profitable one – a 'doddle'. A 'cynosure' is something or someone that attracts attention by its brilliance or 'aura' in any sense. Brigitte Bardot (or your own particular favourite star) would be a 'cynosure' if she walked down the local High Street. The words have unexpected origins. Latin *beneficium sine cura* was a 'benefice without cure' (cure of souls), i.e. the ecclesiastical equivalent of a 'rotten borough'. 'Cynosure' derives from Greek *kynosoura*, literally 'dog's tail'. This was the name of the Polar Star, which forms the 'dog's tail' of the constellation Ursa Minor and was used for guiding or directing.

Sinn Féin/Fianna Fáil/Fine Gael/ Fenians (Irish political party)
'Sinn Féin' means 'we ourselves' and is the name of the left-wing political organisation formed in Ireland in 1902 that today is most widely known for its association with the IRA. Basically it advocates nationalist rule

for the country and complete political separation from Great Britain. 'Fianna Fáil', meaning 'soldiers of destiny', is another nationalist but more conservative party founded in 1926 by De Valera and advocating the establishment of an Irish Republic. 'Fine Gael', or 'United Ireland', is a party formed in 1933 in opposition to 'Fianna Fáil'. The 'Fenians' were members of a revolutionary organisation (the Irish Republic Brotherhood) founded in New York in 1858 with the aim of establishing an independent Irish republic. The name apparently derives either from Old Irish *fen* (Irishman) or *fiann* – the title of a legendary band of warriors in the service of Finn MacCool (or Fionn Mac Cumhail). The first three names are pronounced, approximately, 'Shin Fain', 'Feeana Foil' and 'Finna Gail'.

sirocco see **monsoon**

sissy see **prim**

sit-down strike see **sit-in**

sit-in/work-in/sit-down strike/go-slow/ work-to-rule (type of strike)
A 'sit-in' is not so much a strike as an organised protest, especially against the policy or administration of a place. The protest consists in occupying an appropriate area and sitting in it until, in theory, the authorities change their attitude. Students dissatisfied with the policy of their college principal, for example, may organise a 'sit-in' in his office. A 'work-in' is usually understood as the take-over of a factory under threat of closure by its workers: they simply carry on working. A 'sit-down strike' is rather like a combined 'sit-in' and 'work-in,' when workers refuse to leave the place where they are working as a form of protest or to stake a claim. A 'go-slow' is another form of protest, when work is not stopped, as in an all-out strike, but is done at a deliberately slow pace. This is not quite the same as a 'work-to-rule', in which work is done not so much slowly as by the book, with instructions obeyed to the letter, especially trivial ones, which are normally waived in the interests of expediency. A 'work-to-rule' also means no overtime when this would be caused as a direct result of the 'work-to-rule' itself. It may have, certainly at first, little effect on the efficiency of the place, but is regarded as a suitable measure by a government office, for example, whose staff does not wish to be relocated in the wilds of Scotland as part of a redeployment or decentralisation policy. All these types of strike except the 'sit-in' are varieties of so called 'industrial action'.

sitting/sat/seated (position of person on or in a chair)
'Sat' is increasingly widely used for 'sitting', much as 'stood' is for 'standing': 'There she was, sat in the corner as usual.' There is no ambiguity here, but the usage is one that some find grating. However, since the verb 'to sit' can take an object, as in 'The mother sat the child on her knee', as can 'to seat', there can be no real objection to it on grammatical grounds. Past participles of transitive verbs are often used as a so-called statal passive, i.e. a verb form that expresses a state or condition that remains unchanged, as in 'The table was laid', 'A task has been set', 'We will be put'. 'Sitting', after all, is very much a passive state. So to say 'She was sat' cannot be regarded as 'bad' English – at the most it is colloquial. Possibly the additional fact that the simple past of the verb and the past participle are the same ('I sat', 'I have sat') causes further reluctance for the form to gain general acceptance. 'Seated', which expresses 'sat' in this way, is now used more as a regular adjective, as in a 'seated' model.

skewbald see **dappled**

skimp see **scamp**

skit see **parody**

skittles see **bowls**

skulk see **sneak**

slacks see **trousers**

slander see **libel**

slang/jargon (special type of speech or language)

The term 'slang' has two main meanings. First it applies to words or phrases, or particular meanings of words or phrases, that are regarded generally as being not standard English and that are often used, as the *Concise Oxford Dictionary* puts it, 'for picturesqueness or novelty or unconventionality'. Examples might be 'brolly' for 'umbrella' and 'canned' for 'drunk'. Secondly, 'slang' is the term for words or phrases as used specially by a particular class or profession, such as racing 'slang', thieves' 'slang', or school 'slang'. 'Jargon', apart from meaning 'gibberish' or 'debased language', is the term used to apply to the mode of speech employed by a particular group or profession *as a regular language* (which is where it differs from the second sense of 'slang'). One thus has scientific 'jargon', legal 'jargon', and the 'jargon' used by music critics, say. A form of 'jargon' that has become familiar to the public in general is bureaucratic 'jargon', with its lengthy, pompous and indirect mode of speech. Fortunately much of this, as found in government publications or official notices, is becoming obsolete. In his *Modern English Usage*, Fowler points out that 'slang' implies less dislike than 'jargon' – much 'slang' is quite endearing, in fact – and that 'slang' is commoner in sporting usage since many of the terms used in sport are also 'slang' in the first sense, i.e. are not regarded as standard English. An example of this might be cricket's 'hit for six,' which is used generally to mean 'thoroughly surprise' – 'I really hit him for six that time.' A different distinction between the two is that 'slang' is usually short-lived – it dates very rapidly – while 'jargon', being more 'established', is much more durable in the language. However, both 'jargon' and 'slang' words may be quite old in origin: much legal 'jargon', for instance, is still in Latin, while the 'slang' word 'fence', meaning a dealer in stolen property, was known as long ago as 1600. The words themselves seem to be of unknown origin, although 'slang' may perhaps be related to 'sling'.

slapstick see **comedy**

slate see **tile**

slatternly see **slovenly**

slave/serf (person who is not free and works for a master)
A 'slave' in historic times, and even not so historic, was a 'bondsman' who was acquired by capture (virtually as a prisoner), by purchase, or by birth, after which he or she would be entirely divested of any freedom or personal rights and would be obliged to work for a master. A 'serf', on the other hand, was a 'slave' who had some rights, to the extent that they were preserved by law or custom and were protected by his or her master. However, what really distinguished a 'serf' was the fact that he was essentially 'attached to the soil' and could only rarely be removed from his master's land, so was transferred with it when it passed to a new owner. This feature is the usual one to be singled out when differentiating 'serfdom' from 'slavery'. 'Serf' is the Old French word for 'slave', from Latin *servum*. 'Slave', however, is directly derived from 'Slav', from the fact that the Slavonic races were constantly being conquered in medieval times. Russian 'serfs' were emancipated only in 1861, while elsewhere in Europe they had mostly gained their freedom by the beginning of the nineteenth century.

slaw see **coleslaw**

sled see **sleigh**

sledge see **sleigh**

sleigh/sledge/sled (vehicle travelling over ice or snow on runners)
The 'sleigh', the largest of the three, is usually drawn by horses or dogs and can carry passengers or goods. In the USA and Canada a 'sleigh' can be quite a comfortable conveyance, such as the 'one-horse open sleigh' that features in the Christmas song 'Jingle bells'. A 'sledge' is generally used for conveying loads, but can also take passengers. It usually has to have some kind of motive power, either drawn by horses or dogs or reindeer or pushed or pulled by one or more persons. A 'sled' is either a 'sledge', especially a small one, or an alternative word for 'toboggan', a name more common

in Britain than the other side of the Atlantic. A 'sled' (or toboggan) is the one popular for downhill runs, under its own power – or rather that of gravity – as a sport. A 'bobsleigh' or 'bobsled' is used either for sport, as a toboggan, or for hauling loads, particularly logs. Having said this, many people use two or all of the words interchangeably. The distinctions given are the dictionary ones.

slink see **sneak**

slit/slot (narrow opening)
A 'slit' is a straight, narrow opening or aperture as a 'slit' in a fence or a 'slit' in a skirt. A 'slot' is also this, but is usually designed for something to be inserted, as a 'slot' machine or the 'slot' of a letterbox. The words appear not to be related. 'Slot' in its original Old French form *esclot* meant 'hollow between the breasts'.

slot see **slit**

slough see **marsh**

slovenly/slatternly/sluttish (dirty, slipshod)
'Slovenly' means 'untidy', 'negligent', as 'slovenly' habits or dress. 'Slatternly' means 'like a slovenly woman or girl', so is normally used only of females. 'Sluttish', too, has only a feminine application, since it means 'like a slut', like a dirty, 'slovenly' or immoral woman.

sluggard see **lag**

sluttish see **slovenly**

smallpox see **chickenpox**

**smother/stifle/suffocate/strangle/
asphyxiate/spifflicate** (deprive of air)
The first three words here are quite close in meaning, and all involve the cutting off or reducing of a supply of air or oxygen, which if continued can lead to death. 'Smother' is often used when the agent is something like smoke or feathers. 'Stifle' can also imply a deadening of sound as well as a deprivation of air. 'Suffocate' in turn can mean 'strangling' or 'asphyxiating'. To 'strangle', thus,

is to deprive of air by compressing the windpipe, either with the hands or with a rope or cord or wire. To 'asphyxiate' is to obstruct normal breathing in some way, either by applying physical pressure or by reducing the supply of oxygen. The word is unusual in that it literally means 'stop the pulse' (Greek *sphygmos* is 'pulse'). Yet the stopping of the pulse is not the action of a person who asphyxiates, and medically it is a known fact that the pulse may continue to beat in some cases even after death. Finally, as a lighter word to brighten this rather grim catalogue, to 'spifflicate' is a colloquial word meaning anything from 'flatten', 'crush', which is the nearest it gets to any other sense here, to 'destroy', 'annihilate'. The context in which it is used is normally fairly jovial, however, so that no serious harm has been done. 'We absolutely spifflicated them' may mean 'We won the game with a handsome victory', therefore, or 'I'll spifflicate him' could mean simply 'I'll tell him what I think of him!'. The origin of the word seems to be in rather dated schoolboy slang, suggesting 'spiffing' with a fanciful ending based on words such as 'excommunicate' and 'eradicate'.

snake/serpent (creeping, crawling reptile)
'Serpent', although basically meaning 'snake' – 'snakes' belong officially to the sub-order *Serpentes* – is more common, perhaps, as a metaphorical word for a 'devious' person, or rhetorically (the old 'Serpent', and the like) to mean the Devil, than to apply to the scaly, limbless reptile commonly known as a 'snake'. However, a sea 'serpent', although normally regarded as a huge marine monster of some kind (but not yet scientifically identified), is also a (real) 'snake' of the family *Hydrophidae* that live in the sea. Subjectively, though, a 'serpent' is fearsome and powerful, while a 'snake' is cold and treacherous. As *Fowler* puts it, 'the "serpent" shines in the night sky; the "snake" lurks in the grass.'

snare see **trap**

snazzy see **jazzy**

sneak/slink/skulk (move or behave furtively)

To 'sneak' is to go stealthily or furtively, to leave quietly and quickly, or, as every schoolchild knows, to let out secrets. It has acquired a jocular past tense: 'There was a space, so I snuck in.' This may have been prompted by verbs such as 'slink' which have a vowel change to 'u' in the simple past: 'The dog slunk away with its tail between its legs.' 'Slink' itself means to move abjectly, as well as furtively, especially from fear, cowardice or shame. To 'skulk' is either to move slyly or to lie low, in particular for an evil or cowardly reason. All three words are nicely evocative, and conjure up other 'sly' words such as 'snake', 'skive' and 'lurk'.

snicker see **giggle**

snigger see **giggle**

snooker see **billiards**

snooze see **doze**

snowstorm/blizzard (storm with heavy or driving snow)
A 'snowstorm' is more a general word for a fairly short storm with falling or driving snow, as distinguished from an equivalent 'rainstorm', for example, or 'hailstorm'. A 'blizzard' is a severe and often protracted 'snowstorm', implying a bitterly cold wind, driving snow (and drifting snow), and damage to various structures and vehicles, with much inconvenience and disruption and even loss of life. See also **storm.**

sociable see **social**

social/sociable (pertaining to society)
'Social' is the general word, so that one has 'social' laws and 'social' conduct, as well as the 'social' services. 'Sociable' means 'fond of society', that is, 'enjoying the company of others', so a 'sociable' person likes people to talk to, parties to go to, and is good in company. Confusion is particularly likely between such things as a 'social evening' and a 'sociable evening'. The first is a more or less formal evening spent in company; the second is one spent companionably with one or more friends. However, many 'social

evenings', or simply 'socials', such as those run by clubs, churches and the like, are 'sociable evenings' as well.

socialism/communism (political theory that the community as a whole should own and control the means of production)
'Socialism' (apart from the British sense 'policy of the Labour Party') is usually thought of as having two meanings: (1) an alternative to capitalism on the one hand and 'communism' on the other, especially in western society; (2) a stage on the road to 'communism', via class war and, ultimately, revolution, especially in the Soviet Union (this being the Marxist understanding of the term). Soviet 'communism' is thus a progression of both 'socialism' and Marxism (or Leninist Marxism), and is a policy in which property is vested in the community and each works for the common benefit according to his capacity and receives according to his needs. The term 'socialism' can in fact cover a wide range of political, social (obviously) and religious movements, from 'hard-line' Marxist 'socialism' to Christian 'Socialism' (which when it arose in the nineteenth century did not demand common ownership, as conventional political 'socialism' does) and the self-styled 'socialist' governments of countries such as Ghana and Indonesia which have little in common with 'socialism' as understood in the west. In western society, thus, 'socialism' is contrasted with 'communism' in that the latter involves revolution, but 'socialism' is without insurrection, revolution or other non-constitutional activity. In 'communism', too, the theory is that the state ultimately withers away, while in most forms of 'socialism' the state continues to exist as an established system of political control.

sofa see **couch**

soft drugs see **hard drugs**

software see **hardware**

so-ho see **tally-ho**

solder/weld (join together with melted metal)

One normally 'solders' small objects, such as wires, but 'welds' large ones, such as steel plates. For 'soldering', moreover, one actually needs 'solder' – a fusible alloy applied in its melted state to the metal surfaces, wires or joints to be united. 'Welding' normally also involves the application of heat, but usually directly to the two pieces to be joined, not by means of an agent. There are other forms of 'welding' without using heat. The chief of these are: resistance 'welding' using a heavy electric current; arc 'welding' using an electric arc and then applying pressure; cold 'welding', by pressure alone.

sole see **plaice**

solecism see **sophism**

solfeggio/arpeggio (series of ascending or descending musical notes)
A 'solfeggio' is an exercise for the voice using the so-called 'sol-fa' syllables representing the notes of the scale – do, re, mi, fa, sol, la, ti, do (as familiar from the song in the film *The Sound of Music*). 'Solfeggio' is simply the Italian equivalent of 'sol-fa'. An 'arpeggio' is the sounding of the notes of a chord separately but quickly, often up to the treble or down to the bass – a 'spread' chord, in fact, as heard on the harp. The Italian word for this instrument, *arpa*, forms the root of the term.

solicitor/notary/commissioner for oaths (member of legal profession)
A 'solicitor' is the one with whom most of us have had personal dealings. Basically, he advises clients on their legal rights, deals with a whole range of legal matters from conveyancing (buying and selling houses) to proceedings in magistrates' courts, and puts his clients in touch with a barrister if legal action is necessary at a higher level than he can deal with. (See also **lawyer.**) A 'notary' is a 'solicitor' specifically appointed to deal with such things as 'noting and protesting' bills of exchange (he 'notes' on the bill – for example a cheque – why it has not been accepted or paid when presented), attesting deeds and the like. A 'commissioner for oaths' is another specific 'solicitor': one authorised to administer the oath – oaths are required on many occasions in law – to someone making an affidavit, that is, a written declaration on oath.

solid/stolid/staid/sedate (firm, reliable, not excitable)
As applied to character, 'solid' means 'reliable', 'genuine', as a 'solid' worker, or a man of 'solid' sense. 'Stolid' means 'impassive', 'not easily stirred', either in a favourable sense, as a 'stolid' friendship being a detached, unemotional one, or unfavourably as a 'stolid' stare being a dull, stupid one. 'Staid' denotes a settled or 'sedate' character, as, again, favourably as in a 'staid' companion, or unfavourably as in a 'staid' old maid. 'Sedate' means 'calm and composed': 'She's a most sedate young lady.'

soliloquy see **monologue**

solipsism see **sophism**

sonar see **radar**

sonorous/stertorous/strepitous/stentorian (loud, noisy)
'Sonorous' means 'giving out a resonant sound', especially a deep one, as a 'sonorous' bass voice or a 'sonorous' roar. 'Stertorous' is really a medical term – 'snoring heavily', as of the laboured breathing of someone in an apoplectic fit. 'Strepitous' just means 'noisy'. As the *SOED* points out, its use is mainly in musical criticism. The word's discordant consonants are just right for the purpose. 'Stentorian', which is almost always used of the voice, means 'very loud or powerful' – literally, 'like the voice of Stentor', the Greek herald in Homer's *Iliad* 'whose voice was as powerful as fifty voices of other men.'

sophism/solecism/solipsism
(questionable type of speech or argument)
A 'sophism' is an apparently good but actually false argument, used to display ingenuity or to deceive. (An unintentionally false argument is called a 'paralogism'.) A 'solecism' is a rather grand word to mean simply a lapse of standard speech as 'We

was not going to see no one', (instead of 'We were not going to see anyone'), or otherwise a breach of good manners or etiquette – a sophisticated 'clanger'. 'Solipsism' is the theory that nothing but the self exists, or that nothing but the self can be the object of real knowledge. The term derives from Latin *solus ipse* (only self). The other two words are from Greek, respectively 'clever device' and 'incorrectness of speech'.

soprano see **treble**

sortie/sally (outburst or outrush of someone or something)
'Sortie' is usually confined to military usage: the outrush of troops from a besieged place to attack those besieging, or a particular mission carried out by a group of aircraft, as a bombing raid. A 'sally' can also be used in a military sense (though not of aircraft), but it is mainly found in some figurative sense, as a 'sally' of wit (a sudden outburst of it) or, of one engaged in a conversation or discussion, a brilliant 'sally'. In this sense it applies to a lively remark which is often made by way of a verbal attack. Like several English military terms ('grenade', 'redoubt', 'bombard'), 'sortie' and 'sally' are French words – 'a going out' and 'a leaping out'.

sostenuto/tenuto (musical terms meaning 'sustained')
The words, like the majority of musical directions, are Italian, meaning 'sustained' and 'held'. 'Sostenuto' directs that a note must be sustained to its full nominal value, or even longer than this. 'Tenuto' directs that a note or chord must be held firmly to its full value, or possibly slightly more (as if to be on the safe side). The term is usually used after a staccato passage, or where a staccato passage might be expected, so has the implied contrast, 'not staccato'. The difference is thus very fine.

soufflé see **mousse**

sound/noise (thing heard)
'Sound' is a general word for anything that can be heard, as the wind in the trees, a dog barking, or a supersonic aircraft breaking the 'sound' barrier. A 'noise' is usually thought of as a loud, discordant or unpleasant 'sound' of some kind, as the 'noise' of angry shouting or a motorcycle revving. It can be qualified, though, to mean more or less the same as 'sound', as in the phrase 'to make sympathetic "noises",' that is, conventional remarks. E. M. Forster qualified the word in his famous definition of Beethoven's Fifth Symphony: 'the most sublime "noise" that has ever penetrated into the ear of man.'

sound/strait/channel (narrow stretch of water between two pieces of land)
A 'sound' often connects two seas or a sea with a lake, and in some cases is the word for the water between the mainland and an island, as between the west coast of Scotland and the Hebrides ('Sound' of Mull, 'Sound' of Sleat). A 'strait' is similar, but more obviously a narrow passage of water, as the 'Strait' of Dover (or Straits of Dover, since the word is often used in the plural with a singular meaning). A 'channel' is a wider stretch, as the English 'Channel', or Bristol 'Channel', or North 'Channel' between Northern Ireland and south-west Scotland.

sovereignty see **kingdom**

spa see **health resort**

spar see **mast**

sparse see **scarce**

spasmodically see **sporadically**

spatchcock/spitchcock (meat dish prepared from an animal that has been split and summarily grilled)
The chief difference is in the creature involved. A 'spatchcock' is a **chicken** (which see) or other game bird that has been killed, split down the back and grilled. The word may come from 'spitchcock', itself of unknown origin, meaning an eel that has been similarly despatched and prepared (with grilling sometimes replaced by frying).

specialist see **consultant**

specially/especially (particularly)

A very common pair of confusibles. 'Specially' means 'for a particular purpose', 'in a particular way', and is often found with a verb: 'I did this specially for you', 'He came early specially'. 'Especially' means 'exceptionally', 'to a high degree', 'most', and is usually used with an adjective: 'This is an especially difficult question' or 'This point is especially important.' But the difference often needs careful (or special) distinguishing: if you are 'specially careful' you take care in a particular way; if you are 'especially careful' you are very careful. In the nature of things 'especially' is the much more frequent word – but usually turns up as 'specially', which is of course easier to say.

species see **genus**

specimen see **example**

spectre see **ghost**

spifflicate see **smother**

spine/thorn (pointed part of stalk, stem or leaf of a plant)
A 'spine' is a hard or woody outgrowth on a plant, as on gorse. It is not necessarily sharp. A 'thorn' is a pointed process that *is* sharp, as on a rose bush or hawthorn.

spinet see **harpsichord**

spire/steeple (tapering tower on top of a church)
Strictly speaking, a 'spire' is on a tower or roof, or else forms the upper, tapering part of a 'steeple'. This means that a 'steeple' (related to 'steep') is the whole structure – normally a tower with bells and a 'spire' on top. However, the words are up to a point interchangeable. Ordnance Survey maps have special symbols for 'church with tower' and 'church with spire' as well as 'church without tower or spire'.

spirits see **wines**

spirt see **spurt** (sudden flow or burst)

spitchcock see **spatchcock**

spite/malice (ill will)
'Spite' is a petty expression of revenge or retaliation. 'Malice' is a more fixed state of mind – that of delighting in seeing harm done to others, whether gravely or flippantly. For '"malice" aforethought' see **murderer.**

spleen see **bile**

splutter/sputter (scatter explosively)
Someone talking hastily and confusedly, as when excited or embarrassed, usually 'splutters'; a person almost incoherent with rage or shock may well 'sputter'. 'Splutter' refers more to the actual sound – it is a blend of 'splash' and 'sputter' – and 'sputter', related to 'spout', to the explosive nature of the action. For this reason fat cooking may 'splutter' or 'sputter', but a firework usually just 'sputters'.

sporadically/spasmodically (intermittently)
'Sporadically' means 'appearing or happening at intervals': if you sleep 'sporadically' you have a fitful or disturbed night. The image is that of seeds being sown, from Greek *spora* (seed, sowing). 'Spasmodically' is, in its literal sense, 'characterised by spasms', so basically means 'by fits and starts'. 'He worked spasmodically' means he worked for a while, then stopped suddenly, then started up again, and so on. 'He worked sporadically' means simply that he worked from time to time, rather than continuously.

sport see **game** (activity involving play)

sprained see **strained**

spray/spume (moving droplets of water)
'Spray' is water that is blown through the air, or falls through the air, as from waves, a fountain or a waterfall. 'Spume' is the foaming or frothing water found on an agitated surface, as the 'white horses' that form the crests of waves on a rough sea.

spring/summer (season of growth and greenery and even warmth)
The question is not so much one of identific-

ation but of when, exactly, the one ends and the other begins. If 'spring' ends, for example, at the 'summer' solstice – which seems confusing enough anyway – and this is on 21 June, how can it be that Midsummer Day is only three days later, on 24 June? The answer lies in the definitions, since three different reckonings are in use. Astronomically, 'spring' is defined as beginning in the northern hemisphere at the vernal equinox, i.e. on that date when the sun crosses the equator and makes day and night to be equal in length. This is about 21 March. 'Spring' ends, and 'summer' begins astronomically, at the 'summer' solstice, which is about 21 June and the date when the sun is furthest from the equator and does not apparently move north or south (The 'equator' here is the celestial one, not the terrestrial.) This means that 'summer' ends at the autumn equinox, which is about 21 September. But popularly, and in round months, 'spring' begins in March and continues for April and May, while 'summer' runs from June through to August. Or, if you don't mind not having an exact quarter of the year, you can start 'summer' in May – many people are only too glad to – and 'spring' even, in February (which is usually just wishful thinking). But according to either of these definitions, Midsummer Day on 24 June is hardly the middle of 'summer' by the calendar at all. The third explanation is a religious one: 24 June is John the Baptist's Day, and St John has always been associated in folk tradition with the sun's slow decline into winter. It was St John, after all, who said of Christ and himself, 'He must increase, and I must decrease' (John 3:30), and the days do indeed begin to shorten after 24 June. So when 'summer' starts for you depends on your viewpoint and you can be guided by science, religion, or just plain sixth sense. (The whole thing is even further complicated by the fact that British 'Summer' Time starts around the first day of 'spring'.)

sprint see **spurt** (stretch of fast running)

spume see **spray**

spurn see **scorn**

spurt/spirt (sudden flow or burst of something)
There used to be a distinction. 'Spirt' is the older form, meaning a gush, jet or flow of something, such as water or blood. The form 'spurt', which has now virtually ousted the earlier spelling, came to be used in a figurative sense, as a runner who puts on a final 'spurt' in a race. Now 'spurt' is used in all senses of the word. See also the next entry.

spurt/sprint (short stretch of fast running)
A 'spurt' is a sudden increase in speed of a runner, usually or typically put on at the end of a long race. A 'sprint' is a running race at full speed, especially over a short distance, hence also a separate fast stretch of running before the finish of a long race – differing in this sense from a 'spurt' in that it is not a sudden burst but a reasonably prolonged and premeditated manoeuvre.

sputter see **splutter**

squad see **corps**

squadron see **corps**

squeamish see **queasy**

squid see **octopus**

SS see **Gestapo**

stable/staple (firmly based)
'Stable' means 'firm', 'steady', as a 'stable' government or a person's 'stable' nature, i.e. one that is steadfast and dependable. 'Staple' means 'chief', 'principal', as a 'staple' export or product of a country. Confusion can arise in the phrase 'stable diet': a 'stable' diet is a balanced one; a 'staple' diet is one based on a particular ingredient or food, as a slimmer's 'staple' diet of fish and fruit (or whatever).

stable (place for animals) see **stall**

stack/rick (pile or store of grain, hay or straw)
There is little difference between the two. A 'rick', however, may contain crops other than grain, hay or straw – peas, for example

– and in addition is almost always thatched. A 'stack' may on occasions be unthatched. Possibly 'stack' is also the commoner word of the two.

stag/deer/hart/hind/doe/roedeer (animal with antlers)
The names all have specific applications. The 'stag' is the male of the red or any other 'deer' – the general term for the animal that annually sheds its antlers – especially one in its fifth year. A 'hart' is a male red deer, but *after* its fifth year. A 'hind' is the word for the female of the red deer, especially in, but also after, its third year. 'Doe' is a more general word for a female 'deer' (as the song in *The Sound of Music* reminds us), and is also used of the female of a hare or rabbit. A 'roedeer' is a small species of 'deer' (*Capreolus capreolus*) – seen in Britain in Epping Forest or the New Forest – which still lives in a wild state in many places of the world, even as far east as China.

staid see **solid**

stairs see **steps**

stalactite/stalagmite (deposit of calcium carbonate in a cave)
Two notorious confusibles. The 'stalactite' is the 'icicle' that hangs from the roof, and the 'stalagmite' the one pointing upwards on the floor of the cave. Both derive, unoriginally, from Greek *stalaktos* or *stalagmos* (dripping). One handy mnemonic for distinguishing the two, based on their inclusion of one letter, is 'C for *c*eiling, G for *g*round'.

stalagmite see **stalactite**

stalk see **stem**

stall/stable/loosebox/horsebox (living and feeding place for animals)
A 'stall' is normally a single compartment for one animal in a 'stable' or other lodging place, as a cow-shed. A 'stable' is usually a dwelling and feeding place of a horse, but can also be used for other animals, as cows. Both words are related to 'stand', since this is the basic attitude of the animal when inside. A 'loosebox' is an enclosed and covered 'stall' designed to confine an animal, especially a horse. A 'horsebox' is a van or trailer for transporting a horse or horses – a mobile 'loosebox', in fact. (A 'loosebox' is sometimes called a 'box stall', or simply a 'box'. Since a 'horsebox' can also be called simply a 'box' it is perhaps best to specify which kind is meant when first mentioning one or the other.)

stammer/stutter (utter words hesitantly or with difficulty)
To 'stammer' is to speak with difficulty owing to a 'block', when the words seem to stick, especially at the beginning. It can happen to anyone in a moment of excitement, embarrassment, confusion or similar heightened emotion, as well as be a congenital defect. To 'stutter' is normally understood as 'to repeat involuntarily the initial letter of a word', as 'B-b-b-b-but you s-s-s-seem t-t-t-tired'. The condition is more likely to be an inherent speech defect than the result of an emotional state.

staple see **stable**

star/planet (celestial body)
'Stars' are heavenly bodies similar in nature to the Sun. They are hot, glowing masses that produce their energy by thermonuclear reactions. 'Stars' outnumber 'planets' to the nth degree and our nearest star, which is in fact the Sun itself, is around 93 million miles from the Earth. 'Planets' are heavenly bodies that revolve in definite orbits around the Sun. There are nine known planets. These are, starting with the one nearest to the Sun: Mercury, Venus, Earth, Mars, Jupiter, Saturn, Uranus, Neptune and Pluto. All of them except Neptune and Pluto can be seen with the naked eye, especially Venus, which is also called, confusingly, the **'morning star'.** The most important difference between 'stars' (that twinkle) and 'planets' (that do not) is that 'planets' shine by the reflected light of the Sun, whereas 'stars' shine by their own light. The word 'planet' originates from the Greek meaning 'wanderer'. Historically, the 'planets' were the Sun, the Moon, Mercury, Venus, Mars, Jupiter and Saturn, as these were the only heavenly bodies seen to change their

position or 'wander' against the background of the 'stars'.

starboard see **port** (side of a ship)

start see **beginning**

statement see **account**

statesman see **politician**

statue see **sculpture**

steak and kidney pie/steak and kidney pudding (savoury meat dish)
The difference is not quite that between a pie in the general sense (see **tart**) and a pudding. A 'steak and kidney pie', almost always eaten hot, consists of pieces of meat and kidney baked together in gravy and served in a bowl or dish under a crust of pastry. As bought in shops, 'steak and kidney pies', whether large 'family' ones or individual size, are sold ready to cook either in silver foil dishes or in tins. A 'steak and kidney pudding' has virtually the same contents but these are cooked inside a suet casing, which completely surrounds the meat. In shops, they are usually sold in tins, and whatever the size are either traditional 'pudding' shape (with larger base than top, like a Christmas pudding) or cylindrical (with flat base and top of equal diameter). They are always eaten hot, except by those who do not object to cold, unappetizing suet pudding.

steak and kidney pudding see **steak and kidney pie**

steamy/seamy (improper or shocking)
'Steamy' is a colloquial word meaning 'erotic', such as a 'steamy' love scene in a film or play, or a 'steamy' nightclub. The suggestion is of heat, sweat, passion and even steam baths and nudity as well as general 'temperature raising'. 'Seamy' is more a standard word meaning 'sordid', 'unpleasant', as the 'seamy' side of life that you don't normally see, and a 'seamy' district of a town as its seediest and poorest. The reference is to the seam of a carpet or other piece of material, which is normally hidden on the underside.

steel see **iron**

steeple see **spire**

steer see **ox**

stem/stalk (supporting body of plant)
'Stem' is a more general word, used for the main body of a tree, shrub or plant of any kind that supports its leaves and branches, and for the more slender body, attached to the main one, that supports fruit or flowers. Most 'stems' are thus also 'stalks', since a 'stalk' also supports leaves, fruit and flowers. The word is more often applied, however, to a herbaceous plant, i.e. one with a 'stem' that is not woody and which dies down in winter. This means that a 'stem' is often larger and stronger than a 'stalk'.

Sten gun see **Bren gun**

stentorian see **sonorous**

steps/stairs (treads for one's feet when ascending or descending)
'Steps' is the more general word, although most 'steps' are external ones, as those that form a flight, or a single 'doorstep'. However, single 'steps' exist indoors as well, especially the ones that have to be minded when passing from one room to another – the underfoot version of 'Mind your head'. Ladders have 'steps', and so of course do 'step'-ladders, while a pair of 'steps' is not a ladder that has just two 'steps' but a ladder that has two corresponding sides (like a pair of scissors) and which does not need to be leaned against a wall. 'Stairs', by contrast, are almost always fixed indoor 'steps' on a 'staircase', and a single 'stair', on which children and animals sometimes like to stop and stare, is one of many on a complete set. The only common use for 'stairs' out of doors is as a landing stage by a river, as Horselydown 'Stairs' and George's 'Stairs' on the Thames in London just below Tower Bridge.

stertorous see **sonorous**

stickleback see **minnow**

stifle see **smother**

stimulant see **stimulus**

stimulus/stimulant (something that stimulates or excites)
A 'stimulus' is the general term for anything, especially an incentive of some kind, that incites to action or exertion or quickens action. The thought of a coming holiday may act as a 'stimulus' in dealing with that job or piece of work you had been putting off indefinitely. A 'stimulant' is a drug, or food or drink, that quickens some bodily or mental process. Common 'stimulants' are coffee and alcohol. Both words derive from Latin *stimulus* (spur, goad).

stint see **scamp**

stipulate/postulate (demand specifically)
To 'stipulate' is to make a particular demand or arrangement for something, to require it as being essential, as when one 'stipulates' a condition or a price. To 'postulate' is to claim the existence of something or take it for granted, as well as to demand it as necessary. One can thus 'stipulate' a condition or 'postulate' for a condition. The meaning is the same. 'Stipulate' is much more commonly used, however.

stoat see **ferret**

stockbroker/jobber/broker (financial dealer)
A 'stockbroker' is an intermediary between the public and the 'jobbers' in the business of buying and selling stocks and shares. He acts as an agent for his clients and works for a fixed commission. He is usually a member of one of the stock exchanges. A 'jobber' – properly, 'stockjobber' – acts as a wholesaler dealing in stocks and shares. He, too, is a member of a stock exchange. He quotes two prices: a buying price and a selling price. The difference is called the 'jobber's turn' (selling is always higher than buying) and is his profit. His name comes from the fact that he does a job, or piece of work, for a profit. A 'broker' is a fairly general term for a middleman in some business, or an agent or commissioner of some kind. (The word may, of course, be simply an abbreviation of 'stockbroker'.) There are specialised 'brokers', such as insurance 'brokers', who deal in services rather than goods. The origin of the name is obscure: it is not apparently related to 'break' or 'broke'.

stocks/pillory (old instrument of punishment)
The 'stocks' consisted of a framework with holes for the ankles and sometimes the wrists in which the offender was placed in a

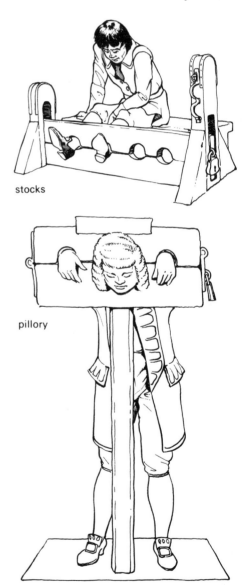

stocks

pillory

sitting position. The 'pillory' was an upright contrivance with holes for the head and hands, but not the feet, in which the criminal was held in a standing position. In both he was exposed to public derision, and could be assailed with verbal abuse or rotten fruit, to choice. In short, he would become a 'laughing stock' – which phrase derives from the former instrument. The origin of 'pillory' is uncertain: the word could perhaps derive from Latin *speculum in gloriam Dei*, 'mirror to the glory of God'. But such an etymology is speculative.

stocks/shares (divisions of company's capital entitling their holder to profit)
The main difference is that 'shares' are issued in specified amounts, such as 25p, 50p or £1, while 'stock' is sold in undefined quantities (which may on occasion be divided into 'shares'). 'Shares' cannot be converted into 'stock' until they are fully paid. 'Stock' is also the term used for government loans. For types of 'shares', see **ordinary shares.**

stolid see **solid**

stomach/belly/abdomen (organ of body in which food is digested)
A 'stomach' is a strange thing. As a word it is of unusual spelling and origin (the Greek for 'mouth', of all things), and is also one of the few words in English whose 'baby version' has become generally if colloquially accepted ('tummy'); as an organ it is of uncertain location and rather vague function – something to do with food, of course, but what? The 'stomach' is in fact situated a good deal further up in the body than most people think it is: more or less under the breast bone, rather than just above or below the belt. It is also only the first stage of digestion that takes place here, since most of the digestive processes occur in the small and large intestines. To make matters even more imprecise, we talk of 'stomach'-ache, not meaning a pain in the 'stomach', but discomfort in the bowels. So what is a 'belly' (sometimes thought of as rather a 'rude' word)? It is either synonymous with 'abdomen', which is the word for that part of the body which contains the 'stomach', bowels, and digestive organs generally, a

sense reflected in the 'belly' landing of an aeroplane (made on its fuselage, or 'belly', without using its landing gear), or it means the same as 'stomach', in particular in the phrase 'an empty "belly"', or 'a full "belly"'.

stone/pip (hard seed of a fruit)
On the whole, 'stone' is used for the larger seeds, as of a plum or peach, and 'pip' of the smaller seeds, as in an apple or orange. However, 'stone' can be used of any hard seed, so that all 'pips' are 'stones'. Even so, fleshy fruits with small seeds are usually thought of as having 'pips'. The word is short for 'pippin', which of course is the name used in certain varieties of apple, as Cox's Orange Pippin and Ribston Pippin, both of which have 'pips' – or 'stones'.

Stone Age/Ice Age (lengthy era in prehistoric times)
The 'Stone Age' was the earliest of the three 'implement' ages: Stone, Bronze and Iron, and was itself divided into the Old Stone Age, or Palaeolithic (from about 3 million years ago to about 8000 BC), when implements were simply chipped into shape, Middle Stone Age, or Mesolithic (about 8000 BC to about 6000 BC), and New Stone Age, or Neolithic (about 6000 BC to about 2000 BC), when stone implements were ground and polished. In Europe the 'Stone Age' began about a million years ago and merged into the Bronze Age about 2000 BC. The 'Ice Age', or glacial epoch, when much of the northern hemisphere was covered with great sheets of ice, corresponds to the late **Pleistocene** (Greek 'most recent') epoch in the geological time scale which in fact largely coincides with the 'Stone Age' of archaeologists.

storm/gale/tempest (strong or violent wind)
A 'storm' is the most general word here, indicating simply a violent weather condition of some kind, whether a strong wind, driving rain, high seas, thunder and lightning, or a combination of these. The word is often qualified, as a 'thunderstorm', 'rainstorm', **'snowstorm'** (which see) or 'hailstorm'. A 'gale' usually implies a strong wind, often one without rain, while a

'tempest' is a more literary word (as in the title of Shakespeare's play) to mean either 'storm' or 'gale'. On the Beaufort Scale, however, which runs from 0 (calm) to 12 (hurricane) to express wind speed, both 'storm' and 'gale' have specific values. A 'gale' is thus force 8 (39–46 mph or 34–40 knots) and a 'storm' force 11 (64–72 mph or 56–63 knots). Moreover, 'strong gale' and 'whole gale' are terms for forces 9 and 10 respectively, with speeds intermediate to these. (The modern Beaufort Scale, too, now has higher, nameless forces from 13 to 17.)

stout see **ale**

stove see **oven**

straight/strait (confined or narrow)
The occasional confusion is something like that of 'plane/plain' – two words strongly suggesting each other. After all, what is 'straight' is often narrow, and a 'strait' is usually narrow as well. And while 'strait' is usually a noun – 'narrow stretch of water open at both ends' – it can also be an adjective, as a 'strait'-jacket (or is it a 'straight'-jacket?). Conversely, 'straight' is more common as an adjective – 'not curved or bent', 'true' – but is also found as a noun, as the 'straight' of a race-course and the proverbial 'straight and narrow'. In origin, 'straight' derives from 'stretch', while 'strait' is related to 'strict'. But this helps only a little with the 'strait' – or 'straight'-jacket. Which is correct? Dictionaries differ. The *SOED* and *Concise Oxford Dictionary*, seventh edition (1982) recognise only 'strait'. Longman's *English Larousse* recognises both, but comments that 'straight' is an American alternative. *Chambers* prefers 'strait' but adds 'formerly also, and still erroneously, **straight**'. The decision must lie in the definition: is the jacket one designed to keep a person's arms and body 'straight' or is it intended to confine or restrain him, which is the sense of 'strait'? The answer must be the latter. So similarly one has 'strait-laced', since a person who has strict or prudish morals was originally a lady who was tightly laced. Confusibles like these can drive one to desperate 'straits'.

strained/sprained (of muscles and tendons – stretched or wrenched)
A 'strained' muscle is one stretched too far or overexerted, as when one has a 'strained' back or a 'strained' ham. 'Sprained' is especially applied to the muscles and tendons of the ankle and wrist, with the sense 'excessively strained', usually as the result of a sudden twist or wrench. For similar confusible discomforts see **wrench**.

strait see (1) **sound** (narrow stretch of water), (2) **straight**

strangle see **smother**

stratagem see **strategy** (plan)

strategy/stratagem (plan)
Both words ultimately derive from Greek *strategos* (a general), so that 'strategy' is literally generalship, or the art of conducting wars and managing armies. (For more on this see **strategy** below.) A 'stratagem', in war or peace, is a trick or ruse for deceiving somebody. *The Beaux' Stratagem,* an early eighteenth century comedy by George Farquhar, recounts how two beaux, Aimwell and Archer, adopt a variety of disguises and devices in order to marry the women they love.

strategy/tactics/logistics (science of warfare)
'Strategy' deals with the planning and directing of projects or manoeuvres that involve the movement of troops, ships, aircraft, etc. The objective is to have the forces moved in such a way that one has the advantage or superiority in conditions, place and time. 'Tactics' deals with the actual process of disposing one's forces, especially when in contact with the enemy. 'Logistics', from the French *loger* (to lodge), deals with the essential but necessarily secondary business of transporting, lodging and supplying troops and equipment – what goes on, in fact, behind the scenes of the actual theatre of war. Thus of aircraft 'strategic' means 'designed to disorganise the enemy's internal economy and destroy his morale', while 'tactical' means 'operating in the immediate support of a local engagement or manoeuvre'. Both 'strategic' and

'tactical' aircraft therefore fire missiles and drop bombs, but for different reasons.

stratosphere see **atmosphere**

street see **road**

strepitous see **sonorous**

stroke/heart attack/coronary (sudden disabling or even fatal attack)
A 'stroke' is the result of a blood vessel bursting in the brain – a cerebral haemorrhage – and destroying the surrounding brain cells by bleeding into them. This has the effect of cutting off the blood to the area of the brain beyond the haemorrhage, and leads to a paralysis in many cases. A 'heart attack' results from the failure of a section of heart muscle. (In turn it can be distinguished from heart failure, which is caused by the inability of the left or right or even both sides of the heart to pump enough blood for the body.) A 'coronary' is in full a 'coronary thrombosis', that is, the formation of a blood clot in the coronary artery (which resembles a crown – hence its name – and supplies the heart with blood). The three conditions thus have quite distinct causes.

stultify see **stunt**

stunt/stultify (impede)
The association is a false one. To 'stunt' is to check the growth or impede the progress of, as to 'stunt' the growth of the economy. To 'stultify' is to make seem foolish or ridiculous, to render inefficient through frustration. One can thus 'stultify' someone's efforts by deliberately undermining his confidence in his ability to succeed. If one does so by belittling his chances of success one is, in effect, also 'stunting' him by cramping his style. However, the words are unrelated: 'stultify' derives from Latin *stultus* (stupid), and 'stunt' is akin to 'stint' and, probably, 'stump'.

stupor/torpor (dulled or numbed state)
A 'stupor' is the state of being almost unconscious because of disease, drugs or shock: a typical 'stupor' is that of a drunk. 'Torpor' is the state of having one's physical powers

suspended, as a hibernating animal. Thus 'stupor' relates more to the mind and the senses, and 'torpor' to the body. Used figuratively, 'stupor' implies a mental dullness or even stupidity, while 'torpor' suggests a lethargic or indifferent state. 'Stupor' is related to 'stupid' and 'torpor' to 'torpid'.

stutter see **stammer**

style see **fashion**

subconsciously see **unconsciously**

subject/theme/topic (matter being considered in a speech or written account)
'Subject' is the general word for whatever is being treated or considered. 'Theme' implies an underlying concept that runs right through the matter and which is usually enlarged on or embroidered. 'Topic' is the 'theme', or 'subject', of a specific type of communication, often a brief or impermanent one such as a speech, a conversation, or an essay. It often, too, relates to a question of the day or a current talking point. The word is unusual in being the English version of the Greek title of a work by Aristotle. This was *ta topika*, 'topics' (literally 'things pertaining to commonplaces') which was a treatise reflecting discussions at the Athenian Academy.

subject(person or thing discussed) see **object**

submerged/immersed (in or under water)
'Submerged' is 'situated under the water', often with the implication that the object itself should not naturally be so, or that it is hidden, as a 'submerged' tree-trunk or, figuratively, 'submerged' fears. Of submarines, of course, 'submerged' is the accepted state. 'Immersed' means 'having been plunged into or under liquid', as false teeth in a glass of water or, in a transferred sense, someone engrossed in work or a book – 'immersed' in it.

subsequent see **consequent**

subtopia see **suburbia**

suburbia/subtopia (residential district outside a city or town)
'Suburbia' was the quasi-proper name first applied in 1896 to the suburbs of London. The word was intended to apply to the characteristic life of those who lived in the suburbs, especially from the point of view of their supposed narrowmindedness. The term now applies to the suburban district of any city or town. 'Subtopia' is a similar name first appearing in 1955 for a '*sub*urban U*topia*'. The appellation was, and is, an ironic one, since it applied to a country area that had been built up by means of tasteless buildings and dreary streets to create the impression of an ideal suburb, a supposed optimum blend of town and country. Surbiton, south London, is an example of 'suburbia' rather than 'subtopia', yet, it, too, was once in the country as its name reveals: 'southern barley town'.

suffocate see **smother**

suite/train/cortège/retinue (company of followers or attendants)
Four French words. A 'suite' usually applies to the followers or attendants of a royal personage. A 'train' is any band of followers, as a 'train' of admirers. A 'cortège' is normally the word for a funeral procession, and a 'retinue', as the term suggests, with its implication of people who have been 'retained' in service, is a 'suite' or 'train' of persons who officially attend or wait upon a dignitary of some kind.

sultana see **raisin**

summary/synopsis/précis (brief or concise account of something)
The difference is rather a fine one. A 'summary' is a brief account or abridgment, a 'summing up' of something, as a 'summary' of the day's play in a test match. A 'synopsis', from the Greek meaning 'seeing together', is a bird's-eye view of something, with an implied compression being made, as the 'synopsis' of a play, that is, not so much a brief account as a condensed one. A 'précis' is similar to a 'synopsis', but usually refers to a written work or extract that is itself somewhat lengthy or turgid and that really *needs* to be

shortened for a particular purpose – if only as a school English language exercise. A 'précis' thus aims to make precise what is seen to be imprecise.

summer see **spring**

supermarket/superstore/hypermarket (large self-service store)
A 'supermarket', originally rather a grand conception – a large self-service store with a wide range of freely accessible goods – is now simply any self-service store or shop, though usually one selling food products. A 'superstore' is basically a large 'supermarket', often on the outskirts of a town, and technically having at least 2500 square metres of selling space, together with a car park and a wide range of non-food merchandise as well as food. The 'hypermarket' is a French innovation, the word itself modelled on 'supermarket' with 'hyper-' used to suggest something that was better or superior or 'more so'. Basically it is a grand 'superstore', technically with at least 5000 square metres of selling space. By 1985 there were 302 'superstores' and 44 'hypermarkets' in Britain, with plans to build many more.

supernatural/preternatural (transcending the laws of nature)
'Supernatural' suggests divine or superhuman properties, as 'supernatural' power or strength. 'Preternatural' implies the possession of supernormal gifts or qualities even to an abnormal degree, as the 'preternatural' silence of the desert or the 'preternatural' sense of hearing of bats.

supersede see **surpass**

superstore see **supermarket**

supine see **prostrate**

supplement/appendix/addenda (material added at the end of a book)
A 'supplement', which can be issued separately or incorporated in a book, is usually for purposes of comparing, improving, correcting or adding. In a sense it not only supplements but complements the main body of the book, that is, it makes it more

complete. An 'appendix' is normally useful additional information without which, however, the rest of the book is complete. In a reference work or dictionary, for example, an 'appendix' might be a table of some kind, or a list of symbols. An 'addenda' – strictly speaking the word is plural, with singular 'addendum' – is a kind of 'appendix' containing additional material which, given other circumstances, would have been incorporated in the main body of the book. An example might be new words at the end of a dictionary: if the publication of the dictionary had been a year later, they would probably have been in the main body of the book. Compare **foreword.**

supplement/complement (additional part)

The two are more frequently confused than they should be. A 'supplement' is something additional to what is regarded as a whole, as a 'supplement' to a newspaper or a 'supplementary' ticket. A 'complement' is an integral second part or portion that makes, with the first part, a whole unit. That is, it is the apparently 'additional' part that makes something complete. A ship will not be complete without its 'complement', or crew of officers and men. 'Complementary' colours are those which, when mixed together, produce white light, e.g. blue and yellow. The confusion between 'complement' and 'compliment' is normally sorted out at the school desk.

suppress/repress (restrain)

The two words are very close, but a distinction can be made. To 'suppress' is to abolish, stop or restrain something that actually or potentially exists, as when one 'suppresses' a riot, an evil practice or the truth. To 'repress' is to check, control, but not necessarily abolish, something – usually something undesirable – as when one 'represses' a thought so that it seems not to exist. To 'repress' a desire is to check it so that it is as little in evidence as possible; hence to 'suppress' a desire is virtually to eliminate it.

surgeon see doctor

surpass/supersede (go further)

To 'surpass' is to be better than, to exceed or excel: 'The results surpassed my wildest hopes.' To 'supersede' (sometimes spelt, possibly wrongly, 'supercede') is to take the place of: 'John Black superseded Bill White, who had retired, as chairman.' No doubt the confusion, where it occurs, is due to the fact that when one thing supersedes another, it is often superior to it, as: 'The car superseded the horse', or: 'Few Victorians could foresee that planes would largely supersede trains for travelling long distances.'

Surrealism see Futurism

susceptibility see sensitivity

swallow/martin/swift (fast, agile bird feeding on insects in flight and nesting under eaves)

The 'swallow' is perhaps the most familiar of the three, with its long wings, swift flight, forked tail, and twittering call. The 'martin' is a member of the 'swallow' family, and in particular the 'house-martin', black above and white below, that builds and nests on the walls of houses, and the brown and white 'sand martin', which nests in sandbanks or sandpits. The 'swift' closely resembles the 'swallow', although it in fact belongs to another family (the one to which humming-birds belong). It can be distinguished by its very long wings and short, stumpy body and its extreme agility

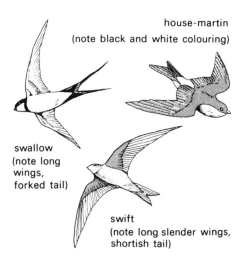

house-martin
(note black and white colouring)

swallow
(note long
wings,
forked tail)

swift
(note long slender wings,
shortish tail)

in flight: it can not only catch insects on the wing but also drink, bathe and even mate. Unlike the 'swallow', too, its tail is not always forked.

swamp see **marsh**

sweater see **pullover**

swede see **turnip**

swift see **swallow**

swing/bop/boogie-woogie (form of jazz liable to periodic revival)
The heyday of 'swing', a form of 'easy' rhythmic jazz with a freely varied melody and simple harmonic accompaniment, was the late 1930s and early 1940s, otherwise 'the swing age'. This was the last great period of jazz proper before experimentation set in. 'Bop', short for 'bebop' (or sometimes 're-bop') was the highly syncopated type of jazz with complex harmonies, that originated in America in the late 1940s. The word originated in an imitation of a typical musical phrase and in turn gave 'teeny-bopper' and 'weeny-bopper' as a term for a 'swinging' teenager or younger girl. 'Boogie-woogie' originated as a pre-war style of playing the blues on the piano, characterised by a persistent bass rhythm. It has since been revived and popularised several times and is by no means moribund. The actual word is of tantalisingly obscure origin. It is tempting to think of it as imitative in some way, but perhaps an American Negro slang word 'boogie' (meaning 'performer'?), with 'woogie' tacked on to rhyme with it, is nearer to the truth. See also **pop**.

swordfish/sawfish (fish with sharp, elongated snout)
The 'swordfish' is, on the whole, not as large as the 'sawfish' – although large enough – with a length of up to fourteen feet. Its 'sword' is its elongated upper jaw which it uses as a weapon for killing its prey. The 'sawfish', which can be anything from ten to twenty feet in length, has a bladelike snout with strong teeth on *both* sides. Its saws are used mainly for feeding, either by digging out animals from the sea bottom, or,

like the 'swordfish', by maiming or killing smaller fish.

sybarite see **sycophant**

sycophant/sybarite (disagreeably selfish person)
A 'sycophant', pronounced 'sickerfant', is a servile, fawning person, one who flatters in order to be praised or rewarded, a 'toady' or 'bootlicker'. A 'sybarite' devotes himself to the pursuit of luxury and pleasure, especially of the voluptuous or sensual. The original 'sybarites' were the inhabitants of Sybaris, an ancient Greek city noted for its wealth and luxury. Greek *sykophantes* means literally 'fig-shower'. 'Showing a fig' was, as it still is in many countries, the classical equivalent of the V-sign (the thumb thrust between two fingers) and a gesture used when denouncing a culprit.

syllabus see **curriculum**

sylph see **nymph**

sympathy/empathy (feeling with or for a person)
'Sympathy' is literally 'feeling with' – a compassion for or commiseration with a person, a feeling of understanding towards him. 'Empathy' is literally 'feeling into'. The term originated in psychology in 1912, as a Greek-type translation of the German *Einfühlung*, to describe the ability to project one's personality into someone and so more fully understand him. The word has subsequently come to mean little more than 'appreciative understanding'.

synchrocyclotron see **cyclotron**

synchrotron see **cyclotron**

synonym see **homonym**

synopsis see **summary**

syrup see **treacle**

systems analyst see **computer programmer**

T

tablet see **pill**

tack see **track** (line of motion)

tact/diplomacy (ability to avoid offending others)
'Tact' suggests a delicate or sensitive touch (which is what the word literally means) in the handling of a situation where it is important not to offend or hurt. It usually implies, too, a personal wish not to offend. 'Diplomacy', which may or may not be personally motivated, suggests a skill in handling delicate matters, often in order to attain one's own ends without any complications or unpleasantness. A professionally diplomatic person is of course a diplomat, who originally held a diploma, or letter of recommendation that once was (literally) folded double (Greek *diploma*) – itself something of a diplomatic gesture.

tactics see **strategy** (science of warfare)

taiga see **tundra**

tale see **legend**

talisman see **charm**

tally-ho/so-ho (hunting call or cry)
Both words are a 'view-halloo' to indicate that the beast has been sighted and to urge riders (or followers) and hounds to pursue it. 'Tally-ho' is or was used in fox hunting (although in its original French *taïaut* it was used in deer hunting), while 'so-ho' is used in hare hunting. The latter cry is said to have given the name of London's district of Soho, which until comparatively recently had fields where the huntsman's cry could be frequently heard.

talon see **claw**

tamper see **tinker**

Tang see **Ming**

tangent see **angle**

tangerine/mandarin/satsuma (type of small orange)
'Tangerines' and 'mandarins' are very alike: they are both small, flat, loose-skinned (and relatively thin-skinned) and a deep orange-yellow in colour. 'Tangerines', however, usually have pips, while 'mandarins' – which is also the name for the canned variety – are seedless. 'Satsumas' are a type of 'mandarin', with the name being a commercially preferable one for the fruit, no doubt because it is more exotic. The names are geographical ones: 'tangerines' originally came from Tangier, 'mandarins' from China, where their colour resembled that of the robes of the Chinese officials called mandarins, and 'satsumas' originally came from Japan, where the word is the name of a former province, also famous for its cream–coloured pottery.

tango/conga/rumba/samba/mambo (Latin-American dance)
The 'tango' is the ballroom dance of Argentine origin with varied steps, figures and poses that became all the rage in fashionable European circles before the First World War. Its music has a characteristic four beats to the bar rhythm, with the first beat strongly accented. The 'conga' is essentially the street dance, of Afro-Cuban origin, that became popular in America and subsequently Britain from the late 1930s. It is performed by a single column of people, each clasping the waist of the person in front, with a 'three-steps-forward-*kick*' progression. There is a slightly jerkier ballroom version. The 'rumba', also of Afro-Cuban origin, is danced with a basic pattern of two quick side steps followed by a slow forward step and is best known for the horizontal 'hip wiggle' of the dancers. The 'samba' is of Brazilian origin, and caught on in western Europe and the USA in the 1940s. It is danced to a four beats to the bar rhythm with a simple forward and backward step and tilting, rocking body movements. The 'mambo' is in effect an offbeat version of the 'rumba', with the slow forward step held through to the first beat

of the following bar and dancers not in standard ballroom embrace but holding one hand only or not touching at all. The cha-cha-cha of the 1950s was a development of it.

tapioca see **semolina**

tar/pitch/bitumen/asphalt (black viscous substance used for surfacing)
'Tar', properly, is the dark, inflammable liquid obtained from the dry distillation of wood, coal or other fuel, and is used for preserving timber and iron and as an antiseptic, for example. Road 'tar' is actually 'pitch', which is in turn obtained from the distillation of 'tar', so that in road construction road 'tar' is used for sealing the wearing surface, which in many cases is constructed from 'tar' macadam (tarmac), a form of macadam or broken stone (as used originally by the civil engineer John McAdam) coated with 'tar'. A binder used for the surface layer of a road is 'bitumen', which is a tarlike hydrocarbon derived from petroleum, and also used is 'asphalt', which is a mixture of 'bitumen' and crushed rocks. 'Asphalt' is also used for roofing and in some paints, while in house construction it provides a protection against rising damp. All four words tend to be used loosely, however, to apply to a range of substances, both natural and artificial, in pure form or in combination, and the meaning will thus vary according to the context.

tarsus/metatarsus/metacarpus/carpus (group of bones in the hand or foot)
The 'tarsus' is a collection of bones in the foot between the **tibia** and the 'metatarsus', which is comprised of five longish bones between the 'tarsus' and the toes. The arrangement of the 'metacarpus' *vis-à-vis* the 'carpus' in the hand is similar: the 'carpus' consists of eight bones that comprise the wrist, and the 'metacarpus' is the group of bones between the wrist and the fingers. 'Meta-' in each case means 'beyond'.

tart/pie/flan/pasty (dish of baked pastry containing fruit or meat)
A 'tart' usually contains fruit or at any rate something sweet, as an apple 'tart' or a treacle 'tart', or it is often small, with no top crust (as once was always the case), as a jam 'tart' or a custard 'tart'. A 'pie' usually contains meat or something savoury, as a pork 'pie' or a fish 'pie'. It is normally enclosed, as earlier it always was. Hence the difference between an apple 'tart' (open) and an apple 'pie' (enclosed). Compare, too, a mince 'pie' – not savoury, but enclosed. A custard 'pie', of course, is not intended for the table. It may start off as an edible 'pie', with flour and eggs, but finishes up with shaving cream or something equally inedible that simulates custard and is suitable for facial application. A 'flan' is usually open, with fruit – as opposed to a pasty, which is enclosed, with meat. Very often, though, it is simply a pastry or sponge cake filled or spread with jam, fruit, cheese, or anything tasty and cookable. A 'pasty' is a chunky 'folded' 'pie', usually an individual one containing something savoury, such as meat or vegetables. A well-known type is the 'Cornish pasty', which is a pastry case filled with cooked minced meat and chopped vegetables, such as potato, cabbage and carrot, and eaten hot or cold. There are also sweet 'pasties', however, especially ones containing fruit, such as an apple 'pasty'. See also **steak and kidney pie** and **pastry**.

tartan/plaid (characteristic cloth and pattern of Scottish dress)
'Tartan' is the name for the cloth, with stripes of different colours and widths at right angles to one another, that is used for the distinctive items of Scottish dress, especially the 'plaid' and the kilt. The cloth's design differs according to the clan that wears it. In this sense, the 'plaid' is the long, rectangular piece of cloth with such a design that Highlanders wear round their shoulders. 'Tartan' is thus not only the cloth but the design on it (so that a 'plaid' is made of 'tartan' and has a 'tartan' pattern). However, both words are loosely used interchangeably, so that 'tartan' can mean any chequered pattern (not necessarily the design of a Scottish clan), and 'plaid' can mean any chequered fabric (with a 'tartan' design). Such casual usage and even abusage is deplored by dyed-in-the-wool Scots, who are sticklers for the correct form.

tax/duty (levy enforceable by law)
'Tax' is a levy on such things as income (income 'tax'), property (wealth 'tax'), goods purchased or services rendered (value added 'tax', or VAT), or gifts made (capital transfer 'tax'). 'Duty' is a levy on such things as import or export (customs 'duty', excise 'duty'), the transference of property (death 'duty', probate 'duty'), and the legal recognition of deeds and documents (various types of 'duty'). 'Tax' is undoubtedly the kind of levy that concerns the general public more, with 'duty' applying to business and commerce in many cases, or chargeable in specific instances. If there is any discernible or significant difference, it is that 'tax' tends to be levied on actual objects (income, property, goods, gifts), and 'duty' on an action or process of some kind (importing, exporting, selling, manufacturing, attesting).

teacher training college/college of education/institute of education (higher educational establishment for the training of teachers)
'Teacher training colleges', or just 'training colleges', are now officially known by the less precise title of 'colleges of education'. They were establishments where, at any rate to 1975, teachers were trained, on a three-year course, to teach in primary schools. In 1975, however, the system of teacher training began to be radically reorganised. Many 'colleges of education' have now merged with each other or been integrated with the rest of higher education with training places concentrated in polytechnics, colleges of higher education and universities. The whole change is because of a general move towards a graduate profession, that is, teachers with degrees in education, not diplomas. 'Institutes of education' are something quite different. They are establishments within a university which supervise and co-ordinate the academic work of the 'colleges of education' in a particular area, at the same time approving syllabuses and conducting examinations. They are closely linked with the faculty or department of education attached to the university which trains graduates as teachers.

technical college/polytechnic/college of advanced technology (specialised further education establishment)
A 'technical college' or 'tech' is an establishment specialising in technical subjects such as mechanical engineering with the aim of preparing its students for industry. 'Polytechnics' provide all types of courses (full, part-time and 'sandwich') in a wide range of subjects at all levels. They complement universities and colleges of education in this respect. The present 'polys' are those that have been formed since 1967 from either 'technical colleges' or colleges of technology. The 'colleges of advanced technology' ('CATS') were set up in 1956. They originally were ordinary 'technical colleges' chosen to concentrate on advanced work. In 1965 they were elevated to university status.

teeter see **totter**

temerity/timidity (state sometimes caused by fear)
'Temerity' is a reckless boldness, a foolhardiness, which may or may not be engendered by fear. 'He had the temerity to tell me I drove too fast.' 'Timidity', seen by comparison with 'temerity', is either fear itself or shyness, and the more common of the two. Possibly the confusion springs not only from the resemblance of the words to each other but also from the tendency of frightened people to perform rash acts. There is no common adjective for 'temerity' – a bookish word 'temerarious' exists – but 'timidity', of course, has '**timid**'.

tempest see **storm**

tenacity see **persistence**

tendency see **trend**

tenor/baritone (male singing voice)
The 'tenor' is the high natural male voice, although there is in fact a higher one, the countertenor (see **treble**). The range of a 'tenor' is roughly from the A below middle C to the A above. The 'baritone', until quite recently spelled 'barytone', is the next lowest male voice, intermediate between 'tenor' and bass and having a range

approximately a third lower than a 'tenor'. Of all male singing voices, the 'tenor' is the rarest and the 'baritone' the most common. (It derives from the Greek for 'heavy tone', the 'bari-' being as in 'barometer', which measures atmospheric pressure or 'heaviness'.)

tense/terse (brief)

'Tense', literally 'drawn taut', means 'characterised by strain', as a 'tense' moment or 'tense' anxiety. To say something in a 'tense' manner or voice might well be to say it abruptly or snappily. 'Terse' has the basic meaning 'brief and pithy' but, similarly, a 'terse' remark could easily be one made at a 'tense' moment.

tenuto see **sostenuto**

tepid/insipid/vapid (lacking warmth, interest or flavour)

The confusion lies not in the basic meanings, as respectively given in the 'common factor' definition, but in the extended uses of the words. A 'tepid' remark, for example, would be one made without enthusiasm, while an 'insipid' remark would be an uninteresting one and a 'vapid' remark a dull – in fact 'insipid' – one. A possible further influence, especially on 'vapid', is 'sapid', which actually means the opposite of 'vapid', i.e. 'having flavour'.

terse see **tense**

Terylene see **poplin**

test see **trial**

testify/attest (bear witness)

The words are close in meaning. 'Testify', however, is more simply 'give evidence', while 'attest' is 'affirm that something is true', i.e. something previously mentioned or known about. Thus one witness can 'testify' that he left the door locked, and another can 'attest' that this was the case since he had been with him at the time.

testy see **touchy**

tetchy see **touchy**

theft/larceny/robbery/burglary (crime of stealing)

According to the Theft Act, 1968, a person is guilty of 'theft' if he 'dishonestly appropriates property belonging to another with the intention of permanently depriving the other of it'; that is, it is immaterial whether taking the property is for one's own gain or benefit or not. This same act repealed the Larceny Acts of 1861 and 1916, in which 'larceny' had to involve so-called 'asportation', that is the 'carrying away' of property with the intent of stealing. Since 1968, therefore, 'larceny' has not legally existed. 'Robbery' is basically stealing with force, actual or threatened. 'Burglary', once the crime of housebreaking at night (i.e. between 9 p.m. and 6 a.m.), has also been redefined by the recent Theft Act. The Act has eliminated the 'breaking' element of 'breaking and entering' with intent to commit a felony or of 'breaking' out of a house after a felony, and has abolished the night v. day distinction. 'Burglary' now is entering any building or part of a building as a trespasser with intent to commit certain offences (such as stealing, or inflicting grievous bodily harm) or, having entered, committing or attempting to commit such offences. 'Aggravated' 'burglary' involves a firearm – even an imitation one – or any weapon of offence, or explosives.

theist see **deist**

theme see **subject**

theory/hypothesis (untested idea or opinion)

A 'theory' is an explanation of something that has become more or less established or accepted as accounting for known facts or phenomena, as Einstein's 'theory' of relativity or the Darwinian 'theory' of evolution. A 'hypothesis' is a conjecture of supposition made in order to explain facts or phenomena – a starting point, in fact, or basis, by which the truth may be reached. Avogadro's 'hypothesis', that equal volumes of gases under the same conditions of temperature and pressure contain equal numbers of molecules, was first made in 1811. It was generally accepted after 1858, so that today it is more generally known as

Avogadro's law. The two terms are therefore really opposite in meaning – respectively facts demanding an explanation, and an explanation leading to the facts – although loosely they are both used to mean 'view' or 'idea': 'I have a "theory" about that', 'Yes, but that's only a "hypothesis".'

thesis see **treatise**

thorn see **spine**

three feet square see **three square feet**

three square feet/three feet square
(measurements of an area)
'Square' units of measurements are used to express the total area of any surface, whether the figure measured is itself 'square' or not (so that a circle can have its area expressed in 'square inches', say). 'Three' (for example) 'square feet' thus expresses the area of a surface of a figure of any shape, such as a table runner three feet long and one foot wide. 'Three feet square', however, is a surface measurement of a 'square' figure three feet by three feet, in other words nine 'square feet'. The two terms are sometimes confused, either because the numerical expression 3 ft^2 is taken to be the same as 3 sq. ft, or because the distinction is wrongly taken to be between 'square' and cubic measures. (See **weight**.)

thrilled/enthralled (highly delighted)
To be 'thrilled' by someone's performance is to be very excited or stirred by it. To be 'enthralled' by someone's performance is to be captivated or spellbound by it, literally 'held in thrall' or 'held captive'. Put another way, to be 'enthralled' is to be so 'thrilled' that one is unaware of anything else.

thymus see **thyroid**

thyroid/thymus (gland in the neck)
The 'thyroid' is the large ductless gland that lies near the larynx and trachea and secretes a hormone that regulates growth and development through the rate of metabolism. The 'thymus', also ductless, is situated at the level of the heart near the base of the neck and in man becomes much smaller with the

three square feet (for example)

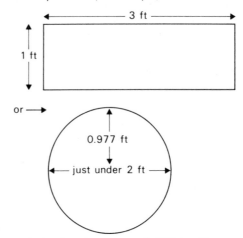

or

a circle of radius approx. 0.977 ft will have an area of 3 sq. ft

three feet square (only possibility)

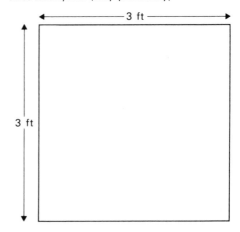

approach of puberty, continuing to shrink with increasing age. Its functions relate chiefly to the newborn, in particular with regard to the production of lymphocytes. The names of the glands indicate their shape: the 'thyroid', from Greek *thureos*, is shield-shaped; the 'thymus' has a shape resembling that of a thyme leaf.

tiara see **crown**

tibia/fibula (bone in lower half of the leg)
The 'tibia' is the shinbone, the inner of the

two bones of the leg that extend from the knee to the ankle. The 'fibula' is the other, outer and thinner of the two. A kick or dig on the shinbone is more likely, in fact, to be a kick on the 'fibula'.

tiddler see **minnow**

tied house see **free house**

tile/slate (thin slab used for covering roofs)
A 'tile', traditionally coloured red, is made of baked clay. A 'slate' is a plate of fine-grained grey, green or bluish-purple rock that can be easily split. 'On the "slate"' is a characteristically British way of saying that a debt has been recorded ('I always go to this pub as they have a "slate"', an English host once said to a mystified American guest); to be 'on the "tiles"' is to be out on a spree, even a debauch. So doubtless one could have a night out on the 'tiles' on a 'slate', if one knew the right hostelry. Such are the delights of the English language.

tiller see **rudder**

timid/timorous (shy, easily frightened)
The words are from the same Latin root, *timere* (to fear), but there is a slight but distinct difference. 'Timorous' has a connotation of 'shrinking back', 'hesitating because afraid', as a 'timorous' remark, one made nervously and apprehensively. A 'timid' remark is simply a shy *or* frightened one. For more about 'timid' see **temerity.**

timidity see **temerity**

timorous see **timid**

tinged/tinted (slightly or lightly coloured)
'Tinged' means 'with a trace or slight degree of colour', as an evening sky 'tinged' with pink. 'Tinted' means 'with a delicate or pale colour', as 'tinted' glasses (delicately darkened) or 'tinted' lines (faint or feint ones). However, 'tint' also means just 'shade', 'hue', as the 'tints' of autumn, with no special suggestion of delicacy and certainly no implication of paleness. Used figuratively, both words mean 'shaded', 'coloured', 'slightly having', as a voice

'tinged' with regret, although 'tinted' is, for some reason, rarely used in a non-literal sense.

tinker/tamper (botch, spoil by poor workmanship)
To 'tinker' with something is to work on it unskilfully or clumsily or at any rate amateurishly, as when one 'tinkers' with the car or a radio. The word is related to 'tinker', the mender of pots and pans who was originally, according to one theory, a worker in tin. To 'tamper' with a thing is to meddle with it deliberately so as to alter or damage it, as someone who 'tampers' with a lock or the works of a clock. The verb is a variation of 'temper'.

tinted see **tinged**

tiredness/weariness/fatigue (feeling of having used up one's strength or energy)
'Tiredness' is the fairly normal sensation experienced by someone at the end of a full or busy day, when a good proportion of one's mental or physical resources has been used up and one feels ready to rest or sleep. 'Weariness' implies a prolonged sensation of 'tiredness', so that one's strength has been worn out and one is constantly 'below par' and listless. 'Fatigue' is not so much prolonged 'tiredness' as an excessive degree of it, so that one is 'done in' and must immediately stop and rest (and probably sleep).

titillate/titivate (touch up)
To 'titillate' is literally to excite a tingling or itching sensation by touching or stroking lightly, and, figuratively, to excite pleasantly – in both senses 'tickle', in fact (although 'tickle' does not always have the implication of a deliberate excitation). To 'titivate', sometimes spelt 'tittivate', is a colloquial word meaning 'smarten up', 'make spruce'. The verb is not used figuratively. It seems to derive from 'tidy' with a modelling on some word like 'cultivate'. 'Titillate' comes from the Latin word of the same meaning.

titivate see **titillate**

titter see **giggle**

TNT see **dynamite**

toad see **frog**

to-do/ado (fuss)
'What a to-do!' The word implies fuss and excitement, pleasant or unpleasant. It derives from the phrase 'What's to do?' meaning 'What's the matter?' 'Ado' used also to mean 'fuss' but now has the meaning of 'activity' or 'doing', as in the phrase 'without further ado'. Shakespeare's *Much Ado . . .* has the old sense of 'noisy fuss', with 'much ado' itself a northcountry phrase meaning originally 'much to do'.

tolbooth see **tollbooth**

tolerance/toleration (degree of allowing something of which one does not approve)
'Tolerance' suggests a lenient or charitable attitude, as towards the expression of some kind of minority right of which one does not really approve. 'Toleration' implies allowing or bearing something that one does not agree with or approve of, as a 'toleration' of loud music or (by a non-smoker) of someone smoking in a non-smoking compartment of a train.

toleration see **tolerance**

tollbooth/tolbooth (place where payment is made or exacted)
Both words can be used identically (with 'tollbooth' also spelt as two words) to mean the 'booth' or collection point where tolls have to be paid on a road, usually at the approach to a bridge. A 'tolbooth', however, is properly a Scots term for a townhall or guildhall or even a prison (which would originally have been under the townhall). One of Edinburgh's most interesting buildings is the Canongate 'Tolbooth' (in the 'Royal Mile'), dating from the late sixteenth century, with its turreted towers and projecting clock. The name literally means 'tax stall' in both cases, with the 'townhall' sense developing out of the earlier custom house where various payments were exacted.

tomb see **grave**

Tony see **Emmy**

topic see **subject**

toreador see **matador**

tornado see **whirlwind**

torpor see **stupor**

torrid see **rigid**

torso see (1)**sculpture**, (2) **trunk**

tortuous/torturous (painful, twisting)
'Tortuous' means 'full of twists and turns or bends' as a 'tortuous' road or a 'tortuous' argument (a complex and involved one). 'Torturous' means 'characterised by torture', as a 'torturous' ordeal. In many cases what is 'tortuous' will also be 'torturous', as 'tortuous' exercises or a 'tortuous' journey.

torturous see **tortuous**

totter/teeter (sway or rock, balance unsteadily)
To 'totter' is to walk with faltering steps, as if very weak and about to fall, or to sway or rock unsteadily – also as if about to fall. 'Teeter', a variation of 'titter', itself a dialect form of 'totter', is a word more common in American English to mean 'move or sway from side to side or up and down', not necessarily with a suggestion of being about to fall. (A specific American meaning of the verb is 'seesaw', so that children go to a playground to 'teeter'.) Both verbs are often used figuratively.

touchy/tetchy/testy (irritable)
A 'touchy' person is one apt or quick to take offence on only slight provocation: 'He's very touchy about his pay'. The word is a variant, by association with 'touch', of 'tetchy', which basically means 'irritable' or 'crochety', as a 'tetchy' old man or a 'tetchy' answer. 'Testy' has the implication of being impatient as well as 'tetchy' or crusty. A 'testy' reply is a hot, angry and intolerant one. The verb has its origin in Old French *testif* (heady, headstrong) from *teste* (modern *tête*) (head).

tower/turret (high structure on top of a building)
A 'tower' can be either a complete building, as the 'Tower' of London, or a high structure *on* a building as the square 'tower' of a church or the round 'tower' of a castle. A 'turret' is a small 'tower' (a 'tower-ette'), which can either rise from the ground or project from a wall, especially at the corner of a main building such as a castle. 'Turret' is also the word for the revolving armoured 'tower' housing a gun and the gunners on a ship, or in an aircraft or tank.

town/city (sizeable populated area)
A 'city' is generally larger and more important or older than a 'town'. More precisely, it is a 'town' that has been created a 'city' by charter, and especially one with a cathedral. In the USA a 'city' is a municipal corporation occupying a clearly defined area. It may have a smallish population (just as an American village may have a sizeable one), so the number of inhabitants only is no guide to the status of a place, as it is in Britain. London, a 'city' if ever there was one, itself contains the 'City' – its business and commercial centre, governed by the Lord Mayor and Corporation.

track/pan/zoom (movement of a film or television camera)
A 'track' is made by a camera in any direction, as forwards or sideways, when in operation, the whole camera moving bodily together with the cameraman. (It very often does this actually on tracks.) A 'pan' – derived from 'panorama' – is a movement of the camera in such a way that a moving person or object is kept constantly in view, especially by swinging the camera horizontally. A 'zoom' is made – with a 'zoom' lens – so as to make a person or object seem either to approach (at the same time growing in size) or to recede (diminishing in size).

track/tack/trail (line of motion or direction)
A 'track', is a line of travel or motion, as marked by, say, a road, path or 'trail'. If you are 'on the wrong track' you are (figuratively) moving in the wrong direction. A 'tack' relates to ships and is either the direction or course of a ship in relation to the position of her sails, as the starboard 'tack', or one of a series of straight runs made by the ship on a zigzag course into the wind. This second sense has given the phrase 'on the wrong (right) tack', where one's course of action or conduct is right or wrong – and differs noticeably from the preceding one. A 'trail' is a path or 'track' made usually by men or animals, especially one across wild country or as followed by a hunter. It is the 'hunting' sense that lies behind 'on the right (wrong) trail' or simply 'on the trail', with the actual objective possibly more in mind than 'on the right (wrong) track' where what is important is the course itself.

trade see **occupation**

trail see **track** (line of motion)

train see **suite**

traitorous see **treacherous**

tramp/vamp (seductive woman)
'The lady is a tramp', as Lorenz Hart immortalised her in *Pal Joey* (1937). As applied to a female, 'tramp' has greater currency in the USA than in Britain. It means 'prostitute', or at the least 'dissolute woman'. (The word would not be readily taken to mean 'vagabond', since in the USA a 'tramp' in this sense is usually called a 'hobo' or a 'bum'.) A 'vamp' is a woman who uses her charms to seduce and exploit men. The word is a shortened form of 'vampire', and dates from 1918, liberation year.

transient see **transitional**

transitional/transitory/transient (passing, short-lived)
'Transitional' means 'passing from one position, state or stage to another', 'intermediate', as a 'transitional' phase of government. The stage itself may be quite lengthy. 'Transitory' means 'lasting only a short time', as 'this transitory life'. 'Transient' means 'passing, and therefore short-lived', as the 'transient' beauty of spring or a 'transient' smile.

transitory see **transitional**

trap/pitfall/snare (device for catching animals or humans)
A 'trap', strictly speaking, has a spring, as a 'mousetrap' or a 'mantrap'. A 'pitfall', rather obviously, has a pit for the prey to fall into. A 'snare' is a device for entangling birds, rabbits or other unwary creatures in order to capture them. Literally, the contrivances are not difficult to distinguish. Figuratively, however, they must be applied more precisely. A 'trap' is usually a scheme planned by one person to catch another, as a 'trap' for the unwary or the 'trap' you nearly fell into when you said that. The latter would not be a 'pitfall' in the metaphorical sense, since this is a concealed danger, error, or source of disaster or 'downfall', as a newspaper editorial that avoids the usual 'pitfalls' (the usual errors). A 'snare' is similar, but figuratively suggests enticement or inveiglement or temptation. 'Kingdoms are but cares, State is devoid of stay; Riches are ready snares, And hasten to decay,' wrote Henry VI in the fifteenth century.

treacherous/traitorous (betraying)
'Treacherous' relates to 'treachery', of course, and 'traitorous' to 'traitor', who is a 'treacherous' person. The difference is a fine one: 'treacherous' implies the abstract quality of 'treachery', as a 'treacherous' action (one that betrays) or 'treacherous' ice (liable to break under pressure); 'traitorous' suggests the personal act of one who betrays or commits treason, 'traitor-like', and therefore can apply only to a person or to a deed, manner, attribute etc. of a person, as a 'traitorous' thought or a 'traitorous' letter. Rather surprisingly, the words are not related in origin. 'Treacherous' (and 'treachery') derive from Old French *trechier* (modern *tricher*) (to trick); 'traitorous' (and 'traitor' and 'treason') come from Latin *traditor* (betrayer), which, also a little unexpectedly, gives 'tradition', the common theme being the 'handing over.'

treacle/syrup/molasses (sweet, sticky foodstuff)
All three are by-products in the process of refining sugar. 'Treacle' (called 'molasses' in the USA) is removed at the second stage of refinement. After further refinement and bleaching 'syrup', sometimes called 'golden syrup', is extracted. (Golden Syrup is a familiar trade name for a brand of this used in making cakes. Its manufacturers define it as 'partially inverted refiners' "syrup"'.) 'Molasses' (in the USA, 'treacle') is what is removed at the *first* stage in the process of refining sugar. The kind used for human food comes from cane sugar; the 'molasses' that is bitter and unpleasantly flavoured and used as a feed for farm animals comes from sugar beet. It can also be used to make alcohol, such as rum. 'Molasses' the word comes ultimately from Latin *mel*, 'honey'.

treatise/thesis (formal account on a particular subject)
A 'treatise' is a book or written account on some particular subject, especially one that explains it or sets out its principles as, for example, Hume's *Treatise of Human Nature*. A 'thesis' is basically a subject or proposition laid down or stated, especially one to be discussed or defended. The word is commonly used, especially academically, to apply to the dissertation itself, as 'Jane's working on her thesis on the influence of moonlight on earthworms'.

treble/soprano/alto/contralto (high singing voice)
'Treble' is traditionally applied to boys' voices and musical instruments of high pitch, as a 'treble' recorder, while 'soprano' is used of women's voices. An adult female 'treble' voice has a range approximately from middle C to 'top' A (a thirteenth above it). Lower than this is an 'alto' voice, whose range is roughly from the F below middle C to the D a ninth above it. This is in fact the lowest woman's voice, and is called a 'contralto' when applied to the voice of a female soloist or operatic singer. An 'alto' voice can also be applied to a similarly low register of a boy's voice, although of a man an 'alto' voice is an artificially high one – a falsetto – similar in range to a countertenor. (The difference here is that the countertenor is not a falsetto voice but a natural extension of the upper tenor voice.) The range of a male 'alto' is approximately the same as a female – possibly a tone or two lower. (For

notably deeper voices see **tenor**.) Usage is fairly firmly established, therefore, although the words themselves are unusual. 'Soprano' comes from Italian 'above', since the 'soprano' voice is the highest. 'Treble' is something of a mystery. Three of what? Singing in thirds, or a voice pitched a third above another? The origin is not too clear. Perhaps once boys sang what was the third part, that is, the higher notes. In fact 'soprano' can also apply to a boy's voice as well as to a woman's although this use is now somewhat dated, as 'Ernest Lough, the boy "soprano"', who with 'O, for the wings of a dove' tugged at the heart-strings of thousands in the 1930s. 'Alto', paradoxically, comes from the Italian for 'high', since the reference is not to the female voice but the male. The term 'contralto' derives from fifteenth-century Latin *contratenor altus*, indicating a voice that is predominantly above the tenor. The two words were subsequently blended, in the Italian form, as *contr'alto*.

trend/tendency (drift in a particular direction)
'Trend' is the general word to apply to an actual drift of some kind, a gradual moving towards, as the increasing 'trend' towards football hooliganism. A 'tendency' is an inclination or disposition to move, proceed or act in some direction or in a particular way, as the increasing 'tendency' towards football hooliganism, i.e. the likelihood, but not certainty, that football hooliganism will increase.

trial/test (attempt to ascertain or establish something)
'Trial' basically indicates trying, as international horse 'trials', where horse and rider try to give of their best, or a piece of equipment available for ten days' free 'trial', to enable a would-be purchaser to see how it works and whether it is what he needs – by trying it out. A 'test' is a more demanding thing: a 'trial' under approved or fixed conditions, or a final 'trial' after a series of experiments. A 'test' pilot thus flies, and subjects to various tests, an aircraft that previously may have undergone a series of 'trials' on the ground only. 'Trial', indeed, often indicates an initial try-out, and 'test' a final one: compare a 'trial' run and a 'test' run in a car.

trip/journey/voyage (course of travel)
A 'trip' nearly always implies 'there and back', whether on foot or by transport, for business or pleasure, short or long, hurried or leisurely. A 'journey' is a longish 'trip', usually by land or air rather than sea, but not necessarily with the 'there and back' idea as a 'journey' by train to Scotland or by air to New York. 'Voyage' primarily suggests travel by sea, and moreover for pleasure, as a cruise. This means that a 'voyage' is normally relatively long in time or distance, with no idea at all of the return section of the travel.

triumphal see **triumphant**

triumphant/triumphal (celebrating a victory or success)
'Triumphant' means 'having triumphed', as a 'triumphant' gesture or look. 'Triumphal' means 'pertaining to a triumph', as a 'triumphal' procession or speech. Whether something that is 'triumphal' is also 'triumphant' will depend on the manner of its performance: a 'triumphal' speech could be a dull and boring one, but if made exultantly it would also be 'triumphant'.

troop/troupe (band, company)
Two standard confusibles, but ones that still turn up fairly often. 'Troop' is the more general word, so that one has a 'troop' of soldiers or scouts, or of animals such as monkeys or giraffes. 'Troupe' is more specialised, and usually confined to performers such as actors, singers and acrobats. 'Troupe' came into English from French (for 'troop') in the first half of the nineteenth century.

troop (military formation) see **corps**

tropopause see **atmosphere**

troposphere see **atmosphere**

trot/canter/gallop (gait or pace of a horse)
A horse's slowest pace, at an average of four and a half miles an hour, is a walk. It is a four-beat gait, with legs moving in the order (for example) near (i.e. left) hind, near fore, off (right) hind, off fore. The 'trot' is the next fastest pace, but a two-beat gait, in which the animal lifts each diagonal pair of

legs alternately – near fore and off hind almost simultaneously, followed by off fore and near hind. This means that at times, noticeably at a fast 'trot', the horse will be altogether off the ground. The next fastest pace is the 'canter', whose name is popularly thought to come from 'Canterbury', since it was the pace adopted by medieval pilgrims as they rode to Canterbury Cathedral to pay homage at the tomb of St Thomas à Becket. (Another version traces the word back to Latin *cantherius,* meaning 'gelding' or 'riding-nag'.) This is a three-beat gait, with first the near hind, off hind, and near fore on the ground practically together, then the off fore on its own, and the final beat being the complete suspension of the animal in the air. A 'gallop' is a fast 'canter' – around thirty miles an hour – so that all four feet are off the ground in each stride, and the horse really makes a series of low leaps.

troubadour see **minstrel**

troupe see **troop** (band, company)

trousers/pants/slacks (garment for lower half of body)
'Trousers' are always an outer garment or an only one (as pyjama 'trousers'). They come in a variety of shapes and sizes, such as short 'trousers' ('shorts') and long men's and women's. 'Pants' is chiefly an American word for what in Britain are 'trousers' or 'slacks'. The term has a certain circulation, however, in spite of the fact that it also means 'underpants' – for which the preferred American word is 'drawers'. (Those anxious to further Anglo-American relations must take care not to get their knickers in a semantic twist). 'Slacks', which can look quite smart and stylish, in spite of being designed for 'slack' or casual wear, are either a male garment, especially for sport, or, more commonly, a female one, although a 'trouser' suit – not a 'slack' suit – is an exclusively feminine affair.

truism see **commonplace**

trunk/torso (upper half of human body)
In spite of 'trunks', as for swimming, your 'trunk' is your whole body apart from your head, arms and legs. A 'torso' is usually the word for the 'trunk' of a human statue (see **sculpture**), but can also be used of a person, often with reference to an idealised or statue-like body: 'He much admired his rippling torso.' A 'trunk', too, can be used of the body of an animal, but with care, of course, when the animal happens to be an elephant.

trunk road see **motorway**

tumid see **rigid**

tumult/turmoil (commotion, disturbance)
A 'tumult' is almost always a noisy affair; a 'turmoil' is a state of disorder or agitation or disquiet, not necessarily a noisy one. Moreover, 'tumult', except in the sense 'mental disturbance', implies a large multitude of people or things, whereas a 'turmoil' is basically just 'agitation', 'confusion'. The etymology of the word is not certain: even *Webster,* who usually comes up with something, has to admit 'origin unknown'.

tundra/taiga (vast stretch of land in the Arctic regions of Europe and Asia)
Both words are chiefly associated with Russia. The 'tundra' is one of a number of treeless plains in the Arctic where permafrost conditions prevail. The 'taiga', by contrast, is a large, coniferous, evergreen forest in the sub-Arctic, especially in Siberia, where it lies between the 'tundra' and the steppe.

tune/melody (series of notes that 'make sense' in music)
The two terms mean almost the same, although 'tune' is quite often used for the upper part in a piece of music, together with an accompaniment, while 'melody' is a more technical word in musical theory, seen as distinct from harmony, rhythm, and so on. Subjectively, a 'melody' is a more poetic and meaningful thing, while 'tune' frequently applies to a rather trivial or superficial line of music. Hence such phrases – which bring out the difference – as 'a haunting "melody"', but 'whistling a happy "tune"'. But although several girls are called 'Melody' – even the name itself is melodious – is there any girl named Tune?

turbid see **rigid**

turf/peat (type of fuel found in boggy soil)
'Peat' is the basic substance, that is, the combustible soil that consists of partially decomposed vegetable matter as found characteristically in bogs, typically in Ireland – where a piece of it is called a 'turf'. (In Scotland a piece of 'peat' is simply called 'a peat'.) 'Turf' also, of course, means a grass covering in general with *the* 'turf' meaning a race course, and a piece of such grass, as used for laying a lawn, for example, is *a* 'turf'. An alternative word for 'turf' in this last sense, but one which is usually avoided because of its undesirable connotations, is 'sod'.

turgid see **rigid**

turmoil see **tumult**

turner see **carpenter**

turnip/swede/parsnip (root vegetable)
All three tend to be something of an unfavourite with children, who may or may not acquire a taste for them in adult life. The 'turnip' and the 'swede' both belong to the genus *Brassica*, which also includes such non-root vegetables as the garden (and common) cabbage and the more exotic kohlrabi. The 'turnip' has a fleshy globular or elongated white-coloured root, while the 'swede' – strictly speaking, part stem and part root – is similar, although somewhat larger, but with white flesh or yellow. (If the latter, it is known as rutabaga.) The 'parsnip' has a longish carrot-type root which is pale yellow in colour. In spite of their unattractive taste, the vegetables have rather interesting names. The 'turnip' was formerly a 'neep', as it still is in Scottish parlance – compare the traditional Burns Night dish of haggis and 'bashed tatties and neeps' (mashed potatoes and 'turnips') – with the 'tur-', however, something of a mystery. The 'swede' really does – or did – come from Sweden, and is properly a Swedish 'turnip'. It was brought from Sweden to Scotland in the eighteenth century (1781–2, to be exact). The 'parsnip' was originally a 'pasnep' but the 'nep' became 'nip' by association with 'turnip'.

The word ultimately derives from Latin *pastinum*, 'dibble' (a two-pronged fork for planting and digging).

turret see **tower**

twat see **twerp**

tweeter see **woofer**

tweezers see **forceps**

twerp/twit/twat (contemptible person)
The terms of abuse are in ascending order of strength. 'Twerp' (or 'twirp') is used to apply to a stupid, objectionable or merely insignificant person: 'silly little twerp!'. 'Twit', often preceded by an adjective such as 'stupid' or 'silly', applies to a foolish or, again, insignificant person. 'Twat' is a far stronger word, although often used by speakers who are not aware of its basic meaning – 'female genitals'. It can be applied, as and if desired, to both males and females. The four-letter word has caused trouble in the past. It appears in its basic sense in the seventeenth century *Vanity of Vanities:*

> His ambition is getting a Cardinal's hat;
> They'd send him as soon an old nun's twat.

This is said to have led Browning to believe that a 'twat' was an article of religious clothing, hence the lines near the end of *Pippa Passes:*

> Then, owls and bats,
> Cowls and twats,
> Monks and nuns, in a cloister's moods
> Adjourn to the oak-stump pantry!

twilight see **dusk**

twit see **twerp**

type I error/type II error (type of error in statistics)
A 'type I error' is a 'rejection of the null hypothesis in statistical testing when it is true'. A 'type II error' is an 'acceptance of the null hypothesis in statistical testing when it is false'. (Both definitions as given in *9,000 Words: A Supplement to Webster's Third*

New International Dictionary, 1983.) It is of course *very* important to distinguish between these.

type II error see **type I error**

typhoid/typhus (acute infectious disease)
'Typhoid' is an infectious, often fatal disease occurring usually in the summer months, with intestinal inflammation and ulceration. It is caused by the 'typhoid' – literally 'typhus-like' – bacillus, introduced with food or drink. 'Typhus' itself is characterised by great prostration and fever with the eruption of purple spots, and is regarded as due to micro-organisms transmitted by lice and fleas. The names derive from Greek *typhos* (smoke, vapour, stupor).

typhoon see **whirlwind**

typhus see **typhoid**

U

UHF see **high frequency**

ukelele see **guitar**

ultra-violet rays see **X-rays**

umber see **amber**

umlaut/ablaut (German term indicating a vowel change)
The 'umlaut', – in German literally 'about sound' – is a change in the pronunciation of a vowel indicated by the addition of two dots over it, or this sign itself. Many German nouns add an 'umlaut' when forming the plural, as *Bruder* (brother), *Brüder* (brothers), or *Kopf* (head), *Köpfe*

(heads). A word with an 'umlaut' may also have a meaning different from the same word without it, as *schön* (beautiful) and *schon* (already). An 'ablaut' – literally 'off sound' – is a term applied to a vowel change in the different forms of a verb (in any language, but especially German and English), as: 'sing, sang, sung'.

umpire see **referee**

unapt see **inept**

unconsciously/subconsciously (without being aware)
'I did it unconsciously' means, loosely, 'I did it without realising I *was* doing it' (even though I now appreciate the fact that I did indeed do it). 'I did it subconsciously' normally means: 'I did it without realising *why* I was doing it' (but now, looking back, I think I can see why I did). Literally, of course, 'unconsciously' means 'without being conscious'. and 'subconsciously' – 'being only dimly or vaguely conscious'. Both terms are from the language of psychology.

undercroft see **vault**

underdeveloped countries see **developing countries**

undertone/overtone (suggestion, implication)
An 'undertone' is the undercurrent of something, often something unpleasant, as in the title of Edmund Blunden's poems *Undertones of War* (1928). An 'overtone' is an additional meaning or implication, often one that is elusive, as the 'overtones' of envy in someone's reply. The term originated in literature, especially poetry, just before the First World War, when it was used to apply to what was suggested or implied by the sound or meaning of the words. 'Overtones', both real and fancied, play a significant part in the generation and currency of confusibles.

undoubted/redoubted (unrivalled)
'Undoubted' means 'undisputed' as in 'He was the undoubted victor of the contest.' 'Redoubted' means both 'dreaded', 'formidable' and 'respected', 'renowned', as an

opponent of 'redoubted' skill or the 'redoubted' champion of a cause. The derivation is from Old French *redouter* (to fear greatly). The 'b' of the word has erroneously crept into 'redoubt' (military field-work), which came to be confused with it in origin.

uninterested see **disinterested**

United Kingdom see **England**

unpracticable see **impractical**

unpractical see **impractical**

unsociable/unsocial (not fond of, or opposed to, society)
'Unsociable' means 'characterised by a disinclination for friendly social relations', as an 'unsociable' colleague. 'Unsocial' also means this, but more positively: an 'unsocial' colleague is one whose behaviour or attitude clearly expresses his dislike of social life (whereas an 'unsociable' colleague is one who grudgingly or unwillingly enters into a social relationship). Even so, 'unsocial' is not as strong as 'antisocial', which means 'hostile to the social order or social relations'. The other distinction is that 'unsocial' normally expresses a standing attitude, while 'unsociable' may define a mood of the moment.

unsocial see **unsociable**

untruth see **lie** (false statement)

uprising see **revolt**

upsilon see **epsilon**

upstage/downstage (at the front – or back – of the stage)
Rather perversely, 'upstage' is at or to the back of the stage, which at one time was higher than the front of the stage and so more prominent. So to 'upstage' someone is to steal attention from him by placing oneself in a more prominent position in some way. Conversely, 'downstage' means 'at or to the front of the stage', which today is the most prominent part of the stage as it is nearest the audience.

Urdu see **Hindu**

V1/V2 (type of German flying bomb)
The 'V1', nicknamed the 'buzz bomb' and 'doodlebug', was the pilotless aircraft or flying bomb launched against England in the Second World War by the Germans. Of the 8,000 or more launched in the period 13 June 1944 to 29 March 1945 about 2,500 landed on London. The 'V2' was not an aircraft but the first military long-range rocket or ballistic missile. It was nearly twice the length of the 'V1', but had a longer range and was nearly ten times faster than the 'V1', which flew at an average of 360 mph. Over 10,000 'V2s' were manufactured, of which about half failed to go off or exploded prematurely. A total of 4,300 were launched; of the 1,402 aimed at Britain, 517 landed on London. The 'V' stood for German *Vergeltungswaffe*, 'retaliation weapon', the retaliation being in return for British bombing raids on Germany.

V2 see **V1**

vacant/vacuous (showing lack of thought or intelligence)
'Vacant' means 'characterised by or showing lack of thought or intelligence', as a 'vacant' look or a 'vacant' smile. 'Vacuous' means 'stupidly vacant', so that a 'vacuous' look expresses a mind quite empty of ideas or intelligence.

vaccination see **inoculation**

vacuous see **vacant**

vagabond see **vagrant**

vagrant/vagabond (tramp or other homeless person)
Many tramps these days – those that still exist – like to think of themselves as 'travellers' or 'wayfarers' or something, but probably not as tramps or 'vagrants', which latter word has a connotation of disrespect-

ability or dishonesty. A 'vagabond', related to it in origin, implies a tramp who is also a permanently dishonest or thieving person – he steals to survive. The word is not used much today, although legally a 'vagabond' is a 'person who wanders about and has no dwelling' and who will become, if he commits one of a number of particular offences, a 'rogue and "vagabond"'. (The definition is that of the Vagrancy Act, 1824, still in force, which classifies 'vagrants' themselves as 'idle and disorderly persons', 'rogues and "vagabonds"' or – in charming but correct legal terminology – 'incorrigible rogues'.)

valiant/valorous/gallant (brave)
'Valiant' means 'showing bravery or valour', 'striving manfully', as a 'valiant' deed or a 'valiant' attempt (which may not be a successful one). 'Valorous' emphasises more positively the attributes of 'valour' such as boldness or firmness, so that a 'valorous' effort will probably be a successful one. 'Gallant' has the overtone of 'chivalrous', 'noble', even in its basic sense of 'brave', as a 'gallant' try or a 'gallant' effort. The pronunciation 'gallant', with the accent on the second syllable, is sometimes used for the sense 'obsequiously or amorously attentive to women'.

valorous see **valiant**

vamp see **tramp**

vampire/werewolf (human being transmogrified as a murderous beast)
At a popular level (where it best flourishes), a 'vampire' is the reanimated corpse of a person improperly buried, and as such is supposed to suck the blood of people as they sleep. 'Vampire' bats, named in their honour, do actually feed on the blood of animals – and even man, if conditions are favourable. A 'werewolf' is a more or less orthodox human male by day, but at night turns into a wolf (retaining human intelligence), and in this guise devours animals, humans or corpses – an omnivorous orgiast. Both creatures owe most of their gruesome popularity to the invention of the cinema and the art of the horror film, as do their brothers in crime, **Frankenstein** and

Dracula. The 'vampire' bequeathed its name to the 'vamp', the female exploiter and seducer of men (but not to the verb 'vamp', meaning 'improvise musical accompaniment', which derives from Old French *avantpié*, 'fore part of the foot', of all things). And as if all this wasn't enough, there is a sinister link between the two creatures, since 'werewolves', after death, are believed to turn into 'vampires'!

vanity/conceit/arrogance (undue self-pride)
'Vanity' is empty pride, the desire for admiration based on a personal achievement or attraction or quality. 'Conceit' is a heightened version of this, even an exaggerated expression of it: putting yourself over as very clever, smart, good or whatever when you're not. 'Arrogance' is an assumed superiority, an overbearing pride: setting yourself up on a higher level than other mere mortals because of your supposed superiority to them. The three are thus in increasing degrees of presumptuousness – and insufferableness.

vapid see **tepid**

varlet/varmint (rascal, rogue)
The colourfully historic words do not quite mean the same. A 'varlet' was a menial servant as well as a knight's page. Such young men were often dishonest, hence the extension of the word to mean 'knave', 'rogue'. A 'varmint' is simply a dated but not quite obsolete word for any unpleasant or obnoxious person or animal. 'Varlet' is related to 'valet', and 'varmint' to 'vermin'.

varmint see **varlet**

varnish/lacquer (preparation giving a glossy surface)
'Varnish' is a resinous solution used to apply a hard, shiny, transparent coating to a surface such as wood or metal. (Nail 'varnish' may be transparent or coloured, of course.) 'Lacquer' can be used to mean a coloured 'varnish' of shellac applied as a coating for brass, but usually the word is taken to apply to a nitrocellulose finish brushed or sprayed on a surface to form a protective film. The colour is provided by

an added pigment, which in the case of a clear 'lacquer' is omitted. 'Lacquer' like 'varnish', also has a use in cosmetics – as a hair spray.

vaudeville see **musical**

vault/cellar/crypt/undercroft
(underground room or chamber)
'Vault is the word either for a place of storage under a building, usually a commercial one, as a bank 'vault' or a wine 'vault', or for a place of interment under a church or in a cemetery, as a family 'vault'. It can also mean apparently the opposite: not an underground room but one with overhead arches – but many underground vaults have arches, too, and this is the common link. A 'cellar' is often a more domestic storage place, as a coal 'cellar' or, again, a wine 'cellar'. A 'crypt' or 'undercroft' – the words are virtually synonymous – is a cell or 'vault' under a church regarded as a private or secret burial place in particular, as distinct from 'vault' as a more general word (also denoting a place larger than a 'crypt'). 'Crypt' is related to 'cryptic', i.e. 'hidden', while an 'undercroft' is a croft – basically the same word as 'crypt' – that is under the church. All the words are useful as the name of a restaurant or wine bar, especially a basement one, since they nicely conjure up wine and an 'olde worlde', historical atmosphere, or even a rather mysterious or spooky one.

vaunt see **flout**

vedette see **corvette**

vegan see **vegetarian**

vegetarian/vegan (person who does not eat meat)
A 'vegetarian' is a person who does not eat meat for moral or health reasons, and so instead has a diet of vegetables, fruit, nuts, cereals and the like. Some 'vegetarians', however, especially so called 'lacto-vegetarians', will also eat animal products such as milk, eggs and cheese. A 'vegan' is a strict 'vegetarian' who would certainly not include animal products in his or her diet. The word is a contraction of 'vegetarian',

and arose in English towards the end of the Second World War, perhaps under the influence of the diet imposed during it, when people had to eat more frugally and so more healthily.

vehement see **violent**

vehicle licence see **driving licence**

vein/artery (main blood vessel)
The 'veins' are the vessels that carry the blood *to* the heart, while 'arteries' take blood *from* it to the rest of the body. Loosely, 'vein' can mean blood vessel in general, as in 'He claims to have royal blood in his veins'. In figurative use, an 'artery' is a main or trunk road, whether thought of as taking traffic to a city or from it, while 'vein' is often used metaphorically to mean 'mood', as a remark made 'in humorous vein'.

venal see **venial**

vendetta see **feud**

venial/venal (sinful)
'Venial' means 'not seriously wrong', 'able to be forgiven', 'excusable', as a 'venial' error or slip. A 'venial' sin, in religious terms, is any sin that is not 'mortal', i.e. does not involve the penalty of spiritual death. The word derives from Latin *venia* (pardon). 'Venal' means 'accessible to bribery', 'prepared to sell unscrupulously', 'corrupt', as the 'venal' sale of a political or influential office (involving bribery) or, in a commercial undertaking, the 'venal' arrangement whereby particular contractors are favoured (by bribing their way to a privileged position). The origin here is in Latin *venum* (goods for sale).

venturesome see **adventurous**

venturous see **adventurous**

verandah see **balcony** (platform in front of a house)

vermouth/bitters (bitter-flavoured alcoholic drink)
'Vermouth' is a white wine flavoured with

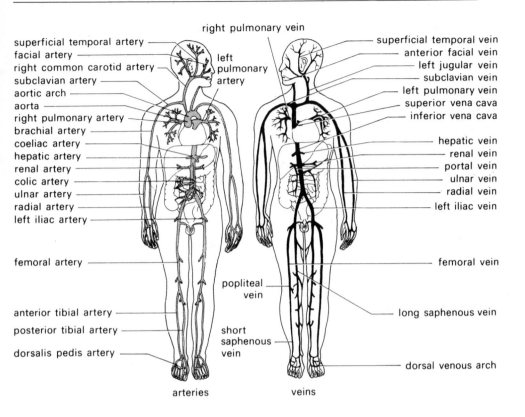

right pulmonary vein

superficial temporal artery
facial artery
right common carotid artery
subclavian artery
aortic arch
aorta
right pulmonary artery
brachial artery
coeliac artery
hepatic artery
renal artery
colic artery
ulnar artery
radial artery
left iliac artery

femoral artery

anterior tibial artery

posterior tibial artery

dorsalis pedis artery

left pulmonary artery

superficial temporal vein
anterior facial vein
left jugular vein
subclavian vein
left pulmonary vein
superior vena cava
inferior vena cava

hepatic vein
renal vein
portal vein
ulnar vein
radial vein
left iliac vein

femoral vein

popliteal vein

long saphenous vein

short saphenous vein

dorsal venous arch

arteries   veins

wormwood or other aromatic herbs. French 'vermouth' is dry, and Italian sweet – the latter being the 'it' that goes with gin. The word is actually the same as 'wormwood', deriving ultimately from the German (*Wermut*). Martini is a cocktail of gin, French 'vermouth' (or Italian), with added orange 'bitters' and the like. 'Bitters' themselves are liquors impregnated with bitter herbs or roots, either to give the appetite or digestion a lift or simply as flavourings. In the latter case they are usually called after their flavour, as orange 'bitters', peach 'bitters'. Campari is a well-known brand of Italian 'bitters', which can be drunk with or without soda. 'Bitters' (plural) is of course nothing to do with that peculiarly English beer called bitter (singular), for details of which see **ale.**

verse see **poetry**

vertigo see **dizziness**

verve see **vim**

veteran car/vintage car (old model of motor car)
The exact years appropriate to each category of car vary from source to source. The Veteran Car Club of Great Britain, however, states that all cars built before 31 December 1916 are 'veterans' and that cars manufactured before 31 December 1904 are 'true veterans' and are eligible for the annual Brighton Run. 'Vintage cars', sometimes called 'classic cars', are those built between 1916 and 1930, with some of the best cars of the 1930s classed as 'post-vintage thoroughbreds'.

VHF see **high frequency**

viaduct see **aqueduct**

vicar/rector/parson/curate (clergyman)
A 'vicar' is a parish priest, historically in a

261

parish where tithes were appropriated, or where he was acting as priest in place of the 'rector' or 'parson', i.e. acting 'vicariously'. A 'rector', by contrast, was a parish priest in a parish where tithes had not been appropriated – that is, they went to him. A 'parson', properly, was the holder of a benefice who had full possession of its rights. In other words, he was a 'rector'! The term is now used, sometimes somewhat condescendingly, of any clergyman. A 'curate', now an assistant clergyman, especially one working with a parish priest, is historically the title for the clergyman who had the 'cure' or charge of a parish – otherwise a 'vicar' or 'rector'. (They order these matters rather better in France, where *le curé* is the parish priest, and *le vicaire* his assistant.) The residences of the first three became respectively the vicarage, the rectory, and the parsonage. For some reason there is no 'curacy' – not as a residence, at any rate.

vice/pace (term referring to a particular person or persons)
Both words are Latin, pronounced respectively 'vicey' and 'pacey'. 'Vice' means 'instead of', 'in the place of' and appears mostly in official reports and military orders to denote that one person is being substituted for another: 'Capt J F Williams is appointed OC Applied Skills Section wef 19 June 1984 vice Capt A L Sanders (sick in quarters)'. The word is much more common as a prefix, e.g. 'vice-chairman', 'vice-captain'. 'Pace', usually printed in italics, means 'with the permission of', 'with due deference to' as a polite term of disagreement: 'I would suggest, *pace* Mr Wilson, that we would do better to defer this project no longer' (Mr Wilson had wanted to defer it).

vicegerent see **vice-regent**

vice-regent/vicegerent (one acting in place of a ruler)
Perfect anagrams. A 'vice-regent' is one who acts in place of a ruler, governor or sovereign, i.e. a substitute for a 'regent'. As *Chambers* points out, the word is 'often blunderingly' used for 'vicegerent' (no hyphen), who is an officer having delegated authority acting in place of another, or any deputy

acting for a superior. The pope, for example, is sometimes referred to as the 'Vicegerent' of Christ. The term comes from the Latin *vicem gerens* (wielding office). There is a rare noun 'gerent'.

Vietcong/Vietminh (Vietnamese political organisation)
The 'Vietcong' were the Vietnamese Communists in South Vietnam who were opposed to the successive American-sponsored South Vietnamese governments in the country and who provoked a civil war which led to the Vietnamese War. As a nationalist movement they had the aim of reuniting North and South Vietnam. The 'Vietminh' – the name is an abbreviated version of the full title meaning 'League for the Struggle for the Independence of Vietnam' – was a resistance movement working originally against the Japanese occupying forces. After the Second World War the movement, which had been founded by Ho Chi Minh in Annam, gained control of North Vietnam with strong support in the South (then under British occupation). In 1951 it was succeeded by a new organisation, the Lien Viet, or Vietnamese National People's Front. North and South Vietnam were finally officially reunited in July 1976 as the Socialist Republic of Vietnam.

Vietminh see **Vietcong**

view/vista/panorama (extensive prospect)
A 'view' is a sight generally, especially from a high vantage point, as of a landscape or valley. A 'vista' is a 'view' seen through a long avenue of some kind, as between rows of trees or buildings. One of London's 'vistas' is the view of Buckingham Palace seen from Admiralty Arch up Pall Mall. (Unfortunately, the focal point is partly obscured by the Queen Victoria Memorial.) A 'panorama' is an all-round 'view', or at least a 'view' over a wide area, as of Paris from the top of the Eiffel Tower. (The word is Greek for 'all view'.)

vigorous/rigorous (forcible)
'Vigorous' means 'full of vigour', 'energetic', 'powerful', as the 'vigorous' growth of a plant or 'vigorous' measures (firm ones). 'Rigorous' means 'full of rigour', 'rigidly

strict', 'harsh'. 'Rigorous' measures are strict or severe ones – which might or might not also be 'vigorous'.

village/hamlet (small populated place)
A 'village', which one almost always associates with the country, although some, as Dulwich 'Village' in London and Greenwich 'Village' in New York, have long merged with a city, is traditionally larger than a 'hamlet' but smaller than a town. It is usually thought of as having less than 1,000 inhabitants and its own parish church. In the USA, a 'village' – which may have well over 1,000 inhabitants – is a small municipality with limited corporate powers. This means that 'hamlet' is a rather more versatile word: at its vaguest it can mean any small 'village', especially a pretty one, and at its most precise – which is not very – it means a settlement smaller than a 'village' with no parish church but belonging to the parish of a nearby 'village' or town. Somewhere in between these two a 'hamlet' can also be a word for a small group of houses in a particularly remote or isolated country area. The word literally means 'little ham', i.e. 'small homestead', but 'ham' now exists only in place-names, as Hampstead, Hampton and Oakham.

vim/verve (energy, vigour)
'Vim', a slang word of American origin, means 'force', 'vigour in action', 'go': 'Put some vim in it!' The word is said to derive from Latin *vis* (strength). 'Verve' is 'energetic enthusiasm', especially in something artistic: 'Sarah Smith played Miss Prism with tremendous verve.' The ultimate origin is in Latin *verba* (words).

viniculture/viticulture (cultivation of the vine)
'Viniculture' is basically the science or study of wine-making (by cultivating the vine). 'Viticulture' is the cultivation of the vine itself, i.e. grape-growing. The derivations are from Latin *vinum* (wine) and *vitis* (vine).

vintage car see **veteran car**

violent/virulent/vehement (forceful, intense, powerful)

'Violent' is the general word, often meaning little more than 'very great', as a 'violent' storm or a 'violent' dislike. 'Virulent' means 'actively poisonous' – the word is related to 'virus' – hence, of a disease, 'violent', in the sense 'malignant', 'evil'. Of people 'virulent' means 'bitter', 'spiteful', as a 'virulent' speech. 'Vehement' means basically 'strong', 'passionate', 'impetuous', especially of a person or his feelings. The connotation is not necessarily evil: a 'vehement' desire is simply a strong or intense one. Less often the adjective is applied to things, as a 'vehement' wind (a strong or even 'violent' one), or the 'vehement' onset of a disease.

violet/purple/mauve/cerise/maroon (shade of blue mixed with red, or red tinged with blue)
Colours can be subjective things, especially when they are blends or shades of other colours, as these are. However, seen as far as possible objectively: 'violet' is the colour at the opposite end of the spectrum to red, produced by a small amount of red with blue, and typically is the colour of violets (the 'purple' ones, that is); 'purple,' the royal colour, is more or less halfway between red and blue, with a variation either way, giving reddish 'purple' or bluish 'purple'; 'mauve' is a bright but delicate pale 'purple' of bluish hue, as sometimes seen rather indelicately on a drinker's nose (it is also a reddish-'purple' aniline dye); 'cerise' is cherry-coloured, but red cherries rather than black or yellow (and also a textile dye, also known as fuchsin, forming a red solution in water); 'maroon' is a brownish crimson or reddish chestnut colour. See also **magenta.**

viper/adder (poisonous snake)
The 'viper' and the 'adder' hardly need distinguishing, since they are one and the same snake – the only poisonous one in Britain. However, the genus *Vipera* covers a number of 'vipers' apart from the British one (*Vipera berus*), such as the horned 'viper' (*Vipera cornutus*), and Russell's 'viper' (*Vipera russellii*) of India – the latter responsible for a number of human deaths. On a wider scale, the whole family *Viperidae* consists of about 150 species of 'viper', found in many countries round the world. Both names have

unusual origins, since both contain an error. The 'viper' (or 'adder') is so called as it was thought to be viviparous, that is, bringing forth its young alive. It nearly is – but not quite, since its young, when born, are enclosed in an egg-type membrane which they immediately hatch out of. This means that the snake is strictly speaking not viviparous, but ovoviviparous. A small inaccuracy, therefore. The 'adder' (or 'viper') also has a name that is slightly wrong: it ought to be 'nadder', but the 'n' was taken to belong to 'an' and became wrongly separated ('an adder' instead of 'a nadder'), as in fact also happened to one or two other words, as 'auger' (which should be 'nauger'), 'apron' ('napron') and 'umpire' ('numpire'). (The opposite happened to 'a newt', which should be 'an ewt'.)

virginals see **harpsichord**

virulent see **violent**

viscount see **duke**

vista see **view**

vitamin A/vitamin B/vitamin C/vitamin D/vitamin E (chemical substance in food necessary for good health and growth)
'Vitamin A', or retinol, is found in liver, yellow and green vegetables, cod liver oil and eggs, among other things. It is essential for normal growth of the skeleton and is well known for its role in preventing night blindness (via the carrots with which it is popularly, although not exclusively, associated). There are various kinds of 'vitamin B'. One of the best known is 'vitamin B_2', otherwise riboflavin, found in milk, eggs, kidney, liver and eggwhite and important for a healthy skin and eyes. 'Vitamin B_1', or thiamine, is influential on mental attitude, muscle tone and appetite, and found to a large extent in yeast and pork. Deficiency of it causes beri-beri. The most recently (1948) discovered vitamin is 'vitamin B_{12}' or cobalamin, particularly important in the nervous system and needed by all cells in the body. Deficiency can occur in vegetarians, since it occurs only in animal foods (liver, kidney, lean meat, milk, eggs, cheese) and not in any plant foods. 'Vitamin C', or ascorbic

acid, is one of the cheapest and easiest to manufacture, although it is found naturally in fruits, especially citrus fruits, and vegetables – including potatoes. A deficiency of it, as is classically known, produces scurvy. It plays a vital part in the process of building and maintaining bones and teeth and in wound healing. (Some claim it can prevent the common cold, but this is still disputed.) 'Vitamin D' is the 'sunshine vitamin', actually provided by sunshine – in which sense it is not a true vitamin, since it does not gain access to the body through what is eaten. It does exist, however, in milk, fish, eggs, butter and margarine. It is a great bone-builder and maintainer, and can prevent rickets. 'Vitamin E' is contained in most foods, especially vegetable oils and whole grains. Health food fanatics therefore get more than their whack of it. Its main claim to fame is that it prevents sterility, although its exact effectiveness in this direction is not proven. The actual word 'vitamin' – originally 'vitamine' when invented in 1912 – is a misnomer, since the substance does not contain an amino-acid. (The 'vit'-part is Latin for 'life'.) When the mistake was discovered, the final 'e' was dropped to try to avoid suggesting a connection with 'amine'. There are other vitamins and vitamin-like compounds with other letters, but these are the ones most familiar from the 'blurb' on the packets of various foodstuffs.

vitamin B see **vitamin A**

vitamin C see **vitamin A**

vitamin D see **vitamin A**

vitamin E see **vitamin A**

viticulture see **viniculture**

vogue see **fashion**

volley see **round**

volleyball see **netball**

volts/watts/amps/ohms (units of electricity)
'Let's put a hundred bulb in – that'll be

brighter', we say, or 'Surely everywhere's 240 now?' 'Watts' in the first case, of course; 'volts' in the second. What *is* a 'watt'? But perhaps we should start with a 'volt'. This is a unit of electric potential – the one that makes electricity 'move'. Technically it is defined as the difference of potential between two points on a conducting wire carrying a constant current of one 'ampere' when the power dissipated between these points is one 'watt'. Thus, an 'amp' is a unit of current, an 'ohm' a unit of resistance and a 'watt' is a measure of energy expended (as we half expected from our light bulb). The four are thus interdependent. 'Volts', 'watts', 'amps' and 'ohms' are named respectively after an Italian, a Scot, a Frenchman and a German, all physicists (Alessandro Volta, André-Marie Ampère and G. S. Ohm) except the Scot James Watt, who was an inventor and engineer. (They were, however, all born in the eighteenth century and all died in the nineteenth.)

volume see **weight**

voodoo see **hoodoo**

voracious see **rapacious**

voyage see **trip**

wake/awake/waken/awaken (rouse, or be roused, from sleep)
One can both 'wake' a person or simply 'wake', as 'I'll wake you up early' and 'I always wake early'. 'Awake' can be used similarly with or without an object, but the application is often figurative: 'Only then

did he awake to the reality of what he had done', 'The book awoke his interest in the subject' (roused it). 'Waken', with an object, often has the meaning 'rouse from inactivity', 'arouse,' 'excite': 'The letter wakened his hopes of getting the job.' Used without an object, 'waken' means exactly the same as 'wake' or 'awaken', but again, is found more in figurative than literal speech. Finally, 'awaken', with or without an object, is simply a stylish or bookish alternative to 'waken'. Usage is thus fairly blurred. On the whole, the shorter verbs are used in a literal sense, and the longer in a figurative. The past and present forms of the different verbs are also not firmly fixed, but the following are reasonably well established and grammatically acceptable:

Present

wake	I wake
awake	I awake
waken	I waken
awaken	I awaken

Past

I woke	I have woken
I awoke	I have woken/awaked
I wakened	I have wakened
I awakened	I have awakened*

(*increasingly heard, rightly or wrongly, 'I have awoken')

waken see **wake**

walrus/grampus (large sea creature)
The 'walrus', from the Dutch *walrus* (whale-horse), is the Arctic creature related to the seal, with flippers and a pair of large tusks. A 'walrus' moustache is one hanging loosely at both ends. The 'grampus', from the Latin, via French, *crassus piscis* (fat fish), is otherwise the killer whale – a member of the dolphin family found in all seas famous for its blowing and spouting – 'puffing like a grampus'.

wander/meander (go aimlessly or casually)
To 'wander' is to go, roam, rove, stray or generally proceed idly, aimlessly or casually. To 'meander' is much more specific: used literally of a river, it means 'proceed by a winding course'. Figuratively it has the sense 'wander aimlessly', 'stroll around'.

One cannot therefore 'meander' down to the shops, only 'wander', but one can 'meander' along the street (with no objective in mind). 'Meander' comes from Greek *maiandros* (winding), originally the name of a winding river, now the Menderes, in Turkey.

war/battle (period of open hostility and combat between nations or other opposing forces)
A 'war' is a larger, generally longer affair, as the Hundred Years 'War', Vietnam 'War' or Trojan 'War'. A 'battle' is usually more localised, and is a fight or combat either at a place or for a place, as is indicated in the names of such engagements as the 'Battle' of Agincourt, 'Battle' of Edgehill or 'Battle' of Brandywine (all at these places), or the 'Battle' for Iwo Jima or 'Battle' for Kohima in the Second World War. (Most battles are named 'of' a place, although many were really 'for' such as the 'Battle' of Stalingrad and even the 'Battle' of Britain.)

warden/warder (administrative head or officer)
'Warden' is fairly common as the title of the head of some body or organisation, as 'Warden' of the Cinque Ports, 'Warden' of the Royal Mint, and the like. The word is also found as the name of a member of a guild or governing body, especially the 'Great' London Livery Companies, and as the title of the head of an educational establishment, as a college or school. (Six Oxford colleges are headed by a 'warden'.) The most common use of the word, of course, is as a short form for traffic 'warden', church 'warden', air raid 'warden' and similar administrative posts. Confusion is perhaps most likely in the matter of prison officials: the head of a prison in the USA is a 'warden', but in Britain a 'governor'. On the other hand a 'warder' is an unofficial and now dated term for a British 'prison officer', who in American prisons is a 'jailer' or, more properly, 'prison guard'.

warder see **warden**

warp/woof/weft (yarns in a spinning loom)
'Warp' is the term for the yarns placed lengthwise in the loom, i.e. across the 'weft' or 'woof'. The 'woof', which rhymes with 'hoof' (not like the 'woof' of a dog), is the name for the yarns that travel across from one selvage (edge of the fabric) to the other, interlacing with the 'warp'. This 'woof' provides the thread for the 'weft', which is basically the 'woof' in woven form. 'Woof' was originally 'oof', but 'w' was added by association with 'warp' which, like 'weft', is related to 'weave'.

warranty see **guarantee**

wary/chary (cautious)
'Wary', related to 'beware', means 'watchful', especially habitually. 'I'm very wary of people who say that.' 'Chary', related to 'care', means 'careful'. 'I'm chary about letting her go on her own.' It has the additional sense 'sparing', 'careful about giving', as one who is 'chary' of praise (ungenerous with it).

wasp/hornet (flying insect with an unpleasant sting)
The 'wasp', with its vivid black and yellow warning colours, formidable sting, predilection for fruit and sweet things, and curiously narrow waist, needs no introduction. So what is a 'hornet'? At its vaguest it is the word for any large kind of 'wasp', especially one with a serious sting. More exactly, it is the name sometimes given in Britain to the 'wasp' known as *Vespa crabro*, although a looser division between the two is to call all members of the genus *Vespa* a 'wasp', and all those of *Vespera* a 'hornet'. (In the USA these two genera are more often known respectively as yellow jackets and 'hornets'.)

waterspout see **whirlwind**

watts see **volts**

weald see **wold**

weariness see **tiredness**

weasel see **ferret**

wedding/marriage (act or ceremony of marrying or state of being married)

'Marriage' is the state of being married, entered into as a result of a 'wedding' – or a 'marriage'. What difference is there? Both words mean 'ceremony of marrying'. 'Wedding' is the more emotive term, conjuring up a memorable ceremony, an emotionally charged gathering of the two families and their friends, and a subsequent reception and honeymoon. 'Marriage' is a more formal word to denote the legal or religious ceremony that sanctions the conscious (and usually deeply committed) decision of a man and woman to live as husband and wife. The word thus anticipates the married state to follow. The difference between the words can be seen in such typical expressions as a 'white "wedding"' and '"wedding" bells' on the one hand (festivities and fun), and '"marriage" ceremony' and 'banns of "marriage"' on the other (formalities and a commitment to the future).

weft see **warp**

weigh anchor/raise the anchor (raise – or lower – the anchor)
To 'raise the anchor' is obviously to haul it up, so that the ship is ready to sail. Over 'weigh' there is a double confusion: of sense and sound. 'Weigh' suggests heaviness – but to 'weigh the anchor' is not to drop it but, similarly, to raise it. The idea of 'weigh' relates to the heaving up of the anchor – when hauled up it will be 'weighed' or balanced. Confusion over sound is between 'weigh' and 'way', so that both 'under weigh' (by association with the raised anchor) and 'under way' (relating to the course of the ship) are found. Is 'under weigh' incorrect? *Chambers* regards 'weigh' as a misspelling, although the phrase is allowed by most other dictionaries. The *SOED* comments that 'under weigh' is a 'common var. of *under way*, from erron. association with the phr. "to weigh anchor".' The *Concise Oxford Dictionary*, however, has simply 'under weigh = under way', although (in the 1982 edition) marking this variant 'D' ('disputed'). In the phrase 'anchors aweigh', though, 'away' would be wrong.

weight/volume/mass (unit of measurement of a body)
To take 'mass' and 'weight' first: 'mass' is the measure of the inertia of a body, in other words the resistance it offers to having its speed or position changed. 'Weight', however, is the result of the pull of gravity and depends on geographical location. This means that 'weight', for example, could be zero – as in space – but 'mass' is a non-varying property (except, as specialists in these things will hasten to point out, at speeds approaching that of light). Put mathematically, if m is the 'mass' of a body, and g its acceleration due to gravity, its 'weight' w is given by the equation $w = mg$, and is expressed in kilograms, newtons or other units (one pound of 'weight' is the equivalent of 4.445 newtons, and one kilogram of 'mass' at the earth's surface weighs about 2.2 pounds, or 9.8 newtons). 'Volume' is the size, measure or amount of anything in three dimensions, that is, the space occupied by a body or substance expressed in cubic units, as the cubic inch, fluid ounce, or gallon.

weld see **solder**

werewolf see **vampire**

wheat see **corn**

whelk/winkle (edible shellfish)
The 'whelk' is the larger of the two, with a pale-coloured spiral-shaped shell about three inches long. The 'winkle' is smaller and fatter, with dark rings on a grey shell about one inch high. Its proper name is 'periwinkle' – nothing to do with the blue flower so called, although the word may have been influenced by the flower's name. (The 'peri-' may derive from Latin *pinna*, 'mussel', but this is only a possibility.) 'Winkles' are traditionally winkled out (the verb comes from the creature) from their shell with a pin or special 'winkle-picker'. There is, apparently, a subtle difference in taste between the two, but what it is exactly, only a gastronomic gastropodophile can say.

whim see **fancy**

whimsy see **fancy**

whin see **gorse**

whinny see **neigh**

whirl/whorl (something that turns or coils)
'Whirl' applies to something that whirls or
has whirled, often in a figurative sense, as
thoughts in a 'whirl' or the social 'whirl'. A
'whorl' is more a scientific or technical term
to apply to something having a circular or
coiled arrangement of similar parts, as the
ring of leaves round the stem of a plant or
a drumlike section on the lower part of a
spindle in a spinning machine that serves
as a pulley for the tape drive. In finger-
printing, a 'whorl' is a complete circle of
ridge-shapes (as distinct from a 'loop' or an
'arch'). Both 'whirl' and 'whorl' are
pronounced alike.

**whirlwind/tornado/cyclone/typhoon/
hurricane/waterspout** (type of
destructive wind)
All the words denote a rotating or circu-
lating wind. A 'cyclone' is the general word
for a 'hurricane' or 'typhoon', with 'hurricane' more a local word applying to such
a wind in the West Indies, and 'typhoon'
relating to the China Seas and adjacent
areas. A violent funnel-shaped wind of small
diameter passing across land is a 'tornado',
occurring typically in West Africa and
America, while a similar one over water is
a 'waterspout'. A 'whirlwind' is a rotating
wind that is less well developed than a
'tornado', and less destructive on the whole,
as well as of shorter duration. (Many 'whirl-
winds' expend themselves fairly harmlessly
as 'dust devils'.) 'Hurricane' is also the
word used on the Beaufort Scale to apply
to a wind of force 12 (or higher, on the new
scale), this being a speed of 73-82 mph or
64-71 knots (compare **storm**). 'Hurricanes'
of the 'cyclone' type have become well-
known internationally from their attractive
but utterly inappropriate designation by
women's names (now superseded by men's).
'Hurricane' Hattie thus killed over 7000
people in 1963 (over 5000 of them in Haiti),
and 'Hurricane' Betsy of 1969 was the most
damaging ever recorded.

whiskey see **whisky**

whisky/whiskey (spirit distilled from
malted barley)
The difference is mainly in the spelling:
'whisky' is from Scotland ('scotch'),
'whiskey' from Ireland, though there are
also corresponding variations in the manufacturing process. (The latter spelling is also
the American one.) Both words derive from
Irish and Scottish *usquebaugh,* in turn from
uisge beatha, 'water of life', Clearly the Celts
are a race with a fine, fiery spirit . . .

whist see **contract bridge**

white magic see **black magic**

White Paper/Green Paper/Blue Book
(official government publication)
Government papers of all kinds presented
to Parliament are called 'White Papers'.
Lengthy 'White Papers', such as the reports
of royal commissions, are bound in blue
paper covers in book form and are called
'Blue Books' (or sometimes Blue Papers). A
'Green Paper' is a type of tentative 'White
Paper'. It sets out the proposals for a future
government policy that must first and foremost be discussed (rather than be regarded
as a commitment to a particular action). It
is printed on green paper to distinguish it
from a 'White Paper'. In the USA a 'Blue
Book' is a (non-governmental) book in blue
covers giving details of US government
officials, or other prominent persons. (The
non-governmental Black Papers that arose
in Britain in the late 1960s to criticise
educational policies had a name patterned
after the 'White Paper')

whitewash/distemper (solution suitable
for painting on walls or ceilings)
The difference lies mainly in the composition and application of the substance.
'Whitewash' is a solution of quicklime or
whiting and size for brushing over walls and
ceilings to make them clean. 'Distemper' is
a water paint (as distinct from an oil paint)
containing powder colours and is used
mainly for painting internal walls and
scenery.

whorl see **whirl**

who's/whose (relating to 'who')
'Who's' is the colloquial form of 'who is' or
'who has', as 'Who's going first?' and
'Who's been sitting here?' 'Whose' is the
form to use for 'belonging to whom' as
'Whose chair is this?' For a similar distinction, see **it's**.

whose see **who's**

Wild West see **Middle West**

wince see **flinch**

winch/windlass (device for hoisting or
hauling)
A 'winch' is the crank or handle of a
revolving machine, so that a 'windlass',
which is the whole lifting or hoisting device,
has a 'winch'. However, 'winch' can sometimes apply to a complete hoisting gear,
especially when a simple or basic one, such
as that over a well. A 'windlass' is often a
fairly complex powered device, as that on a
ship for raising the anchor. Both are related
to 'wind' (turn). Windsor, of castle fame,
has a name that may mean 'slope with a
windlass'.

windlass see **winch**

windward see **leeward**

wines/spirits (type of alcoholic drink)
When is a wine not a wine? There is no
doubt about the well-known table 'wines' of
France and Spain, say, or Germany and
Italy. But what about sherry or port, for
example? These are fortified 'wines', so
called – fortified in fact with brandy – so
that they have an alcoholic content of
around 20 per cent as against the traditional
table 'wines' whose content is around 10 per
cent. Madeira, muscatel and marsala are
other fortified 'wines'. 'Spirits', with an
alcoholic content of 40 per cent or more, are
distilled liquors in which the concentration
of ethyl alcohol (the intoxicating agent) has
been increased above that of the original
fermented mixture. So although fortified
'wines' are fortified with brandy, a 'spirit',
they are not themselves classed as 'spirits',
which are the familiar 'hard' drinks such as
gin, vodka, whisky and rum. Fortified
'wines' in America are usually known as
dessert 'wines'.

wink/blink (brief closing of the eye)
A 'wink' is usually a rapid closing and
opening of one eye done deliberately to
convey some signal or meaning, as a friendly
greeting or a 'glad eye'. A 'blink' is an invol-
untary rapid closing and opening of both
eyes, either as a natural process frequently
repeated to lubricate and cleanse the eye or
as the result of a sudden blow or shock or
dazzling light.

winkle see **whelk**

wit see **humour**

witch doctor/medicine man (tribal
magician having powers of healing)
There is little difference in the function of
the two – although a 'witch doctor' can both
heal *and* harm. The chief distinction is in
their area of operations: the 'witch doctor'
is found among African tribes, the 'medicine
man' lives among the American Indians.
(The Canadian city of Medicine Hat is said
to be named after a 'medicine man' who lost
his hat while fleeing from Blackfoot warriors
who had massacred his tribe.)

woebegone see **woeful**

woeful/woebegone (full of, or showing,
woe or distress)
'Woeful' means 'full of woe', 'wretched',
'unhappy', as a 'woeful' tale or a 'woeful'
sight or 'woeful' ignorance. 'Woebegone'
means 'affected by woe', especially in
appearance, as a 'woebegone' expression
which is a mournful, miserable one. The
'begone' element derives from a former
verbal construction in which the object was
governed by a compound tense of 'bego'
(meaning 'beset', i.e. 'surround by'). An
example would be 'Me is woe begone', literally: 'Woe has beset me'.

wog/wop (abusive term for a foreigner)
'Wog' is mainly used of a dark-skinned foreigner, especially one from the Middle East
or North Africa, and in particular an Arab

or Egyptian. 'Wop', not so commonly used, is a derogatory epithet for an Italian, or any Italian-looking foreigner. The derivation of the term is perhaps in the Neapolitan dialect word *guappo* (dandy). The origin of 'wog' has been much debated. The most likely candidate would seem to be 'golliwog'. Unlikely candidates are the various acronyms from such words as *w*ily *o*riental *g*entleman, *W*orkers *o*n *G*overnment *S*ervice (in the construction of the Suez Canal), and Egyptians serving as porters and handlers of *W*ar *O*ffice *G*eneral *S*tores. Four-letter terms of abuse often upstage the many three-letter ones, as: oik, erk, yob, git, nig, Nip, nit, Yid, and the two in question. In the main, such words are more racial and social than sexual and scatological.

wold/weald (tract of open or wooded country)
Both words derive from Old English *wald* (wood, forest). In Britain, the 'Wolds' are those elevated tracts of country, especially in Yorkshire and Lincolnshire, that resemble the downs of the southern counties. The word is also found in the 'Cotswolds', whose first element is not, in spite of the association, 'cot' or 'cottage' – picturesque cottages are a feature of the district – but the Old English personal name Cod, pronounced (approximately) 'Code', that is, 'Cod's wood'. The 'Weald' is the name of the former wooded district of south-east England in Kent, Surrey and Sussex, now primarily put to agricultural use. 'Weald' is found in a number of English place names, as Harrow 'Weald' and various villages called 'Weald'. Both words, in changed form, crop up in such place names as Northwold, Southwold, Waltham and Harrold.

wood/forest/grove/copse/coppice (collection of trees)
A 'wood' is smaller than a 'forest', is not so primitive, and is usually nearer to civilisation. This means that a 'forest' is fairly extensive, is to some extent wild, and on the whole not near large towns or cities. In addition, a 'forest' often has game or wild animals in it, which a 'wood' does not, apart from the standard quota of regular rural denizens such as rabbits, foxes and birds

of various kinds. Many newer 'forests' in Britain are of planted trees, while the famous 'forests' of medieval Britain, such as the New 'Forest' (created by William the Conqueror, as a royal hunting ground, therefore decidedly old), although originally partly 'man-planted,' are now regarded as natural extensions of their former confines. A planted 'wood', as distinct from a natural one, may often be recognised from the predominance of one particular species of tree. A 'grove' is a smallish group of trees and is normally cleared of undergrowth; it may also contain fruit or nut trees, as an orange 'grove' or a walnut 'grove'. 'Copse' is simply a shortened form of 'coppice', and is a small 'wood' of undergrowth and small trees that are grown to be cut from time to time.

woof see **warp**

woofer/tweeter (type of loudspeaker)
These attractively juvenile names are respectively for a loudspeaker that will reproduce low-frequency sounds, and one (smaller) that will reproduce high-frequency sounds. Both form part of a hi-fi unit or music centre, for example. See also – on the same sort of lines – **wow.**

wop see **wog**

work-in see **sit-in**

work-to-rule see **sit-in**

world/earth (planet on which we live)
The 'world' implies not just our terrestrial globe but the people who inhabit it. Someone who sails single-handed round the 'world', therefore, will doubtless have his or her exploit reported all over the 'world'. The sense 'mass of population' is used more narrowly in such terms as the Western 'World' or the Third 'World' (for definition of which see, if necessary, **developing countries**). The 'earth' is more the globe seen either as a scientific entity, specifically astronomically (the planet 'Earth') or geographically (the 'earth' and its natural resources), or, from a religious viewpoint, as contrasted with heaven and hell (it was the 'earth' God created in the beginning,

not the 'world'). In general, too, 'earth' is a more lofty or poetic word than 'world', especially where the senses are the same: compare 'the people of the "earth"' and 'the people of the "world"'

Worship see **Lordship**

wow/flutter (perceptible variations in pitch in sound reproduction)
Both words are imitative. 'Wow' is slow fluctuation of pitch, most clearly detected in long notes. 'Flutter' is the term for rapid variation in pitch or in loudness. Both are caused in irregularities in the speed of the turntable or tape, either in recording or in playing. (Neither should be confused with **woofer** and tweeter, which are similar types of jokey name but relate to something different.)

wraith see **wreath**

wreak see **reap**

wreath/wraith (symbol of death and the dead)
Where 'wraith' is confused with 'wreath' it is usually the association with graves and ghosts that causes the trouble. A 'wreath' is not only a band of flowers left at a grave but also a term to describe a curling mass of smoke or vapour. A 'wraith' is principally an apparition of a dead – or living – person, as well as a word describing something pale, thin and ethereal, as a plume of vapour or smoke. The words are not related: 'wreath' is akin to 'writhe', while 'wraith' may come from an Old Norse word meaning 'guardian'.

wrench/rick (strain or sprain)
To 'wrench' an ankle is to overstrain or injure it by a sudden violent twist. To 'rick' one's neck or back is to sprain or strain it in a similar manner. For further diagnosis, see **strained.**

wyvern see **gryphon**

X-rays/infra-red rays/ultra-violet rays/gamma rays (invisible rays used in medicine or for special applications)
'X-rays', so called as their original nature was unknown, are the ones discovered by Roentgen in 1895 and widely used to examine the interior organs of a person or the nature of an opaque object. They are of a shorter wavelength than light. 'Infra-red rays' are ones beyond the visible red rays at one end of the spectrum. They are largely used in photography, in heat therapy, and for night-viewing devices, such as for military surveillance. 'Ultra-violet rays' are the opposite: beyond the visible violet rays at the other end of the spectrum, with a wavelength between visible light and 'X-rays'. One of their most popular uses is for so-called 'sun lamps', which produce an artificial suntan. 'Gamma rays' are streams of gamma radiation, that is, electromagnetic radiation of shorter wavelength and higher energy than 'X-rays', especially that portion of the electromagnetic spectrum that has a frequency greater than about 3 by 10^{19} hertz. They are so named since they were discovered (in 1900) as a third component of the radiation from radioactive materials, the others being alpha-particles and beta-particles (and alpha, beta and gamma being the first three letters of the Greek alphabet). 'Gamma rays' have uses in radiotherapy and in the detection of flaws in metal castings.

yachting see **sailing**

yang see **yin**

yard see **mast**

yearning see **longing**

Yiddish see **Hebrew**

yin/yang (one of two fundamental principles of the universe in Chinese philosophy)
The two are opposite yet complementary. 'Yin' is regarded as the feminine, passive (or negative) and yielding principle, associated with cold and wetness. 'Yang' is the masculine, active (or positive) and assertive principle, associated with height, light, heat and dryness. The two interact and combine to produce all that comes to be in the universe. The basic meanings of the words are respectively 'dark' and 'bright'.

Z

zany/zombie (stupid person)
A 'zany' is a clown or silly person. The word comes through French from the Venetian Italian *zanni* (clown), related to the Italian proper name Giovanni. A 'zombie' (or 'zombi'), of West African origin, is the snake or python god worshipped in voodoo

ceremonies in the West Indies and certain parts of the Southern States of the USA. The god has the power of bringing someone who has died back to life, hence the transferred sense of the word to mean 'dead person brought back to life' and its modern extension to refer to a dull or apathetic person, one resembling the walking dead. The term is often wrongly used in such phrases as: 'There I was tearing round like a zombie'; no 'zombie' would do that, but a 'zany' might.

zeal/zest (enthusiasm)
'Zeal' is 'ardour', 'eager desire', 'enthusiasm': 'He attacked his steak with zeal.' 'Zest' is 'keen relish', 'hearty enjoyment', 'gusto': 'He attacked his steak with zest.' The word originally meant 'flavouring', and although of ultimate uncertain origin comes from obsolete French *zest* (now *zeste*) (orange peel).

zebra crossing see **pedestrian crossing**

Zen/Zend (eastern religious philosophy)
'Zen', from the Japanese (ultimately Sanskrit) for 'meditation', is a Buddhist sect popular in Japan – and now with a certain following in the West – which advocates self-contemplation as the key to the understanding of the universe. The religion was introduced to Japan from China in the twelfth century. The 'Zend' is not itself a religious faith but the traditional translation and exposition of the Avesta – the Books of Wisdom, or sacred scriptures, of Zoroastrianism. This was the dualistic religion of Zoroaster or Zarathustra, its Persian founder in the sixth century. The combined text and commentary is called the Zend-Avesta. 'Zend' derives from Persian *zand* (interpretation).

Zend see **Zen**

zest see **zeal**

zither/cittern (stringed musical instrument played by plucking)
The 'zither' is a folk instrument of the Austrian Tyrol. It consists of a wooden box, acting as a resonator, with about thirty to

forty-five strings stretched over it. The instrument is played flat, on a table or the knees, with a plectrum (hard pointed device for plucking the strings) and the fingertips. It became very popular from its association with the 'Harry Lime Theme' played on it in the film *The Third Man* in the early 1950s. The 'cittern' (also rendered as 'cither', 'cithern', 'gittern' and 'zittern') is an old instrument related to the guitar, with a flat, pear-shaped sounding-box and wire strings. 'Zither' derives from Latin *cithara*, the name of a musical instrument of ancient Greece (*kythara*), and it is a blend of this Latin word and 'gittern' that gives 'cittern', which, together with all its variants and 'zither' itself, is related to 'guitar'.

zombie see **zany**

zone see **belt**

zoom see **track** (movement of camera)